To Barbara!
Miriam Freund
Rosenthal

IT TAKES A DREAM...

THE STORY OF HADASSAH

IT TAKES A DREAM...
THE STORY OF HADASSAH

gefen גפן
publishing house בית הוצאה לאור

Published and distributed by:

Gefen Publishing House Ltd.   Gefen Books
POB 36004, Jerusalem   12 New St., Hewlett
91360 Israel   N.Y., U.S.A. 11557
972-2-5380247   516-295-2805

and Hadassah, The Women's Zionist Organization of America, Inc.
50 W. 58 St., New York, New York 10019
Tel: 212-355-7900   Fax: 212-303-8282

Typesetting: Marzel A.S. - Jerusalem

Cover Design: Yaacov Agam

ISBN 965 229 179 X

Edition 9 8 7 6 5 4 3 2 1

Printed in Israel

Library of Congress Cataloging-in-Publication Data
Levin, Marlin.
It takes a dream--: the story of Hadassah / Marlin Levin:
foreword by Elie Wiesel: afterword by Teddy Kollek.
        p.   cm.
    Includes index.
    ISBN: 965-229-179-X
    1. Hadassah, the Women's Zionist Organization of America.
I. Title.
DS150.H4L49   1997
320.54' 095694--dc21   97-19184
                                                     CIP
                                                     r97

for my parents

ISADORE AND ROSE

CONTENTS

FOREWORD

by Elie Wiesel

It is a given in the Jewish world: if you want a project to come to fruition, if you want an initiative to have a follow-up, you think of Hadassah.

Hadassah is more than an organization; it's a family – a family that loves and is loved. It loves to help those in need, the weak, the ill, in short, those who need help. And it is a family that is loved because it does these things with as much devotion as competence. Is it because Hadassah is made up of and run by women? And is it because these women are more dynamic, endowed with a more pragmatic sensibility than men? Far be it from me to even think of hiding behind the "Fifth Amendment." In the case of Hadassah, I am sorely tempted to answer "yes." The women of Hadassah have always been successful in guarding against the scatter-shot approach and the piling up of activities and goals. They know what they want to do, and they do it well.

As for Hadassah's history, it can be found meticulously and, of course, warmly recounted in Marlin Levin's narrative – the beginnings of the dream, the challenges, the apparently insurmountable obstacles, the victories won on Mount Scopus, overlooking Jerusalem. Who is not acquainted with Hadassah's Hospital, which attracts researchers, physicians and patients from the whole world?

The originality of Hadassah stems from its preoccupation with the education of its members, teaching them that it's not enough just to collect money, that it's just as important to be cognizant of the meaning of what they've undertaken.

Several times, I have had occasion to be a participant in their regional and national meetings. Each time I was pleasantly surprised by their organizational talents as well as by the thoughtfulness of their discussions.

Do I idealize Hadassah? Let's just say that I propose the romantic view. That's because, even today, one can still find in Hadassah the inspiring devotion and enthusiasm that were the hallmarks of the early Zionist movements.

A memory: Moscow, 1966. It's my second visit. The holiday of Simhat Torah. My impressions, I have given them elsewhere. The singing, the dancing, the courage of our Jews who, before anyone else, had defiantly dared to confront the Kremlin's terror. Suddenly, I heard some familiar voices: some one hundred Hadassah women had had the very same idea as I did: to come celebrate, with those admirable Russian Jews, the most beautiful of Jewish holidays. Like myself, they would go over to talk to the young people there, they would slip a few siddurim to the aged, they would establish relationships, they would deliver a few words of encouragement: they were everywhere.

Back in America, I happened to mention to one of Hadassah's leaders how happy I had been to see so many of her associates in Moscow. "How many of us were there?" she asked. I answered: "More than a hundred." She burst out laughing: "There were twenty five of us there." It was my turn to laugh: "You were involved in so many activities that there appeared to be four times as many of you as there were."

I was grateful to them. Hadassah had been among the first Jewish organizations to work for the Jews of the Soviet Union. As for the others, it was impossible to motivate them, to make them take action. May I remind you that, in those days, in the sixties, "the Jews of Silence" were not the ones who were living in fear in the Soviet Union, but rather their brothers who were living in security, if not in happiness, in the West.

Does that mean that Hadassah's past, however glorious, is without fault? That would be an exaggeration. There is no human endeavor without a blemish. For example, I am not convinced that even Hadassah did enough for the Jews of Europe during the Holocaust. Nor, of course, did anyone else. But let's leave that for another time. Today, it is incumbent on us to recount simply all the pride that Hadassah inspires in the hearts of so many Jews in Israel, in America and around the world.

Today, let us say to Hadassah, to its leaders and to its members: thank you for existing, thank you for all the honor you bestow on Jewish womanhood.

— *Elie Wiesel*

Translated from the French by Joseph Lowin

PREFACE

Looking back at the changes in American Jewish life which I myself witnessed, I would put the growth and influence of Hadassah high on the list. Out of a little volunteer group of Zionist women organized some sixty years ago has come a force of great dimensions, a force for health, education and the salvation of human beings. Hadassah has been making a contribution of basic importance to the development of the State of Israel and – clearly because of this – to the survival and enhancement of the Jewish community in the United States. Notably it has, at the same time, developed in thousands of women skills and talents unknown even to themselves.

All this emerges in rich detail from the pages of *Balm in Gilead*. Interweaving the story of Hadassah with the unbelievable, often tragic, political struggle of Jews in Palestine, the book shows Hadassah's efforts in true perspective, not as philanthropy but as nation-building in the face of great odds. Beginning at the turn of this century, Mr. Levin makes us see and feel the filth, poverty and disease of Turkish-ruled Jerusalem. This was the distress that inspired Henrietta Szold to make of American Jewish women "the healing of the daughter of my people."

Those American women were to bring the neglected land modern medicine at its most advanced – hospitals, the training of doctors and nurses, university medical research. It is a great and daring story, from 1913 when the first two nurses came, to 1918 when the Medical Unit arrived in the war-stricken, starving country, to vital aid in successive outbreaks of anti-Jewish rioting. Medicine was supplemented by vocational education and the magnificent Youth Aliyah program that saved thousands of Jewish children from the extermination camps which snuffed out the lives of a million of their young brothers and sisters in Europe.

I cannot forget the meeting I participated in during the siege of Jerusalem in 1948, when Hadassah's representatives decided to hold on to their hospital on Mount Scopus as long as possible and, in doing so, helped to divert the brunt of Arab attack from the Jewish Quarter of Jerusalem. Until the liberation of Jerusalem in 1967, we were cut off from Mount Scopus where so many Arabs had been healed by Hadassah. Having lost Scopus, Hadassah energetically planned and built its hospital complex in Ein Karem. Later, many of its medical staff were lent to Asian and African developing countries, as I know very well from my days as Israel's foreign minister. And sadly, though gloriously, the Hadassah Hospital at Ein Karem is known to so many of us in Israel as the place that cared for hundreds upon hundreds of wounded soldiers during the Six-Day War and thereafter.

This is the record of an extraordinary alliance between Jewish women in the United States and their people come to life again in the Land of Israel – one of the great chapters in the integral relationship between the State of Israel and Jews throughout the world.

— *Golda Meir*

Reprinted from *Balm in Gilead*

INTRODUCTION

Marlene Edith Post rises weekday mornings at 5:15, and after a small breakfast rushes out of her Long Island home for Manhattan. Leaving early, she misses the morning crush of traffic and reaches her seventh-floor office in Hadassah House on 58th street in 45 minutes.

The President of Hadassah turns over a mountain of paper work that she finished last night to her secretary and goes over the day's schedule awaiting her. There are sessions either with leaders of other organizations or with National Board members. She can spend hours discussing specific issues with department heads or in an Executive Committee meeting. There are budgets to scan, requests for funds, new projects, a convention to prepare, and, as always, letters to answer.

Lunch is at her desk, if at all. "I am a cookie and M&M eater," Marlene admits. Consultations with leaders from out of town often run over into dinner. If Marlene manages to leave the office by 9 or 10 o'clock at night, she will drive back to Long Island. Otherwise she will stay over in a Hadassah apartment close by.

So much for the normal working schedule. During Marlene's first year in office she traveled tens of thousands of miles. Every six weeks finds her in Israel where she is closeted with heads of the Hadassah Medical Organization or conferring with political or Jewish Agency leaders or attending dedication ceremonies of one project or another. While she is away, one of the Posts' three daughters – all of whom were married within 18 months of each other – cares for their father.

Marlene confides that she could never maintain the grueling schedule without the support of her husband, who is a prominent physician at the Queens Division of New York Hospital. By pre-arrangement, they manage holidays and an occasional weekend together in their East Hampton getaway cottage.

Marlene sometimes is asked why she devotes her life to Hadassah to the exclusion of nearly all else. Like most others in her position, she finds it difficult to reply. "I know I have neglected my children. Maybe I should have been home more for my husband and children." And after a moment of reflection, she adds, "It's a passion... it's hard to explain."

Being President of one of the world's largest volunteer women's organizations places enormous responsibility on this former nurse. It also makes her one of the most influential women in American and Jewish affairs.

The President of Hadassah oversees the fortunes, among others, of two major medical centers, a college of technology, a youth movement. She supervises educational programs and social action projects. She is the leader of more than 300,000 women, controls an annual budget of nearly $400,000,000, and commands an ardent army of women who will respond instantaneously to her call for action.

"If there is an issue in Washington that concerns us," says Executive Board Member Ruth Cole, "we issue Action Alert papers. When we ask our leaders to write in, we can depend on 5,000 letters."

Directing the Women's Zionist Organization of America places the President in the public limelight. As head of Hadassah, she is a member of many influential groups, among them the powerful Conference of Presidents of Major Jewish Organizations. She is invited to the White House for special occasions. She dialogues with Cabinet members and leaders of the Congress. Israel's leaders seek her out when she is in the country. She discusses issues with Arab leaders, among them Egypt's President Hosni Mubarak and Jordan's King Hussein. Marlene's special interest in the disabled has placed her on a number of committees and commissions, state, federal and local, for the disabled in the U.S.

With Hadassah chapters located in every one of the 50 states and Puerto Rico, she spends a lot of time on roads and in the air. "I believe that as a National President you need to be out there with the people," she says.

People are what Hadassah is all about – whether they are the inhabitants of Kinshasa, Zaire, who need a new hospital; the earthquake victims of Armenia, war victims in Sarajevo, or Jews searching for their identity in Beijing or Hong Kong. Hadassah has taken on a dazzling number and variety of causes whether it be to free Russian Jews, help Ethiopian Jews, act in Congress on behalf of women, or get out the vote in a presidential election.

Hadassah has funded projects that have saved countless lives regardless of nationality, religion, or gender, friend or enemy. It has prepared young men and women for high technology jobs, honed the skills of doctors from many places including the University of Chingdao on the northeastern coast of China, and made land fruitful by building dams and draining swamps. It has made American Jewish families more conscious of their heritage, got the President of the U.S. to speak out on behalf of Zionism, and offered curbside mammography tests to American women.

It Takes a Dream attempts to portray in narrative form Hadassah's political, educational and social action efforts at home, and its often death-defying adventures in Israel over the past 85 years. I have tried to weave the Israeli saga within the political revolution and social upheaval of the times. In many instances, the events of the period were told to me by the very pioneers who experienced them.

The "dream" began in the vestry of Temple Emanu-El in New York at Purim in 1912. Since then, the achievements of these pioneers and their successors have been prodigious. They have saved the bodies and souls of thousands of children, taught more than 28,000 trainees from 112 countries how to heal, established a permanent presence in 34 countries. Few other humanitarian organizations have had an equal impact.

It Takes a Dream had a previous life under the title *Balm in Gilead* which was published shortly before the Yom Kippur War in 1973. That volume grew out of a feature article I had written in 1958 on Sam and Madeleine Lewin-Epstein, who were members of the American Zionist Medical Unit that Hadassah sent to alleviate the suffering of the Jews of Palestine following World War I. Before his death, Sam told me about his first trip to Palestine when he surreptitiously took gold to Jerusalem under the nose of a Turkish despot. Madeleine was a nurse who worked in cholera-stricken Tiberias and infuriated a British officer when she dropped a pair of panties in the gas tank of one of his vehicles. Here were Hadassah heroes of a character I had never met. Their true-to-life stories electrified me and made me eager to chronicle Hadassah's history.

In 1960, the opportunity arose when I wrote an article for *Time* on the new Ein Karem Medical Center. Friends I had cultivated among Hadassah's leadership during my work as a journalist – Rebecca Shulman, Esther Gottesman, Judith Epstein, among others – invited me to do a book.

Balm in Gilead was the product of years of research. It was used as source material by many writers and served as an educational tool for Hadassah. After three printings, when the book was no longer available, I received constant requests for copies, some from as far away as Australia.

Toward the end of 1995, the Hadassah Medical Organization's spokesman, Yossi Shoval, recommended to President Post that *Balm in*

Gilead be republished in English and Hebrew. Marlene agreed and appointed a former President, Bernice Tannenbaum, to supervise. I could hardly have asked for anyone better. Bernice is a prototype Hadassah leader who combines drive and loyalty with creativity and dynamism. I profited by her wise counsel and her speedy replies to my countless queries.

As my liaison at Hadassah House, Bernice had an onerous task. On the one hand, I was free to select the material and tell the story as I saw it. On the other, she was under an obligation to peers who, understandably, sought to have their considerable achievements fairly represented in the work. Not all could be fully obliged. That she was able to manage conflicting pressures with great poise and aplomb bespeaks well of her experience, maturity and leadership.

Bernice and I were ably assisted by Rose Goldman, whose vast knowledge of Hadassah was of great help. Rose reviewed the text with sensitivity. Susan Woodland, Archives Director, helped in the selection of photographs and quickly located background material. Bernice's secretary, Henrietta Wolinsky, efficiently handled the voluminous communications that passed between us. HWZOA Executive Director Beth Wohlgelernter likewise read the manuscript and saved the work from a number of awkward errors.

In Israel, Wendy Elliman assisted me from the beginning in researching and interviewing. She provided material from her abundant archive of articles written for *Hadassah Magazine*, checked facts, read proofs and assisted with the index.

In computerizing the manuscript and making copious changes, some of them which she suggested, Jean Max, long-time office manager of the TIME-LIFE News Bureau in Jerusalem, was an indispensable aide. The courtesies generously extended by *TIME*, my employer for more than 30 years, were most helpful in the successful production of the work. My appreciation is due as well to Gefen Publisher Ilan Greenfield, both for his expertise and understanding; to Alex Auswaks, a fine editor whose incomparable command of language and style did much to improve the text; and to Marsha Twersky for keeping me on schedule so that I was able to produce the manuscript well ahead of the deadline.

As with the first volume, I again had the benefit of advice at Hadassah in Jerusalem from two valued friends. Marian Lewin-Epstein, whom I have known since Young Judaea days in the U.S., and Annabelle Yuval since her arrival in Israel in 1952. Both are models of the Hadassah volunteer without whose devotion the organization could not thrive.

Hinda Gross, the indefatigable and courageous President of Hadassah-Israel, early on suggested that *Balm in Gilead* be republished and provided valuable assistance. Ethel Carmel, the executive secretary who keeps the wheels turning efficiently at Hadassah headquarters in the Straus Center, and her assistant Sharon Ben-Dor, were precious assets in keeping my communications flowing smoothly with the New York office.

My gratitude goes out as well to Hadassah Medical Organization Director-General Shmuel Penchas and his entire retinue of physicians, nurses and staff who found time from incredibly busy schedules to be interviewed. Although I could not possibly use all the fascinating material they provided, it served as excellent guidance in shaping the tale. To them and to all those who labor in the Hadassah College of Technology and Career Counseling Institute, in Young Judaea, the Jewish National Fund and Youth Aliyah, I extend my deep appreciation.

With all the foregoing help and advice, this book would not have been possible had it not been for the one person who was always there for me, even when I shut myself in my study. For more than a year she accepted without complaint my shunning social activities. She was empathetic as I worked under the strain and stress of meeting a difficult deadline. Without her love, understanding and wise critiques I certainly could not have prevailed. I refer, of course, to my wife of 50 years, Betty Schoffman Levin. I want our children – Sara, Oren and Don – our daughter-in-law Michal and our four lovely granddaughters to know that on the many occasions I was not there for them, they were always in my thoughts.

A word about the writing. Just as a building contractor prefers to tear down an old structure and build anew, so I found that it would have been simpler to rewrite the Hadassah adventure from the beginning. But, alas, time was not available. And so I had to pore over each page of the old volume and where possible continue the story. In places where updating would have interrupted the flow and rhythm, I liberally used footnotes, something that I had avoided in the first edition.

Here, then, is one of the most extraordinary narratives it has been my good fortune to tell in more than 50 years of reporting.

— *Marlin Levin*

Jerusalem, April 1997

MISSION: JERUSALEM

Jerusalem entered the nineteenth century with the eyes of the Western world focused upon it. In 1799, Napoleon Bonaparte stormed the gates of Acre and Jaffa, pushed inland and reached Nazareth where he spent a night in prayer. But his conquest was short-lived. The Ottomans on land and the British at sea defeated his overextended troops and prevented his triumphal entry into the Holy City. Bonaparte's presence in the Holy Land nevertheless electrified Europe and by the first half of the nineteenth century, pilgrims were on a new crusade.

Jerusalem has over the centuries been called by a hundred names: City of Heaven, City of Peace, Navel of the World. To Europeans it was more than a city of flesh and blood; it was not really of this earth, but a gleaming golden, fantasy city of sun-burnished castles guarded by hovering angels. The first pilgrims who followed Bonaparte indeed found Jerusalem sublime in its natural beauty, but hardly the glittering capital of some celestial realm. To their dismay they found that the God who reigned over its indolent residents from beneath a golden dome on the Temple Mount was Allah. Except for some shrines, Jerusalem was in fact a neglected city – its venerated streets defiled by stinking heaps of sewage and feces and built upon layers of refuse that had accumulated to a height of over fifty feet since the days of the Second Temple. The sanitary condition of the City of God was such that anyone who sought to spend his last days on earth there could look forward to fulfilling that ideal with dispatch.

The word of Jerusalem's degradation soon spread to the religious councils of Europe. Missionaries and emissaries rushed to the scene from Russia and Britain, Prussia and France. These self-sacrificing souls, unaccustomed to either the ways or the filth of the Middle East, nonetheless attacked disease and ignorance with fervor. But their primary aim was spiritual salvation. By 1840 the local population of 7,000 Jews and 5,000 Moslems looked upon the rapidly increasing number of Christians in Jerusalem (3,000 in 1840) as the beginning of the insidious crusade. To the Orthodox Jew and Moslem the threat of conversion was much more real than the danger from flies, mosquitoes or microbes. Just as disturbed by the missionary menace were the medicine men who balmed the sick and dying with amulets and talismans. As missionary schools, hospices and clinics began to appear in the walled city, bitter murmurings spread through the marketplaces and the houses of worship:

> Ha! Christians, you say? Nonsense. Not with names like Gershman and Bergheim. Converts! May their names be erased!

> At the English Mission a Jew will step inside with a fever and come out cured of both his fever and his Judaism.

The physician Gershman and the pharmacist Bergheim arrived in 1838. By the early 1840's the sick and the lame – Jew and Moslem alike – were trooping regularly to mission clinics and getting quicker cures than they could ever expect from the quacks. As conversions multiplied, the rabbis sent frantic messages to Jewish notables in Europe. One of the first to reply was the Italian-born, British philanthropist Sir Moses Montefiore, who made many visits to Jerusalem, the first in 1827. Sir Moses sent a Chelsea physician, Shimon Frankel, with medical supplies, but Frankel did not stay.

The missionaries did and the Jews of Jerusalem wrote more urgent warnings to their brethren on the continent. What was in reality the forerunner of a European invasion of the Holy Land was to them a Christian conquest of the Holy City. The crisis for the Jews reached its peak by 1853 when the Crimean War between Russia and Turkey erupted. As a result, *halukah* (charity) from Russia, on which half the city's Jewish population depended, came to a halt and its alternative to starvation was to take the free food, medicine, and clothing dispensed by the missionaries. The situation was similar in Tiberias, Safed and Hebron. As the seers of Palestine saw matters, it was only a question of time and pills before Jewry in Eretz Israel would silently disappear.

In that year of 1853 there appeared at the gates of Jerusalem a distinguished, bearded French-speaking gentleman who introduced himself as Baron Gustav de Rothschild. To the spiritual leaders of the community he was one of the city's hovering angels in disguise. The baron was appalled by the conditions in which the Jews lived. He recognized the threat from the missions and sent his father in Paris an urgent message which said in essence: "All that our brethren in Jerusalem say is true. Their needs call for the most urgent action." In the French capital, his father, Baron James, summoned to his drawing room one of his most trusted friends, Albert Cohn, a scholar and a devoted Jew who directed the educational work of the Rothschild family. The baron gave Dr. Cohn a simple mandate: Save the Jewish community of Jerusalem.

In June 1854, Albert Cohn left Paris for Vienna en route to Jerusalem. In the Austrian capital he called on Emperor Franz Josef I, who five years earlier had granted his Jewish subjects full civil rights. Dr. Cohn faced the emperor with this proposal: If Franz Josef agreed to be the patron, a hospital would be built in Jerusalem with Rothschild funds that would serve all, regardless of race or creed, in the spirit of the empire's liberal new constitution. The Catholic Franz Josef readily assented, and with an empire firmly behind him, Dr. Cohn set sail for the Holy Land with a traveling companion, Michael Ehrlanger. They landed at Jaffa on July 7, and two days later they stood at Jerusalem's Jaffa Gate. There the entire Jewish community awaited them. Dr. Cohn wept both out of joy and grief, and paraphrasing the words of the prophet, he asked, "Is this the city that is more beautiful than the whole land and now is sighing?" Refusing to rest, he requested to be taken directly to the Western Wall where he wished to pray for the success of his venture. Every Jew in the city, Ashkenazi and Sephardi, infant and aged, man and woman, followed reverently in his footsteps.

Negotiations for the purchase of a hospital building began immediately. The most suitable structure in the Jewish Quarter was a religious school belonging to the Sephardi community. It was located on the slope facing the Wall and the Al Aqsa Mosque. With £1,000 in gold available, the negotiations were not unnecessarily protracted, but there was a fly in the ointment. Under Ottoman Law a European was not permitted to own property in Palestine. Dr. Cohn suggested that he take a lease on the building on condition that when the Rothschild Hospital moved to other quarters the premises would be returned to the Sephardi community. Thirty-five years later, in 1888, that is actually what happened. The Rothschild Hospital moved outside the walled city and the Sephardi community replaced it with its own Misgav Ladach Hospital.

Only seventeen days after Albert Cohn arrived, the conversion of the Sephardi yeshiva into a hospital of eighteen beds (nine for men, nine for women) was completed. It was Rosh Hodesh Menahem Av, July 26. The dedication on that hot, dry summer day was done in the typical Rothschild manner. Turkish and Arab dignitaries of the city attended. So did the consuls of Austria, England, France and Prussia. So did the tailors and the rabbis, the beggars and the carpenters, the scribes and the yeshiva boys. Dr. Cohn spoke in faultless Hebrew, Arabic, French and German. He gave notice that the hospital was under the protection of Franz Josef's flag and that it would be open to the sick of all faiths. The Talmud Torah children, proud to appear before so distinguished an audience, lustily sang Psalm 119 (the longest in the Psalter) and the equally proud rabbis besought the

Divine to pour his blessings on the sultan, the kings of Europe and the Rothschild family. The hospital was a declaration of status, a symbol to the non-Jewish residents of the city of Jewish determination to survive. Just as important, it was an assurance to the Jews that they had not been forgotten by their fellow Jews in the Diaspora. In turn there was little doubt they would ever forget the Rothschilds. On the courtyard gate they put up a Hebrew sign transliterated in Latin characters which read: "For Mayer Rothschild from his sons Amschel, Solomon, Nathan, Karl, James Barrane von Rothschild." From each of the eighteen beds in the green-walled wards hung a plaque bearing the names of members of the family plus those of Sir Moses Montefiore and Lady Judith, Albert Cohn and his wife, Mathilde.

Before leaving Jerusalem later that month, Dr. Cohn provided funds for the establishment of a boys' vocational school and a girls' school. The latter was named for Evelina de Rothschild and is still in existence in western Jerusalem. Prior to embarking from Jaffa, Dr. Cohn addressed a letter to the Jews of Jerusalem in which he pointedly summed up his month-long stay. He wrote, "Ashkenazim and Sephardim! No longer need you ask the missions for aid." On his way home he called on the Turkish minister for foreign affairs in Constantinople and received an unusual letter assuring the Rothschilds that all rights accorded to the Gentiles of Jerusalem would likewise be accorded to the Jews. He stopped in Vienna to report to Franz Josef and invited him to visit the hospital which, in fact, the emperor did sixteen years later. Back in Paris he arranged for a steady flow to the Rothschild Hospital of pharmaceuticals, surgical equipment and a substantial supply of hernia belts. To the schools he shipped libraries in five languages.

The hospital itself was always crowded. Medical care was free. Anyone could visit the out-patient clinic three times a week and obtain all medicines without charge. The Rothschild Hospital doctor was permitted to take a fee only for house visits: two francs during the day and four francs at night. Administration of the hospital was turned over to a mixed Ashkenazi-Sephardi committee, but such were the intercommunal squabbles that the committee was finally disbanded and the hospital was turned over to Dr. Bernard Neumann, who had been resident in Jerusalem for seven years. In Paris, Dr. Cohn received regular reports of the institution's progress. At the end of the first year he happily informed Baron James that of the 542 patients served by the hospital, 502 walked out cured. In that first year, men of many faiths and nations were served. The meticulously kept records include among the patients "33 Moldavians, 21 Italians and 2 Americans." A glance at the occupations of some Jewish patients is revealing: "1 painter, 2 watchmakers, 5 bakers, 6 laundrywomen and 83 scribes," among others. Expenses were listed down to the last sou: of the 14,510 francs expended the first year, 9,490 were spent on food and administration. Albert Cohn returned in 1856 and went away heartened. A year later Alphonse de Rothschild (brother of Gustav) paid a visit and took back to Paris a stirring report that both the death and conversion rates of Jews had fallen. Baron Alphonse set up a fund of 250,000 francs from which the annual interest of 14,000 francs would keep the hospital operating on a permanent basis. In gratitude, the *yishuv* promised that the memorial prayer for the dead would be recited annually in the synagogue hospital for all Rothschilds.

The Rothschilds' word being as sound as their checks, the hospital never lacked means of support. Obligations were kept, sometimes in bizarre ways. During the Franco-Prussian War, for example, Paris was cut off by siege. In September 1870, Dr. Cohn wrote the following letter to the hospital's administrator in Jerusalem:

> This letter will reach you by means of a balloon, if it reaches you at all. We are under siege this Sunday, September 18. Today is the 33rd day of the siege but we are well, thank God.
>
> My two sons are in the army. God has protected them until now. Just now I have written by balloon post to London and I have asked Mrs. Lionel de Rothschild to send by way of the

London branch to Mr. Valero in Jerusalem 5,000 francs that
we will repay, God willing, after the siege is lifted.

In the same year that the Rothschild Hospital was opened, a will was
probated in New Orleans, Louisiana, that had a decisive effect on the
fortunes of Jerusalem's Jewish community and their hospital. It was the
will of the shipowner and philanthropist Judah Touro. He, too, had heard
the agonizing cries that came from the Holy City and provided $60,000
from his $1.5 million estate for settling the Jews outside the walls of
Jerusalem so that they would be assured "the inestimable privilege of
worshiping the Almighty according to our religion, without molestation."
Except for monks who lived in seclusion in fortress monasteries, no one
lived beyond the walls of Jerusalem nor dared to venture beyond them at
night. Beasts and brigands, both real and imaginary, roamed the barren
hills of Judea. But life within the walls had become so intolerable, a break
finally had to be made. Touro's bequest was given to Sir Moses Montefiore
who directed the construction of "almshouses" across the Valley of
Hinnom, which in Biblical times was used by the Canaanites for human
sacrifice. There, only a few hundred yards away, the walled city was close
enough for comfort, yet sufficiently distant to escape the ministrations of
missionaries and the fevers of plagues. A year after the Rothschild Hospital
was in operation the almshouses were dedicated. Named Mishkenot
Sha'ananim (tranquil dwellings), they were beautiful homes for their
times; so well built, in fact, that a century-and-a-half later they were still
being used. Touro's money soon ran out but Sir Moses kept them going.
Later, another neighborhood was added with a windmill that became a
landmark. As a tribute to Montefiore the new project was named Yemin
Moshe (right hand of Moses). Sir Moses, knighted by Queen Victoria for
his philanthropy to Jews, placed an illustration of the Mishkenot
Sha'ananim-Yemin Moshe site on his family seal.

In 1875, with money for the almshouses gone, the poor moved back to
the Old City. The wealthy Jews of Jerusalem leased their own homes within

the overcrowded walled city and moved into the almshouses, living in them rent-free and paying only for their upkeep. In that same year the new head of the hospital began to press the Rothschilds to move the institution outside the walls. Recurrent epidemics made administration difficult and the more well-to-do Jews were leaving the Old City to build new homes beyond the ramparts. The hospital, the pioneer director reasoned, should be in the vanguard of Jewish settlement. The arguments made sense to Alphonse de Rothschild, who got the necessary firman from Sultan Abdul Hamid II and work soon began on a one-and-a-half acre plot not far from the Russian Orthodox Church compound. One week before Rosh Hashanah, in 1888, the hospital – a dignified, three-story edifice costing 211,000 francs and described by a diarist as "the nicest building in our city" – was ready. Originally, the hospital was fitted out with eighteen beds but was quickly enlarged to twenty-four. Later, a children's ward was opened which permitted mothers to live in with their infants. By the turn of the century the hospital could boast of the city's first maternity ward and its own ophthalmologist who was taken on to combat the rocketing incidence of trachoma. Baron Alphonse increased the capital fund for the hospital from 250,000 francs to a round one million and the income increased accordingly. In 1904, Alphonse began receiving reports of budget "irregularities" – money for the hospital was ending up in private pockets – and ordered the physician in charge to turn over the administration to a special committee "appointed from among the best Ashkenazim and Sephardim." He sent a physician from Paris to assume control of the medical organization, but such were the antagonisms between the communities that the committee could not function effectively. The baron, by now old and ill, threw up his hands and turned over the hospital administration to Kol Israel Haverim (better known as the Alliance Israelite Universelle), the Jewish communal organization in Paris. Within a year the books were straightened out and in 1905 the hospital boasted thirty-three beds, two physicians and an administrator, as well as separate quarters for the three men and their families.

To most diaspora Jews, as to the Gentiles, Jerusalem had become a mystical, dreamlike place. For the Jews the city's glories were in its history – in the chronicles of the kingdoms of David and Solomon, in the heroism of the Maccabees, in the magnificence of the Second Temple. *Yerushalayim* was a holy word to repeat in prayers; and its rebirth in this world would be a gift brought by the Messiah. Then in the mid-nineteenth century the crucial mission of a man named Cohn served to change Jewry's view of Jerusalem. He had come to save a remnant and as a result the city again stirred for Jews everywhere. With the passage of time ordinary Jews began to acknowledge the fact that on top of the weather-beaten, treeless Judean hills, at the end of an aimless road located on this globe at 32°45' latitude, 35°13' longitude, Jerusalem breathed.

It would be ludicrous to imply that Jerusalem of the Jews was restored only because the Rothschild Hospital of eighteen beds was established. There is little question, however, that it was a significant beginning. Later on, other hospitals were established, but in the first fifty years none of them managed to prevent epidemics or even undertook large-scale public health campaigns. Jerusalem still suffered from malaria, trachoma, cholera, typhus, typhoid, ringworm, malnutrition and pox. But at least the city's Jewish population could have good care without paying for it either with money or with their consciences. There was another important development, too. Mothers began going to hospital to have their babies and infant mortality dropped.

The Rothschild Hospital helped lift Jerusalem out of the Middle Ages, brought it into contact with the medical sciences of the Western world and, perhaps as important as anything else, provided the focus from which Jerusalem would be catapulted into the best that medicine of the twentieth century could offer. But that would not take place until after World War I and until after a few brave pioneers in skirts came to Jerusalem and looked into the sad, sick eyes of its children.

FLIES IN NOVEMBER

November, 1909. On the uneven stone pavement outside the Old City wall, on Jaffa Road, three women stood for a moment chatting in a foreign tongue. From where the barefooted beggar woman sat, up against the wall of the apothecary, she could see that the eldest of the three had tears in her eyes. These were definitely Ashkenazim from a foreign land, judging by their clothes. The beggar woman adjusted the scrawny dozing infant in the crook of her arm, extended her hand a bit farther and pleaded, "Matliq, matliq."

The old Ashkenazi matron sent one of the younger women over with a coin. The beggar looked up into a face that was grim, into eyes that were as sharp as the bite of mosquitoes. The mouth of this Ashkenazi lady was saying something in a strange Hebrew accent: "Why don't you brush the flies from the child's eyes?" As the lady deposited the coin she swooshed her hand past the baby's fly-infested eyes. The baby jerked its head as though something familiar were being snatched from it. The beggar woman's own watery, squinting eyes lost some of their vapidity for a moment as she began to explain, "They will only come back." They were part of her abysmal life, like begging and like her chronically ill husband who had to stop work in the carpentry shop because of his consumption.

What did these strangers want, that a poor mendicant should do the sultan's work for him and rid Jerusalem of its flies! "May God bless you and keep you well and give you a safe return home," the beggar murmured. The matron called out, "Come on, now, we have only a few hours to the Sabbath, Henrietta, and we want to make it to the Wailing Wall." Henrietta Szold, then only a month from her forty-ninth birthday, turned and, lost in thought, walked off mechanically to join her mother and friend. Soon they were lost in the crowds of the marketplace.

Not far from the beggar woman a haughty, elderly doctor was receiving patients from the back of his ragged brown mule. "What is *your* complaint?" he asked with a touch of annoyance in his voice.

"Doctor, doctor," half-cried the young man holding his hand to his brow. "My brains feel like they are boiling."

The doctor bent low to probe for the patient's spleen and stated the diagnosis, "ague," in the tone of a magistrate fining a hungry thief for stealing bread. He scribbled a prescription on a piece of notepad paper, took the *grush* that was extended to him and looking at his watch, shouted, "Next!" An elderly man complained of loose bowels and terrible cramps. "Bismuth for you. Next! Hurry up! The Sabbath is approaching."

Prescriptions in hand, the sick turned and stepped past the beggar woman into the pharmacy. In the opening years of twentieth century in Jerusalem, quinine and bismuth were the magic cure-alls. Physicians took up their stations outside pharmacies because it was both practical and profitable. Doctors and the druggists cooperated as partners-in-trade.

In the first years of the century not more than a dozen Jewish doctors with fairly good training practiced in Jerusalem. Because there was no medical association or effective health department to control standards, quackery and medicine existed side by side. Even physicians who had genuine diplomas scoffed at new methods of diagnosis and treatment. A thorough medical examination was unknown. When one young physician arrived with a lab microscope from Europe as late as 1914, the resident doctors laughed in ridicule. What kind of doctor has to examine blood specimens before he diagnoses malaria?

As for the pharmacists, not all, to put it mildly, had academic training. A large number learned the rudiments of the profession as apprentices. Turkish law did require a certificate showing professional competence before issuing a license to open a drugstore, but this regulation was easily circumvented. All one had to do was to pay a practicing pharmacist to open another shop in his own name. He would then permit his young apprentice to run the apothecary. Working together with a physician or a quack, they made a good living by splitting the profits.

One of the most popular pharmacies of the day in Jerusalem was that of the Greek Kaitonopoulos, well-located just off Jaffa Road. There the medicine men would gather. The well-to-do would work from the backs of mules. The others, usually younger men, would sit on stools near the beggars, smoke water pipes and, while waiting for customers, exchange the latest in folk medicine. Understandably, some patients had more faith in pharmacists than in doctors. The druggists had the advantage of being less expensive; going straight to the pharmacist was like bypassing the middleman. When there were no physicians near, pharmacists would encourage direct contact. "Why ask the doctors?" a druggist would confide to a patient, "I can do as well." Medical problems were simply solved. Complaints were put into a few general categories. Every pharmacist knew that a few drops of silver nitrate would cure trachoma, and if the eye disease was already in a chronic stage, then a touch of copper stick, serving as a cauterizing agent on the conjunctiva, would give relief. It was as simple as that.

Jerusalem had four Jewish hospitals. But many Jewish mothers placed their faith primarily in traditional preventive measures and remedies. In late summer, for example, the children should be very careful of ripe melons. Melon juice must not be rubbed into the eye otherwise it will become sticky with the sickness. And if the child does contract trachoma, the best relief is egg yolk and a mustard plaster over the temple. If the baby's sleep is disturbed at night because of stomach pains, burn white herbs of the field under the cradle. The fragrance, seductive as a lullaby, will caress the child back to sleep. If the pains continue, then drive them away with a burning stick applied to the chest or stomach.

Basically, all ills had their root in the evil eye and there was no safer, better guardian than a well-prepared amulet. Going into hospitals was so risky! Is it not a fact that many who go in never come out alive? If you are going to die, then what better place than in your own bed, among your own sympathetic family. It is better to die peacefully than to take your chance in the French, German, Greek, Russian or British mission hospitals. They may serve kosher food, but they are the devil's delicatessens! The government hospital? Who would ever think of putting his life into the hands of the Turks! Jewish hospitals? They were probably the safest of the lot, but better wear the *Kame'a* and stay well.

There was another segment of the population – less primitive, more courageous and willing to take a chance – that would call a physician or a quack to the home; whether the former or latter, depended on the family's financial position. If the doctor's advice did not immediately cure the patient, then another doctor was called the following day. After a number of physicians were consulted, then all the prescriptions were taken to the pharmacy and the pharmacist was asked which he thought was the most effective.

A relatively small community of enlightened souls took advantage of the few reasonably good doctors and hospitals in Jerusalem. They went to the excellent eye hospital established by the Order of St. John of Malta. They entered the Jewish institutions which, for all their administrative problems, gave exceptional medical care. But the best of medicine in Jerusalem was only palliative in the face of enormous problems. When Henrietta Szold and her seventy-seven-year-old mother stared at the flies in children's eyes in Tiberias, Jaffa and Jerusalem – a scene that invariably brought tears to the eyes of Mrs. Szold – they were looking at a problem whose dimensions were social and educational as much as medical. The need for a vast public health program screamed out. Mamma Szold and Henrietta heard the cry. Throughout their month-long trip to the Holy Land in November 1909, as they visited schools and religious sites and saw beggars in squalid streets, it was tearful Mamma who prodded Henrietta, "Here is work for you. This is what your group ought to be doing."

Henrietta's group was a study circle that was formed as the Daughters of Zion by Emma Gottheil in 1898. Emma had accompanied her husband, Semitics Professor Richard Gottheil, to Basel where he was a delegate to the Second Zionist Congress. While there, Emma met Theodor Herzl, who encouraged her to organize American women in the cause of Zionism. On her return home she invited young women from New York's East Side to study Zionist and Jewish subjects at her elegant Fifth Avenue home. A few years later, at the suggestion of some of the participants in the group, the name was changed from Daughters of Zion to Hadassah in memory of Hadassah Gottheil, Emma's mother. Similar study groups sprang up in Harlem, then a center of Jewish life in New York City. Most of them were called Daughters of Zion and a few, Hadassah. They were small and met sporadically. The girls, who were in their late teens or early twenties and had some Hebrew education, were concerned about their identity as Jews. In their discussions they eagerly sought Judaism's answers to such problems as social inequality and militarism.

One of the better known group leaders was the brilliant but complex Jessie Sampter, a pacifist and intellectual, who traveled to Zionism and back to Judaism by a devious route, through the Ethical Culture movement, Unitarianism, and socialism. She influenced a number of young women who later were to become leaders on the American Zionist scene. One of the more successful study circles called Hadassah was formed by Lotta Levensohn at the encouragement of Rabbi Judah Leib Magnes, of Temple Emanu-El, for whom she worked in his capacity as honorary secretary of the Federation of American Zionists (later to become the Zionist Organization of America). In discussing prospective members for the group, whose primary purpose was to acquaint Jewish women with

Zionism and Palestine, Rabbi Magnes suggested to Lotta that his prestigious pacifist friend Henrietta Szold be asked to join – in an honorary capacity, of course. Lotta later recalled that she was reticent to approach so eminent a scholar and editor as Henrietta Szold and asked Rabbi Magnes to make the approach. He did and Henrietta replied that she would be happy to join but as an active participant not as an honorary do-nothing member. That assured the success of this particular study group. From its inception in the autumn of 1907 it met in the YMHA on Lexington Avenue in New York City.

Henrietta was twice the age of most of the young women, so it was natural that she should be their leader. Later, she brought in a few older women ("They will keep me company," she told a friend), among them Emma Gottheil and Mathilde Schechter, wife of the president of the Jewish Theological Seminary. Henrietta set the tone of these meetings. "Wherever she sat," Lotta Levensohn recalled years later, "Henrietta Szold became the head of the table."

On returning from the Palestine adventure in January 1910, spurned in love, Henrietta lost herself more and more in Zionist work. She served as honorary secretary of the predominantly male Federation of American Zionists. But after eight months of trying to straighten out the organization's hopelessly desperate financial affairs, she gave up. That experience, coupled with her mother's urging to "do something" and her own poignant recollections of life in Palestine, quickened within her the idea that a national women's Zionist organization must be formed to carry out practical projects. She arrived upon the scene at the right moment.

Women from the former study groups of Harlem created the nucleus. There was Emma Gottheil, the third woman of the triumvirate that toured Jerusalem. There was Gertrude Goldsmith, with whom Henrietta worked closely on the early plans of a national organization. And there were Mathilde Schechter, Lotta Levensohn, Sophia Berger and Rosalie Philips. "I would be ashamed to attend another Zionist Congress," Emma would say, "and report that we did nothing but talk." That was the sentiment of the hour and it was embodied by these seven Zionist women in the brief invitations sent out to prospective members in the second week of February 1912. "The time is ripe for a large organization of women Zionists," their invitation read. Their purpose? "The promotion of Jewish institutions and enterprises in Palestine and the fostering of Jewish ideals."

Sometime after 8:00 p.m. on February 24 1912, in the vestry room of Rabbi Magnes's Temple Emanu-El, a group of fewer than 20 (the precise number is not known) met for what was to become the founding session of Hadassah as a national Zionist organization. Henrietta Szold spoke of her trip to Palestine and of the need for a "definite project." Eva Leon, who had been to Palestine more recently and was Emma Gottheil's sister, brought home the need for wider maternity service in the Holy Land. One such service, she reported, was run by the Christian missionary London Jews' Society whose price of admission to the hospital was the agreement of mothers to baptize their babies on departure.

A constitution was later drawn up. Article I gave the old familiar name Daughters of Zion to the projected national organization. Henrietta held that the organization could not really be considered national in scope until more chapters were established. This constitution, then, was really the by-laws of the New York chapter called Hadassah (from the Hebrew for myrtle). The name was a natural if only because the founding meeting was held on the Feast of Purim and Hadassah was also the Hebrew name of the Biblical heroine Queen Esther. In the spirit of the holiday the opening session decided that all future chapters of Hadassah would likewise take on the names of Jewish heroines. (It was historic justice that in later years Henrietta Szold would be among the most popular of all Hadassah chapter names.) Other articles in the constitution spelled out the purpose of the organization and provided that associate membership be given to women who did not consider themselves Zionists. Later, associate membership was dropped when the constitution was amended to foster Zionist ideals in America.

At the first meeting there was a discussion on numerous projects that the Daughters of Zion might initiate: a day nursery, a girls' workshop to make lace, a maternity hospital, a school to train midwives, a district nursing scheme, sending nurses to Palestine. Finally, Henrietta Szold was elected president and nineteen members were made either officers or members of the board. Altogether thirty-eight women were listed as founding members. At the first board meeting, held at the home of Mathilde Schechter on April 4 and chaired by Henrietta, the ten members present agreed that if practical projects were not to be mere flights of fancy, the organization would need a membership of three hundred. By the end of the first year, that goal had not been reached: there were 157 regulars and 37 associates, and the cash box had $542.00 from dues. But the organization did have a motto taken from Jeremiah 8:22 (*Arukhat Bat Ammi* – "Healing of the Daughter of My People"*), which was suggested by the Jewish Theological Seminary's Professor Israel Friedlander. And it had an emblem – a Star of David – on which the motto and Hadassah in Hebrew were superimposed. That was the work of Victor Brenner who gave the United States the design for the Lincoln penny. In February 1913, Hadassah Chapter finally had sufficient money – "tribute" as Henrietta Szold described it sarcastically – to affiliate with the Federation of American Zionists. In June of 1914 the first and last Daughters of Zion national convention was held in Rochester, New York, where seven of the eight chapters were represented (Boston's Deborah was missing). At that convention Rabbi Magnes took an active part. His lasting contribution was to urge the delegates to adopt the more concise Hadassah as the name of the national organization. It was done and Daughters of Zion became a footnote in Zionist history.

Apart from its founding day, there is no date in Hadassah's first years that was so significant and hopeful for the organization as January 1, 1913. On that day an extraordinary meeting of the board was called at the home

---

* Although this has been a standard translation, especially appropriate for Hadassah, the phrase is more accurately translated "Healing of My People."

of Emma Gottheil. There, Henrietta Szold brought the exciting news that the department store magnate and philanthropist, Nathan Straus, had agreed to help finance both traveling expenses and four months' salary for a trained nurse, to be chosen by Hadassah, to open a health station in Palestine. But he set two conditions: one, after the first four months Hadassah would have to pay the nurse's salary – that would mean $2,500 for two years – and, two, that she would be ready to leave for Palestine with Mr. and Mrs. Straus by January 18.

Hadassah was facing its first crisis. "When I heard the proposal, I was terrified," board member Alice Seligsberg wrote many years later. With only a few hundred dollars in the till these women were about to undertake a major responsibility that could, through failure, make them the laughing stock of the Jewish community. Already, male Zionist leaders were grousing that the women were dividing the movement. An undercurrent of feeling grew at first among board members that it was too big a challenge for so young an organization. But Henrietta and Emma were insistent. Their self-confidence swung the other members and when a vote to underwrite the mission was taken, all ten hands went up in favor. Everyone was aware that should they fail, the organization would be badly crippled. But should they make a success of it, chances were good of winning over large numbers of American Jewish women.

Henrietta Szold was sold on the idea of establishing in Jerusalem, for a start, a district home-nursing system. She wanted to model it after Lillian Wald's Settlement House and District Visiting Nurses, then being tried with success in New York City. Nathan Straus, too, was aware of the need. He visited Jerusalem in 1912 and on the spot set up a soup kitchen and a health bureau. The latter was run by a German-Jewish doctor, Wilhelm Bruenn, who on his own had been fighting malaria, trachoma and backwater fever.

There was a political side to the quick opening of the health bureau. When Straus appeared in Palestine, he found that the German government, expecting a war in Europe, was sending doctors and sanitary engineers to

Jerusalem. The Kaiser considered Palestine strategic because it protected the flank of the Berlin-Constantinople-Baghdad railroad line. It was therefore necessary to clean up the area for the German soldiers who might have to be stationed there. The Kaiser ordered the Hamburg Tropical Institute to send doctors and sanitary engineers, one of whom was known to the Jews of Jerusalem as a dangerous and rabid anti-Semite, to close cisterns and give quinine prophylaxis. It was this added factor – to provide a counterweight to the German activity – that convinced Straus to answer the urgent call of Dr. Bruenn and the Jewish community.

When Nathan Straus returned from Jerusalem, he told Henrietta Szold in explanation of opening a soup kitchen, "Once long ago, I suffered the pangs of hunger. I was starving; I had no money for even a single meal. I have never forgotten the sensation. In so far as lies within my power, no man that crosses my path shall go hungry." He then told Henrietta that he had heard about her desire to initiate a nursing project in Jerusalem. "Why don't you do it?" the philanthropist asked Henrietta.

"But we have only $283 in our treasury," she replied.

"That doesn't matter," both Strauses said in unison. "Start!" Nathan Straus commanded.

Henrietta insisted there was no money, and Nathan Straus repeated, "That has nothing to do with it!" Henrietta was befuddled for a moment. Then her eye caught Lina Straus standing behind her husband's chair nodding frantically as if to say, Henrietta later recalled, "The Lord will provide." Henrietta was encouraged although doubt still lingered.

The day after that confrontation took place, the Strauses called at Henrietta's apartment. They went through the same "start work – no money" routine until Nathan Straus finally broke it off with the offer that Henrietta somewhat breathlessly reported to her board on January 1. The Lord had indeed provided.

In the following weeks, hectic interviewing took place. Henrietta talked to twenty-one applicants. In the midst of the search for a suitable nurse came a bombshell message from Eva Leon. Non-Zionist friends in Chicago, she reported, offered to grant $2,000 a year for five years to send a nurse to Palestine and they insisted that Hadassah choose and supervise the nurse. The crisis was over. It was now possible to send two nurses with the Strauses and possibly a third and fourth later on.

On January 18, as planned, the Strauses sailed again for Palestine taking with them Eva Leon and two trail-blazing Hadassah nurses – Rose Kaplan and Rachel Landy. Little more than two months later, on March 23, 1913, Hadassah for the first time brought healing to Jerusalem.

WAR, DISEASE, STARVATION, DEATH

T he four horsemen of the Apocalypse had already begun their long, wild ride in the Balkans when the two nurses set sail for Palestine in the bitter cold winter of January 1913. Highly skilled as the nurses were, they were not prepared for the hardships ahead.

Short and stocky, Russian-born Rose Kaplan was the older of the two and had a long distinguished career in nursing at Mt. Sinai Hospital in New York. Tall and blonde, Cleveland-born Rachel Landy was a light-hearted, fun-loving woman who had supervised nurses at Harlem Hospital Dispensary in New York. Rose signed up for two years, Ray for two-and-a-half. The assumption was that they would introduce a district nursing system under the guidance of Dr. Bruenn, head of the Straus Health Bureau. Things turned out differently.

When the nurses, together with the Strauses and Eva Leon, arrived in Jerusalem, public health work was being done by a number of independent organizations. Dr. Bruenn had gone to Tiberias to fight a cholera epidemic, then left for Germany. An eye clinic, Lema'an Zion, was functioning under a popular young German-Jewish physician, Albert Ticho. Anti-trachoma clinics were operating under the Austrian-Jewish doctor, Arieh Feigenbaum. Rose and Ray hardly knew where or with whom to begin.

With financial aid from the Strauses they furnished a stone house located in the ghetto-like, ultra-orthodox quarter of Mea Shearim, opposite the Hungarian Houses. A fragrant lemon tree grew in the courtyard. On the iron gate entrance a sign was hung: "American Daughters of Zion Nurses Settlement **HADASSAH**," and – as fate would decree – at Purim time, on March 23, 1913, they accepted their first patients. In the beginning they took maternity cases, but trachoma was so rampant that under the guidance of their neighbor, Dr. Ticho, they began to care for the sick eyes of Jerusalem. One year later, they reported to Hadassah that they had treated five thousand children for eye disease, 20 percent of them trachoma.

The Strauses and Eva Leon, who had been asked by Henrietta Szold to represent Hadassah in Jerusalem, soon left. Hard work and loneliness took a double toll of the nurses' spirits. They had hoped they would be accepted with open arms by the community. In fact, they were greeted with suspicion and skepticism by both residents and professionals because in those days nurses who went to Jerusalem were nuns. Rumors were spread that Rose and Ray were spies who had come to infiltrate the Jewish community. They plugged away nevertheless against Jerusalem's spiritual and bodily malignancies. Their monthly reports contained an encyclopedia of illnesses: enteritis, dysentery, typhoid, paratyphoid, trachoma and, as they wrote in one, "starvation." What disturbed them most was the high maternal mortality rate. It seemed that at least every other mother died while giving birth. They found one source of the problem in the untrained women who were acting as midwives. Ray and Rose were horrified to discover that these "midwives" would supervise births without even washing their hands. To ease difficult labor the ignorant attendants would pour impure oil into the womb and unintentionally induce septicemia which was usually fatal.

The nurses immediately scoured Jerusalem for Jewish women who had received some training abroad in obstetrics. They discovered four, all graduates of Viennese and Constantinople schools, and employed them to pay regular visits to pregnant Jewish women in the city. Rose and Ray also formed a class for "big sisters" to whom they taught personal hygiene and child care.

When they were not in the settlement house tending to patients, the two nurses helped destitute families with a little money or food, sometimes giving them linen or a layette, and generally building confidence and faith in genuine medical practices. Where they could not help with medicines or money, they would ease social problems with sympathy and understanding. Gradually a feeling of kinship grew between the nurses and the Jewish community. Soon they were among the most loved visitors in Jerusalem. Their warm, gentle manner, their easy Yiddish talk had won out. Where once they were called spies, they were now called angels. In schools, where teachers had refused to permit the nurses to examine the children's eyes, they now eagerly greeted them. With the pupils Rose was gravely persistent; Ray was smilingly insistent. The nurses' personalities were complementary and they got along well. (Ray always had an added inducement in her pockets when the going got rough with the children: hard candies.)

When they diagnosed serious eye trouble, their most difficult task was to convince the patients, or the parents in the case of children, to enter Dr. Ticho's eye clinic for treatment. Once the patients did risk it, they found the cure well worth the treatment. As a result, fear and prejudice gradually declined and the queues outside the settlement house grew longer from week to week. One of Ray's favorite stories to her stubborn patients was about a Bedouin who brought his young wife to Dr. Ticho's clinic. The Arab asked the doctor whether he could restore the sight of his bride's one bad eye. Ticho found that her sight had been impaired by tissue that had grown over an old inflammation and he operated. A short time later the woman could see well again. Her proud husband, profuse in his gratitude, said to Dr. Ticho, "I took a chance and I won, thanks to you. I bought this woman cheaply because she had one bad eye. Now she is worth twice as much."

Jerusalem had a deep effect on the nurses. Rose was no Zionist when she left for Palestine and she never seemed to have considered the possibility of settling in the Holy Land. But in her letters home she wrote of the joy she felt when she visited schools, particularly the secular Gymnasium, where she saw hundreds of bright and alert children who had emigrated with their parents from Eastern Europe. She also wrote despairingly of the poor children she treated in Jerusalem's Tin Quarter, so-named because the hovels in which they lived were made from discarded Standard Oil Company tin cans. So bad were conditions of other Jewish families living in cramped, underground cavelike rooms, she said, that even a little bit of sunlight would have made an immense difference in preventing and curing illnesses. She reported back to Hadassah the general feeling of the small professional community that social conditions of hygiene were the prime factors influencing the health of the Jewish community, but the problems were so enormous that a large-scale public health effort would be needed to change the picture.

A few months before World War I erupted, the noted Baltimore eye physician, Harry Friedenwald, spent two months' volunteer service in Jerusalem. He saw that the nurses were doing fine work, but there was no overall coordination. Health institutions were duplicating each other. Besides four Jewish hospitals there were the Straus Health Bureau and Pasteur Institute, Dr. Ticho's Lema'an Zion, Dr. Feigenbaum's clinics and Hadassah. Competition among them caused animosity and friction. For their part, the nurses worked around the clock – in the schools, at the settlement house, in Dr. Ticho's clinic, with pregnant women, teaching midwives. In the United States it was impossible for Hadassah leaders to get a clear picture of what was taking place. Frantic correspondence went back and forth over the 6,000 miles between New York and Jerusalem. Hadassah was troubled that the nurses were fighting trachoma in schools when they should have been setting up a district nursing system, and besides why wasn't the Straus Health Bureau doing the anti-trachoma work? The fact was that so much had to be done by so few competent people that everything was being done on an emergency basis. It was clear even before Dr. Friedenwald arrived in Jerusalem that two more nurses were urgently required. Eva Leon reported to Hadassah early in 1914 that the nurses needed help to get their district visiting system underway. She said she planned to return to help them. After hearing Eva's report in January 1914, Hadassah's central committee in New York adopted two principles that fixed the guideposts for its future work in Palestine. In agreeing to Eva's return, it requested her to send frequent reports and to consult on essential matters first with the home office, "even at the risk of delay." The reason for the latter principle was simply that even as early as January 1914, Hadassah was thinking in terms of a permanent presence in Palestine and that final responsibility for all the work overseas had to reside with the home organization. Hadassah was to be no mere fund raiser but a dynamic American-based Zionist movement.

The war exploded in August 1914. Communications with Palestine were broken. Eva Leon did not return as planned. The additional nurses could not sail. Dr. Friedenwald reported his experiences to Henrietta Szold and suggested that Hadassah establish a lying-in hospital in Jerusalem. His was the first serious suggestion that Hadassah build a hospital. Henrietta reported this to the central committee in October. By then the war was two months old. The committee decided to ask Rose Kaplan to consider remaining at her place until a replacement could be sent. Ray Landy's contract was to expire in July 1915, and by then, it was felt, the war would be over. The request never reached Rose and her letters pleading for instructions never arrived in New York.

Conditions in Jerusalem were fast deteriorating. The war added another misery to the lives of the city's Jews. They were panic-stricken at the thought of being trapped on a potential battlefield, but even more so that sons and fathers would be drafted into the sultan's army. Hundreds of families packed their bags and prepared to flee to Egypt. The Turks expelled all non-Turkish citizens. The French physician heading the Rothschild Hospital, Jacob Segal, returned to Paris and joined the army. Dr. Bruenn, of the Straus Health Bureau, sailed for Germany to enlist. Bruenn's successor, Abraham Goldberg, was inducted into the Turkish forces. Later on, Ticho and Feigenbaum would have to leave the city on perilous adventures. The prospects were not bright for the American nurses. The Jewish agronomist, Aaron Aaronsohn, world-famed for discovering the original species of wheat in eastern Galilee, warned the nurses to return home. Rose was in a dilemma. The last ship was about to sail from Haifa. She was not aware that Hadassah urgently wanted her to remain. Her contract was expiring. Refugees were pouring out of Jerusalem. She had little money left and no prospects for getting more. Aaronsohn, who was aware of the international political situation, pleaded with her to go. Rose bent to the pressures, but with a purpose in hand. She sailed with the Jewish refugees, meaning to care for them in three camps set up in Alexandria. Hadassah was completely in the dark about Rose. Then, while the central committee was meeting in New York on February 15, Rose walked in. The committee members were startled. What they soon learned was that Rose could not stay on in Egypt because she needed urgent medical care. After an operation, she insisted on returning to the refugee camps in Alexandria. She set sail in November 1915, but the Greek steamer she had taken sank in the Atlantic as a result of a fire in the engine room. She was rescued and finally got to Egypt in early 1916. There, she served in the camps until, on August 3, 1919, she died of cancer.

Ray kept on with the maternity and anti-trachoma work in Jerusalem after Rose's departure. "Although it is not very pleasant living here alone, especially just now," she wrote to Alice Seligsberg in January 1915, "I am perfectly willing and satisfied to keep up the Hadassah work, as long as I have funds."

Bravely but lonely, in a tense unpredictable situation where the Turks were daily becoming more anti-American, Ray tried to maintain a normal regimen of work. Every Thursday morning she continued to give classes in what she called her "School of Home Nursing."

She wrote:

> I find these classes very interesting. We have taken bed-
> making with and without a patient in bed – lifting helpless
> patients. I gave one of the children a bed sponge bath. We
> have made linseed poultices, mustard pastes and foot baths.
> The girls are very clever and enjoy the classes very much. The
> last few weeks I have been teaching bandaging, so as to be
> up-to-date. We all find it very fascinating. I just give practical
> work and then give them notes. The girls are from 15 to 17
> years of age – only seven of them – but small classes are
> always better...

Around Ray's island of normalcy the whirlwind of terror grew daily. Jews in Jerusalem were a suspect alien element. They were liable to sudden arrest, banishment, torture. They were at the will and whim of Jamal Pasha, a tyrant who was answerable exclusively to the sultan and, on occasion, only to Allah. Little wonder that anyone who could escape the city did so. So many left that midway during the war only three Jewish physicians remained. And hard as they worked they were helpless in the face of chain-reaction epidemics. Malnutrition set in on a large scale soon after the hostilities began. Day in, day out, families lived on *tzibile mit shires* (onions dipped in sesame seed oil), a few spoiled vegetables that were brought to market by Bedouin, a bit of bread and a little goat's milk. Children suffered from a lack of vitamins, and as the war continued their stomachs became bloated. They were a pathetic picture as they walked the streets of Jerusalem searching garbage cans for scraps of food. Ray never forgot the scene:

> Never in my life will I forget these last few weeks. You should
> see the people in the streets. They are perfect studies of pain,
> misery and starvation. I never saw such faces. You can
> imagine how it feels to meet people who you can see are

hungry, yet you don't like to approach them and they are ashamed to approach you. The Straus soup kitchen is open. What a blessing it is! I passed it one morning and I never witnessed a more pitiful sight. You can imagine the number of applicants – such screaming and pushing – women fainting... I was watching some children of the Sepharad Talmud Torah eat their midday meal yesterday. Some had a piece of bread and the green leaves and stalks which come off a head of cauliflower. I have often wondered how these children can be happy – for they really seem to be. They are very amusing – perfect little devils. I have a right jolly time with them once in a while...

Two weeks later: "It is all I can do to treat the Sepharad Talmud Torah. The children seem to be getting smaller and thinner every day. They are developing idiotic expressions on their faces and are such pitiful sights."

Then the locusts came. Voraciously, as though they too were victims of the growing famine, they ate fabrics, curtains, rugs. Infants had to be protected with heavy clothing. They fastened on to the garments – even the underwear – of adults.

Debilitating diseases became widespread – diarrhea and intestinal ailments were common, spread by unattended cesspits that poured rivers of sewage into the streets. Few residents boiled their water. Paratyphoid, typhoid, typhus swept across the city in waves. In summer, water in the cisterns sank low. Arabs would fill the cisterns by bringing supplies in *tennikes* (oblong oil tins), strapped to the backs of donkeys. A whole day's work would fill a cistern, but the wells were left uncovered and the anopheles thrived in the water. The Old City of Jerusalem swarmed with mosquitoes and few residents escaped malaria. Trachoma cases multiplied and Jerusalem became known, along with its traditional names, as the City of the Blind. Spotted fever made an appearance, then cholera. On and on rolled the list of diseases and the registers of the dead.

Jerusalem was a ghostly city. In mid-morning, Jaffa Road was deserted except for the movement of military traffic. A few old people who seemed immune to death, showed up regularly to sweep the streets. Men of military age dared not go out lest they be pulled into the sultan's forces by Jamal Pasha's police. And that was worse than a thousand plagues.

The situation might have been somewhat relieved if sources of money had not dried up. But Jerusalem was as poor as it was sick. Soon after the war began, families sold furniture, pillows, bedsheets and rugs to buy food. They would barter it to the Bedouin who came in out of the wilderness with vegetables. As the war went on, families were left living in bare houses, sleeping on stone and tile floors with nothing but the clothes they wore.

At this time, Ray wrote in one of her letters, "There is a lady physician here, an obstetrician and I have asked her to help us in our maternity work."

Helena Kagan was her name. Spurned and scorned by professional colleagues when she first arrived in Jerusalem from Switzerland in 1914, she was later to carry on the Hadassah nurses' work when they left, and to treat Jerusalem single-handedly when the last two Jewish male physicians were forced out of the city. She was to become a legend in her own time.

In those days Helena Kagan kept a cow in her backyard for no other purpose than to provide milk for the children who visited her clinic. But it was only a drop in an ocean of need. To save the Jews of Jerusalem, transfusions of money and supplies were needed on a grand scale. They arrived in a most dramatic way.

Young as it was, Hadassah was making urgent inquiries at top political levels in Washington to send relief to the Jews of Palestine. Acting on its behalf was Louis Levin, a noted social service worker and brother-in-law of Henrietta Szold. Levin knew that a Navy collier, the *Vulcan*, was about to sail for the Middle East. He asked the Navy Department whether Hadassah could send along a physician and supplies. Inexplicably, the *Vulcan* was not permitted to take a physician but space was made for 900 tons of food and medicines, sent by Mary Fels, wife of the founder of the Fels-Naphtha soap company, who till she died at aged 90 in 1953, was an active Zionist. Levin and a young dentist, Samuel Lewin-Epstein, were authorized to travel along with the relief.

The *Vulcan* put into Jaffa port four days after Passover in 1915, too late for its supplies of *matzot* to grace holiday tables. Awaiting the *Vulcan* were the Turkish police with orders to arrest Levin and Lewin-Epstein the moment they set foot on shore. The charge was that they were agents of the Allies who had come to incite a revolt against the Turkish regime. But the Turks were stymied by the American consul in Jerusalem, Otto Glazebrook, an Episcopalian minister who went aboard and announced that the two men had the diplomatic protection of the neutral U.S. government. The two men turned over to Glazebrook $100,000 in gold which they had brought from American Zionist organizations for the Jews of Palestine. The consul returned immediately to Jerusalem with Lewin-Epstein who later checked into a Jerusalem hotel. Levin remained with the *Vulcan*.

One day, Jamal Pasha called on Lewin-Epstein, and in the presence of the consul invited him to dinner. Suspecting that the Pasha intended a plot against the American, Ellis Gillette, the interpreter, stepped on the foot of the consul and said, "But Dr. Glazebrook, you already have asked our guest for dinner." With that Lewin-Epstein was rushed to the safety of the consulate. In a few days, the *Vulcan* was to sail for home. Lewin-Epstein had to make the ship, but the consul had been warned that Jamal Pasha was not going to let him leave the country alive. It was suggested that he leave in disguise, but the proud Glazebrook would have none of it. "He arrived here as an American. He will leave as an American."

Telegraphic messages passed urgently between Jerusalem, American Ambassador Henry Morgenthau in Istanbul and the State Department. Finally, Glazebrook was authorized to inform Jamal Pasha that if Lewin-Epstein was harmed before he reached the *Vulcan*, the U.S. cruiser *Tennessee*, steaming off the coast of Palestine, would fire its guns on the port of Jaffa.

Jamal Pasha quickly indicated that the man need not worry about traveling to Jaffa. The ride to port went off without incident.

Back in Jerusalem, Jamal Pasha's agents began searching for the gold. Glazebrook had handed it over to David Yellin, then chairman of the Va'ad ha-Kehila (committee of the Jewish community), whose headquarters were located in the Street of the Prophets not far from the Rothschild Hospital. One night, Yellin raced across the street to Helena Kagan, hauling the hot gold. He pleaded with her to hide it, arguing that the Turks would not lower themselves to search the premises of a single, young woman. Years later, Dr. Kagan recalled, "I almost fainted when I saw all that gold, because I knew that if I were ever found with it, I would have been hanged." Working at night, she and Yellin dug a hole next to a palm in her backyard and buried the money there. From time to time, as they needed it, Dr. Kagan would dig it up and turn as much as was needed over to a special committee of the community. The treasure did not last too long. Nor did the relief supplies, half of which were confiscated by the Turks.

Through the summer of 1915, Ray Landy worked together with Helena Kagan. Her own money was down to practically nothing. Hadassah sent messages through Ambassador Morgenthau to Glazebrook to find out how she fared. Ray replied that even though her contract had run out, she was willing to stay on if everyone at home agreed. But Ray's parents in Cleveland were terrified by news reports from Palestine and implored Hadassah to recall their daughter. Finally, the central committee cabled: "Come home." Ray could hardly believe that she was to seal the doors of the settlement house. She wrote to Hadassah, "I don't know whether I had malaria or whether my fever was due to your telegram, but my temperature went up to 39 degrees C. (101.6) and stayed there off and on until I sent you a reply."

Ray settled her affairs, distributed supplies that she had received from the *Vulcan* and closed the settlement house. But she remained in Jerusalem until the very last moment. She disliked Jaffa so much that she asked Consul Glazebrook to telegraph her from the port precisely when the ship was to leave. As she sat for several days waiting, she wrote, "I still wish I would be obliged to stay until you could send nurses. I don't know whether it is Jerusalem or these trying times, but I have become so attached to everything and everybody that it gives me a sinking feeling when I think of leaving it all at this stage, especially since I have been through the worst. It upsets me very much to break up the Settlement. I had looked forward to leaving it in a different fashion."

Her last words from Jerusalem in September were to ask Hadassah to raise the salaries of the two local "probationers." Wrote Ray, "No matter what or how much I asked them to do, they always did it cheerfully." And the midwives were underpaid, too, she wrote. She hung on, but finally the moment of her departure was at hand. At the specific request of Hadassah, Dr. Kagan and Dr. Ticho continued the medical work. Glazebrook took fond leave of Ray. He had written Hadassah, "Miss Landy is one of the most useful people in Jerusalem. She is a splendid woman and is accomplishing most excellent work. I congratulate your society on having such a representative."

In New York, Hadassah had no word after it sent the "Come home" cable. What happened to Ray? It sent more cables to Glazebrook through Morgenthau. "Why does Landy not come home?" Finally, on October 8 a telegram arrived from Ray in Naples. Two words: "Sailing *Cretic*." The *Cretic* left two days later, and Ray was home two weeks later. The following day she reported to a meeting of the committee. It was a gathering full of emotion and pride and some disappointment too. Ray reported that Albert Ticho was continuing with the anti-trachoma work. In one school she visited, she said, trachoma had been eradicated, but it would return. Helena Kagan was caring for the maternity cases. Ray pulled a letter out of her purse written by Dr. Kagan in which she asked that a small polyclinic for female diseases be established. At a later meeting the committee accepted the suggestion on condition that the work be done in the name of Hadassah and in Dr. Kagan's office, and that she submit monthly reports.

But back in Palestine there was little hope of setting up such a clinic. Through 1916 and 1917 the community of Jerusalem dwindled. Corpses lying in the street were becoming a common sight. The new Jaffa suburb of Tel Aviv, begun with great hope and spirit in 1909 on the sands north of the port, was inhabited by ghosts. When the war broke out, Jamal Pasha ordered the evacuation of all Jews. Some ran back into Jaffa, others fled north, but most sought refuge in Alexandria. Tel Aviv, then consisting of nothing more than four main streets, was left without population. By the beginning of 1917 it looked like a deserted set of a Western film. Papers and packing materials were whisked up and down the sand-covered streets by the winds blowing in from the sea. Doors banged and echoed through the hollow town. Empty windows looked out on empty streets. Occasionally a guard from Jaffa shuffled through the quarter, coming and going like a mirage out of the dunes.

In November 1917, the Balfour Declaration was issued, promising a Jewish National Home in Palestine. But the Jews of Palestine knew nothing about it, and even had they known, they would have despaired that the only Jews left by the time the British could arrive would be dead ones. The Turkish authorities were aware, of course, of the declaration. General Edmund Allenby (known as "the Bull") was on his way from the south at the head of the British forces. It would be a month until he entered Jerusalem. The Turks became increasingly suspicious of the Jews who remained in Jerusalem. Of a prewar population of over 50,000 fewer than 25,000 remained, most of them women and children, old men and some frightened young men, many of them in hiding. As Allenby's men took El Arish and were on their way to Beersheba, Jamal Pasha insisted that every Jewish male of Jerusalem be called into service. Turkish police rounded up any man who could walk. A few young Americans studying in yeshivas were told to report to a police station to register as aliens. When they found they had been tricked into the Turkish army, they protested and waved their American passports. That brought sneers of contempt. They were corralled with all the rest.

Rothschild Hospital was taken over by the Turks and was then closed altogether. Three other Jewish hospitals remained open but had no funds and no nurses and could do little for patients.

Shortly before the British entered Jerusalem, Jamal Pasha arrested the heads of the Jewish community. Consul Glazebrook used his influence to have them released on the pretext that they had to hand over the affairs of the Va'ad ha-Kehila to others. Once out of prison they ran into hiding. A favorite refuge, as we have already seen in the case of the gold, were the quarters of Helena Kagan.

A sharp rap on the door scared the wits out of Dr. Kagan, that cold, rainy night of December 7. At first she refused to reply, fearing that the Turkish army had decided to conscript women as well. The knock came harder and harder, again and again. The pounding became unbearable. Helena opened the door to prevent it from being broken. Meekly she asked who stood out there in the dark. Through the crack she could make out two figures. One was Rachel Feigenbaum and the other her father, Yosef Baran Meyouhas, one of the leaders of the Jewish community.

Said Meyouhas, "Helena, I must hide here. They won't look for me in your house. I must stay the night."

Helena hesitated, then reluctantly agreed. She went to her kerosene stove to warm food for a drenched, shivering Meyouhas. Then, another brisk knock came at the door. Meyouhas ran for cover inside the house.

Helena opened nervously. Another member of the Va'ad, Siegfried Hoofien, was looking for refuge.

"I'm coming from Glazebrook," whispered Hoofien. "He said he could not keep me another minute. Let me in. Quick."

"Where is Thon?" Helena asked. Ya'acov Thon was then head of the Palestine office of the World Zionist Organization.

"Over at Hadassah House."

Helena ordered Hoofien to take cover with Meyouhas. She then wrapped a shawl around her shoulders and ran over to Hadassah House (as it was then popularly known). On the way she slipped through lines of

Turkish soldiers moving out of the city. She banged violently on the door, but the frightened Thon refused to open. She continued knocking and shouting until he finally relented.

"Meyouhas and Hoofien are at my place. Come with me. Quickly."

Thon followed her back through the storm. Once all were together she gave refuge to one of the men in her clinic, put another in an empty house next door, and a third in the flat of Dina Meyer. Helena asked Meyouhas for news of Arieh Feigenbaum, the eye specialist. Meyouhas said he heard Feigenbaum had been taken prisoner and was being held with hundreds of others in the Dominican monastery near Damascus Gate.

At dawn the next day, December 8, Helena Kagan headed for the monastery. Her plan was to bribe the guards to release the ophthalmologist. But the place was empty when she arrived. She found a deaf mute and wrote out an instruction to take one hundred pieces of gold to Feigenbaum. She figured that since the messenger could not talk, he would not be questioned. The deal was that if he brought back a note from Feigenbaum saying that the doctor had received the money, he would receive a reward of ten gold sovereigns. It was taking a chance, of course, but two days later, the honest deaf mute was back at her home with a receipt from Feigenbaum whom he had met on the road to Jericho.

Dr. Feigenbaum had been arrested while making his rounds of the Old City. When asked why he was being taken to the *nookta* (police station), the policeman replied, "Doctor Feigenboom, you are a Zionist. The British have promised Palestine to the Jews. Therefore, you Jews are the enemy of the sultan." It was the first inkling that any Jew of Jerusalem had of the Balfour Declaration.

On the way to Jericho, the miserable group of men – Moslem Arabs, American Jews, Palestinian professionals and beggars – were strafed by British planes. They walked all the way to Jericho, a distance of twenty miles. En route one night they were held in an empty cistern. From Jericho they were taken across the Jordan River in German lorries to e-Salt. Then they marched to Dera'a and boarded a train to Damascus. In all, it was an eight-day trip. They found chaos in Damascus and many escaped, among them Feigenbaum. He moved south, walking, hitching rides, and got as far as Kfar Saba where he waited for the British advance. But it was long in coming. He saw horrible scenes of men and women dying of starvation. The fleas were incredible. People dropped dead everywhere from typhus.

Dr. and Mrs. Ticho had, in the meantime, fled to Damascus on their own and kept on going to Istanbul, returning to Jerusalem after the war on a refugee ship.

On December 9, 1917, Allenby took the surrender of Jerusalem in what is today the Romema Quarter of the city and signed the peace terms in Sha'arei Tzedek Hospital, Jerusalem's oldest existing hospital. For the Jews of the city the war was over, but it still raged farther north, and it would be yet another year until the Armistice stopped all fighting. An American Red Cross unit moved in with the British forces, but it was woefully inadequate to deal with the dreadful health problems of Jerusalem. What the *yishuv* needed was radical and complete medical rehabilitation, not just supplies and pills.

It would be another eight months and a long hard winter before that kind of aid would arrive. Unknown to the survivors, it was on the way.

THE UNIT

Broadway, "the Gay White Way," as it was then known, was neither gay nor white that second week of June 1918. Fourteen months previously, President Woodrow Wilson asked Congress for a declaration of war. Now, 25 American divisions were already in France and fresh ones were leaving weekly. In Belleau Wood, the green American Marines were stopping the massive German thrust toward Paris. Mightier, bloodier battles were still ahead, but the stand of the Marines was welcome relief to the growing numbers of casualties that would total more than 100,000 American dead and twice that number wounded before armistice five months hence.

The group of Hadassah doctors and nurses who gathered on 42nd Street in the early evening of June 11 were making an effort to be happy and carefree their last day on home soil. At midnight they would report at the pier for duty overseas.

One of the keyed-up young nurses suggested, "Let's all go to see the 'Garden of Allah'."

One young physician had a less romantic proposal. "You nurses can watch a Broadway show if you like. We'll be in Allah's garden for a whole year. What I want to do is say good-bye to the biggest, juiciest steak I can find." And with that, he and two concurring colleagues went off to a restaurant.

Two other nurses demurred as well. They wanted to go to Coney Island to have their fortunes told and off they flitted in a shower of gleeful titters.

Even at midnight the weather was hot and humid. Tense, heavy-eyed, the small band of doctors and nurses gathered at the wharf beneath a looming troopship. In peacetime it was the luxury liner S.S. *Megantic*. Now, great and grey, its only marking was a giant number "19" on the prow.

"How was the show?"

"How was your steak?"

"Could've been better, but there *is* a war on you know!"

"What did the fortune-teller have to tell you?"

"I'm going on a long trip and I will marry a dark, handsome man…"

"So what else is new?"

"And there will be a tragedy before it's over. And I will not come back."

Only a sharp call to get moving up the gangplank saved the nurse from being dumped into the river.

Three thousand American men and women moved into the ship. Most were soldiers in khaki. Others were Red Cross and social welfare personnel. Forty-four, most of them doctors and nurses, wore a badge that no one had ever seen before: a red Star of David encircled by the words "American Zionist Medical Unit." At 4:00 a.m. on June 12, number 19 cast off from its moorings, joined eleven other ships in the predawn haze and sailed in convoy into the U-boat-infested Atlantic.

AZMU – as the Unit was popularly known – was long overdue. It was conceived two years previously, in June 1916, after the World Zionist Organization (WZO) in Copenhagen cabled an urgent appeal to the Provisional Executive Committee for General Zionist Affairs in New York City to send a medical force to Palestine. The committee passed the request on to the Federation of American Zionists, which in turn fielded the ball to Hadassah. That July, Hadassah was holding its third national convention in Philadelphia. The treasurer reported that the organization was in the black to the tune of $2,880.65, and membership was at a record high of 1,937. The goal of 2,000 members would certainly be reached before the end of the year. Henrietta Szold, who was also Hadassah's representative on the Provisional Executive Committee of WZO, disclosed that money had been raised to send two more nurses to Palestine. But then in the name of Hadassah's central committee, she announced that what was really needed from Hadassah was to organize and contribute to the dispatch of an entire medical unit. The Federation of American Zionists had set a budget of $265,000, of which Hadassah would be required to raise only $25,000. "Only!" whispered a horrified delegate from Boston. "Only eleven times more than we have in the bank!" Henrietta made it sound simple. If every member saved on carfares, each could certainly donate up to $15. And that would do it. Henrietta's leadership won the day. The world had gone mad, so why should Hadassah be an exception. The project was endorsed.

Across the nation, as far as Kansas City, then Hadassah's westernmost chapter, and Galveston in the south, Hadassah women saved nickels and dimes for the project. Henrietta had once said to her New York chapter, "The emergency should be used as an opportunity." It was. AZMU became a cause to believe in and work for. Membership rose. And so did costs. By the end of 1917, Hadassah sent out word that its share in the project was now $30,000.

But money was only one of the problems in forming AZMU. Transport was another. Trans-Atlantic shipping was scarce for all but the military; AZMU was to aid Palestine – a low priority – when, for America, the war was in Europe. Visas were a problem because the Turks held Palestine. Then, when the British issued the Balfour Declaration in November 1917, an entry permit from the Turks was unthinkable. In December, after Jerusalem was conquered by the British, the Unit's organizing committee began to negotiate with the British ambassador in Washington. By March 1918, authorization for the Unit had been received from Washington and London through the personal intervention of Supreme Court Justice Louis Brandeis, a leading Zionist. At first, the plan was to send AZMU to

Palestine via the Cape of Good Hope, but finally sanction was given to permit the medical team to sail directly to Europe, on an American troopship. Adolph Hubbard, who had been active in obtaining passports for the Unit, wrote later, "This passport matter was not altogether simple. It was war-time and everybody was subject to suspicion, so that in a number of instances it was necessary to cut corners." Most problematic was Alice Seligsberg, a pacifist, who was granted her passport only hours before sailing time.

Originally, the Unit was planned for two doctors, two nurses and a half-ton of supplies. By the time it got underway, there were twenty nurses, a dermatologist, obstetricians and gynecologists, an orthopedist, a pathologist, pediatricians, dentists, a pharmacist, eye and ear-nose-and-throat specialists and a sanitary engineer. Five administrators were assigned to the Unit. The manager, white-goateed Eliahu Lewin-Epstein, who was secretary of the Provisional Executive, had sailed on ahead. Alice Seligsberg, a children's welfare leader in New York, represented Hadassah.

Henrietta Szold wanted to go but stayed behind to help raise funds. She chose Alice to replace her. Henrietta described Alice as "a rare human being, wise, devoted to duty to the point of self-effacement." However, Henrietta refused the pleas of another friend, Jessie Sampter, to join the mission. To Jessie, a poet, she wrote, "What your pen could add would not, to my mind, be so valuable as to justify changing what I conceive the character of the Unit should be – a strictly professional undertaking."

The pharmacopoeia and supplies that were shipped separately included 2,000 cases of medicines, two ambulances, eight vehicles, uncounted gallons of anti-louse fluid, instruments, blankets, linen and clothing – all told, enough to open a 50-bed hospital. A great deal of thought went into the choice of summer and winter uniforms. The women had light cotton greys with panama hats and veils (to protect sensitive skins) for summer wear. Dark grey woolens and velour hats were the uniform for winter. According to prevailing fashion the hemline was maxi – just above the ankles. The men wore khaki cottons or woolens. For shipboard emergency, each member was given an outlandish life-saving unit that was as big as a tent when inflated. When the commanding officer of the troopship saw the lifesaver, he exploded. "Anyone who inflates one of those tents in an emergency will be shot on the spot." He had a point. The suits were so expansive that they would have blocked the ship's companionways.

For all Henrietta Szold's meticulous preparation, the Unit went off without a medical director. Dr. Isaac Max Rubinow, a medical statistician from Washington, who had accepted the post, suddenly backed out at the beginning of June at the insistence of his family. Szold appealed to Adolph Hubbard to go as an administrator in charge of equipment, personnel and finances. He agreed.

Thirty thousand Americans sailed in convoy that day, but only AZMU and a group of American Judeans (who volunteered to fight with the Jewish Legion in Palestine) sailed through three submarine zones – the Atlantic, the English Channel and the Mediterranean. The two-week crossing of the Atlantic was hard from the outset. Homesickness was aggravated by seasickness, which in turn was brought on by violent storms that lashed the ship for the first few days. Anxiety over submarines was so great that few of the members of the Unit undressed to sleep. Most climbed into their berths even with boots and overcoats on and kept lifebelts at arms' length. Lifeboat drills two and three times daily did nothing to reassure them.

At 4 o'clock one morning, close to Scotland's shore, sirens sounded the submarine alert. Members of the Unit hurried to their lifeboat stations.

> We waited in silence. It was dark except for a thin glow of light on the horizon to the east. The minutes passed by in agony. Three thousand men and women thinking a single thought. Most of them were soldiers who had to be there. They had no alternative. But we were volunteers. We could have remained home. We nurses were all about 25 years old. Most of us never ventured beyond our home states. Some of us had gone for the adventure. When we finally faced it, we

were scared. Some were here because they simply got bored at home doing not much of anything and this was one way of serving both our country and our fellow Jews. The pay was certainly good. One hundred dollars a month and maintenance for nurses. For the doctors, two hundred and twenty-five dollars. But at four o'clock in the morning, standing on top of a hunted ship, the pay was not so good as it first seemed... We heard muffled explosions off in the distance. Our escort cruiser, the San Diego, spotted the sub and sank it. The eternity was over. All-clear sounded. Later, when we learned that the San Diego went down in the Atlantic while returning home, we all cried a little.

That was how, many years later, one of the nurses recalled the terror of that night.

Blacked-out Liverpool was a blessed sight. It was the night of June 24. The nurses marched down the gangplank waving tiny British and American flags. Two of the women were taken to hospital on stretchers, one with pneumonia and one with Spanish flu.

In London, the Unit split, some bedding down at the Regent Palace in Piccadilly, the others at the Strand. With Vera Weizmann, Chaim Weizmann's wife, and Rebecca Sieff as their hosts, the nurses quickly got their fill of sightseeing, theaters, parties and teas. Wherever they went they were greeted as the AZMU's. One night at a vaudeville show the noted comedian George Robey greeted them from the stage to the applause of the crowd.

But the most remarkable welcome of all took place in the regal London Opera House on the afternoon of July 14. Posters all over London proclaimed: "A Public Meeting to Welcome the American Zionist Medical Unit on its Way to Palestine."

Zionists who packed the opera house were in high spirits. The previous November, the British government had sent Lord Rothschild a short note saying that it looked with favor on the establishment of a Jewish home in Palestine. As a follow-up Chaim Weizmann had gone off to Palestine in March as head of the British section of the Zionist Commission to survey conditions in preparation for implementation of the Balfour Declaration. In June, Weizmann had his first meeting with Emir Feisal, leader of the Arab world, with whom he was to come to an understanding on Arab acceptance of a Jewish state. In two weeks, the cornerstone of the Hebrew University would be laid on Mt. Scopus in Jerusalem. Thus, the Zionist program was rolling forward rapidly and AZMU's presence in London added vigor to the momentum.

Lord Rothschild, who chaired the meeting, was interrupted nine times by applause and cheers during a five-minute opening welcome address. "I consider the sending out of a fully-equipped Jewish Medical Unit as a very great tribute to the progressive means by which modern Zionists are seeking to solve the problems of the new Palestine."

The most rousing speech of the day, however, was made by a non-Jew, Member of Parliament George Barnes who represented the war cabinet. In a long-forgotten, but nevertheless highly significant address, he said to mounting crescendos of hand clapping, "The British Government proclaimed its policy of Zionism because it believed that Zionism was identified with the ideals for which good men and women are struggling everywhere. That policy is the policy of the Allies with us in this war. It is the policy to which we are pledged. It is the policy which we believe accords with the wishes of vast numbers of the Jewish people." Barnes glorified the Unit: "They are taking help and hope and succor to people long-oppressed and down-trodden.... They are taking to a liberated East the knowledge and science of the modern West."

Another cabinet member, Sir Alfred Mond (later to become Lord Melchett) followed: "What we have been promised in a declaration of policy made on November 2nd by the British Government, and which has since been gladly endorsed by the Governments of our gallant allies, France and Italy, is the establishment in Palestine of a Jewish National center, to which Jews from all over the world, who wish to unite in spreading the influence of Jewish thought, Jewish industry and Jewish energy throughout Palestine *and the adjacent countries*, can do so in complete harmony with the other people living in that territory." Then Nahum Sokolow, the great Hebrew writer and early Zionist leader, referred to the Balfour Declaration as the "Magna Carta of the Jewish people" and declared that the AZMU was the "beginning of the result of that Declaration."

Among the greeters was a member of the Armenian National Delegation who hoped the Unit would maintain "the high and noble Samaritan traditions of the American people"; the highly popular and good-humored Colonel Josiah Wedgwood: "You are going to lay a foundation stone that will convert a race into a nation," and David Lloyd George who later became prime minister and had just come back from Palestine: "I have been working alongside the Arab Army and I want to say there is plenty of room in that country for the Jewish people, for the Arab people and for all the peoples that are in it."

Alice Seligsberg and Lewin-Epstein replied on behalf of the Unit. The last to speak was Sergeant Gershon Agronsky (Agron) on behalf of the American Judeans. In the forthright manner that was later to make Agron a popular Zionist speaker as well as a fine editor of *The Palestine Post*, which he founded, he told the audience, "Bid us, if you will, good-bye or farewell but for a very short time, because we shall see you all in Palestine. In these circumstances, you cannot speak to us of homecoming in the sense of returning or of seeing us on a return when we shall pass through England again, because it is not our intention to come back."

Originally scheduled to remain ten days, the Unit was now in England three weeks. The meeting in the Opera House had been arranged partly to keep up morale. It would still be another week before they could continue. Adolph Hubbard and a few others spent the time digging out as much information as they could on the conditions prevalent in Palestine. Having learned something of the terrifying situation awaiting them, they thanked heaven that they had the foresight to take along about a half-ton of medical supplies, since the four hundred tons being shipped separately would most certainly be delayed en route. Now they could begin work the minute they stepped off the ship.

Finally, on July 22 the Unit was on the train to Southampton. From there it sailed for Le Havre, in what Hubbard called "a dirty little tub." More delays awaited the group at Le Havre, then the seat of a rump Belgian government. Hubbard was given a list of names, including his own and that of Alice Seligsberg, who were to be questioned by American Army Intelligence about their pacifism. But Hubbard used a ruse – he never revealed what it was – to bypass the investigation.

The group arrived in Paris past midnight to find a dozen army-requisitioned taxicabs waiting to take them in a grand convoy to their hotel near the Place de l'Opera. Only next morning did Hubbard learn that AZMU had been given the status of official guests by the French government because Baron Edmond de Rothschild had assumed "sponsorship" of the group. The war-bankrupted government, eager to maintain good relations with the financier, had laid out the red carpet. Hubbard, Alice and engineer Louis Cantor called on the baron, who was so impressed by their mission that he agreed to their request to turn over the Rothschild Hospital in Jerusalem to the Unit and to help maintain it financially. The baron authorized James de Rothschild, then serving with the Zionist Commission in Palestine, to draw up a contract. Addressed to Eliahu Lewin-Epstein on October 17, 1918, the agreement provided that while the Unit would be responsible for managing the hospital, it would always carry the Rothschild name. The three-year contract likewise provided that the furnishings and equipment would be returned to the Rothschilds on its expiration. But that provision was never invoked. At the end of three years the accord was not renewed, but the hospital remained in Hadassah's hands and subventions from the House of Rothschild were continued until 1940 – 300,000 francs in the first three years and 2,000 Egyptian pounds thereafter.

Paris was bubbly, even in wartime, and French food made up for the grey, hard weeks of scarcities in London. On July 26, the little taxi convoy took the much happier contingent to the railroad station. But on the train they had no facilities for washing, dining or sleeping. Some tried dozing on the floor. The nurses had thoughtfully brought along tins of sardines and French cheese to which the doctors generously helped themselves. "Those doctors wanted to be mothered. So we mothered them, but the result was that *we* went hungry," one nurse remembered many years later. In Rome, they toured the catacombs, Vatican City and the big synagogue on the Tiber where psalms of joy were sung in their honor by an organ-accompanied choir. A troubled Hubbard had no time for touring. "Nothing went right," he recalled later. "Most of our two days in Rome I spent getting our papers in order. Were it not for the aid of the British naval attaché, we would have had even more delays. And to prove that nothing could go right, when it came to getting the final papers a clerk told us that he had orders for us to remain in Rome until the camp at Taranto, our next stop, was prepared to take us."

Hubbard was impatient. When he figured that it would cost about $350 more daily to remain in Rome, he charged ahead to the camp at Taranto, despite the orders. "I decided to go on, trusting to be able to talk us out of trouble, if trouble came."

Taranto was located on the burning sands of a gulf on Italy's heel and was the principal reception center for Allied troops and supplies moving from Europe to the Middle and Far East. The heat hovered around 120 degrees at times, but nothing was so fierce as the British commanding officer's temper on hearing that Hubbard's contingent had arrived against orders. The Unit remained only because no transport was available to take them back. According to Hubbard's itinerary, the Unit was to ship out to Alexandria within forty-eight hours. But a submarine raid in the Mediterranean delayed them for ten days. One evening a group of Palestinian and British officers discovered the Americans and serenaded them with Hebrew songs. One of the Palestinians was botanist Aaron

Aaronsohn, soon to die in a mysterious plane crash. Another was Major Ormsby-Gore (later to be colonial secretary), who had been hunting for the Unit high and low in his capacity as British military liaison officer to the Zionist Commission then in Palestine. From Aaronsohn and Ormsby-Gore the Unit received a sobering picture of raped Palestine. The war was still in a critical stage; Jerusalem was in British hands but northern Palestine was not. The American Red Cross unit, headquartered in Jerusalem, was not equipped to cope with Palestine's basic medical and rehabilitation problems. In sum, the Unit was desperately needed.

On August 9, AZMU shipped out on an Indian transport convoyed by three Japanese destroyers and an Italian hydroplane. As the ship slipped out of Taranto, the nurses and doctors glumly stared at the hulks of sunken vessels. The *Kaiser I. Hind* sailed into Alexandria two days later, but not without a scare. Several hours before arrival all hands were told to put on life belts and stand by at lifeboat stations. Submarines were lurking about at the entrance to the harbor, but the danger passed without incident. On hand for their first welcome to the Middle East was Chaim Weizmann who regretted the delay in the Unit's arrival and said that departure for Palestine would be given top priority even though most transport was then being used by the military.

The doctors and nurses spent four days in Alexandria and two in Cairo. The Unit put up at Cairo's Shepeard's Hotel and the wealthy Mosseri family who dominated the Jewish community was their host. They dutifully visited the sixty-bed Israelite Hospital where the director told them, "If it were not for the Jews of Palestine who came to Egypt during the war, we would not have had this hospital. It was they who infused us with a new spirit and it was with that spirit that we built this institution."

There was just time enough for the group to see something of Egypt before leaving. The impressions never left them. They were horrified by the mud villages along the Nile, the oxen yoked to the water wheel, the sickly peasants ploughing the earth with scraggy camels. In the city itself, they tasted and smelled misery wherever they went. Poverty, filth, rotting refuse in the streets, dirty naked children, blind beggars and everywhere flies – billions of flies spreading an invisible germ canopy over the teeming, milling metropolis. What made the experience grotesque was that, amid the destitution, fabulous wealth, luxuriant living and high culture were enjoyed by a small ruling clique. This then was the gateway to the lurid, alluring Levant, a loud and sluggish region, illiterate, indigent, a diamond on a garbage heap, intoxicating in its tawdriness, frustratingly inconsistent, magnetically enigmatic, a mosaic of contradictions that no Westerner would begin to understand.

By Saturday evening, August 17, 1918, the British had cleared space on troop trains to send AZMU on the last leg of its voyage to Palestine. Leaving one nurse behind to take charge of the camp of Palestine Jewish refugees in Alexandria, the group boarded double-decker berthed trains and, according to one scholarly version, traveled the route into the Holy Land chosen by Moses to take the Israelites out of bondage. Across the horizon, as they chugged along in the bright moonlight, they could discern long caravans of camels. By early morning they crossed the Suez Canal and were in Qantara. The northern coast of Sinai, along the Mediterranean, was anything but romantic. A sand storm swirled up out of the desert and all views were lost in the gritty winds.

Eighteen hours after they started out, the train finally arrived in Lydda (Lod), a sandy tent town that could offer not a single shade tree against the August heat. The railroad terminal was a rickety shed. Sitting on valises for two hours, waiting for someone to greet them, left the group depressed. Several nurses fainted from the oppressive heat and fatigue.

Their presence in Palestine was a source of contention between the Zionist Commission and the British authorities. The British had decided that AZMU would not be quartered in Jerusalem. But Chaim Weizmann put their case before General Allenby who, while not overly sympathetic toward Zionist aims, was fair. Allenby argued that since the American Red Cross had already pitched its tents in Jerusalem there was no need for a second mission there. In the end, Weizmannn's charm and persuasive arguments won out. As a compromise the two agreed that the Unit would split up, with AZMU establishing its base in Tel Aviv and a detachment working in Jerusalem. But both certainly knew what would happen in the end. There was an air of permanence about AZMU and only Jerusalem could then be headquarters for any Zionist organization.

Despite the agreement the largest number of AZMU members entrained for Jerusalem. The others – Executive Headquarters – set out in vehicles over the limestone road through the citrus groves for Tel Aviv. In Tel Aviv, the Unit occupied the only three houses located on what is now Allenby Street. These houses marked the limit of the town. Beyond, all was sand dunes. With emergency supplies that were brought along, squads began work immediately. In Jaffa, a sanitary unit sprang into action to supervise garbage collection, food inspection, cattle examination at slaughter houses, malaria control. In a short time an emergency hospital of ten beds was operating.

Not long after the Unit was functioning, Tel Aviv stirred with military activity. Moving at night in long shadowy columns, British troops tramped through toward Petah Tikva. On the evening of September 18, two members of the Unit were returning from Lydda when they reported an extraordinary sight – an unending line of camels loping northward, each animal carrying two tanks of water. There were 25,000 camels. On a nearby road, trucks and ambulances moved in the same direction. The next day muffled booming of heavy artillery could be heard in the streets of Tel Aviv. Allenby's offensive to capture northern Palestine had begun. Later on, trains and ambulances brought in the wounded. Several of AZMU's physicians were put into service at a casualty clearing station set up in the Gymnasium on Herzl Street.

Soon the Turks were routed and the north of the country was open. All of Palestine waited to be cared for and only the American doctors and nurses were prepared to cope with the long, bitter task.

PANTIES IN THE GAS TANK

Jamal Pasha, the Turkish tyrant, could not have cared less about the miseries of Jerusalem when he retreated from the British in December 1917. He told an aide, "There is enough bichloride of mercury (mercurochrome) in the drug shops for all of them." Nine months later, the Holy City was a terminal patient suffering its last agonies. Rarely had microbes grown in such favorable conditions. Apart from the usual endemic ailments, cases of typhoid and meningitis were common. The men and women who could still walk were shells. Well did the Wailing Wall live up to its name. There, mothers lay on the stone pavement weeping, praying, beseeching the Lord to save their children.

The Unit sought out the sick. As they visited Jewish homes, one picture emerged. In unlighted hovels, humans writhed on rag-covered floors. Their furniture was gone, sold to Bedouin for vegetables. Sunken-eyed, bearded men shook violently from chills. Disheveled women held scrawny infants at dried-out breasts. Even the houseflies were skinny. The stench was overpowering. One nurse commented at the time that living quarters were so bad it would have been necessary to fumigate to turn them into dog kennels.

The moral climate of the city was in raucous tune with the general war atmosphere. The army was an intoxicated troop. Off duty, the men's cry was, "Here today, gone tomorrow – so let's have a time, lads." Girls kept alive by turning to prostitution.

Jerusalem's most pitiful sight was its little army of orphans and abandoned children. Their mothers were either dead or too feeble to care for them and their fathers were behind Turkish lines. The lot of one such typical tot has been recorded. His name was Yitzhak and his father was impressed into the Turkish army. No one knew who or where his mother was. A Hadassah doctor found him roaming the streets, emaciated and blind, begging for bread. When the air turned cool, Yitzhak knew it was evening, so he fell where he stood and went to sleep, to be awakened by the sun the following morning. He managed to stay alive because he was a familiar figure on the streets of Jerusalem and people saved crusts for him. Even when he had his fill of bread, he would still go on begging for more. It was his way of asking for love and care. The doctor picked up Yitzhak and took him into Rothschild Hospital. He was cleaned, fed and pampered, and a couple of days later his appetite was satiated. One afternoon the doctor asked him whether he wanted more bread.

"*Neyn, neyn,*" he replied in Yiddish.

"Cake, perhaps?"

"*Neyn, neyn.*"

"Well, then, what can we give you?"

Yitzhak raised his head and whimpered, "*Ich vill mein eygelach.*"

Yitzhak could not have his eyes, but his body was rehabilitated and he was eventually reunited with his family.

An estimated four thousand waifs roamed the streets of Palestine, most of them in Jerusalem. Alice Seligsberg, who had dedicated her adult life to solving the problems of neglected children in the United States, went about the country establishing orphanages and foster homes, and searching for parents.

From August until November 1918, AZMU handled Palestine's unfortunates on a basis of emergency care. Before it could do more basic work, the Unit had to settle in and acclimatize. On their arrival in Jerusalem, the physicians were housed in the Hotel de France and the nurses in a small house on the Street of the Prophets. Their first few days were hectic. On the first morning after their arrival, the nurses awoke to find their faces dotted with red spots. Most thought they had caught a dread tropical infection. Others diagnosed it as measles. A doctor hurried over and after a quick examination announced his diagnosis to the women: "Sand flies! And don't be too hard on them because they haven't had the pleasure of such well-fed animals in years." Three days later a more serious affliction gripped the Unit: enteritis, or as most referred to it then, "Gyppie tummy." What made the affliction particularly unpleasant was the lack of a modern plumbing system in Jerusalem. Water was carried by Bedouin to the nurses' quarters in goatskins. More fortunate householders had cisterns. Cooking was done on smelly kerosene stoves. Kerosene was likewise the fuel for lighting. Daily, the Unit had to take quinine against malaria.

Language was a problem. Few AZMU members spoke Hebrew or Yiddish sufficiently to make themselves understood. There was friction between the Unit's doctors and the few Jerusalem doctors who survived the war, the latter believing that the newcomers had no experience to handle the medical problems peculiar to the Middle East. At night there was no entertainment except for one cinema which played the same film for a solid year. In winter the unpaved streets turned into quagmires. In summer the air was polluted by clouds of gagging dust.

By September 1918, the Turks were on the run. Nablus, Nazareth and Haifa were all yielding to British forces. Refugees streamed southward into Jerusalem as they did to Jaffa and Tel Aviv. Then, Tiberias fell to the Allies and the flow of refugees to Jerusalem was even greater.

Friday, September 27, 1918, was a memorable day in Jerusalem. It brought the season's first rain. Those who escaped the Turks up north and had recently returned were in better physical condition than the people who had remained in the city. Elated, they walked through the muddy streets of the city observing the festival of Sukkot. They were a mixed crowd of Yemenites and Bokharans, Hasidim wearing their holiday *shtreymlach*, North African Jews in fezes – all singing and dancing lustily. The Sephardim carried their white-bearded *hakham* (rabbinical leader) on their shoulders; Jewish soldiers of the British army whipped through the streets on horseback. It was bitter-sweet merrymaking because Jerusalem was a ghost city and the holiday jollity resembled a wake. In between the Sukkot processions bands of ragged Turkish prisoners, starved and gaunt, interspersed with the better-fed, straight-backed Germans, ambled along to POW camps under the wary eyes of victorious Australian soldiers and bearded Sikhs in white turbans.

The more areas that were liberated from the Turks, the more the Unit was called upon to do. Its members traveled south to Hebron, the most orthodox Moslem town in all Palestine. One AZMU doctor recalled:

> I and my assistant and a nurse would leave at dawn in our Ford tin-lizzie. The car was crammed with medical and surgical supplies and basic food items. It was only 25 miles but it took us two hours in those days. On the way to the dilapidated, tumbling town of stone houses and narrow crooked streets we would pass a wayside tavern called the 'Oak of Abraham.' It was presided over by a bearded, one-eyed ogre, indescribably and wretchedly filthy. We had been told that to pass the ogre without partaking of his sickly sweet, syrupy coffee would set off a signal to his henchmen who lay in ambush farther down the road. We always stopped. In Hebron, the Jewish hospital had been stripped of every movable item by the retreating Turks. We treated more Arabs than Jews. Their most common ailments were malaria and trachoma.

In the Jewish schools of Hebron about 40 percent of the two hundred pupils were suffering terribly from malaria. "As night came on, we always had the choice of spending it in the vermin-ridden 'Oak of Abraham' tavern or returning to Jerusalem. We preferred returning despite the narrow, hilly roads, the sharp curves, the fog and our Ford's weak lights." In that same month of September, the Sea of Galilee area was liberated. One day, the Unit's manager, Eliahu Lewin-Epstein, got an urgent call from Allenby's headquarters in Tiberias. He was told that a cholera epidemic had broken out in the wake of the Turkish retreat. Lewin-Epstein hired a droshka, fitted it with supplies and sent two doctors, a sanitary engineer and three nurses. Along the way the evidence of the war was everywhere. The rotting bodies of Germans and Turks were a common roadside sight. On the desolate road the team was stopped by a British officer and an escort with rifles at the ready. "And where are you going at this time of night?" the officer asked with his pistol drawn.

He suspected that the doctors and nurses were disguised German spies returning from a behind-the-lines foray. The forgetful doctors had left their passports behind, but fortunately one of the nurses had hers. After sharing coffee from a Thermos with the reassured Tommies, they got a good send-off on the last lap of the trip. As it turned out, the route they were traveling was taking them directly into the German-Turkish lines. The British officer set them straight.

It was dawn when they arrived on top of the hills overlooking Tiberias and the Sea of Galilee. The trip had taken them forty-eight hours. The sun was just rising over the Golan Heights and the vast panorama below made them gasp. Never had they seen a picture so sublime, so full of nature's wonders. But even more surprising was the welcome they received. There before them on the road were scores of Jews. All night long they had waited in expectation of the "Amerikanim." Some were crying, some were laughing. All chanted in unison a single prayer: *sheheheyanu, ve'kiyimanu, ve'higiyanu lazman hazeh.*

The Unit was overcome both by the welcome and by the conditions in which the Jews lived. Dr. Joseph Krimsky wrote in his diary:

> In the main bathhouse, the water was changed once in three days. Hundreds of people, many of them suffering from skin diseases, immersed themselves in this water. It was an abomination. In the poorhouse, men, women and children reclined, haggard, sunken-eyed, hollow-cheeked with skin the color of yellow parchment, their eyes with lustrous feverish unnatural brilliance, lips graying blue, emaciated limbs. They could not sleep at night because of the vermin. They were fed only once a day. Even then they could not eat.

The team was horror-stricken when they saw that before burial, corpses were being washed in the Sea of Galilee at the same spot where women were filling water jugs. Most of the Jews in Tiberias were so weak that they could not dig graves deep enough to bury the dead properly. Dogs and jackals scratched open the shallow graves and pulled out the corpses.

The Unit found that 75 percent of the town had cholera, a disease transmitted by bad water, and usually fatal if not checked within a few days. Hadassah's doctors immediately ordered the populace to stop using the Sea of Galilee water and the British army fenced off the most frequented sites. The entire town was placed under quarantine. Truckloads of food and medical supplies were sent by Hadassah from Jerusalem. Inoculations were given to hundreds. Most cholera patients were treated at home, but the Unit opened an emergency ward in a private house for 40 of the most seriously ill. Ray Malin-Cutler, one of the nurses, later recalled:

> I was the sole nurse in the house, but I had help from hired people who agreed to work only for very high pay. Taking care of the cholera patients was nothing more than hard, physical labor. No medications. Just drinks, drinks, drinks and hot water bottles and massage, all day and all night long.

Wells were chlorinated. Over-chlorinated to be exact. So much chlorine was dropped into the water that the distressed nurses found their hair standing stiff as chicken wire after they washed it. One of the doctors helpfully suggested they add lemon juice to the rinse. The Unit had more serious problems, however. A nurse fell ill with malaria and at one point was close to death. Lice were the staff's nemesis. On one occasion this led to tragicomic consequences. "We wore long flowing caps, like those of the British nurses," nurse Madeline Epstein* recalled many years later. "Not only did the lice camp on our heads, but they traveled. The clothes we wore were conservative; you just couldn't scratch yourself wherever you wanted to. Nor was it easy to give a hypodermic with one hand and relieve an itch with the other. The steel corsets we wore were partly to blame for our discomfort."

One day as Madeline stood on the balcony of the Tiberias Hotel where the team was housed she noticed a long line of army trucks and cars parked outside. It dawned on her that they held the solution to the lice problem. Asking no one's permission she picked up a stick, hammered a nail into it, furtively headed for the trucks, opened the cap of a gas tank and then proceeded to dunk her underclothes in the gasoline. The solution was effective although somewhat irritating to the skin, but it was better than the vagrant vermin. The daily rinsing of clothes in military gas tanks went along smoothly until one day Madeline carelessly let a pair of pink panties slip off a nail.

Early next morning, Nurse Epstein stopped short on her way to the dunking ritual. She saw a British officer severely reprimanding one of the army drivers. The soldier was pleading that he knew nothing "about it."

---

* Madeline was the young nurse to whom the Coney Island fortune-teller had foretold she would not return and she would suffer a tragedy. She did not in fact return because she married dentist Samuel Lewin-Epstein, son of the Unit manager, and lived the rest of her years in Jerusalem. Tragedy struck in the death of her father and, during World War II, in the death of one of her two sons. Her second son, Ya'acov (Jack), a prominent oral surgeon, was dean of the Hebrew University-Hadassah School of Dentistry. He died in 1988. His widow, Marian, active in Hadassah affairs for over 50 years, lives in Jerusalem.

Later that day, Madeline was ordered to report to the headquarters of the commanding officer. As she entered the staff room, she faced the granite faces of the C/O, his aide-de-camp and officers in charge of military transport. The C/O was direct.

"Sister, do *these* belong to you?"

He held high a pair of pink panties, now bleached white.

"I suppose so," mumbled Madeline, pink-faced.

"Sister, can you explain this act of sabotage?"

The C/O listened patiently, drumming his fingers on the desk. When she concluded, he remonstrated icily. "Do you realize that you put four Staff HQ vehicles out of commission. *Four!*" Only later that day did Madeline understand that the lice that she had killed in the gas tanks had clogged the feed lines of the vehicles. Next morning, a tin of petrol was placed at the door of her room marked "For Personal Use ONLY!"

Tiberias's off-limits status posed a problem as the British military machine pushed on toward Damascus and Constantinople. As it went, the conquering army freed more Palestinian Jewish refugees and the road home for the war victims led through Tiberias. One morning a group of five hundred riding on hay wagons suddenly appeared at the city's gates. In the city, the health risk was great. The weather had turned stormy and the frail refugees could not continue to Jaffa and Jerusalem in their wagons. At the intercession of Nurse Epstein, the British agreed to send them to their homes in a military convoy. After being fed and housed by the Unit, the refugees trudged up Tiberias's hills to the takeoff point, which they reached by midnight. At 2:00 a.m. a message was received by the Unit at the Tiberias Hotel that the convoy was nowhere to be seen. Enraged, Nurse Epstein dressed, jumped on an unsaddled horse and dashed after the truant convoy. She found the British officer-in-charge several miles beyond the appointed place, calmly shaving. He explained airily that he did not intend to take the civilians because they were not the responsibility of the British army. A fierce argument ensued, with Nurse Epstein doing most of the arguing and gesticulating. When she threatened to report him to army HQ in Jerusalem, he finally gave in, turned the convoy around and picked up the refugees. It occurred to Nurse Epstein only after she returned to the hotel at dawn that she had rarely ridden a horse and never bareback. Frightened, she pulled the covers over her head and went to sleep.

As Hadassah made it a rule never to distinguish between Arab and Jew, so did its doctors not distinguish between British, German and Turk in Tiberias. The British kept a large number of ill POW's in an administration building behind the Scottish Mission Hospital, which had been turned into a general hospital. Hadassah treated the prisoners – as it later would Arab terrorists – with the same professional care given to Jews.

Members of the Unit soon moved north from Tiberias into the Hills of Canaan where lay the mystic town of Safed, venerated home of sages and kabbalists. No more charming site existed in the Middle East. But the war had left its scars. When a Hadassah doctor arrived in the winter of 1918-19, he headed straight for a Jewish elementary boys' school. After the physician finished examining the pupils, none more than ten years old, the teacher addressed them softly: "Children, it's now time for *minha* (the afternoon prayers). Those of you who must go to synagogue to recite *kaddish* (prayer for the dead) may now leave. Now run along quickly."

The doctor looked up from putting his stethoscope in his bag. He was shocked to see half the class leaving to say *kaddish*. That night in his room in Safed he wrote in his diary:

> Safed. 8,000 Jews before the war, only 3,000 left. 3,000 died of hunger and pestilence. The rest fled. Town is full of little orphans, many homeless and destitute. Pitiful to see these thin, wizened children with their solemn appealing faces framed in straggling unkempt hair and long curly earlocks. Safed's Jews live off *halukah*, sent from abroad. When war cut off the charity, they sold homes and belongings to Arabs. Problem of Safed is the problem of the entire Jewish population of Palestine. Healthful, livable conditions and

remunerative labor are the solution. Water must be provided. Marshes must be drained. On the way up to Safed we passed enough swamps and morass to poison an empire.

A typhoid epidemic hit Safed early in 1919. AZMU provided the town with three physicians, five trained nurses and 12 student nurses, who took over a 50-bed hospital that had been erected by the Rothschild family. The American Red Cross unit that was then disbanding sold AZMU its equipment and by June 1919, a five-ward hospital was formally opened. It provided free out-patient service to all of Galilee and did the surgical work for the entire north of Palestine. Because of Safed's long dry season it was a favorite site for tubercular patients. By June 1926, Hadassah Hospital had opened a ward for 28 consumptives.

At the western gateway to Galilee, in the little port town of Haifa, AZMU opened a clinic and introduced a school hygiene service soon after the war. But immigration so heavily taxed the city's resources that by 1922, Hadassah established a small hospital which it continued to subsidize until the late 1930's. Between Safed and Haifa, the Jewish settlers of north Palestine were cared for fairly well. Tiberias was not to have a hospital until May 1930, although money for the construction of an institution had been contributed by Mr. and Mrs. Peter Schweitzer as early as 1921. Maintenance funds were not available for nine years when finally Hadassah assumed responsibility.

In Jaffa in 1919, an epidemic of relapsing fever and bubonic plague broke out. AZMU opened an emergency ten-bed hospital in Mordecai Ben-Hillel Hacohen's two-story house. In the summer of 1920 an out-patient clinic and 45 beds were added. Eight years later the Tel Aviv area would have its first modern, fully-equipped hospital. In the late 1930's Hadassah turned it over to the Tel Aviv municipality, but for more than 50 years the name Hadassah Hospital would linger on.

Jerusalem was still Hadassah's capital, however, and the immediate need in Jerusalem was to open the Rothschild Hospital which had been entrusted to AZMU. "I shall never forget the first day we saw the hospital," said one nurse. "We walked right in and we walked right out." Jewish community leaders, expecting the Unit, had done their best to clean up the worst of the mess left behind by the Turkish Army, which had stabled its horses there. Charwomen were not available, so the nurses assaulted the building. The cleaning took nearly a week, and having been done, hundreds of cases of medicines, instruments and food were unpacked. Hadassah had forgotten nothing. The only item that was in oversupply was toilet paper; it was several years before the original inventory was depleted.

The ceremonial opening of the Rothschild Hospital took place eight days before the end of the war – on November 3, 1918 – as part of the celebrations marking the first anniversary of the Balfour Declaration. In retrospect, the presentation of the hospital to AZMU was a milestone in Palestine's medical history. Present at the ceremonies, held on the steps of the building, were the Grand Mufti of Jerusalem, who blessed the project in Arabic as well as the highest ranking British officers in Jerusalem at the time, headed by General Arthur Money, and diplomatic and ecclesiastical representatives of France, Italy, Spain and Armenia. The United States was represented by the Spanish consul. For the occasion, Jerusalem's Bezalel Art School fashioned a silver key which the goateed Eliahu Lewin-Epstein, looking all the while like King George V, accepted from the monocled Major James de Rothschild.

By the end of 1918 the hospital had received 255 patients, but conditions were far from ideal. In the first few months the atmosphere was more that of a field hospital. In the operating theater, kerosene lamps provided light. During the operation the task of an unfortunate nurse was to hold the lamp high over the anesthetized patient.

At the official opening the Rothschild Hospital was an institution of 90 beds, six departments with out-patient clinics and three laboratories. The two largest departments of 24 beds were set aside for internal medicine and pediatric patients. The others were obstetrics, ophthalmology, dermatology and general surgery. An isolation hut, morgue, machine shop, garage and laundry were soon constructed and bacteriological and pathological labs were installed. The demand for beds was so great that within a short time 22 were added. AZMU's most valuable innovation was the introduction of an X-ray institute. At first it was poorly equipped and could provide only emergency services, but by 1921 the institute had a specialist and new equipment provided by the American Jewish Physicians Committee. It helped make Rothschild the most important medical institution in the country. In the four months of operation from September 1918 to the end of the year, Hadassah treated 15,000 ambulatory patients who made 59,000 visits. Another vital statistic: In the first full year of AZMU's work in Jerusalem, 20 out of every 100 patients were Arab.

The foundations were now established for the Hadassah Medical Organization (HMO), which would run all medical services usually under Hadassah's retiring President.

Hospitals had been activated up and down the country – probably a unique undertaking in medical history for a foreign, private volunteer women's organization. Twenty years later when Palestine's first medical center was opened on Mt. Scopus in Jerusalem by Hadassah, over 200,000 patients were being treated in Hadassah's institutions annually. That amounted to nearly 60 percent of all Jewish patients treated in Palestine hospitals. By the end of the century the number of annual visits, including hospitalization, to all Hadassah institutions would grow to nearly one million.

As early as January 1919, AZMU had made a great impression in the United States. We may today read with wonder that Henrietta Szold in New York should write to Alice Seligsberg in Jerusalem:

> Are you noticing in Palestine the change that is taking place in the name of the Unit? Here Hadassah is fading out of sight and mind. *The Palestine News*, I see, still refers to it as the Hadassah expedition. I should like to make a suggestion. Eventually the name Hadassah will have to disappear, but

> would it not be well and fitting if we could at least secure its attachment to the little hospital that Dr. Kagan established before the Unit came out?... If you think well of this suggestion and if the little hospital still exists, will you propose its keeping the name Hadassah Hospital as a memorial to our pioneer medical undertakings in Palestine? Would it not be lovely if Hadassah were to be memorialized through a children's hospital?

Alice must have reacted with astonishment because Hadassah was rooting itself deeply into the life of the country. As she read the letter, a sanitary commission made up of Hadassah doctors was on a six-week tour of the settlements to determine the health situation of the "colonies." Hospitals were fine institutions to build, but what was needed just as much by the *yishuv* was a network of preventive and educational services which only AZMU was in a position to create. This, the commission was to recommend and it was to lead to the beginning of nurses' training, school hygiene and mother and child care. Odd indeed were Henrietta's words. Perhaps they would have been different had she been with the commission when it stopped at seven-year-old Degania, mother of kibbutzim, and heard one of the settlers speak to it:

> The heat is unbearable, for as you well know this spot is located over 200 meters (600 feet) below sea level. To work in such heat requires superhuman effort. To sleep is well nigh impossible. We are constantly drenched with perspiration and we drink gallons of water. This pouring water into our systems while we are overheated as well as the poor quality of the food and the irregular hours of work and sleep have made everyone here a confirmed dyspeptic... We are now confronted with this question: shall we continue or are we fighting a losing battle? We believe that we cannot carry on here much longer unless conditions are made more

endurable. It is for you, gentlemen, to see that it is done. We colonists form the vanguard of our nation in Palestine. We are trying to hold a front which is unsanitary, unhealthful, unlivable. You must remedy these evils for us.

The commission found that backwater fever, a pernicious type of malaria, had already claimed a number of Degania pioneers. All the settlers had malaria, including the infants, and most suffered from anemia. One of the commission members observed, "The colonists are all intelligent looking but have a yellowish pallor. They are our most promising forces. We must establish a system of public health and hygiene and harness the Jordan River to drive every labor-saving motor in every farm and homestead in Palestine."

The commission continued its investigation and Hadassah's Dr. Joseph Shapiro noted in his diary:

At Rosh Pina, 40 settlers, 100 hired laborers. Sephardim, Persian, Ashkenazi Jews dressed in rags. Homes are one and two rooms in which five to 10 humans huddle. Diet: durrha bread, tea, green vegetables. No medical help except the local druggist who dispenses quinine and eye applications.

Mishmar Hayarden: An old greybeard tells this heart-breaking story... "Turks, Arabs, Germans, Arabs, British, Arabs followed one after the other and each contributed something to our destruction. Horses, cattle, food. All are gone. We are sick. We have no medicines."

Metulla: With adequate sanitation and mosquito control, this could be the health resort of Palestine.

Yesod Hama'ala: Pop. 200. Wide muddy streets with two rows of one-story stone houses. We sink into the mud to our knees. All plans for sanitary improvement must take into

consideration the Arabs in the villages around. Bad as is the
Jews' sanitation, the Arabs' is one thousand times worse.

Poriya: A few Americans here among 60 settlers. Cisterns
impure.

Sejera: Arab village of 300. Kurdish Jews among them.
Misery, misery.

Merhavia: 25 men and women. At least one member of every
family down with fever. Despite fever, they work.

Zichron Ya'acov: Pop. 1,000 of whom 100 are Yemenites.
Hospital built by Baron de Rothschild is neglected. They're
waiting for him to come up with money to repair it...
Colonists are apathetic, indifferent, nursed on charity.

Shfeya, Karkur, Bat Shlomo, etc.: Malaria, trachoma, all the
usual things.

Hadera: Turks destroyed 1,000 eucalyptus trees. Seven years
ago, 300 enthusiastic Yemenites arrived. 200 died, some
returned home, 70 left. Filth, poverty, overcrowding, low
wages, malaria, trachoma, tuberculosis.

The six-week tour of the colony mapped the needs of the *yishuv*. The
commission's findings showed that if the land was ever to be turned into a
Jewish home as the Balfour Declaration had promised, more than curative
and preventive medicine was required. Solutions and remedies had to be
found for neglected children, ignorance and indolence, communal and
intercommunal strife. As the war ended, there was nobody on the scene
capable of coming to grips with these problems except the American
Zionist Medical Unit which was fast becoming known to everyone in
Palestine as, simply, Hadassah. The Unit itself was beset by enormous
internal administrative, personnel and financial problems at the time.

Financially, the Joint Distribution Committee played a life-saving role in keeping the venture going. Between 1919 and 1923, it provided over $800,000 – first to AZMU and then to Hadassah when the name of the Unit was changed to Hadassah Medical Organization, a change authorized by the Twelfth World Zionist Congress at Carlsbad in 1921. But, more than anything else, Hadassah was kept alive by the *yishuv's* need to survive. And Henrietta Szold would admit in 1929 that she had been wrong about Hadassah's name disappearing. Said she: "The Hadassah Medical Organization came into the country as a war relief organization and remained in the land as a peace organization."

"JEW! SPEAK HEBREW!"

At nineteen, beautiful Shulamit Yedid-Halevy could be excused for having more nerve than sense. But her father, well-known and well-to-do in the Jewish community of Beirut, Lebanon, was at the point of exasperation. Girls of traditional families simply did not go in for nursing careers. That was a job for nuns, not for good Jewish daughters. But Shulamit inherited a healthy portion of her father's will power, and she threatened that if he did not let her become a nurse, she would run away to some foreign school to study. So, as most loving fathers do, he compromised. She would remain at home in Beirut and study nursing at the American University Hospital.

The same determination that overcame her father's objections also helped Shulamit through a strange, even hostile, new environment in training. She was pained to be obliged to attend Christian prayer services in the university chapel on Sunday mornings. The curriculum was based on church mission ideology, because nurses were expected to heal bodies and souls alike. In this foreign world she dreamt of going to Palestine where one day she would help organize a Jewish nursing school. As she studied late into the night her thoughts would meander – Jerusalem was so close – only 150 miles to the south – and yet so far.

In September 1918, word reached Beirut that the Hadassah Unit had reached Palestine. By then, Shulamit was a registered nurse. She satisfied her longings for Jerusalem by joining the Maccabee Zionist Organization. One day in December, the coastal vessel *Geula* (*Redemption*) called at Beirut. On board were war refugees returning to Palestine from Constantinople. Only males were permitted on board. The exception was the wife of a prominent eye specialist. Shulamit's cousin was emigrating to Palestine and Shulamit pleaded with him to take her along as a stowaway. In a moment of weakness he agreed and hid her on deck behind a stack of camp beds. Shulamit's cousin warned her to remain there for the overnight voyage to Jaffa. But when the returning Palestinians gathered on deck to sing and to dance, the temptation was too much for her. Shulamit came out of hiding to join the joyous males. Almost at once the captain roared, "Who's this young woman?" Discovering that she was taking a free trip, he ordered the helmsman to return to Beirut.

Shulamit ran to the doctor whom she found to be a Jewish physician returning to Jerusalem. He was Albert Ticho.

"Dr. Ticho," she pleaded. "I am a registered nurse. I know that the Zionists have come to Palestine from America to help and I want to join them. Please influence the captain to let me go on."

The famed physician was at first dubious. How, he asked, could he know that she was telling the truth.

"My cousin is on board. You can ask him."

"He is your cousin, is he?" Dr. Ticho was skeptical.

Members of the Maccabee organization came to Shulamit's aid. They pleaded with Mrs. Ticho, who convinced her husband to vouch for the girl and her fare. The captain grudgingly ordered another turnabout.

On landing in Jaffa her joy was unbounded. She noticed signs everywhere addressed to immigrants. "Jew! Speak Hebrew!" Thanks to her father she had been given a good Hebrew education and could read easily. But Shulamit's joy was quickly eclipsed. When she applied to join AZMU, the doctor told her abruptly, "We don't need nurses." Shulamit could not know then how wrong he was. She had the choice of returning to Beirut or of taking a post as an operating nurse in the Catholic St. Louis Hospital and once again working under the sign of the cross. She chose the latter. About six weeks later, she noticed a doctor wearing a Star of David on his military uniform. He had come to St. Louis Hospital to observe operations and to seek out a Jewish nurse who he had heard was working there. He was pathologist Benjamin Roman, acting medical director of AZMU.

"We are in a predicament in Jerusalem, Shulamit. We have taken in 40 students who want to be taught nursing – but only in Hebrew. The girls are refusing to attend classes if they are taught in any other language. Do you by any chance know Hebrew?"

Her heart pounding hard, Shulamit barely managed to say, "I do."

In February 1919, Shulamit reported to Dr. Roman at the Hotel de France, Hadassah's headquarters in Jerusalem. She moved into the Hughes Hotel across the street where the nurses now lived. The following day she began teaching.

Shulamit's Hebrew was classical rather than colloquial, and she read better than she spoke. At first, she would write out lectures in English, then with the help of two Palestinian-born members of the staff, she would translate them, always keeping two lessons ahead of the class. Shulamit, who was soon to marry the Unit's sanitation engineer, Louis Cantor, would even write down replies to a long list of questions she was sure the students would ask her. They rarely did ask the ones she prepared.

As halting as her spoken Hebrew was, it was much better than that of the other nurses. Even the students themselves were not too good at the language, most of them being Russian and Polish immigrants. The Hebrew was fractured, but thanks to their tenacity, the Hadassah school became the first anywhere to instruct nurses in the language of the Book. It did present difficulties. No texts were available in Hebrew nor were there Hebrew typewriters to prepare them. So a scribe was engaged to transcribe the lectures and these were given to the students. Most members of the Unit not only had no knowledge of Hebrew, they had no readily available translations of scientific words. On occasion the father of modern Hebrew, Eliezer Ben-Yehuda, would sit up long nights with members of the staff creating Hebrew medical terms. Some words, such as "vitamin," defied translation and remained unchanged.

Professional standards were high and the curriculum was wholly American. In charge at the beginning was Russian-born, American-educated Rose Klombers. Shulamit took charge for a short time. She was relieved by Anna Kaplan. Anna, a nurse with long experience in New York hospitals, started out with the Unit, but remained behind in a London hospital gravely ill with flu. During her tenure as head of the Nursing School she broadened the curriculum, introduced textbooks and established a permanent staff of instructors. But not without periodic crises.

To begin with, the Americans on the staff and the others, like Shulamit, were worlds apart in outlook. The Americans were high-and-mighty about their superior training. This often expressed itself in a supercilious attitude toward non-Americans. Many picayune, personal battles were fought with non-American staff members. Objection was raised, for example, to Shulamit's wearing the same uniform and pin as the Unit's nurses or even eating together at the same table. Acting Director Roman did much to calm tempers, but new irritations constantly erupted.

The European physicians at Rothschild had their own idiosyncrasies. They objected strongly to a three-year period of training for nurses, which they thought was overlong. They considered theoretical classroom work a waste of time. On the Continent, nurses learned all they knew in the wards. They were never expected to utter more than an obedient "Yes, sir" or "No, sir." And here was Hadassah teaching them all sorts of preventive work that was the private preserve of the physician. The German-born Jewish doctors, who had always worked with nuns, thought that regular hours for nurses was madness. They could not quite accustom themselves to the fact that nurses were human. The Russian-born doctors objected particularly to nurses who had something to say about the condition of the patient. On one occasion when a nurse reported a change in a patient's symptoms, a European-trained doctor cried out in exasperation, "Nurses should have feet, hands and eyes! They are not supposed to think! They should *do, see,* and *rush. That's all!"*

Working and teaching conditions of nurses always leave something to be desired. But in Jerusalem in the early years after the war they were downright primitive. Anna Kaplan recalled:

> We had no classrooms. We taught wherever we could find an empty room, even in the laundry. The nurses' Home was some distance from the hospital. We had no transport and the students had no suitable wearing apparel. When I opened the Surgical Department, the plumbing was not yet completed. Equipment came from America but not furniture. We saved the shipping cases from the Palestine Supply Department and from these made bedside tables, chairs and cabinets. Electricity was only a dream in those days. Ice was unheard of.
>
> After the first year at the Hughes Hotel, we moved to more spacious quarters in the Musrara Quarter of the city, but even then there was considerable overcrowding with as many as five girls sharing a single room. A terrible snowstorm, unprecedented in Palestine, visited us – the roof caved in, two nurses were injured and the house was no longer fit for use. The snowstorm lasted twenty-four hours but it caused us trouble for weeks. During the storm the doctors and the nurses had to sweep the snow off the roof of the hospital for fear that it too would cave in.

The first class of student nurses was assembled on November 3, 1918, the same occasion on which the Rothschild Hospital was formally opened. What a group they were! Most came from rural areas. Some had been employed in menial jobs at the hospital. Few of them had as many as eight years of formal schooling. A number of the girls had sneaked through Turkish lines in northern Palestine after they heard a nursing school was being organized. They were a ragged, sickly group of refugees. But what they lacked in physical appearance they made up in high spirits. Matured by war and hardship, they were highly independent. On one occasion one of the girls took off without permission for an overnight trip to Tel Aviv together with a doctor of the Unit. She was temporarily suspended on her return. Her enraged fellow students, claiming that the Don Juan physician was at fault, went on strike. They won. Strikes were frequent among the nurses, but they did not always succeed. Their most successful protests opposed the use of Yiddish, English and all languages other than Hebrew.

With it all Hadassah upheld its high, if martinet, standards: "You are expected to give respectful attention to your superiors," read the rules, "to obey orders promptly and unquestioningly, to refrain from carrying on conversations while on duty, to speak in a low voice, to move about gently, not to indulge in familiarities with patients or discuss their illness with them."

The school soon developed a strong feeling of responsibility among the students. Once the question arose before the five-member governing committee whether a nurse should be punished for giving a patient the wrong medicine.

"Definitely not!" replied Anna Kaplan, to the shock of the committee members. "Nurses must not be afraid to report such errors. On the other hand, failure to report should be severely punished."

As the first year passed, the school insisted on more stringent screening of students. After Henrietta Szold arrived in 1920 to head Hadassah's work in Palestine, she personally scoured the country for candidates.

"Do you owe any debts to your parents or to anyone else, and how much do they amount to? Do you suffer from rheumatism, headaches, emotional upsets?"

These and twenty other questions were routinely asked. If the students' debts were too large they were disqualified, because they would then have to take on outside work to repay the loans. They had to be twenty-one years old (today: nineteen), had to know Hebrew, the Latin alphabet, and remain on probation for six months. They were not permitted to treat sick relatives at home or in the hospital, except in the line of duty. They received a small allowance for the first six months. The working day was twelve hours with three hours off for homework and recreation. The students got one afternoon off a week and had a two-week annual vacation. Lights-out was 10:00 p.m. with late leave until 11:30 p.m. once a week. Today, student nurses do not reside on campus. On graduation nurses were assured of work and a starting salary of the equivalent of $50 a month (today $400). And yet they did have a measure of self-rule. The girls had their own committee which dealt with complaints against both students and nurses, and could mete out light punishment for disciplinary infractions. The committee later grew into a national nurses student organization.

Only 22 nurses of the original 40 made it through the first three years. But those who were graduated did well. Six became principals of schools or supervisors in hospitals. Several made excellent reputations in public health nursing. Later on, Shulamit Yedid-Halevy Cantor, the stowaway from Beirut, would succeed Anna Kaplan and serve a long and distinguished career as Hadassah's supervisor of nurses and director of the school.

Graduation exercises are set and staid affairs. But the rites of the first class were an exception. Since the school's dedication coincided with the first anniversary of the Balfour Declaration, the graduation ceremonies were set for Balfour Day, 1921. In the last week of October, the Hebrew-English invitations were about to be dispatched by two Yemenite runners (they were more reliable than the local mail service) when a representative of the Zionist Executive asked Henrietta Szold to postpone the festivities. Rumors were wild that the Arabs would observe the anniversary as they did in 1920 and again at Passover in 1921 by shooting and stabbing Jews.

The rumors turned out to be true and fortunately Henrietta took the advice to delay the ceremonies for one week. On Balfour Day, November 2, blood-thirsty Arab mobs ran screaming out of the Old City of Jerusalem. They burned and pillaged. Before the day was out, five Jews were dead and 20 wounded. British Governor Ronald Storrs's police neglected to intervene energetically, though Storrs himself, whom Henrietta described as "an evil genius," had taken refuge in Hadassah Hospital during the Passover riots under the pretense of "protecting" the Jewish community. Zionist officials demanded his removal. But Storrs remained and riots continued periodically through the 1920's and 1930's. On November 4, 1921, a massive funeral procession left the Rothschild Hospital compound. More than 1,000 persons marched in silence behind the stretchers on which the *tallit*-draped bodies were borne. When a month of mourning was declared, the graduation exercises were postponed again to December 2. Henrietta insisted the date be left unchanged as a sign "of unquenchable hope for the future of the Jewish people."

Dressed in crisp white uniforms and caps on which was emblazoned a blue Star of David, the graduating class of 1921 was led into the hall of Bet Aminoff, on Jaffa Road, the new nurses' home, by Anna Kaplan. Henrietta Szold presided and Lady Samuel, wife of the first British high commissioner, handed out the diplomas. Szold commented in her address:

> For this day you have waited three years, and across the ocean (in the United States) there are thousands of women who have waited for it nearly ten years. When they sent two pioneer nurses over here to inaugurate District Visiting Nursing, they thought of this evening. When the summons came to enlarge the number of nurses from two to twenty, they rejoiced for the sake of this evening.

Now, as if in payment for the loan of the 22 nurses that America had sent before and after the war, the *yishuv* was contributing 21 of its own. And none too soon. Only two of the original AZMU nurses were still on duty at Rothschild Hospital by the time graduation had rolled around.

Immediately after the exercises were over, six-month courses were begun in midwifery, operating-theater nursing and public health. Later, these would be integrated into the undergraduate studies.

By the end of the first decade, 135 registered nurses were graduated by the school and the standards of the profession were fixed. In its 11th year, the Hadassah School of Nursing was adjudged by the International Association of Graduate Nurses to be the finest in the Middle East.

Still, the demand for graduates was insatiable. Hadassah started courses for male orderlies partly to make up for the lack and partly to care for those Arab and Jewish Orthodox patients who refused to be tended by women.

Hadassah was the main source of highly qualified registered nurses until 1935 when Kupat Holim Clalit, the health fund of the Jewish Federation of Labor (Histadrut), opened a school. A municipal school was opened in 1940 in Tel Aviv. Both these institutions drew heavily on Hadassah's experience and personnel.

In 1952, Hadassah transferred to the Government the responsibility for nursing care in the public schools as well as for other public services. Soon Hadassah would be called upon to upgrade the profession. The need for even more qualified nurses became apparent during the war of June 1967 when the Medical Center at Ein Karem treated nearly 1,000 cases in 72 hours. It could do so not only because of the dedication of its staff but because medicine had become more specialized, its tools the products of a revolution in technology.

Higher education was obviously needed if nurses were to cope. Besides, a better education would attract talented candidates who at the time were moving to more lucrative professions. In 1975, Hadassah initiated the first basic academic nursing education program. It awarded a Bachelor of Nursing Science (BNS) to graduates after four years' study. That created a new generation of highly-educated nurses for Israel's hospitals.

In 1987, Sara Levi, daughter of Holocaust survivors in Rumania, became the first at Hadassah to earn a doctorate in nursing (at the University of Pennsylvania). Three years later, she was appointed head of the school. Says Dr. Levi, "An academic education has enabled the nurse to function in today's technologically sophisticated health system."

The nursing school, nearly 80 years old, had taught 3,000 nurses but only now after years of inequities the sisters in white were coming into their own as women and as professionals. By 1996, 35 percent of Hadassah's nurses held academic degrees, with the percentage growing annually, and some RN's were returning to the classroom to earn a BNS.

Israel today has 29 nursing schools, most of them offering academic degrees. With so many, competition for students increased to the point where the old taboo against married women was abandoned. Still, Hadassah managed to fill its quota of 50 students a year. Of these, an average of 40 were graduated.

All told, Israel now has nearly 21,000 Registered Nurses and 17,700 practical nurses. That provides the country with one nurse for about every 130 citizens vs. 63 in the U.S. At Hadassah 1,600 nurses (75 percent RNs) were not nearly enough. One reason was budget but there were others as well.

Even with the introduction of an academic program, the profession had still not attained the dignified status it deserved. Part of the roadblock was a conservative medical profession that anticipated a challenge from academically-trained nurses. Some MDs held to the belief that nursing was at best a semi-skilled job. They argued that academic studies were not needed to carry a bedpan or to follow orders. What need had nurses for academic literature or post-graduate study? These doctors rationalized with some justice that higher education would make the nurses loath to carry out menial jobs – making a bed or emptying a patient's urinal. Even worse, they might no longer take orders without question.

In practice, both fears came true, but not only because the nurses were better educated. More specialized medicine was making heavier demands on nurses' time and on their skills. They were no longer mere ward maids. Many were overworked; they claimed they had little time to carry out menial tasks.

Inevitably, members of families complained that their kin were being neglected in emergency rooms and in the wards. Mothers and fathers, wives and children felt compelled to spend long hours at bedside. What the nurses had little time to do, the family did.

In an address to nurses in 1996, former nursing services director Ahuva Regev-Michel aptly defined nursing as "caring." But she complained that nurses were being required to ensure quality in "an ever more demanding environment."

"Other needs" often took precedence – needs which "others can also meet," she said.

Families obviously felt they should not be those "others."

Challenges from conservatives in the medical community and the public led some Hadassah leaders in the U.S. to take unprecedented steps. They mobilized thousands into nurses councils and, as we shall see later, sparked a radical change in the profession.

To at least one veteran nurse, however, there was in all this a sense of *déjà vu*. As a girl of 16 in 1922, nurse-to-be Hava Shohat-Karlin was admitted to a Hadassah hospital suffering from exhaustion. "Then as now, there was a severe nursing shortage, so I got out of bed and began bringing other patients glasses of water and bedpans," she recalled years later.

With budgets growing tighter there seemed to be no ideal way out, but nursing was not the only profession where women faced an uphill battle. Nor was this new to Hadassah. Long before Israel was born, Hadassah women who tried to break new ground and old habits remembered how they were told, plainly, that they were wasting their time.

"YOU'RE WASTING OUR TIME, DOCTOR!"

A year after World War I ended, the third great wave of Jewish immigration began to hit the shores of Palestine. It also brought a small number of immigrants from the United States, among them Henrietta Szold and Golda Meir. Nearly 10,000 Jews from Central and Eastern Europe arrived in a single year. They left their homelands for many reasons, but essentially they had taken the Balfour Declaration literally and yearned to be in Eretz Israel for the founding of a Jewish state. The immigrants were rugged idealists. They trooped off to the marshes of northern Palestine, joined the colonists in building roads and draining swamps. By the end of 1920 more than 60 labor centers were organized throughout Galilee. Living conditions for the pioneers were primitive. The region was a morass that spawned malaria, typhus and typhoid. Roving doctors and nurses from Hadassah provided the only medical aid. Public health teams from Jerusalem tried to teach elementary rules of hygiene, but the Hadassah workers soon found that if they wanted to subdue the louse, the fly and the mosquito, they would first have to overcome the mulish, senseless opposition of the *halutzim*, the pioneers. As a matter of course, the laborers refused typhoid inoculations. Not even the offer of an American cigarette could entice them to submit to the needle. Some spurned an injection even when they were lying flat on their backs with soaring fevers.

The largest of the labor centers was located at Migdal on the western shore of the Sea of Galilee.

"Your toilets are lousy," the enraged Hadassah public health doctor Joseph Shapiro spluttered in a mixture of weak Hebrew and Yiddish. "You've got to cover them. Besides that, you men have just got to stop taking your drinking water out of the Sea of Galilee because that's where your sewage is being dumped. You'll all soon be dead if you keep going on like this and then what good will your Zionism be to anybody?"

The camp foreman gave a half smile. "Now look, Dr. Shapiro. We had worse conditions when we first came and we've survived."

Of the 500 men and women at Migdal, nearly every one had malaria. Yet the foreman insisted that they were willing to struggle and – to die. Let the shopkeepers of Jerusalem and Jaffa worry about things like chlorinating water or building toilets. *Halutzim* had to do just as well as the Arabs and under the same conditions.

Defying the *halutzim*, Dr. Shapiro put in a filtration plant to purify the water at Migdal. The workers boycotted it and kept taking their water from the lake. The foreman told his men: "The Arabs don't drink antiseptic water. We've got to live as they do." And to Shapiro he said, "You're wasting our time, Doctor."

It was a point of view, but that was all. What the men realized only later was that the mortality rate among the Arabs was calamitous and only their enormous birth rate saved them from extinction. As they would later find out, the Arabs were glad to accept aid from the Hadassah teams.

What Dr. Shapiro could not do, nature did. Soon, a typhoid epidemic struck with terrible swiftness and stopped work in the labor centers. Common sense finally won out and in answer to an urgent appeal, Hadassah set up a 38-bed field hospital at Migdal.

But there was a point beyond which one could not reasonably ask a pioneer to go. He would now grudgingly agree to take a shot in the arm, but to demand that he eat oatmeal for breakfast? "What are you giving us?" the Russian Jew with the heavy beard demanded. He held a bowl of brown porridge in his hand, but looked at it as though it were poisoned mud.

The pretty young nutritionist, Yehudit Aaronson (later to become Mrs. Alex Dushkin) fresh from the United States, stammered, "You *must* eat it. You and all the other men are eating the wrong kind of food. You need a good diet to keep you going." She had put the bowls of steaming, enriched oatmeal on the mess tables as a surprise one morning and watched from the kitchen as one worker after the other stared at it, sniffed it and passed it down to the end of the table where the bowls were now piled, untouched. The Russian glowered at Yehudit, "All our lives we men have done without this. We like herring and we will continue to eat herring. Don't throw this stuff at us again."

Yehudit was one of the few graduate Jewish nutritionists of her time. Highly successful in her field, she became a staff dietician of the American Red Cross and agreed at Henrietta Szold's request to serve with AZMU. In fact, she accompanied Henrietta to Palestine early in 1920. The Unit's new medical director, Isadore Rubinow, who arrived in Jerusalem after the war, had cabled an urgent plea for a nutrition expert because there was not one qualified dietician in the country at the time. Soon after their arrival, Henrietta, Yehudit and Rubinow toured Galilee, and Yehudit agreed to solve the nutrition problems at Migdal.

No one spoke to her when she arrived. On her own she went to the kitchen and began peeling onions. At the end of work on the second night, Jennie Landsberg, who was in charge of the kitchen, took Yehudit aside.

"You must be wondering why we ignore you," said Jennie. "Try to understand. We could not tell our people we were bringing in a nutritionist. As it is, you are suspect. You come from America where everything must be sterile and everyone must be healthy or life cannot go on. But here, these people are followers of Tolstoy. They deny the importance of the body. To them the power of the spirit of ideals is everything. Remember that. I know you mean well. But go slowly.

Yehudit did not realize how slowly. She tried introducing oatmeal and that was already a bust. So, using a bit of psychology she worked right along with them. She began by doing a hated job – washing pebbles out of the rice. Eight girls normally spent a full day at it, griping because they were not out on the road working with the men. The water for rinsing the rice was carried in buckets from the lake. After a few days on the job, Yehudit suggested that she might save the campers the bother of rice-washing if they could get her a donkey and the use of a tinsmith for one day. They were all for this and in no time Yehudit had an ass and an artisan. Outside the kitchen wall she built a heap of stones. On the stones she placed a barrel to which the tinsmith attached a pipe. The pipe led into the kitchen through an opening made in the wall. A spigot was fitted to the end of the pipe. Yehudit hired a boy who would fill the barrels with water and transport them on the donkey. The result: running water. It cut the rice-washing crew in half and Yehudit could now move on.

The basic diet in the camp was bully beef, herring, mushy rice and jam. The heavily spiced, British army tinned beef and the salty herring burned the scurvied men's bleeding, spongy gums. The bread was badly baked. Actually, as Yehudit found out, it was cooked. Yehudit solved this problem by making friends with a British officer who gave her a field oven from military stores in Afula. Better bread won her additional merit.

Slowly, at spaced intervals, she introduced peanuts, fresh vegetables and dried milk to the tables. The supplies had to come all the way from Haifa and for that purpose a marketing agency was set up by Yitzhak Sadeh, who became famous as commander-in-chief of the Haganah in 1945, while the marketing agency that he set up later became Hamashbir Hamerkazi, the Histadrut's giant retail outlet. From vegetables, Yehudit went on to a highly nutritious, somewhat sophisticated dessert which she convinced the men was a delicacy from America. The dessert was Jell-O and it was sent to Palestine by the Zionist leader, Justice Louis Brandeis.

Yehudit was now at Migdal nearly six weeks and she was ready for her greatest triumph. One day, a delicious pudding reached the tables. It was dark brown in color and it was served in bowls. By now, the men had learned to trust Yehudit and they dug in. After the first mouthful, there was some hesitation, but a burly, bearded Russian Jew shouted, "All right men! This we eat for the sake of *havera* Yehudit!" And with true Tolstoyan sacrifice they licked their bowls clean of pudding-disguised oatmeal. That night Yehudit held a party for some of the men and women and she served herring. By now, all the malnutrition symptoms had disappeared.

Yehudit's oatmeal victory was far-reaching. By the time she left the camp, the leaders of the women's liberation movement at Migdal were convinced that their rightful place was in the kitchen. It happened that when one of the camp's 50 girls was found to have a defective heart she was forced off the road. "Well, food conquered our health problems, so it certainly isn't a disgrace to cook," she rationalized to the other girls. In a noble act of comradeship they all decided to join a permanent corps of cooks.

Malaria was a more difficult problem to beat. The answer of the pioneers was to take quinine, but the bitter pill was only a repressor. When the pill was not taken, the symptoms surfaced. The only effective control was to drain the swamps and to rid the country of its mosquito-breeding grounds. Malaria was endemic; it fevered the cities as well as the farms. The work against the blight in the urban areas was the exclusive domain of the Mandatory government's health department, which began to function in the latter part of 1920. At first, Hadassah was forbidden to do any sanitary work in the cities and towns, most probably for political reasons. Recent arrival Henrietta Szold was furious: "The prohibition would be just and proper provided the Government fulfilled its functions. It has a corps of Arabs, low-class inspectors, who are charged with practicing graft. They sell the petrol entrusted to them for (pouring into) wells, cisterns and puddles, and accept *baksheesh* (bribery) from householders who desire not to drink petrolized water."

The Mandate government, under its first high commissioner, Sir Herbert Samuel, soon saw the error and authorized Hadassah's sanitary engineer Louis Cantor to direct squads of inspectors in an all-embracing anti-malaria campaign. Sir Herbert probably reasoned that Hadassah was, after all, killing mosquitoes that were biting both Arabs and Jews and even an occasional Englishman. Cantor's efforts were long remembered by all sections of the community. He introduced toilets and garbage disposal units in Arab villages. He drew up the first plan for draining quarters in Jerusalem that were avenues of running sewage. He gave the first course of instruction on how to install plumbing ("installators," as plumbers are still known in Hebrew). And what some distinguished Zionist leaders long remembered him for was the hot shower installation that he introduced into the Hotel de France, Hadassah's headquarters. It soon became a regular Friday afternoon rite for the captains of the *yishuv* to wash themselves down under Lou Cantor's showers.

By 1921, Hadassah-directed teams under Dr. Israel "Kleeg" Kligler neutralized the anopheles in the rural areas. The breakthrough came when Justice Brandeis provided $10,000 for experimental work in malaria control. Kligler's teams found that countrywide 25 percent of the Jewish and 50 percent of the Arab populations were chronic malaria sufferers. With methods proven in Panama during the construction of the canal, new cases were reduced by 90 percent. Sanitary inspectors stood guard over swamp areas during the breeding season. They forced quinine down the gullets of Arabs and Jews alike. They even went as far as to repair dripping faucets in town, village and camp. By the end of 1921, the nation's worst pest holes had been eradicated. At one cooperative farm near Migdal, all but two of the 80 workers suffered at least two malarial attacks in the summer before the work was begun. By the beginning of 1922, only five cases were reported in the same area. Henrietta Szold was ecstatic: "The men sleep in the open without nets and remain unstung! It's a miracle."

Not everyone was so happy about the results. The government's health department chief, Colonel George Heron, was a physician of questionable sympathies. He had been transferred to the Colonial Office from the army when the military administration made way for the civilian Mandate administration in 1920. On one occasion he was asked to approve a big anti-malaria project and to provide a token sum toward the expenses as a demonstration of British concern. When the project landed on his desk, he demanded, "Who owns the land?" His subordinate replied, "The Palestine Jewish Colonization Association, sir." Replied Heron, "Then, damn it, let them pay for it." After all, the mosquitoes were carousing on private land.

It was not until 1931 that the Mandate government finally agreed to pay the bill for killing mosquitoes, public or private. Hadassah had turned over the responsibility for malaria control to Sir Herbert Samuel in 1922. The men who now fought the good fight under British supervision were either former members of the Unit or trained by it. And the Jewish Joint Distribution Committee financed the work until 1931.

Work with pioneers in the marshes of Galilee led Hadassah to participate in the healing of the land through reclamation projects undertaken by the Jewish National Fund. Founded on December 29, 1901, at the Fifth Zionist Congress in Basel, the JNF was created for one purpose: "...to buy lands in Palestine." Such lands, according to the founding declaration, would be "the inalienable property of the Jewish people." But reality decreed otherwise. Within a short time the JNF, known worldwide for the little blue-and-white coin boxes that still grace Jewish homes, was not only buying land but draining swamps, rehabilitating river beds, cutting new roads, planting forests, creating picnic areas and parks, and making desert soil fertile.

Near the end of its first century, the JNF has planted more than 200 million trees and owns 17 percent of the land on which Israel exists. The annual budget has reached one-quarter of a billion dollars. For this money, when current projects are completed in the year 2000, Israelis will have one-half million acres of forest.

Having extended far beyond its mandate, no other institution could boast at having fulfilled Zionist aspirations as could the JNF. It was to this star in Jewish life that Hadassah firmly hitched its Zionist mission. Killing mosquitoes in the Galilee had given this healing society a hearty appetite for more projects to revive a land that, after centuries of neglect and rape, was nearly terminal.

Beginning in 1926, Hadassah over the next 70 years would spend $50 million to finance 25 diverse schemes through JNF. These programs would among others: redeem 4,000 acres in the Haifa Bay area, 10,000 acres in Galilee, drain the Huleh Lake to create 33 villages and, in the 1990's, participate in recreating part of the Lake to preserve the ecological balance. It created a grassy shore that the western side of the Kinneret (Sea of Galilee) never had. In 1949, it set up a hospital in Beersheba when the village consisted of only two dirty streets. Four decades later through the JNF it would replace the scrub and sand of Beersheba (1995 pop.: 153,000) with a park and playground at the entrance to the city.

For all their ingenuity none of Hadassah's founders would have imagined their members would one day build dams in a desert. But in 1986 that is just what they did. One of the largest soil barriers in Israel – 56 feet high – was partially financed by Hadassah. The Hadassah-Eshet dam has spawned a 10 million cubic meter blue, sweet water lake in the Arava along the border with Jordan. Floodwaters that formerly ended up in the Dead Sea or in Jordan now recharge depleted aquifers and provide water for 3,000 settlers in 10 villages. In a wasteland where once there were only snakes, scorpions and tumbleweed, water has produced winter crops of melons, mango, persimmon and avocado that feed the markets of Israel and Europe.

Not far away, near Kibbutz Sde Boker, another Hadassah dam blocks winter's flash floods, providing water for flocks of sheep and orchards of acacia, pistachio and tamarisk.

But that was yet to come. Back in the early 1920's relations between the Zionists and the new British colonial government were testy. The fact that Sir Herbert Samuel was a Jew and pro-Zionist made little difference to Colonial Office bureaucrats many of whom, like Heron, had transferred from the army or the Occupied Enemy Territory Administration to what they hoped would be adventurous, well-paid, easy jobs in Palestine. Many had served in Cairo and knew how to "handle" Arabs. Jews, ideologically motivated and anxious to establish a state, were another cup of tea.

In Haifa, for example, the anti-Zionist military governor had remarked that the overcrowded and unsanitary conditions in which Jewish immigrants were living endangered the health of the Arab population. This, despite a dispensary that was being run for Jews and Arabs by Hadassah.

In reply to the military governor's challenge, Hadassah rushed Joseph Shapiro into the port town. His public health survey concluded, even to the satisfaction of the British governor, that the Arabs were less likely to fall ill from the Jews than from the drinking water which they were taking from shallow wells or from the garbage they were spilling into the streets or from the sewage that was running by their houses or from the open barrels of water which they used to wash clothes – which bred mosquitoes. Shapiro proved that the health and sanitation conditions of the Jews were just as good as, and in many cases better than, those of their Arab neighbors.

Shapiro's biggest challenge was the common louse. By mid-1920 immigrants were entering Haifa and Jaffa ports en masse and were bringing with them an unprecedented plague of East European lice. Delousing of their bodies was not much of a problem since there was plenty of chlorine at hand. The problem was how to deal with the clothes. The British had invented an apparatus called a Serbian Barrel to sterilize clothes, but it was not yet available in Palestine. Shapiro improvised by taking empty alcohol barrels and making them air-tight. He then fitted them with false bottoms which were filled with water. Placed over a fire, the barrels became giant pressure cookers. In a short time the clothes placed in the Shapiro Barrels, as they became known throughout the country, were free of lice.

By mid-1922, Hadassah asked the Mandate government to take over rural sanitation along with malaria control. In any case, inspection of newcomers ceased to be a great problem since immigration had been curbed. Thus relieved of preventive medical work Hadassah could expand its medical services throughout the country. From the Jordan to the

Mediterranean, from Galilee to Judea, a string of 60 Hadassah clinics soon functioned in towns and villages. Clinics serviced nearly all the moshavim (cooperative villages). In 1931, the rural medical service was turned over to Kupat Holim Amamit, a health maintenance organization founded by Hadassah. It thrives today as Kupat Holim Meuchedet, now one of the largest in Israel.

Throughout the 1920's the Hadassah horse-and-buggy doctors and nurses who traveled the dirt paths into remote settlements were familiar figures. At the beginning of the 1930's they worked under different auspices, but that did not alter the fact that Hadassah was the first to send them on their appointed rounds. Henrietta Szold later paid them the ultimate tribute when she said, "The itinerant doctors had become the lineal successor to the priest in the camps of ancient Israel."

Few people living today have a full understanding of the extent to which Hadassah – young, poor and inexperienced – fashioned the future of the *yishuv's* medical history in the third decade of the century. When Americans were only beginning to dream of national health insurance, Hadassah in Palestine was forcing an amalgamation of the health funds that were started by the two existing political labor parties. Both parties were serving as contractors on the road-building and swamp-clearing projects in Galilee and each demanded separate field hospital services from Hadassah. The Unit's acting director at the time was Henrietta Szold. She put her foot down and issued an ultimatum for the two to amalgamate. That decided the issue. The result was Kupat Holim Clalit of the Histadrut, Israel's Federation of Labor. Until 1931, Hadassah institutions at first took on all Kupat Holim cases free of charge. With financial help from Hadassah, Kupat Holim built its first hospital in the Jezreel Valley in 1929. A second, Beilinson, was constructed in Petah Tikva seven years later. These two institutions took considerable pressure off Hadassah and permitted Hadassah to reach for new horizons. Kupat Holim Clalit covered nearly the entire Jewish population. In time the others would be cared for by three private health funds.

In 1995, the Knesset decreed that all Israelis be covered by one of the four. Fees set by the Government were deducted from salaries like social security payments in return for which residents received blanket coverage. Trouble was that the expense for such care far outran Government funding. Thus the four, constantly facing bankruptcy, could not pay their hospital bills. Hadassah's medical institutions together with others were always out of pocket to the tune of millions of shekels. In fact, at the end of 1996, the foundering four funds owed Hadassah $50 million. To relieve that pain, Hadassah had the satisfaction that its good medical care was helping give Israelis longer lives than nearly all other peoples.

Just as in Galilee Hadassah pioneers were being told that they were wasting time, so in Jerusalem they were being similarly rebuffed. As in Galilee the Americans refused to accept "no" for an answer, so in the Holy City they persisted until the population accepted them. Often they had to use bizarre stratagems. No single Hadassah worker was more persevering than a dynamic mite of a public health nurse by the name of Bertha Landsman. Her charges would relate how in the summer of 1921 she issued orders with the cadence of a top sergeant marching into battle against a dangerous enemy. "If they don't let you in the front door, go in the back door. And if they don't let you in the back door, go through the window. But get in!" It was a battle cry no one believed could possibly emerge from pink-cheeked, blue-eyed Bertha.

In some ways Bertha's story was much like that of Shulamit Yedid-Halevy Cantor. At about the same time that Shulamit was threatening her father that she would run away from Beirut to go to nursing school, Bertha was doing the same. She told her father in no uncertain terms that nursing was definitely for her and if she could not study in her native New York City, she would flee to Washington, D.C. The poor man agreed, providing she remained near home. So Bertha trained at Mt. Lebanon Hospital, in New York, the source of many of AZMU's first nurses. After graduation she served in mother and infant welfare stations established by philanthropist

Nathan Straus in New York City's underprivileged neighborhoods. But her heart was in Palestine and in 1921 she followed it there.

To the newcomer, Eretz Israel has always been seductively rich in challenges; Henrietta Szold would say, "Where everything is needed, everything needs to be done." Bertha looked at the needs and saw that in Jaffa-Tel Aviv four out of every ten babies never lived to celebrate their first birthday. In Haifa, the mortality rate was 30 percent and in Jerusalem 20 percent. To keep babies alive, then, was her challenge. She reached into her experience and pulled out a plan to adapt the Straus mother and infant stations to Palestine. She organized a platoon of nurses, opened the first center in the ancient walled city of Jerusalem and then went out to drag in the reluctant mothers. In the beginning, the male members of the Jewish families beat off the nurses, sometimes physically. Most of the nurses did not wear marriage bands, so they would be taunted with: "Hah! You are not even married and you are going to tell us how to take care of our babies!"

The unfortunate nurses were caught in a crossfire. From one flank they were being driven on by Bertha's exhortations; from the other they were being pushed away by irate husbands. At times they took Bertha's orders literally and climbed through back windows to plead, to cajole, to tempt mothers to come to the stations. Inside, they found dark, dank rooms where babies lay bundled like mummies, their hands and feet tightly tied "to give them good postures." The infants looked more like packages ready for mailing than human beings ready for living. Their eyes were watery from the smoke of charcoal cooking fires. Windows were kept closed even in temperate weather because the families believed it was the only way to keep out unseen germs – and the evil spirit. For extra protection, a *hamsa* (brass hand) was hung in every room. Flies and vermin plagued the tots, but they were disregarded because they were "too small" to do harm. When mothers had insufficient milk to nurse, they gave the infants unpasteurized goat's milk.

Bertha broke the opposition. She began by offering free layettes and pasteurized formula milk to parents on condition they give birth in

Rothschild Hospital. Once the mothers were in the hospital Bertha would exhort each one, "Bring your babies to our station regularly and I promise you they will live to bless you with many grandchildren."

The Drop of Milk (Tipat Halav) station, as it was known, had a kitchen and two rooms. Each day in the kitchen hermetically-sealed vats of milk would be lifted on to a three-headed kerosene stove. When the milk reached close to boiling point, the vat would be hurriedly shifted into a bathtub filled with ice where it would be quickly cooled. The result was the first pasteurized milk in all of Palestine, probably in the Middle East. Nurses and volunteers, headed by the wife of the director of customs, Mrs. Harold Solomon, would then prepare formulas, fill bottles and wait for the mothers to appear. Those who came for the first time would receive a free tin container to carry the bottles home. The word quickly passed from mouth to mouth in the Jewish quarter of the Old City that Hadassah was giving out a new type of milk, milk that did not turn rancid quickly. That appealed to mothers and their numbers at the Drop of Milk station grew. Some began coming from quarters outside the walled city, but many were still hesitant.

Bertha was impatient. If mothers did not come for milk, she would see to it that the milk was taken to them. And so was established the Donkey Milk Express. The bottles, each labeled with the baby's name, were packed in ice and put on a donkey cart whose sides carried the name "Tipat Halav" in Hebrew, Arabic and English. Each weekday morning, the Donkey Milk Express began its journey from the David Street station, joined the raucous traffic of horses, camels, carriages and tin-lizzies on its life-giving mission to the Rothschild Hospital, which was the New City's milk distribution point. There, volunteer women of the Hebrew Women's Federation (Histadrut Nashim Ivriot) handed the sterilized bottles to waiting mothers.

So popular was the Donkey Milk Express and its cargo that housewives from Western countries who had no infants clamored for pasteurized milk. One well-to-do American mother once approached Bertha to provide her with pasteurized milk because her daughter disliked drinking boiled milk.

Bertha's reply was in character: "Of course we will provide you with our product. Just send someone each morning to pick up a pint. And send along 50 cents for each bottle." Hadassah's Robin Hood explained that she was charging the outlandish price to help cover the cost of the milk for several children whose parents could not pay one cent. Actually few got it free. Except for the destitute, mothers were required to pay something, even though it be a pittance. Bertha intended to drive home the lesson that mothers and fathers must care for their own children, that charity should not replace responsibility. Bertha and her nurses struggled with this problem as they had struggled to get the mothers to visit the station in the first place. Mostly, the fathers were the ones who objected. For this kind of luxury they expected the Americans or Europeans to pay. Mothers cried on Bertha's slim shoulders begging her to help convince their husbands. For those who did have more generous spouses Bertha would keep precise accounts of the mils the women paid and each Saturday would remain at home making out individual receipts which they could show their husbands. At times, exhausted, Bertha was tempted to give up the idea, be done with the accountancy and hand out the milk free. Then one day a pretty, young Orthodox mother came to her, smiling coyly, and told a story that convinced Bertha the battle was won.

The mother had always complained that she could not get milk money from her stubborn husband. This day she showed up with the coins clenched in her fist and a promise that she would no longer have to plead for milk money.

Bertha was surprised. "How did you do it?" she asked.

The mother's cheeks turned pink and she dropped her eyes. She wanted to talk to Bertha privately. They stepped aside and the mother whispered, "It was very hard, but my husband does not like sleeping on the floor."

Bertha's eyes opened wide with an unspoken question.

"It was the day I was supposed to go to the *mikveh* (ritual bath). I absolutely *refused* to go until he gave me the money for milk. He won't refuse again," she said with a twinkle.

Forty years later, Bertha recalled the story and said that it was the turning point in her personal battle. Never again did she waver.

Soon, the milk program was running smoothly. Bertha now felt sufficiently sure of herself to move into related fields. She sent her nurses into homes to advise mothers how to prepare cereal, how to refrigerate, how to nurse. And by mid-1923 they were all going through the front door. At the station, Bertha insisted that babies be weighed regularly. Some mothers objected because they said it would invite the evil eye, so they fed their children before they took them to the station and then insisted that there was no need to weigh them. The nurses overcame that obstacle by forcing the mothers to leave the children at the center for three hours before going ahead with a test feeding and a weighing-in. Periodically, the children were examined and fortunately for everyone concerned, Jerusalem's first pediatrician was Helena Kagan, whose understanding and kindliness earned her the respect and gratitude of generations of parents.*

So popular was the station after a time that the non-Jewish mothers in the neighborhood began to ask for aid. Everyone was accepted, Jew and non-Jew alike. In 1923, with a gift from Nathan Straus, another station was opened in the lower Musrara Quarter near Damascus Gate where the population was predominantly Arab. Even during the bitter Arab riots, a Jewish and an Arab physician would remain on duty at the station. Veteran nurses in Jerusalem still remember with a smile the diminutive Dr. Abu Saud, who had to stand on a bench to examine the taller children's eyes and throats and whose favorite – and effective – treatments for many ailments were barley water or castor oil. The nurses, too, courageously carried on through the bloodletting, keeping to their rounds in both Arab and Jewish quarters.

One of those nurses was Hanna Elkayam who was sent into the village of Siloam (Silwan), in the southern environs of Jerusalem, to open a station. The village was mainly Arab, but about 100 Yemenite Jewish

---

* On July 31, 1958, Mayor Gershon Agron and the city fathers bestowed upon Dr. Kagan the coveted Freedom of Jerusalem, the first woman to be so honored.

families lived there peacefully. From 1925, Hanna lived in Siloam and served the community as nurse, confidante, pharmacist, social worker. All problems came to Hanna for resolution: how much to spend on a bar mitzvah party, what clothes to buy for the children, how to reunite a separated couple. Hanna was the mother of the village.

One night the leading Sheikh of Siloam, Haj Ghuslan, did Hanna the unique honor of calling upon her. After the usual formalities were ended, he asked whether she would go to his house to deliver his wife's child. Not a little tremulous, Hanna agreed. She found the woman in difficult labor, but Hanna delivered the baby after a few tense hours. As the Sheikh's son uttered its first cry, the grandmother threatened the nurse, "That child you have brought into the world will grow up one day to throw a rock at you at the Wall." Sheikh Ghuslan never forgot Hanna's kindness. During the riots of 1929 he placed guards over the property of all the Jews of the village and nothing was stolen or touched during their temporary absence.

The lone milk station that was opened by Bertha Landsman in 1921 had by the end of the decade multiplied to 22, not counting numerous sub-stations throughout the country. One result was that the Mandate government's slow-moving health department was obliged to emulate Hadassah, opening its first infant welfare center for Arabs in 1925. By the end of the decade it had 14 going. The idea spread beyond the borders of Palestine. In Cairo, WIZO (Women's International Zionist Organization) asked for the loan of a Hadassah-trained nurse to run a center. Nurses from Iraq were sent to Jerusalem to observe Hadassah's work and returned to Baghdad to organize similar operations. A center based on the Hadassah pattern was likewise opened in Amman.

Fruits of the infant welfare work were quick and sweet. Mortality dropped dramatically. In 1922, 144 Jewish children out of every 1,000 throughout the country died before their first birthday. By 1930, the rate had dropped by more than half to 69. Unfortunately, the net was not so large that it could provide blanket coverage for all Arab communities. Although Hadassah served both sectors of the population, its work was done primarily in predominantly Jewish areas, so that in the same period infant mortality rates of the Arab community rose by three percent. Had the welfare stations not been in operation, however, there is little question that the Arab rate would have climbed more rapidly than it did.

By the end of the decade Hadassah closed the Drop of Milk kitchens. In nine years the Jewish population had accepted as a matter of course the necessity of proper milk preparation. In the 1960's, the stations were transferred in Jerusalem to the Municipality and in the rest of the country to the Ministry of Health. Although now officially known as "Well-Baby Clinics," the original name Tipat Halav (Drop of Milk) has endured.

The pulse of every undertaking in preventive medicine and in education initiated by Hadassah in Palestine came from the heartbeat of the child. When the generation of Yitzhak Rabin, Shimon Peres and Moshe Dayan was in its infancy, Hadassah was there doing its best to protect and nurture it. When AZMU arrived in Palestine trachoma afflicted the eyes of upward of 40 of every 100 Jewish school children. A similar number had scalp and skin ailments. Home inspection was tried, but Hadassah soon learned that the most efficient place to attack these maladies was through strict control in the schools where one child was more apt to infect another. No agencies existed to carry out inspections in schools in 1918 and 1919. So, as Henrietta Szold reported back to New York in finger-snapping prose, "A School Hygiene Department was organized."

To beat trachoma, Hadassah doctors and inspectors dispersed throughout the country. Itinerant ophthalmologists made regular calls at remote settlements. One of the first eye specialists who traveled the trachoma circuit on the back of a donkey was Haim Yassky, then on the threshold of a brilliant career that would end in tragedy. Hadassah took responsibility for children in the regular school system but also went into the homes of youngsters who studied at private schools. At one time 30 specially trained nurses were treating children under doctors' supervision. The results were spectacular. By 1930, trachoma was practically beaten; by 1938 only four out of every 100 children had the disease, even though immigration from Near East countries constantly brought new sources of infection. By comparison, both the Arab community and the Mandate government neglected trachoma. The result: 65 out of every 100 Arab children still had the disease in 1938, the year it practically vanished among Jewish pupils.

Hadassah's service to Jewish pupils was the most comprehensive in the world. At the start of each term the child was weighed, measured, tested for tuberculosis, examined for defective eyesight and hearing, and periodically vaccinated and inoculated. A child absent from school for more than two days was visited at home by a school nurse and treated before being permitted to return. In an average year 80 percent of all Jewish public school pupils received some kind of medical help.

Under the energetic direction of department chief Mordecai Brachyahu, pioneering work was carried out in mental hygiene. Kindergarten teachers reported emotionally unstable or mentally backward children to Dr. Brachyahu, who ran guidance clinics in Jerusalem and Tel Aviv.

At the end of the first ten years – by which time Straus Health Centers* provided the roof for all of Hadassah's preventive medical work – the School Hygiene Department was supervising more than 250 schools in eight urban areas and 64 rural settlements. Altogether, 25,000 children were being examined yearly. And in that decade Hadassah dispensed to school pupils alone more than 10 million individual treatments.

By 1927, Hadassah wove its network of infant welfare stations and school hygiene services into a countrywide child welfare program that was years ahead of its time. By the latter part of the 1920's Hadassah was not only bringing children into the world, feeding them and making them disease resistant, but it was also attempting to supervise their recreation. This came about after the first playground in Palestine was opened in 1925

---

* The Straus Center in Jerusalem now houses Hadassah-Israel and Hadassah International, the Hadassah Council and the Career Counseling Institute. Most of Hadassah's complementary (alternative) medicine services are provided there. Annually more than 55,000 treatments are given in everything from Chinese medicine to osteopathy.

at the edge of the Jewish Quarter inside the Old City of Jerusalem. The money for the playground came from a $100,000 fund set up by Bertha Guggenheimer, of Lynchburg, Virginia, aunt of former Hadassah President Irma Lindheim. Until the lot was opened the slum children's favorite games were playing cards, throwing dice or scrounging in ash cans. In February 1928, the trustees of the fund under which the playground was established turned over responsibility to Hadassah. A teacher in the Old City, Rachel Shwarz, wife of a noted Jerusalem attorney, whose two daughters later married Moshe Dayan and Ezer Weizman, was placed in charge. She moved to a larger area outside the city walls and brought in a Hadassah doctor to examine all the children who registered to play. The playground was beautifully equipped. It even had showers and therein lay the cause of opposition from Arab parents. The following account was left by Eva Dushkin, who was sent to Jerusalem by the Guggenheimer family to observe the work:

> When a rumor went around that showers were being installed, the Arabs in the neighborhood were indignant. They never saw anything like it and could not imagine that a shower could be taken inside a room. They thought that showers were taken in open public places and I was called by several of the Arabs in the neighborhood, particularly the Moslems, and asked to understand that they would not stand for any such immorality. They did not propose to have their several wives look through the window and see little boys and girls bathing nude in the street. When they were given to understand that these showers would be taken inside four walls with a roof over their heads, they consented to hold back their anger for the opening day. Since then, there have been constant streams of Arab visitors who come and see and stand back with great admiration and awe over the fact that

children may come and bathe at leisure without being forced
to either pay for the water or bring it themselves.

The playground project was so successful that it quickly spread to all parts
of the country. But when a plot was opened in the Mahane Yehuda Quarter
of the new city of Jerusalem, opposite the Etz Hayim Yeshiva, the principal
of the school was enraged. He complained bitterly that his children were
not paying attention to their Torah and Talmud lessons and instead were
gazing out the windows at the boys and girls playing below. Repeatedly he
implored Rachel Shwarz to close the field, using the argument that it was
sinful according to Jewish law to permit boys and girls to romp together.
The principal was all the more disturbed because his own granddaughter
was playing there. Rachel stubbornly stood her ground, countering with
the argument that his pupils might study better if they had time off daily
to kick a ball around. But he would not be moved and he applied to the
Jerusalem rabbinical court to issue a summons calling on Rachel to give
good reason why the playground should not be closed.

Rachel had no choice but to appeal to the rabbinical eminence of the
day, Chief Rabbi Abraham Isaac Halevy Kook. Rachel stood before the
saintly mortal and pleaded, "Our children have a natural instinct to play.
How can a rabbi deny it to them?"

"My daughter," he said reassuringly without committing himself, "go
back to your work and all will be well."

Objections evaporated as fog before the sun. The summons was
withdrawn, the playground flourished and municipal authorities all over
the country made increasing demands on Hadassah's experience in helping
establish them. But a last bailiwick of opposition remained – oddly, in the
kibbutzim. There, members argued that children already had sufficient
open spaces in which to run free and that in any case land was much too
scarce to use for swings and ball games. Hadassah reasoned that
playgrounds were more than sites for idle frolicking; when run Hadassah's
way with properly trained staffs, they were educational instruments that

sharpened leadership qualities and moulded good bodies and minds. Irma Lindheim finally broke the ice with the first kibbutz playground at Mishmar Haemek, located at the entrance to the Jezreel Valley, where she established her home after giving up the presidency of Hadassah in 1928.

By 1950, nearly 50 playgrounds had been set up by Hadassah while numerous others profited from Hadassah's expertise. In that year all the grounds were turned over to the Israeli government.

The British authorities looked upon the project with benevolent grace. In 1934 they even went as far as to turn over to Hadassah a one-half acre plot in Jerusalem and then at the end of the year cited that act of charity in a report to the League of Nations as a major contribution to the Jewish population of Palestine.

BUTTER FOR THE PARSNIPS

O ne miserably cold day in December 1922, a tall, gaunt figure with sad, bespectacled eyes and a finely-trimmed goatee stood before Henrietta Szold in her Jerusalem office. He was beloved as a teacher and principal of a girls' school in the Old City.

"Not a day goes by," sighed Yeshaya Press, "that one of our children does not faint in the classroom. They come to school with nothing in their stomachs. When they go home, they are lucky if they find bread and a few vegetables to eat. I have found some of them raiding garbage pails. How can I expect them to do their lessons? Can't your American organization help us get some warm food into their bellies?"

Press would not admit it, but Henrietta knew that his teachers were just as hungry as the pupils and there were instances where they had collapsed as well. Palestine was then paralyzed by economic stagnation. The country was not paying its way. Imports far outpaced exports. There was little industry and many of the plants that had opened soon went bankrupt for lack of working capital. Fifty years later in Jerusalem, Prime Minister Golda Meir would smilingly recall those days to an economic conference of millionaires: "I remember when I first came in 1921. The only 'heavy' industry was chocolate. But the chocolate it produced was full of sand and when I asked why, I was told that sand was the country's only natural resource."

So poor was the country that in the struggling kibbutzim and villages, farmers had nothing more to eat than the vegetables they grew. Their patron, the World Zionist Organization, was having trouble finding money to carry both them and the Unit over their initial period of development. AZMU got some support, as we have seen, from the Joint Distribution Committee, the Rothschilds and from the young Hadassah organization in the United States. Partly because of a severe economic depression membership in Hadassah in 1921 was little more than 10,000 and so was not big enough to bear single-handedly the burgeoning burdens of the pioneers in Palestine. Hadassah's weakness was also partly organizational. From 1918 to 1921, it was affiliated and subordinate to the male-dominated Federation of American Zionists. Full independence came only in 1933 when Hadassah stopped paying affiliation dues to the Federation's successor, the Zionist Organization of America. Growth was slowed as well by the intellectual and political climate in the United States. The Jewish masses, engrossed in sopping up American culture, were practically untouched by Zionism. After some initial enthusiasm over the Balfour Declaration, apathy quickly set in when the British pledge failed to instantly produce a Jewish nation. Hadassah's problem was a small reflection of the general American lack of interest in the Zionist movement.

In the early 1920's the largest fund raiser on the American scene was the Joint Distribution Committee which, in the main, channeled funds to the poverty-stricken Jewish communities in Europe. So it was that Palestine's requirements far exceeded Zionism's ability to meet them. In Jerusalem, Zionist headquarters was so badly off that electricity and telephone services were shut down periodically for nonpayment of bills. The World Zionist Organization cut its budget for Hadassah's work by two-thirds and thus forced it to the brink of bankruptcy. Grocery bills piled up. Suppliers of pharmaceuticals pounded on Henrietta Szold's desk. Hadassah employees went for months without salaries. On one occasion they were paid in linen. Medical Director Rubinow had to close a clinic in the Old City and the hospital in Tiberias and reduce the number of beds in the Tel Aviv hospital. The pressure was so great that Rubinow repeatedly threatened to quit. Into Henrietta's lap fell the whole sorry mess. She was then 62 years old and ailing. She knew very well that the only logical thing to do would be to disband the Unit but, she rationalized, even that was impossible because there was no money to pay off the doctors. She wrote her sister Rachel, "If the Unit and I survive the winter, it will be a miracle."

Early in October 1922, Henrietta Szold desperately fought to keep the Unit alive by calling on Baron Rothschild in Paris. As she walked past great works of art in his ornate mansion in the Rue de Faubourg Saint-Honoré, she day-dreamed that all the old man would have to do to save the Unit would be to say: "Over there is a little thing of the school of Leonardo da Vinci – take it." But he did not say it. Rather, he used the occasion to berate American Jews in general and Zionists in particular for not supporting what they started. The only constructive part of their meeting was the lavish praise that the baron voiced for Hadassah's work. Bitterly, she later commented, "I have heard that too often now to be flattered. Fine words butter no parsnips and keep no hospitals going."

The baron's advice to Henrietta was to go to America to raise the money. She would have done so even though she detested the idea, but poor Rubinow in Jerusalem had frantically cabled he was about to leave for good. From the baron's she returned to her hotel and, nursing a bad cold, she consoled herself by dining on a bag of roasted chestnuts. She wrote home, "French laundresses are artists and must be paid like prima donnas, and colds consume handkerchiefs."

Henrietta was not back in Jerusalem very long when an old friend, having heard of her distress, cabled $20,000. The money was from Nathan Straus, but much as it was appreciated, the dollars covered only one-fourth of the Unit's debts. The problem now was whether to use it to pay salaries or to pay the baker or the drug manufacturers. "I know the agony of an honest bankruptcy," Henrietta said. "Hour by hour I sit in the office and count and calculate." Happily, the Unit's administrative staff and "even a few of the doctors" were prepared to sacrifice. They were ready to forgo their back pay to allow the work to continue, accepting Henrietta's promise that one day they would receive their money in full.

It was at that hour in the gray fortunes of the Unit that Yeshaya Press stood before Henrietta Szold. She told him that she had no money to buy even a piece of chalk, but ever optimistic she repeated to him her overworked slogan, "Where everything is needed, everything needs to be done. And it will be done." Press walked out of her office empty-handed, buoyed by Henrietta's faith that help would come. Shortly after that, an American tourist, Rabbi Maurice Harris, of New York, burst into Henrietta's office. He introduced himself as a religious educator. He said he was appalled to see how badly nourished the school children of Jerusalem were. As it happened, the rabbi went on, he had brought a small sum of Hanukkah money with him, contributed by his school, and he thought Miss Szold could put it to use to feed the unfortunate pupils. It was not nearly enough to help everyone, but what would Miss Szold think if he started a campaign in the United States to provide lunches for Jerusalem's needy pupils? Would Miss Szold ask Hadassah in New York to help him?

Henrietta could hardly encourage Rabbi Harris to return soon enough. And Yeshaya Press was, of course, the first to be told. Rabbi Harris did go back and together with Leon Lang organized a school lunch program committee on which Hadassah was represented. Soon thereafter the project was transferred to Hadassah. At first, appeals for lunch money were made almost exclusively to pupils of religious schools throughout the United States. The slogan was simple: "Give a penny so a child in Jerusalem can eat." Pennies rolled in by the basketful. Children sold brochures on Palestine to raise money. Hadassah women organized thrift luncheons whereby they would cook and serve the same meal that was served to the Jerusalem pupils. But they would charge each guest from five to ten times more than the cost of the meal given in Palestine. A typical lunch was oatmeal, soup, cole-slaw and date and raisin compote. On Fridays the children got free cocoa and bread at 10:00 a.m. recess because mothers gave them no solid food for breakfast in anticipation of the Sabbath evening meal. With a healthy donation from Hadassah the first hot lunches were served in Yeshaya Press's school in September 1923. A small kitchen and dining room were equipped. At first, only some of the girls could afford the one-half piaster (2.5 cents) for a meal. When the Hadassah committee under Nellie Straus Mochenson saw other girls standing "in tears at the door of the dining room looking on the feast," it was decided to include every child in the school. No one but Press knew who paid and who did not.

But that was only the beginning of the story. It was Henrietta's policy that no project would be an end in itself. Each endeavor must serve wider educational aims. A cook was hired to supervise the six weekly meals, but the pupils in the higher grades were required to prepare them. They were taught not only how to cook but how to serve and clean up, and most important, the fundamentals of nutrition. Henrietta's ultimate goal was to introduce domestic science in the school's curriculum. In 1923 as the lunch program started that goal was remote. Among the girls of Press's school there were some who were not accustomed to sitting on a chair or at a table to eat. Before they could be taught how to plan a balanced meal, they had to be taught how to use a knife and fork. At the end of the first year Henrietta reported, "Eventually the school luncheon program will be the means of teaching the food values of the rich variety of cereals and vegetables obtainable in Palestine which are largely disregarded now, particularly by the newer arrivals."

Teaching dietetics was not exactly new. Yehudit Aaronson Dushkin introduced the idea in the labor centers of Galilee. Student nurses in Jerusalem took cooking lessons for three hours every morning in a converted stable at Rothschild Hospital. The cadet nurses liked their lessons on the whole and the more proficient were chosen to cook part of the lunches served to the 120 patients and 105 staff members in the basement dining hall – originally built as a mammoth cistern.

Hard times in Palestine grew harder in 1927 and 1928 and the penny lunches were extended to kindergarten children, but even they did not get away with merely filling their little stomachs. The five-year-olds were also taught how to use cutlery, how to set a table and how to ask politely for the bread plate. By the turn of the decade 1,000 children were being fed from eight centrally located kitchens in Jerusalem, Haifa, Safed and Tiberias. So extensive had the project grown that Hadassah set up a Nutrition Department in the newly-opened Straus Health Center in Jerusalem.

In charge was a Dutch-born nutritionist, Sara Bavli, who opened the first course to train domestic science teachers in December 1930. As the teachers became available, the lunch programs broadened. By the time Israel was founded in 1948, 28,000 children were being fed daily in 300 schools and when Israel was ten years old, the number increased to 130,000 children. That was more than 25 percent of the entire school population of the country. By now the government itself was carrying most of the budget and the parents were only paying 10 percent of the bill. Meantime, Mrs. Bavli had, in 1953, opened up The College of Nutrition and Home Economics in Jerusalem.

Sara Bavli's college taught nutritionists for hospitals, clinics, schools and senior citizens homes until 1981. It was then split. Part formed the basis of a school for Nutritional Sciences in the Hebrew University's Agriculture Faculty, the only source in the country on world-wide nutrition research. And part introduced nutrition to the curriculum of the David Yellin Teachers College in Jerusalem. In 1993, Sara Bavli died.

What had started out as a frantic measure to ease the hunger pangs of a few score children (and teachers) in the Old City of Jerusalem had within 25 years grown into a ramified educational effort. Girls were being taught more than nutrition. Their courses included everything from child development and child guidance to interior decorating and stain removal. Hadassah's School Luncheon Committee made inroads into the kibbutzim where the science of food preparation was generally ignored in favor of the business of food production. Teachers in a number of kibbutzim asked Hadassah to set up cooking lessons even though, oddly enough, kibbutz parents objected. After an experimental lesson in one collective succeeded, the idea caught on and many set up kitchen committees. Hadassah knew it had succeeded when one kibbutz finally put hated spinach on the menu in the children's dining room. The kids ate it because they themselves had prepared it.

THE BLOOD OF AUGUST

Tired and tense, close to midnight on Friday, August 23, 1929, the administrative director of Hadassah Hospital in Jerusalem, Reuven Katznelson, scrawled a cable to Hadassah in New York:

> WE HAVE ELEVEN DEAD AND TWENTY-FIVE WOUNDED. ARABS ATTACKING SEVERAL JEWISH HOSPITALS.

On Saturday night, August 24, he wired:

> ANOTHER SEVEN DEAD AND EIGHT OF YESTERDAY'S WOUNDED HAVE DIED ALSO. MORE THAN THIRTY WOUNDED. THE ARABS ARE ATTACKING MEKOR HAIM, TALPIOT AND MOTZA. NEW SURGERY DEPARTMENTS HAVE BEEN OPENED. WE ARE CALLING ALL DOCTORS WE CAN. BABIES HOME HAS BEEN TRANSFERRED INTO TOWN. NEED MONEY BADLY.

That was only the beginning. Arab rioting lasted eight days, spanning the whole of settled Palestine from Safed in Galilee to Hebron, city of the

Patriarchs, south of Jerusalem. The violence was the bloodiest since the end of World War I: Arabs killed 133 Jews and wounded 330; British police killed 110 Arabs and wounded 232 and the Jews killed six Arabs. The riots illuminated the inadequacies of the British police and the need for a better Jewish system of defense. Zionist leaders in Jerusalem took immediate remedial measures that transformed the underground Haganah, forerunner of the Israel Defense Forces, into a skilled fighting unit.

The Arab riots of 1929 were the outgrowth of a quarter of a century of political struggle and intrigue. Throughout, Hadassah had a unique role to play, particularly during the height of the bloodletting. And everything that Hadassah accomplished in the Land of Israel from the arrival of the two nurses in 1913 seemed in retrospect to have been fated as preparation for those eight bloody days in August 1929.

The seeds of the riots, which were a turning point in Middle East history, were watered by the turbulent political crosscurrents of the late nineteenth and early twentieth centuries. Jewish nationalism in the form of Herzlian Zionism, dramatized by the formation of a political movement at the First Zionist Congress in Basel in 1897, was only a hop, skip and jump ahead of a similar movement then forming in the Arab world. Herzl was dead only a year and the Zionist platform was just beginning to sweep over the Jewish communities of Europe when the first serious call was heard for Arab secession from the Ottoman Empire. In 1905, a Christian Arab publisher, Neguib Zaouri, envisioned an Arab empire stretching "from the Tigris and the Euphrates to the Suez Isthmus and from the Mediterranean to the Arabian Sea." Interestingly, he excluded Egypt from his Arab nation because, as he wrote, "The Egyptians do not belong to the Arab race; they are of the African Berber family."

During World War I, the British and French secretly arranged in the Sykes-Picot agreement to divide the spoils of war and to establish two protectorates over lands the Ottoman Empire had held for four centuries: the French were to rule Syria and Lebanon and the British would control Iraq and Palestine. No provision was made for Jewish autonomy.

In Cairo the British high commissioner was goading the Bedouin of the Arabian peninsula to join the war on the side of the Allies. Toward that end Sir Henry McMahon made contact with Sharif Hussein Ibn Ali of Mecca. In his letters from Cairo, McMahon pledged British support for the Sharif's dream to place the Arab world under one caliphate. That convinced Hussein to fight the Turks.

By June 1916, Hussein got the Arab revolt under way against Ottoman rule. Lawrence of Arabia, a British agent who was assigned to assist Hussein's forces, glamorized the revolt. But as things turned out the Arab contribution to the overall war effort was not so effective as either the British or the Arabs had hoped it would be. Sharif Hussein planned a bold strategy. He intended to drive straight north and capture Syria. Once that was done he would install the commander of his troops, his son Feisal, as the king of a united Arab monarchy in Damascus, but the power behind the throne would remain in Mecca with Sharif himself.

While this scheme was being hatched, the noted chemist Chaim Weizmann, unaware of the Sykes-Picot agreement, was organizing a Zionist lobby whose purpose was to encourage the British government to establish a Jewish nation in Palestine once the Turks had been defeated.

Feisal's forces, together with the British, did not reach Damascus until October 1918 and did not take all of Syria until a fortnight before World War I ended. What the Arabs tried to do in battle, Weizmann had already succeeded in doing on paper. He had helped the British war effort by inventing a cheap method to produce explosives and he had convinced the British to support the establishment of a national home for Jews in Palestine. The Balfour Declaration was issued on November 2, 1917, a month before General Allenby reached Jerusalem and nearly a year before Feisal got to Damascus. Arabia was stunned by the Zionist victory. The British tried to allay Arab fears and at the same time urged them to fight on by promising, in June 1918, to work for Arab independence as well.

Little more than a month after World War I ended on November 11, 1918, the Allies solemnly gathered in Versailles for the peace conference.

Zionist and Arab leaders were present too, among them Chaim Weizmann and Emir Feisal. The two were no strangers to each other. In June 1918, they met in Feisal's tent on the shores of the Gulf of Aqaba in an attempt to pave a path to Arab and Jewish co-existence. Later that year they met again in London where, with the assistance of T. E. Lawrence, they drafted an accord which was to have tied the destiny of their two peoples. But the agreement came to nothing. Poor Feisal fell victim to British-French power politics and the extremists among his own people. The latter pressed him to lead a revolt against the French who had taken over from the British in Syria. He was forced to renege on his pledges to Weizmann and from Damascus he began to mouth vicious anti-Zionist propaganda.

Feisal was at the mercy of an extremist group called the General Syrian Congress. The congress was created by Arab nationalists in July 1919, with the aim of creating an independent Syria that would include Lebanon and Palestine. Once the French took over Syria and Lebanon, as laid down by Sykes and Picot, the congress shifted to violence. On March 1, 1920, it instigated an attack on two Jewish farm settlements in Galilee – at Tel Hai and at Metulla – in which seven pioneers died, including the noted Russian-born Zionist, Captain Joseph Trumpeldor. One week later, the Congress crowned Feisal king of United Syria and sent gangs into Galilee. At Passover time, April 4 and 5, Arab mobs ran amok in Jerusalem killing six Jews and wounding 211.

The Allies counterattacked, dealing a mortal blow to the Congress. Toward the end of April, the Allied powers met a few miles east of Monaco in the Italian town of San Remo. They had still not concluded a treaty with Turkey and since the situation in the Middle East was fast deteriorating, they gathered at San Remo to work out a permanent settlement for the peoples of the area. Three mandates were set up: two went to Britain to administer Palestine and Iraq and one went to France to govern Syria and Lebanon. Most important for the Zionist cause was the rider on the Palestine mandate that obligated the British to implement the provisions of the Balfour Declaration.

Little more than two months after the San Remo conference ended, the French sent King Feisal packing into comfortable exile (on the shores of Lake Maggiore, Italy) and brought independent United Syria to an ignominious and abrupt end. In that same month of July, the British appointed a prominent, pro-Zionist Jew, Sir Herbert Samuel, to be the first high commissioner of the Mandate government of Palestine.

As Jewish and pro-Zionist as Sir Herbert may have been, he was still committed to British colonial policy. Then, the policy was called "the equality of obligation." In our day, it might be known as "even-handedness." Eight months after he took office, in the worst decision of his career, Sir Herbert appointed Haj Amin el-Husseini to be Grand Mufti of Jerusalem. The wily Husseini was a rabid anti-Zionist and was regarded as one of the leaders of the Passover riots in Jerusalem. Sir Herbert mistakenly believed that the Arabs would now be mollified.

In March 1921, Winston Churchill appeared on the scene. He was now colonial secretary and as such he was responsible for the Mandate. New to the area's problems, he was determined to clean up the mess that had been created by contradictory British promises to Jews and Arabs. His ultimate aim was to pacify the area so that he could remove all British military forces. In his view the Arabs were the injured party and in characteristic Churchillian style he moved boldly. He called Emir Feisal out of Italian exile and rigged an election that made him king of Iraq. Churchill then sliced off that portion of Palestine that lay east of the Jordan River, including the hills of Moab from where Moses saw the Land of Israel and put Feisal's brother, Abdullah, on a separate throne. Abdullah was to rule an area to be called Trans-Jordan, later to be renamed the Hashemite Kingdom of Jordan.

The Arab dream was shattered. Arab nationalists despaired of uniting their peoples under the Syrian flag. So they turned their energies to and found unity in fighting Zionism in Palestine. To Churchill's credit he did not renege on promises to Zionists even while he championed the cause of Arab independence. When a delegation of Moslem and Christian Arabs asked him in Jerusalem to rescind the Balfour Declaration and to stop

Jewish immigration, Churchill replied, "That is not in my power and it is not my wish."

Zionist leaders did not kick up much dust at Churchill's handing half of Palestine to Abdullah. Only at the end of the decade, when a British Labour government turned against the Zionists, would Revisionist Vladimir Zev Jabotinsky cry out that the Jordan River passed through the middle of the Land of Israel. In retrospect, Churchill did not succeed, but unlike others who tried to solve the problem of Palestine, he executed his failure with brilliance and flair. He did not achieve a rapprochement between Zionists and Arabs. He fractured the idea of a single Arab state, apportioning slices to the favorite sons of Sharif Hussein. (Hussein himself would in short time be overthrown as the ruler of Hedjaz by Ibn Saud and Saud would give his name to the kingdom of Saudi Arabia.) The result was that Arab nationalists remained dissatisfied and the Jews grew apprehensive.

Churchill was gone from the scene little more than a month when violence again erupted. In Tel Aviv, now twelve years old, members of the socialist Zionist Ahdut Avodah party held a May Day parade. A rival parade was staged at the same place by the Trotskyite party. The two met head on with banners flying. Being an all-Jewish riot, there were no serious casualties. Arabs, watching from Jaffa, picked up arms and while the Jews were scuffling, went on a rampage of killing. Martial law was declared, but the "disturbances" continued sporadically for a full week. The Arabs had been provoked with rumors that atheist, Bolshevik immigrant Jews who recently arrived in Palestine were going to raze the mosques.

The first Arab target was an immigrant hostel in Jaffa. Twelve men and one woman who had just arrived from Russia were hacked to pieces. The Arabs raced on toward the center of Tel Aviv where they were held off by Jewish veterans of the World War. It was the first successful defense of the all-Jewish city. But farther north, Petah Tikva was sacked by hundreds of angry Arab peasants. Hadera, Kfar Saba and Rehovot were invaded by Arabs who destroyed crops and vineyards and made off with farm equipment and livestock. Henrietta Szold happened to be at lunch in Jaffa on the day of the riot. Halfway through the meal she rushed to the Hadassah dispensary. The 300 dead and wounded lined the floors and crowded neighboring buildings. She immediately phoned to Jerusalem for additional medical personnel and supplies. Then she went about talking to eyewitnesses and residents. Her conclusion was that the riot, far from being spontaneous, had been well-planned.

Faint-hearted Herbert Samuel tried appeasement again, this time by suspending Jewish immigration. It was another major *faux pas*, for the Jewish community of Palestine never trusted him wholeheartedly after that. In London, attempting to mediate the problem, the Colonial Office met separately with a Moslem-Christian Arab delegation and with Zionists. The talks which began in 1922 went on for a year, but the Arabs would not accept anything remotely like the Balfour Declaration and the Jews would not accept anything that diluted it. Winston Churchill tried to mollify both groups by issuing a White Paper in which he defined the meaning of the declaration as giving the Jews a national home in Palestine but not over all of Palestine. He thus laid the groundwork for eventual partition. He candied the pill for the Jews by adding that they were in the Holy Land by right and not on sufferance. Weizmann wisely convinced his colleagues to accept the White Paper, although with some reservations. The Arabs rejected Churchill's formulation totally. They also rejected a plan to set up a legislative assembly in Palestine in which they would hold a majority.

The immediate effect of all the Arab "no's" was to hamstring some of their firmest supporters in England. And the outcome in 1923 was a decision by the British that effective administration of the Mandate was feasible only if the Balfour Declaration and the Zionist cause were given full support. The deadlock between Arabs and Jews had become so hardened during the discussions that the British even considered giving up the Mandate altogether. What won the day for holding on to Palestine was the argument that the area might be needed at some future time to protect the Suez Canal.

A lull of almost five years then dominated Palestine affairs. Strangely, Zionism suffered thereby despite some progress. In Palestine, Hebrew was fast catching on. The Histadrut had taken roots as a powerful trade union and out of the road-building projects in the north had sprung the first major construction company, Solel Boneh. But the kibbutzim were still struggling. Land was hard to come by and Arab landowners demanded steep prices, even when a transaction was completed. Mandate officials often interfered. The brightest star of the mid-1920's was the opening of the Hebrew University on Mt. Scopus in Jerusalem. Arthur Balfour, architect of the controversial declaration, was present. Wherever the white-haired, white-moustached diplomat traveled, cheers rang out – but only from the Jews. Arabs prepared plots, but either through good security or bad planning he escaped harm.

Quietly, Haj Amin el-Husseini, the Grand Mufti, organized his forces against the Zionist settlers. On the surface it almost seemed that co-existence between Arabs and Jews was possible, so much so that Zionist land developer Arthur Ruppin founded an organization called Brith Shalom (Peace Covenant). This group, in which Henrietta Szold and Hebrew University Chancellor Judah Magnes were active, foresaw a bi-national state in Palestine where Jews and Arabs would enjoy equal rights and equal duties. Chaim Weizmann himself was likewise lulled into thinking that peace was really possible with the Arabs. At the Fourteenth Zionist Congress held in Vienna in 1925 he said: "Palestine must be built up without violating the legitimate interests of the Arabs – not a hair of their heads shall be touched... Palestine is not Rhodesia."

The tranquility that enveloped the land can be explained in a number of ways. In these years a general malaise gripped the Zionist movement. The Arabs, seeing that the idea of a national home was not taking hold among Jewish masses, decided to wait patiently for Zionism's collapse. There was good reason to believe that might happen. In the years following the setting up of the Mandate, American and European Zionists fought bitterly over two contradictory philosophies. The prevailing feeling of most American Jews was to give priority to raising money for special projects in Palestine that would establish facts on which future political decisions could be based, while the Europeans saw Palestine as the last stop on the way home for millions of Jews living abroad in "exile." To the Americans, Palestine was more cause for the philanthropist and the investor; to the Europeans, Palestine was the site for the fulfillment of the prayers of generations to rebuild the third Jewish commonwealth by settling the land through a universal ingathering.

In the United States, Zionist ranks came under the strong influence of Louis Brandeis, a justice of the Supreme Court.* Still Weizmann and the Europeans had their supporters in the U.S., most notably Louis Lipsky, a maverick within the establishment. The differences between the American and European approaches came to a head with the establishment by Weizmann of the Keren Hayesod (Foundation Fund) as the principal fund-raising arm of the World Zionist Organization. The Brandeis group insisted that money raised in America by the fund be used mainly for economic and industrial projects in Palestine. The Weizmann-Lipsky group urged that the money be used for settling immigrants on the land. These differences split the Federation of American Zionists. When Weizmann's view finally prevailed, the Brandeis group resigned from the American Zionist leadership. The dispute had a decisive effect on the future of Hadassah, most of whose leaders sided with Brandeis. The organization felt a growing need for complete autonomy and at Hadassah's national convention in Pittsburgh, in 1921, delegates voted to break the amalgamation with the Federation of American Zionists, which it had voluntarily accepted three years earlier.

---

* Brandeis, a fervent Zionist and champion of liberal causes, was appointed to America's highest court by President Woodrow Wilson. The first Jew to sit on the court, he served with distinction for 23 years. President Franklin Roosevelt compared Brandeis with "Isaiah."

Because immigration to Palestine was less than a roaring success, the Arabs had good reason to suspect that Zionism was a flash in the pan. The Jewish multitudes in the Diaspora did not rush to enter the gates of the Holy Land. Palestine's only good year was 1925 when about 35,000 Jews immigrated, most of them prodded by economic depression and raging anti-Semitism in Poland. Toward the end of the decade the numbers fell to a point where by 1929 more Jews were leaving the country than settling in it. Palestine was not particularly attractive to many Jews. A devastating earthquake struck in July 1927. A severe financial crisis hit the Jewish economy; Tel Aviv, the much-touted all-Jewish city, was bankrupt.

Fortunately for Palestine the British appointed a fine high commissioner, Field Marshal Lord Plumer, one of the most brilliant officers of World War I. He replaced Herbert Samuel in August 1925, and quickly built a reputation for fairness and firmness. He created an air of goodwill by reducing the security forces of the country, but Plumer's tenure was all too brief. He left in July 1928 and about six weeks later the peace of Palestine was ended.

When the Jews did not sink from the weight of their woes, Arab patience ran out. Only a small spark was needed to set the two communities on fire and that was provided by a British official. On the eve of Yom Kippur, in 1928, Jews gathered for Kol Nidre prayers at the Western Wall. Hemmed in by a warren of Arab hovels, only several hundred worshipers could crowd into the narrow alleyway in front of the Wall. But a few thousand always tried to crush in during the holy days. To separate men and women, the rabbi at the Wall put up a screen. Two pieces of flint could not have provided a sharper spark. Although the screen had been there on Rosh Hashanah, a British official now declared its presence to be a major violation of the status quo in Jerusalem.

On the morning of Yom Kippur, as the Jews were reciting the sacred Amidah prayer, British police arrived to remove the menacing divider. The aforewarned Arabs were right behind. Fortunately, no one was killed in the melee that followed, but the tempers of Jerusalem immediately began simmering.

A countdown on the inevitable blow-up began far from the scene in Zurich on July 28, 1929, when Zionists gathered for their Sixteenth Congress. There, Chaim Weizmann crowned seven years of labor by formally establishing the broadly based Jewish Agency, composed of both Zionists and non-Zionists. The establishment of the Agency was authorized by the Mandate, which was decided upon at San Remo and later ratified by the League of Nations. The Jewish Agency was the executive arm of the World Zionist Organization and was designed to work hand in hand with the British for the implementation of a Jewish national home. As it turned out, the Agency developed into a shadow government of the incipient state.

At the same Zurich congress, firebrand Vladimir Zev Jabotinsky spoke passionately about the borders of the national home. In a widely reported oration, he pronounced, "The Jordan River does not mark its frontier but flows through its center."

To the Arabs of Palestine the Zurich congress was clear evidence that the Zionists planned a takeover in Palestine. This, coming on top of all the frustrations that had built up since the World War, primed the bomb of mob violence.

One day in August a Jewish boy, who ran into an Arab courtyard after his ball, was knifed to death. Zionists turned his funeral into a protest march. Tishah b'Av, the fast day when Jews mourn the destruction of the Temple, occurred shortly thereafter on Friday, August 22, and it was then that the Arabs struck.

Crowds gathered to worship at the Al Aqsa Mosque on the Temple Mount above the Western Wall. On this Moslem sabbath day the Grand Mufti, leader of the Supreme Moslem Council, chose to address the congregants. British police officers noticed that many of the worshipers were carrying weapons. When they made inquiries, the Grand Mufti assured them they only wanted to protect themselves from possible Jewish revenge for the murder of the boy. The assurance was accepted. Shortly after the noon hour, a single shout was heard. Then several more. Someone began running in the direction of the Jewish Quarter opposite the Wall. The mob followed.

The Arabs' timing was good. British forces had been moved to Egypt and only a few hundred policemen were available. The new high commissioner, Sir John Chancellor, who had been at his post eight months, was out of the country. All the important members of the Jewish Agency were abroad at the Zionist Congress. The violence spread like wildfire beyond Jerusalem. Jewish settlements were laid waste. Wholesale murder and pillage struck Safed, Tel Aviv, Haifa and Hebron. In the course of eight days 820 Jews and Arabs were either killed or wounded.

Hadassah in Jerusalem faced its own crisis. Henrietta Szold was attending the Zionist Congress. Director Ephraim Michael Bluestone had resigned and the responsibilities for supervising the medical services were left in the hands of the one-time itinerant ophthalmologist Haim Yassky. Administration was under Reuven Katznelson. Yassky, too, was in Europe. When the storm hit, it was Katznelson aided by Chief Nurse Bertha Landsman and Mrs. Katznelson who ran the show. Fortunately, they had prepared for trouble. A week before the riots began, 50 extra surgical beds were made ready in Hadassah-Rothschild Hospital. In the Old City, an emergency first-aid station was opened. The spanking new Straus Health Center was set to house and feed refugees; it finally catered to 3,700.

Newspapers ceased to publish, so Hadassah became an information center for the outside world simply because it alone had telephone contact with its units throughout the country. For eight days in August, Hadassah in Jerusalem filled the role of an operations center. Telegrams arriving from abroad asking for information about relatives were delivered to Hadassah. Medical communiqués were issued not by the Mandate's department of health but by Hadassah.

The man who controlled communications was Haim Shalom Halevy, who began at Hadassah in 1927 as the keeper of statistics and went on later to develop the first modern hospital record department in the Middle East. He noted at the time:

> I slept with the phone at my ear so that I could answer a ring in the middle of the night. It was the only telephone with connections to all parts of the country.
>
> On Saturday night, Hadassah had 13 victims in the mortuary. Katznelson said that we must make arrangements to bury them today because tomorrow it might be necessary to bury other patients – it might even be necessary to bury them in the courtyard.
>
> The young boys from the Haganah and others refused to go to the Jewish cemetery on the Mt. of Olives. They said they were ready to face any danger to protect the living but not to bury the dead. After a lot of discussion the Burial Society agreed to take the bodies and we had two laymen along besides myself. I went as Hadassah's representative. We were ten in that party. We had assured ourselves of a *minyan*.

Edward Joseph, a massive man with massive hands, arrived in Palestine from his native New Zealand in 1928. He had fought at Gallipoli in 1915, studied medicine and came to Israel after three years at Rochester's Mayo Clinic. A follower of Jabotinsky, Dr. Joseph was convinced that Israel was the place for him after he read a boast of the Grand Mufti of Jerusalem: "The Jews want to make a National Home in Palestine. We Arabs will turn it into a Jewish national graveyard." He arrived at Hadassah to find himself in charge of the small surgery unit. The chief was on three months' leave. Sooner than he expected, he was saving riot victims, working day and night in the stifling August heat, bare to the waist. He later recalled:

They suffered mostly dagger wounds. We had no antibiotics. Surgical treatment was rather primitive. If there was active bleeding into the lung, we would go in and try to find the source and control it. Otherwise we would let things alone. If there was too much blood accumulated in the pleural space pressing on the lung, we would withdraw it with needles and hope it would stop. If it didn't stop, we would have to go in and try to suture the blood vessel.

We had no plasma but I remember introducing blood transfusions. That was the citrate method. Problem was we had no saline for the people. We used the saline as an anti-shock treatment but even so everybody got reactions. Today it is routine. Nobody gets a reaction. In those days it was so dangerous we were afraid to use it.

During the riots the hospital was fired at by Arabs passing in the streets, but no one was hurt. We had no security. So, our orthopedic surgeon, Dr. Treu, and I decided to barricade the hospital to keep out the invaders. Treu was a little man but very courageous. He would venture out into the night to call on his patients. I warned him against it. He held up a huge Arab key and said, 'This is enough for me. If anyone comes near me, I'll slug him with this.'

In Jerusalem, Hadassah was not the only hospital that took in the wounded. But in other cities Hadassah was the sole source of medical care and supply.

News of the riots in Jerusalem reached Tel Aviv on the afternoon of August 23. There, twelve girls at Hadassah prepared bandages. Weekend leave was canceled for everyone. On August 25, three operating tables were made ready with a surgical team for each. First-aid corpsmen stood alert at the hospital doors with stretchers. Jewish policemen were given 300 bandages cut from diapers. By noon, the first 16 wounded, attacked near a mosque, were brought in. Their names were posted outside the hospital. The hospital could not get to its laundry so improvised one in the yard. The municipality was in charge of the 700 refugees who sought shelter in the Ahad Ha'am School, but in fact Hadassah nurses looked after them.

In Haifa, Hadassah received all wounded from Galilee. Expecting riots to break out, Hadassah prepared the Technion (Israel Institute for Technology) to take in refugees. August 26 was the worst day. Arabs used firearms as well as knives, stones and clubs. Thirty-eight wounded flooded the hospital. Medical personnel accompanied by British escorts went into the thick of the fighting to drag out the victims, among them Arabs whom the British authorities asked Hadassah to treat. By nightfall of August 26, 3,000 Jews were evacuated from their homes by the British.

The Galilee town of Safed was alerted by Jerusalem on the 23rd. Next morning, to the roll of drums, Arabs gathered at the mosque. At noon they raced from the mosque screaming hysterically and throwing stones at Jews. They did not move into the Jewish Quarter that day and only one person was hurt: an Arab had been hit on the head by a stone thrown by another Arab. He was treated at Hadassah. The situation remained tense until August 29 when at the hour for the afternoon prayer, they attacked the Sephardi Quarter, started fires that kept the city illuminated all night, killed 20 and destroyed over 100 Jewish dwellings. The first wounded was an Arab policeman. The first dead was a Hadassah worker, Yitzhak Maman. (A second victim was Hadassah physician Haim Israeli who died defending his home in Be'er Tuvia.) Three hundred refugees filled the Safed hospital. On September 2, Dr. Yassky, home from Europe, organized relief work and ordered expansion of medical facilities in the town.

> When we arrived [reported Dr. Yassky] many of the ruins were still smoking and it was impossible to attempt to remove corpses. The stench was unbearable. Whole streets were razed as though they had been bombarded and the city presents a picture of desolation and suffering that cannot be

described. Things happened there during the riots that do not
bear the telling. The people are in a state of extreme hysteria.
The city and the roads leading to it present a picture of war
times – armored cars, automobiles with armed escorts
bringing medical supplies from Haifa and returning with
refugees.

The most macabre orgy of killing took place in Hebron where Jews had
lived for centuries side by side with their Moslem neighbors. Life with the
Arabs was amicable, although the Jews there were always second-class
citizens: no Jew was permitted into the tombs of the Patriarchs because a
grand mosque had been built over them. For the seven hundred Jews of
Hebron it was sufficient to be able to live and to study the Law close by.
Haganah men were sent to the yeshiva, but they were summarily dismissed
by the rabbis who said that their presence in the town was a provocation.

On August 24, the Sabbath, armed Arabs reached Hebron. Arab
policemen watched them race through the town, enter an inn where Jews
had taken refuge and hack 23 to death. The mob then marched to the
yeshiva where about 40 Jews were massacred. Their bodies were butchered
as though they were cattle. Not long after the riot in Hebron, the former
president of Hadassah, Irma Lindheim (1926-1928), who had moved with
her family to Palestine, visited the scene. She recollected:

> Manya Shochat and I went to Hebron with the chief of police,
> Fred Partridge. We visited the yeshiva. The moment Manya
> entered she said it was a pogrom, because in a pogrom they
> always ripped open the mattresses to look for money and
> broke the windows and mirrors. We walked on feathers and
> glass, a most God-awful combination. Blood had soaked
> everything. From there we went to the Hadassah clinic. The
> place was a shambles. Every wall was down. Every floor was
> up. Every test tube was smashed. Hadassah had a first-class
> clinic and it was smashed completely. Why? Because the

Arabs wanted nothing of the world that Jews represented. Hadassah had done a wonderful job in Hebron, did more than any other group to build real Arab-Jewish friendship. Miss Szold did it consciously.

In 1929, Hadassah was in its eighteenth year. One Hadassah eyewitness to the riots, an American tourist from Pittsburgh, returned home a month later and reported the words of an unidentified Haifa resident. "If Hadassah had done nothing else in the land during its years here, this one week of its activities would be worth all the money it has spent."

All Hadassah services were suddenly integrated into a smooth-functioning life-saving machine. Refugees were shepherded to the Straus Health Center, newly opened to house Hadassah's preventive health-care work. The homeless were fed by the school lunch service. Meals were cooked and diets prepared by Hadassah's nutritionists. Tots were cared for in the infant welfare stations. Even the school playground project became vital as it set up special recreation activities for children who were separated from parents.

Chaim Weizmann later wrote, "If the riots were intended, whatever their effect on our nerves, to overthrow the structure of the National Home, they came too late. We had built too solidly and too well."

The British government fumed and fumbled in the years that followed the disturbances. High Commissioner Chancellor issued a caustic statement blaming the Arabs for "savage murders." But for balance – and to soften Arab protest – he announced that a commission would investigate "Arab and Jewish responsibility." The commission, headed by jurist Sir Walter Shaw, concluded that the attack on the Jews had not been premeditated. This august commission was immediately followed by another, chaired by Sir John Hope Simpson. His task was to investigate land sales to Jews. He concluded that Palestine could economically hold only 100,000 more immigrants – Jews and Arabs.

On October 21, 1930, the colonial secretary, socialist leader Sydney Webb (Lord Passfield) issued a White Paper, based on the reports of the commissions. The White Paper in effect restricted Jewish immigration into Palestine and land sales to Jews.

One outcome of the riots was to rally Jewry behind the Zionists and the Zionists made the most of it. In the United States, Hadassah joined the men's Zionist organizations in a political demonstration. Hadassah's President was then Zip Szold, Savannah-born wife of attorney Robert Szold, cousin of Henrietta.

> We went to Washington [says Zip Szold] with Rabbi Israel Goldstein as our spokesman. We wanted our Government to stop the riots in Palestine. I don't believe we were very effective but we did speak to many Congressmen, Senators and one or two Cabinet members. This was probably the first time that Hadassah had taken part in a political act.

Arab extremists emerged from the crisis stronger than ever. The Grand Mufti lost his battle to throttle the Zionist effort in Palestine, but he became a national hero nevertheless because he had won strong British support for the cause of Arab nationalism.

As Palestine entered the 1930's, the stage was set for a drama in which three motifs would play simultaneously: Arab against Jew, Jew against Arab and both against the British. These were cruel years. America was agonizing in economic depression. Germany was watering the weeds of Hitlerism. Russia, suffering under Communist dictatorship, was actualizing George Orwell's "Animal Farm."

In Palestine, oddly, economic recovery was quicker than in almost any other place in the world. Investment in Zionist projects ran relatively high. Construction picked up and despite the restrictions, Jewish immigration was heavy. There would be a brief eruption of violence in 1933 as the Arabs, having failed to frustrate the Zionists, would suddenly turn against the

British. In 1936, the Grand Mufti would try for three years to rid the country of the infidel Jew and would buddy up to Hitler toward that end.

In the new storm that was gathering, Hadassah would brave the winds along with the rest of the *yishuv* and emerge from the decade strengthened many times over, for it was in these years that membership would mushroom, new and vigorous leadership would rise and genuine independence would send Hadassah into a Zionist orbit of its own. In short, Hadassah was on its way to becoming the most forceful single Zionist organization in the world. All this could be traced in part to Hadassah's efforts to save children from the Nazi inferno.

THE CONTRACT

One cold February afternoon in 1932, Recha Freier was musing in the study of her home near Berlin's Alexanderplatz. She was the wife of a prominent Orthodox rabbi, the mother of three sons and an author of fairy and folk tales for children. Writing fantasies helped Recha escape the wretched world that was rising around her. Here in Germany, the Weimar Republic of Chancellor Heinrich Bruening was collapsing under the twin sledgehammer blows of an economic blizzard and Hitler's hypnotizing cry for a new order. Across the frontiers, dictator Benito Mussolini held Italy in the vise of Fascism and was about to undertake a restless escapade into Africa. Fickle France's Third Republic was changing governments as fast as fashions. England languished under an austerity economy led by ailing Prime Minister Ramsay MacDonald. Across the seas, mighty America agonized under a depression that put millions of men out of work and militaristic Japan, having subdued Manchuria, began its imperial march into China. What then was there for a poetic soul like Recha to do but to write and dream and "call up memories of my early childhood in Norden on the North sea at the turn of the century... of Sabbath afternoon strolls into town with the family and of one special Sabbath when we came upon a white paper with a black border posted on a gate... "We stop to read it. I am only four and cannot understand but I hear what the others are saying. They say the sign reads **ENTRANCE FORBIDDEN TO DOGS AND JEWS**. Soon we move to another town and there I am the only Jewish girl in the class and the pupils ridicule me when I say that my religion does not permit me to ride on the Sabbath... how homesick I am for a town I can really call home. In my childhood I know of the Land of Israel but I believe that it is unreachable because it is in heaven."

A knock on the door roused Recha. Her caller was a pale, thin sixteen-year-old boy who introduced himself as Nathan Höxter, son of the late Rabbi Höxter.

"Why have you come to me?" Recha asked.

"I thought that you might be able to help us."

"Us?"

"Yes, my five friends and me. We are members of the Brit Ha-Olim, a group of Zionists. Our problem is that we have been thrown out of our jobs. They said they no longer wanted Jews. Maybe we can find work in the mines in the Rhineland. We don't know where to turn."

"Bring your friends to me and let us discuss it. We will work something out," replied Recha.

Next day she ran to the office of the Jewish Labor Exchange of the Zionist movement. Yes, the secretary knew the problem, but insisted with a shrug that it was only temporary. With the Norden experience strongly in her mind she could not accept his assurance. She sat in her study at night and pondered:

> How I always dreamed of an exodus of Jewish youth to Palestine! But this was only a dream that was never practical. Maybe, just maybe, now is the time. How helpless that boy made me feel. And how joyous, too. This certainly must be the hour. I must dream no longer. I must make reality my partner. Palestine is their home. They must go to it. It is my home too.

Recha called on Enzo Sereni, an Italian-born Zionist living in Palestine, who was in Germany as the representative of a kibbutz movement. Later, during World War II, Sereni was killed by the Nazis after he parachuted into Italy to organize underground rescue operations. She explained to him that she would like to organize large groups of German youth to live in the kibbutzim. Sereni fairly jumped out of his chair as she spoke.

"Do it. Do it at once and you will revolutionize the entire German Zionist movement," Sereni explained.

When Nathan Höxter returned with his five friends Recha said, "I will not help you go to the mines. There is no future for Jewish youth in Germany. Eretz Israel is your home. You must go there. You can work in a kibbutz. And if you so decide, I shall help you."

The boys immediately agreed. At Sereni's suggestion, Recha wrote the Histadrut in Tel Aviv for assistance to arrange places in kibbutzim. The Histadrut was encouraging but Berlin's established Zionist leadership was not supportive. When Recha called on Zionist leaders, they dismissed the idea. Several told her to send the boys to German farms where, as one advised, "They'll really learn to work and to spend money properly."

In the spring of 1932, Recha was ready to give up the idea when the Histadrut's education and cultural chairman in Tel Aviv, Yaacov Sandbank, wrote that three agricultural settlements, Geva, Ein Harod and Nahalal, were ready to accept the boys. Recha went back to the German Zionist Organization, to WIZO (Women's International Zionist Organization) and to EZRA, a Jewish agricultural society. All rebuffed her.

"In the kibbutzim they will become Communists."

"You cannot separate adolescents from their parents."

"The kibbutzim are not kosher."

Only young Zionists showed enthusiasm. "In them I kindled a spark that burst into a flame," Recha later recalled. After she spoke to teenagers in Jewish schools, they rushed to her to register for Palestine. The excitement of the youth moved Georg Landauer, a member of the Zionist Executive in Berlin, to agree reluctantly to Recha's plan on condition that the Va'ad Leumi (National Council of Jews in Palestine) arrange for the care of the young immigrants. The head of the Social Welfare Department of Va'ad Leumi was then Henrietta Szold. Recha wrote to Henrietta. Henrietta replied that no funds were available in Palestine for the poor children already there; a large influx of parent-less children from Germany might strain the limited resources of the *yishuv*. The memory of Norden and the exuberance of the youth around her pushed Recha on.

In June 1932, Recha, still unable to mobilize sufficient aid, had a visitor from Palestine. He was Siegfried Lehmann, founder of the Ben Shemen youth village. He liked Recha's idea and was ready to arrange twelve entry permits for her boys if they would agree to study farming with him. Recha's ideal was the kibbutz, but she agreed. Forty teenagers met with her and twelve were chosen. She now worked feverishly to raise money for their care at Ben Shemen. Recha fought stiff opposition from parents and peers. But she had a few friends who helped. One raised 4,000 marks by pawning her jewelry.

On October 12, 1932, the first group of boys left Berlin by train en route to Ben Shemen. When Nathan Höxter and his friends landed in Jaffa on December 2, they became the vanguard of the mass movement of children who traveled to Palestine under the banner of an organization, unique in history, that was soon to be known in Germany by its bilingual name *Jugendaliyah*, or Youth Aliyah.

Great movements, like great rivers, rise from many tributaries. In the latter half of the nineteenth century, liberal Jewish community leaders in pogrom-mad Russia tried to form save-our-children organizations. They too met heavy opposition. Opponents argued that children must remain with their parents. In 1870, Carl Netter, a learned and wealthy Strasbourg merchant who championed rights for Jews in France, opened a farm school called Mikve Israel outside Jaffa. Netter moved to Mikve Israel with a group of Polish orphans. Shortly thereafter, Israel Belkind, a leader of the Bilu, the earliest Zionist agricultural colonists, tried to set up several schools for orphans of Russian pogroms. He attempted one at Shfeyah, but it failed because he could not raise sufficient money. In Baltimore, in 1917, Hadassah's own Alice Seligsberg stated publicly that the only solution for Europe's Jewish orphans was to open schools for them in Palestine. Later, as adviser to Junior Hadassah, she was largely responsible for the success of Meier Shfeyah Youth Village. In 1927 Siegfried Lehmann established a "Youth Republic" (a kind of Boys' Town) at Ben Shemen, amidst the gnarled olive groves near Lydda, and took in a group of orphans of the Russian revolution from Kovno, Lithuania. Lehmann saw the possibility of expanding Ben Shemen in 1932 with young German immigrants. And so he called on the visionary Recha Freier in Berlin.

Among the Jewish youth of Berlin, Recha became known as "the dreaming woman." She did not mind and she would say, "I happen to come from the world of fairy tales. There as you know, everything is anonymous. So I would like to remain anonymous, too. It's the youth, not me, that want help. I only want to turn dreams and fairy tales into reality."

Recha spoke incessantly, at times obsessively, about sending 10,000 German youth to Palestine. That only enhanced her image as a dreamer, for even her closest colleagues thought in terms of 50 or 60. Time and genocide would vindicate her.

Early in January 1933, the Histadrut's Sandbank wrote Recha that she must come to Tel Aviv if she wanted to further her cause. In that same month Henrietta Szold decided to retire. It wasn't for the first time. In 1931 she returned to Palestine from the United States only at the urgent insistence of *yishuv* leaders to organize the haphazard social services of the incipient Jewish nation. Now, she wrote to her sister Bertha that she wanted, at last, to finish out her years with her family in Baltimore.

Back in Berlin, Recha prepared to go to Palestine. On the last day of January she gathered together in the office of a notary, Hugo Fuerth, seven young Zionist leaders, some of whom were not yet 21. They called themselves the Aid Committee for Jewish Youth, carefully avoiding any hint that their real purpose was emigration to Palestine. But among themselves they referred to the project as *Jugendaliyah*, Youth Aliyah. At nightfall they left Fuerth's office and as they turned into Berlin's broad Unter den Linden boulevard, they saw masses of jack-booted Brownshirts marching in a mammoth torchlight parade in celebration of the coming to power, earlier that day, of Adolf Hitler.

Persecution of the Jews became a major function of the new German government and even in that day of primitive international communication it was not long before the Jews of Palestine felt the foul winds blowing in from Europe. By April 1933, Berlin decreed a boycott on all Jewish enterprises but then at the last minute canceled it when Mussolini convinced Hitler the time was not ripe. Chaim Arlosoroff, head of the Political Department of the Jewish Agency in Jerusalem, went to Berlin to try to convince the German Zionist organizations to prepare for the emigration of Jews to Palestine. They knew he was right. The Zionist opponents of Youth Aliyah made a quick turnabout and formed one joint committee to prepare youth and to raise money.

Henrietta Szold's personal plans were now complete. She invited sister Bertha to Palestine to show her all the sights, after which they would return home together; for Henrietta, home was still America. But the Jewish leadership in Palestine pressured Henrietta to give up the notion of retirement. They were now forming a committee to do something about German-Jewish refugees and they insisted that she head it. Bertha went home alone.

In Tel Aviv at the end of May, Recha attended a Histadrut rally at the Jascha Heifetz Hall where a large audience heard labor and kibbutz leaders call for the immigration of German youth. One even mentioned the number 10,000. The meeting passed a resolution opening the settlements to the youth. After the rally, Recha rode to Jerusalem where she had her first meeting with Henrietta Szold. No two more dissimilar personalities ever faced each other. Recha failed to convince Henrietta that it was urgent to flood the gates of Palestine immediately with German youth; Henrietta could not convince Recha that the *yishuv* was not prepared for mass immigration. What, asked Henrietta, would happen to German youth left unattended on the wharves of Jaffa and Haifa unless homes were waiting for them? In the back of Recha's mind was the frightening torchlight parade on the evil night of January 31 and all that it portended. Henrietta was concerned that the kibbutzim were simply not prepared to cope with German teenagers.

Recha went home that summer only slightly encouraged by Palestine's noted land developer and pioneer of the kibbutz movement, Arthur Ruppin. He promised to try to convince Henrietta of the worth of Recha's idea. In Berlin, Recha pestered Zionist groups to organize training camps for the youth. Already entire German-Jewish families were beginning to leave. In 1932, total Jewish immigration into Palestine was 9,553. In 1933, the year Hitler came to power, immigration of Jews into Palestine was 30,327, two-thirds of whom were Germans. But Recha was interested in the youth and especially in those whose naive parents had faith that Hitler was a passing fantasy.

In Jerusalem, the committee that Henrietta headed had no guidelines. Housing was short. So many refugees had already arrived that they bedded down underneath the sky on Tel Aviv's beaches. That made Henrietta all the more dubious about the idea of encouraging large numbers of German youth to immigrate. Then, the kibbutzim agreed to accept 1,000 children. Recha was jubilant. Henrietta insisted on inspecting kibbutz housing facilities. Finding that they were not up to her high standard, she suggested a compromise whereby some youth would go to the settlements. But when she went to the British authorities for certificates, they refused, saying that none of the facilities were ready. Immigration in those days was limited to "capitalists" (those with the equivalent of $5,000) and to those youth for whom two years' sustenance was available. Henrietta personally urged the settlements to begin building for the youth she knew would come.

The Eighteenth World Zionist Congress met in free but threatened Prague on August 21, 1933. While Hitler's shadow grew darker over Germany, the political debate at the Congress was marred by the deep rift between the Labor and Revisionist parties. But the Congress did take up the German question and established what became known popularly as the "German Bureau" under the chairmanship of Chaim Weizmann in London. Henrietta did not attend the Congress, but Arthur Ruppin, who chaired the Jerusalem section of the German Bureau, implored her to take over as head of a new *ad hoc* office of the Jewish Agency devoted to Youth Aliyah affairs. That October, at a worldwide meeting in London of Jewish organizations called to declare a boycott on all German goods, Henrietta heard more of the disaster that was overtaking the Jews of Germany, so off she sped to Berlin. In the German capital she deliberated day and night with Zionist leaders. She expressed dismay at the lack of understanding they had for life in Palestine and at the absence of an organized effort to raise funds and prepare youth for their new life.

If ever she had any doubts that the youth must leave, they were now dispelled. Before departing, she succeeded in arranging for the early "conditioning" and transfer of 63 boys and girls, aged 15 to 17, under the leadership of Hanoch Reinhold. Henrietta did not meet Recha Freier in Berlin and Recha resented it. But Henrietta did appreciate Recha's role. At the Nineteenth World Zionist Congress held in Lucerne in 1935, Henrietta Szold said: "I would like to say a word of thanks to the organizer of this movement [Youth Aliyah], Mrs. Recha Freier. It was she who conceived the ingenious idea and carried it through despite all difficulties and obstacles. We are grateful that she held with such devotion to her idea, which in the beginning found little support."

Recha reached Palestine only in 1941 after a harrowing journey through Eastern Europe. By the time Henrietta returned to Palestine the British government offered Youth Aliyah 350 permits for German-Jewish children. Immediately, she left for Kibbutz Ein Harod where she personally whipped the kibbutzniks into frenzied building of housing for the expected newcomers.

In mid-February 1934, the winter's worst gale hit the shores of Palestine. On the high seas opposite Jaffa was the *S.S. Martha Washington*. On February 18, the ship tried to drop anchor off Jaffa, but the weather was so bad she headed north to the recently opened port of Haifa. There on Monday, February 19, the first organized group of Youth Aliyah children walked down the gangplank – precisely two years after Recha Freier met Nathan Höxter in her Berlin apartment. Henrietta smiled as she watched the well-turned-out youngsters from Germany standing on the quay with their mandolins and their skis and rucksacks on their backs. Some had brought along bicycles and even flagpoles. No one seemed to mind the pelting rain. Henrietta greeted each child by name. It was a custom she was to follow for the rest of her days. She escorted them to Ein Harod, spent the first day with them, even joined them in a *hora* in the kibbutz dining hall.

From that day on Henrietta's life was taken up with the affairs of Youth Aliyah. All the tremendous vitality that she could mobilize went into raising funds, supervising training, struggling for permits. By the end of 1934 a dozen groups totalling about 500 arrived and Henrietta wrote: "This great constructive movement has only begun. Five hundred young people is not more than five percent of the number that should be drawn out of Germany into the productive, promising life of Palestine."

Her toughest problem was money. It always was. But money now meant young lives. On her way back from Berlin in November 1933, she wrote, "If only there were funds... the Joint Distribution Committee has practically nothing to give." Raising cash in Palestine was difficult. Henrietta went to one wealthy landowner in Jerusalem and came away, after much pleading, with a paltry 50 pounds. In one letter home she wrote, "The public does not like the German Jews." Cash was being collected in Germany by a joint committee, the Arbeitsgemeinschaft. The first appreciable sum that flowed into the organization's coffers grew out of a pageant, "The Romance of a People," that was produced at the Century of Progress Fair in Chicago by Meyer Weisgal. The pageant took place on "Jewish Day," July 3, 1933, before 130,000 people jammed into Soldiers Field. At Weisgal's insistence, Chaim Weizmann traveled 8,000 miles to make an appearance. Weizmann's speech was good for the unheard-of sum of $100,000. He received $25,000 on the spot for refugee relief. The remaining $75,000 was presented a few months later by Weisgal in London to the director of the German Bureau, Martin Rosenbluth, with the words, "Here is money you can use for Youth Aliyah. Now you're in business."

In its infancy Youth Aliyah was thwarted by the harsh immigration restrictions of the Palestine government, by the indecisiveness of world Jewry and by a dearth of funds. The free world had not only been put off balance by Hitler but had been impoverished by a financial crisis. In the United States, wellsprings of philanthropy were dry. All the while, young German Jews waited. Separated from the European scene by 3,000 miles of ocean, the people of the United States were not adequately aware of the significance of Hitler's rise to power. Even in England, ever so much closer to the whirlwind, Winston Churchill was jeered for demanding national preparedness. How much more so those few voices who shouted into the wind in far-off America. But voices there were, few but powerful, like that of Stephen Wise, who warned that Hitler was not a temporary aberration.

In New York City during 1934 there was a woman who in some respects was the counterpart of Recha Freier. Tamar de Sola Pool, Hadassah's national president from 1939 to 1943, was also a visionary and a treasure-trove of madcap ideas. But she had charm and she had megatons of energy. And no matter what the opposition, Tamar had an abundance of resilience that always kept her afloat. She was then president of the New York City chapter of Hadassah. With her husband, the courtly Rabbi David de Sola Pool, she had been abroad many times. She knew Palestine well. Now she was back from her most recent trip with a "bug" in her head that Hadassah must enter, as she put it, "immigration work." Tamar sensed that an immigration project was essential to maintain a high level of involvement in Hadassah at the grass roots. Many of the National Board agreed, but the responsibility was a tremendous one and the leadership, while moving in that direction, decided to move cautiously. Many years later, Tamar would remark with justification, "The National Board had no confidence in me.

They thought I was scatter-brained, that I was not a good organizer. But I must admit I do have a talent for creative thinking."

Hadassah was then in the midst of a devolutionary program, which in simple terms meant that it was transferring some of its responsibilities in Palestine. In line with the principle laid down by Henrietta Szold, Hadassah turned over its projects to municipal or other local public authorities as soon as they were ready to maintain them. The transfer of hospitals, preventive medical stations, school hygiene programs and tuberculosis care outside Jerusalem was hastened in the early 1930's because of the financial squeeze caused by the depression and because of Hadassah's eagerness to move ahead on Mt. Scopus with the construction of the most modern medical center in the Middle East. In October 1934, Henrietta Szold laid the cornerstone of that center. Hadassah was then 50,000-strong, but board member Judith Epstein, a great champion of the center, would later recall: "We suddenly found that our world could not be bound by Palestine and the medical work we were doing. Nobody saw clearly in 1934 in what direction an expanded program would go."

To find new direction and purpose, Hadassah President Rose Jacobs left for Palestine in the summer of 1935 on a mission for the National Board. An intimate friend of Henrietta Szold, Rose Jacobs was a powerhouse of energy armed with an iron will. Some found her school-marmish and criticized her for expecting to be followed blindly into the unknown. But few faulted Rose Jacobs on her decisiveness. During Henrietta's presidency, Rose often served for long periods as acting president. She wore Henrietta's mantle and had her confidence.

In Palestine, Rose Jacobs pondered two non-medical projects for Hadassah, Youth Aliyah and vocational education. She drove herself to exhaustion in the two months she spent there. Henrietta was her mentor, but she did not suggest that Hadassah assume the responsibility of funding Youth Aliyah. What Rose saw confirmed Tamar de Sola Pool's earlier observations.

Youth Aliyah was first on my list... When one follows the youth groups from the port of entry in Palestine into the settlements [Rose wrote from Palestine], one is prone to forget that what one sees is connected with a desperate situation in Germany and that their being in Palestine is the challenge of a tragic dilemma. Youth Aliyah looks like the beginning of a movement, initiated by German youth, to save itself from destruction. It may be faced with the despair of homelessness.

She wrote vividly of meeting the ships bringing Youth Aliyah children, of following them together with Henrietta to the kibbutzim. Rose reported that in Merhavia one frightened youth fresh from Berlin suggested that the windows be closed so that their conversations would not be overheard. In a kibbutz near Haifa, the children arrived with books by Schiller, Goethe and Heine. The kibbutz children jeered when they saw the German writings. Reported Rose:

I shall never forget Miss Szold. She turned to the German children and said, "It is wonderful what you have brought; you have brought prize possessions from Germany which Germany itself does not value. Don't forget the cultural things, the fine part of Germany that you have learned. Try to forget the other things." The children of the kibbutz bowed their heads, ashamed. Thus did Henrietta Szold lay the basis for mutual respect in the relationship of German and Palestinian youth.

Rose also saw the need for vocational training and wrote a report on it, although she leaned toward Youth Aliyah. But she planned to take both proposals back to New York and let the National Board decide. In August, Henrietta and Rose traveled to Lucerne, Switzerland, where the Nineteenth Zionist Congress convened. Chaim Weizmann returned to the presidency after four years out of office and Henrietta reported on two years of Youth Aliyah. To a hushed hall she said:

> Before I left Palestine last week I took a trip through all the kvutzot where our young boys and girls are placed, in order to see at close hand the full extent of my responsibility. I was gripped by the thought of the children whom we have lost during the course of generations. I thought of the children who were sent to the Island of St. Thomas by the Inquisition, of the cantonists in Russia, of Edgar Mortara in Italy, and I thought also of the crimes we are committing against our own children – that we have not gathered the funds which Palestine needs to solve the most important problem – the problem of the Jewish child.

Seventy-five-year-old Henrietta was the star attraction of the congress. Rose Jacobs was as proud as though she were Henrietta's own daughter. There was no longer any doubt that the National Board would accept Youth Aliyah as its own ward in America. Attending the Congress, too, was Georg Landauer, director of the German Settlement Bureau in Jerusalem. With Henrietta's acquiescence, Rose and Georg drew up a confidential letter on August 27, 1935, which spelled out the terms under which Hadassah would be the sole agency for Youth Aliyah in the United States. The five-paragraph statement, addressed to Rose as president of Hadassah and signed by Georg, specified that Hadassah would be the sole representative of Youth Aliyah in the United States for an experimental two years during which Hadassah undertook to cover the expenses of 100 German and Polish youths at the rate of $500 each. It stipulated that if the Hadassah convention due to meet in November declined or reduced the number from 100, the Arbeitsgemeinschaft in Berlin would carry out its own campaign in the United States. But if the convention did accept, then "no organization for Youth Aliyah shall be established in America."

In the annals of American Zionist history, it would be difficult to find a document that raised more dust than that one. Both Georg and Rose were vaguely aware that they had overstepped the limits of their authority. The Zionist Congress had just passed a resolution prohibiting separate fund-raising appeals apart from those which were already established. Yet Georg Landauer committed the Zionist Organization to doing just that and he was to suffer great embarrassment for his sin. With Henrietta's support, Rose was confident that Hadassah would prevail, but she too had certainly gone far beyond her terms of reference.

By the end of September, Rose was back in New York. She immediately convened a meeting of the National Board. "The saving of European Jewry is the crying need of the hour," she said with deep emotion. "Hadassah is that channel through which the appeal for the rescue of our youth can be made effective. We can help convert the Youth Aliyah project into a great movement." With the still-secret contract in hand, Rose obtained the Board's unanimous consent to accept Youth Aliyah as Hadassah's newest major project. No sooner was the meeting over than Rose rushed off to Atlanta to be at the bedside of her ailing father. Acting for her, Judith Epstein wrote Landauer in Jerusalem of the Board's unanimous acceptance and of its intention to recommend it to the convention opening in Cleveland on November 28. No one was more jubilant than irrepressible Tamar de Sola Pool. She wrote a letter to Henrietta in Jerusalem saying how happy she was that Hadassah had accepted Youth Aliyah and said that she was sure Hadassah would raise at least $100,000, not $60,000. (As a matter of record, Hadassah raised $250,766.76 in the first two years.)

On October 29, one month before the convention was to meet to approve the Youth Aliyah project, the Jewish Agency Executive in Jerusalem annulled the Landauer-Jacobs contract.

Louis Lipsky, the chairman of the board of the American Palestine Campaign, had not heard of the agreement until October 11 – a full six weeks after it had been signed. He immediately wrote indignantly to Rose Jacobs that a separate campaign for Youth Aliyah run by Hadassah would "inevitably lead to the disintegration of the Zionist Movement of the United States." The gladiator of American Zionism was wounded. There were good reasons for his concern. Organized Jewish philanthropy for domestic and overseas causes was in turmoil. Part of the problem was that there were simply too many mouths to feed and there was too little to go around. After the depression of 1929 hit America, the American Palestine Campaign joined the Joint Distribution Committee (for all non-Palestine causes) to form the Allied Jewish Appeal. But that mixed marriage foundered on the rocks after the first year. Zionist and non-Zionists found it impossible at that time to work together.

In 1934, they tried again – this time under the family name, United Jewish Appeal. That marriage lasted two years, but at the end of the 1935 campaign the JDC asked for a divorce. Lipsky, as head of the American Palestine Campaign, was terribly concerned. He found sympathy and relief at the Zionist Congress in Lucerne where delegates urged consolidation and unity in Zionist ranks, especially in fund-raising. Toward that end, the American Palestine Committee joined with the land reclamation and land purchasing agency of the Zionist movement, the Jewish National Fund, in what was then called the United Palestine Appeal. In the latter part of 1935, Hadassah was about to fall out of line. Lipsky would not suffer this breach of Zionist discipline and there then began what became known as the "battle of the cables."

Lipsky began the offensive from his headquarters in New York on October 22 when he cabled "strong protests" to the Jewish Agency Executive in Jerusalem. He insisted that "a coordinated front for Palestine fund-raising was imperative." Otherwise, "the entire Zionist program is menaced."

On October 27, in a stormy meeting with Hadassah, Lipsky insisted that Hadassah forgo its exclusive rights. Later, Lipsky reported on the Hadassah leaders' reaction in what must have been the understatement of any year. "They remained unimpressed." He added, in a fit of self-righteousness, "They thought as always only of their own Hadassah fund-raising without seeming to care for one moment what the effect would be on the rest of the fund-raising in America. They would hear of no arrangement other than the one which they *think* [Lipsky's underlining] they have concluded with Landauer." Immediately after the meeting broke up, Lipsky protested against the Jewish Agency Executive's entering into the contract "without our consultation, communication or advice." There, he obviously had a point and it was a point that stuck.

Two days later, on October 29, the Zionist Executive met in Jerusalem. Treasurer Eliezer Kaplan was in the chair. Among the other eight present were Moshe Shertok, Jewish National Fund President Menachem Ussishkin, David Werner Senator, Rabbi Yehuda Leib Fishman and Georg Landauer. On the agenda was an urgent item: "Special Campaigns."

Kaplan had before him Lipsky's cable of protest. Obviously angry, Kaplan eyed Landauer and said it was obvious that American Jews would not contribute twice in the same year to a Zionist appeal. Therefore, the Congress had wisely forbidden separate fund campaigns. Landauer asked for the floor. He took a practical line: Youth Aliyah needed about $200,000 for those children already registered to emigrate from Germany and Poland. "The Keren Hayesod [fund-raising arm of the World Zionist Organization] simply cannot provide that kind of money for Youth Aliyah," Landauer said. "The Joint Distribution Committee is propagandizing for the children to be sent to America. They will not provide funds for them to come to Palestine. The question is where the money is to come from. Without America we simply cannot do it. Hadassah has informed us that it has the capability to carry out a separate campaign and has guaranteed to care for 100 children. I would favor a United Zionist Campaign if it would guarantee to raise the money Hadassah is willing to raise. But if it won't, then I suggest that Hadassah do it."

Landauer was outnumbered. Ussishkin, a double-fisted stalwart of classic Zionism, expressed astonishment that Landauer should have dared to violate discipline by signing the agreement with Hadassah. To have been so harshly attacked by a veteran of the movement must have been the ultimate hurt for well-meaning Landauer. The stern-eyed Rabbi Fishman, supporting Ussishkin and Kaplan, said that unity of the Jewish people and its campaigns overrode all other considerations.

The balanced, precise Shertok came mercifully to Landauer's support. "The money must be found," he said. "Separate appeals have been made for this purpose elsewhere. In any case, Hadassah conducts campaigns for other projects and I see no sin committed if this year it includes Youth Aliyah in its general appeal." Senator supported Shertok. But they were in the minority. Zionist discipline was all-important. In deference to Shertok, Kaplan was a trifle more flexible at the end of the debate saying that Hadassah could go ahead and raise funds for Youth Aliyah but only within the framework of the overall united appeal in America. In effect, however, he abrogated the contract. His strictly conservative stand won a majority.

In an attempt to forestall a fraternal war in the American Zionist camp, Kaplan instructed his colleague stationed in London, affable Berl Locker, to hurry to the United States. The cable he received would have floored a giant and Berl stood just over five feet: "Bring back an agreement between Hadassah and the American Palestine Campaign that will satisfy the just demands of Hadassah, that will assure the participation of the American Palestine Campaign and will safeguard the interests of Keren Hayesod."

On October 30, Kaplan ordered Lipsky to go ahead with his plans for a united Palestine drive and to "include youth immigration in the slogan." Kaplan also cabled Hadassah an official repudiation of the Landauer-Jacobs contract. The Hadassah board went into emergency session. On Friday, November 1, it drafted a cable to the Jewish Agency that matched Kaplan's slap with one of its own: "Repudiation of the contract would hurt the Youth Aliyah project and Hadassah's effectiveness in Palestine."

Hadassah's cable went on to explain cogently that its way of running a campaign – on a year-round, day-to-day basis – was much more effective than the one-shot drives run for a short period by the united campaign. And then the cable ended: "Your failure to honor the contract will stunt Youth

Aliyah's future development in America and force Hadassah to adopt a substitute specific project."

With that cable Hadassah, perhaps unknowingly, entered the major league of Zionist politics. It had challenged the Jewish Agency and therefore the World Zionist Organization, as well as the organized, male-dominated Zionist Organization of America. Hadassah, now 21 years old, had come of age with flair.

Two days later, Kaplan in Jerusalem cabled Lipsky in New York: "Hadassah has cabled a demand for revision on the basis of the agreement with Rothenberg in Lucerne."

This cable referred to an oral agreement made at the Zionist Congress between Rose Jacobs and Morris Rothenberg, President of the ZOA, to permit Hadassah to run the Youth Aliyah campaign.

That same day a livid Lipsky replied: "Neither Rothenberg nor myself in Lucerne knew of Hadassah's intention of taking exclusive possession of children's aliyah in America. Would not have agreed then. Cannot agree now."

The Hadassah board exploded at that and went on preparing its campaign to sell Youth Aliyah to its membership which by now had reached 60,000. The American Palestine Campaign people were becoming edgy. Executive Director Robert Silverman cabled Jerusalem on November 13, only two weeks before the Hadassah convention: "Despite Jewish Agency Executive rescinding exclusive contract, Hadassah insists continuing the children's campaign, threatening a serious conflict."

Hadassah received support from outside the Zionist fold. Maurice Hexter, non-Zionist member of the Jewish Agency Executive and key figure in American-Jewish philanthropic work, cabled the Jewish Agency: "Your decision concerning Youth Aliyah will repeat the civil war reminiscent of 1921.* Strongly urge revision in favor of Hadassah."

---

* This was a reference to the bitter battle between Weizmann-Lipsky and Brandeis forces over the aims of American Zionism.

If there was one thing on which both Hadassah and the Lipsky-Rothenberg-Silverman group agreed, it was that the presence of Berl Locker in America was pointless. On November 18, ten days before the Hadassah convention, Silverman cabled Jerusalem to that effect and then added in anger: "Urge Executive ignore Hexter cable supporting Hadassah." The next day Hadassah's cable message was firm: "Useless send Locker. Insist Executive honor contract."

That same day, the Agency Executive wired Hadassah in tough no-nonsense language. Obviously, the leaders of the movement had had their fill! "Executive anxious to settle conflict by agreement without resorting to the imposition of our decision. Therefore deputizing Locker with the approval of Szold and Halprin for mediation with instructions to safeguard the interests of Hadassah, American Palestine Campaign (Ampalc) and the integrity of the Zionist Organization."

Into the war of cables there now entered a gun of heavy caliber. David Ben-Gurion, as chairman of the Zionist Executive, thought the situation sufficiently serious to force a solution. His message was addressed personally to Rose Jacobs: "Conflict liable to endanger the integrity of the Zionist Organization. Object to the intervention of non-Zionists in internal Zionist affairs. After consultation with Szold, advise settlement by agreement through the intervention of Locker as an impartial deputy."

Ben-Gurion's reference to "non-Zionists" was to Hexter and others such as the Arbeitsgemeinschaft who were solidly behind Hadassah. The final cable that arrived on that climactic November 19 was from Henrietta Szold and Rose Halprin, then Hadassah board representative in Jerusalem, and was addressed to Rose Jacobs: "We've been shown your cable to the Executive. Advise acceptance of the intervention of Locker whatever else you may do."

That settled it. Locker left on November 20 and arrived six days later in time for the opening of the Cleveland convention. The Hadassah board carried the fight from New York to Cleveland. Its members had been in continual negotiations with Lipsky and Rothenberg; they even carried the debate to an all-night beanery opposite Hadassah's New York office at 111 Fifth Avenue. In Cleveland, the sessions between the National Board and Locker went on throughout the night before the convention formally opened. He pleaded with Hadassah leaders to let go of their exclusive right to Youth Aliyah. They held on like tiger cats and then informed Locker that the entire issue would be put before the delegates. Forlorn, frustrated, alone on foreign soil, Locker retired for what was left of the night.

On the following day Rose Jacobs addressed the delegates at a session lasting from 10:00 p.m. to 2:00 a.m. Marian Greenberg followed with an exposé of the cable war, the acid messages, the acrimonious negotiations. The delegates gave both women an ovation. With that, Locker knew his mission was lost. He gallantly seconded Rose Jacobs's resolution affirming Hadassah's role as the sole agency in America for Youth Aliyah.

Recalling the convention fight, Rose said in 1957, Berl was no match for our women, who proved they could stay up all night, if necessary, to win their right to a project... In the end everything worked out beautifully. Youth Aliyah was a great success, the United Palestine Appeal was not destroyed, a Jewish State came into being and Hadassah gave Lipsky a citation.

In January 1936, a peace-making formula was worked out whereby Hadassah could begin its Trojan toil in earnest and still satisfy the needs of the United Palestine Appeal and the Jewish Agency Executive in Jerusalem. Hadassah agreed, in exchange for its exclusive rights, to confine its campaign to women (a pledge made to be broken) and to credit the Palestine Appeal with the money it raised. Thus, the UPA reported that during its first drive from January 1 to October 15, 1936, it raised $1,779,454, *including* the $125,000 raised by Hadassah for Youth Aliyah.

Even before the formula was worked out, the dynamo began to hum. In December, Henrietta Szold, who had fought gamely for Hadassah in Jerusalem, arrived to a hero's welcome. The night was cold and wet when her ship tied up at Hoboken, but reporters were there for interviews. She was rushed to a newsreel studio for a statement that appeared on screens across the nation. Later, Mayor Fiorello LaGuardia handed her the key to New York City. She spoke at a mass rally. "I come to you not only from Palestine, but from Germany, Austria and Holland," she began. There was hardly a dry eye in the crowd when she finished. Her trip netted thousands of dollars for Youth Aliyah. She was the pampered guest at the luxurious home of Mrs. Felix Warburg, where the first National Youth Aliyah Committee was set up.

Hadassah's "massed motherhood," as Marian Greenberg phrased it, fought for the children with every gimmick it could devise, approached Zionist and non-Zionist, Christian as well as Jew, to fulfill its contract. Thousands of Hadassah workers were in the field rousing America to the need. They mobilized the most prominent women in America, among them the wives of Secretary of the Treasury Morgenthau, Senator Robert Wagner, Supreme Court Justice Louis Brandeis, Governor Herbert Lehman. Elinor Morgenthau, a close friend of Eleanor Roosevelt, brought Youth Aliyah to the attention of the First Lady. Later at a meeting in the Blue Room of the White House with Hadassah representatives, Mrs. Roosevelt accepted an honorary post with Youth Aliyah and on the death of South African Field Marshal Jan Smuts* became the second World Patron of Youth Aliyah.

Of all the star-studded names that went on the official letterhead and on the posters, none worked more conscientiously for Youth Aliyah than Eddie Cantor, the comedian. He was brought into the act by Tamar de Sola Pool who, with the campaign now officially on, went into a state of perpetual motion. In February, she raced off to the Hollywood Beach Hotel in Florida where Eddie was staying. In her hand she held an article written by the right-wing columnist Westbrook Pegler, in which he denounced Hitler's war on children. Eddie was having his breakfast when Tamar bounced in. She showed him the article and asked him to work for Youth Aliyah. "For this cause," the pop-eyed father of five girls said, "I'm ready

---

* Smuts accepted the titular post of World Patron at the behest of an active Youth Aliyah worker, Vera Weizmann, a leader of WIZO and later First Lady of Israel. Following Mrs. Roosevelt's death, the title went to Baroness Alix de Rothschild.

to give my life." One month later, in March 1936, when Hadassah ran the first donor lunch in New York for Youth Aliyah, Eddie appeared. He surprised everyone with the announcement that he had already collected $44,000 – in those days a considerable sum.

In Madison, Wisconsin, the local Hadassah president, Mrs. Herman Mack, found that it was too much to ask the members to raise $360 each to take care of a child in Palestine. For some, that was four months' salary. She got the idea of holding a *minyan*: ten women would gather weekly or monthly for teas or parlor meetings and each would ante-up a few dollars until the $360 sum was reached. The *minyan* idea spread throughout the country.

Junior Hadassah, Hadassah's young adult group which was organized in 1920, carried out its own campaign. At their convention in Washington, in December 1936, 1,000 delegates pledged to expand the children's village of Meier Shfeyah to care for 150 young refugees. Junior Hadassah had adopted the village in 1925. It retained the responsibility for financing it until 1957 when Hadassah merged Junior and Young Judaea into a single, short-lived youth organization called Hashachar (The Dawn).* Later its title reverted to Young Judaea.

Hadassah used German refugees for nationwide speaking tours. Among them were three members of the Warburg families: Ilse, Ingrid and Gisela; and Yettka Levy-Stein. Speakers were advised not to talk at rallies about the atrocities taking place in Germany because the Nazis were listening. The Gestapo grilled Ilse's father-in-law after an American newspaper wrote a story about her under the headline, "Blonde Victim of Nazi Persecution Refuses to Acknowledge Atrocities."

---

* Sadly, Junior Hadassah, an exuberant organization that had attracted the cream of young American women, did not survive the transplant. But, as will become evident, Hadassah breathed new life into the Zionist youth movement. In the latter half of the 20th century, Zionism received massive infusions of new blood from both the old Young Judaea and the new Hamagshimim, an organization of post-high school students.

In Palestine, Henrietta was unbelievably active. Nearly 80 years old, she awoke at 5:00 a.m. every morning and after her usual calisthenics, dived headlong into a long day on behalf of Youth Aliyah. In June 1936, she wrote Rose Jacobs, "Three days a week I get to bed at two and rise at five; the rest of the week I have from four to five hours' sleep, including the nap. I never, never relax. I never read unless it is a memo. I am inhuman."

The Arab riots of 1936-1939 had already broken out. The British government searched for a way to ease tension and typically started by handing out fewer immigration certificates to Jews. In December 1936, Henrietta appeared before a royal commission, set up to hear Arab and Jewish grievances, but when she appealed for more certificates for Youth Aliyah she was told, "We have heard all that before." When she persisted, again she was cut off. The situation looked desperate. In October 1937, Henrietta attended Hadassah's Jubilee Convention in Atlantic City. The convention elected Judith Epstein president. Retiring Rose Jacobs then became the first woman to be named a member of the Jewish Agency Executive. With more than 2,500 delegates present, it was the largest Zionist gathering held in the United States up to that time. Henrietta told the delegates, "My office is the center of a cobweb; threads run out of Germany to the youth in Palestine."

On March 10, 1938, the British government suddenly changed course and notified the Jewish Agency that it was establishing a new category of immigrant – students. Certificates would be unlimited on condition that housing was made available for the students. On the following day, March 11, when Germany marched into Vienna and annexed Austria, 200,000 Jews sought to leave. Most wanted to go to Palestine, but in Palestine there were places – in the kibbutzim primarily – for only 1,000 youths. In New York, Youth Aliyah Chairman Marian Greenberg called a meeting at the home of Mrs. Roger Straus. An emergency committee of 1,000 was organized with the aim of raising enough money to pay for 1,000 youths in Palestine by September 30, 1938.

Responding to urgent pleas by Hadassah to step up his work, Eddie Cantor cabled Hadassah, "Except for Sundays and Mondays, Hadassah's time is my time."* He was Youth Aliyah's single biggest money raiser. Eleanor Roosevelt came to Hadassah's aid with endorsements of the rescue movement in her "My Day" column. When the September 30 deadline arrived, 903 of the 1,000 were already in Palestine and the remainder were on the way. Hadassah had managed to triple its Youth Aliyah income in that period.

1939 was a year of frantic effort. Hadassah dramatized the appeal by organizing meetings featuring noted British women, among them the wives of Foreign Secretary Lord Halifax and the Marquis of Reading. They told poignant stories of refugees arriving in England. In Washington, Hadassah board member Denise Tourover pounded the sidewalks between the White House and Congress, even appealed to foreign diplomats to bring pressure on the Germans on behalf of Youth Aliyah. In June, Marian Greenberg flew to England to meet leaders of the Arbeitsgemeinschaft at a Youth Aliyah conference; the previous year the Berlin office of Youth Aliyah was closed by the Nazis and headquarters were now located in London.

On September 1, the Luftwaffe bombed Warsaw. Two days later Britain and France declared war on Nazi Germany. Trapped behind the iron gates now closing on the Continent were nine million Jews.

The war marked the end of Youth Aliyah's first phase. Between February 1934 and September 1939, Youth Aliyah rescued 4,886 children. By the close of the war 7,446 children would be moved to Palestine from Europe by Youth Aliyah. The total saved from Nazi Europe would thus number 12,332, which does not include about 4,000 additional children from Asian and African countries. During that period more than two million young Jews were murdered in Hitler's extermination and concentration camps.

Rose Jacobs was not the only one to evaluate Youth Aliyah as a success. Eleanor Roosevelt said, "I have always felt that Youth Aliyah is one of the

---

* "My time is your time" was the theme song of his popular radio program.

most creative accomplishments in history and that its importance is reaching far beyond the borders of Israel." On its 25th anniversary, in 1959, Youth Aliyah won the coveted Israel Prize for "rescuing nearly 80,000 children and youngsters." Education Minister Zalman Aranne said, "There seems to be no similar exodus of children and youngsters of this scope in the annals of mankind." As the fourth decade of the organization's work closed, it could be justly proud of its rehabilitation work; 350,000 young people had benefited from its pathfinding in education and human reconstruction.

That having been noted, the question arose whether Youth Aliyah could have saved more children from Nazi Europe. There can be no satisfying reply. When the Hitler cataclysm erupted, no one was prepared. In their inability to understand what lay ahead, Jews rationalized. Pogroms had been common in Europe. They were understood to be temporary storms, usually limited to specific periods of time and locales. Nothing in living experience prepared the world for the commission of evil on so vast a scale and in such broad dimensions as that which Hitler unleashed on one single, defenseless people.

The few years that it took for normally sensitive Jewry to interpret in full the signals emanating from Berlin were precious years lost, precious time that only now can be counted in numbers of dead. It was not until 1943 when the war was half over that the Jewish Agency Executive accepted full authority and established the Department for Child and Youth Immigration.

Henrietta Szold was a woman of impeccable character and boundless energy. She was, as David Ben-Gurion has said, the most outstanding Jewish woman of the 20th century. When she was asked to manage the affairs of Youth Aliyah, she was already in her seventies. She did the work that should have been done by a legion of imaginative younger men and women. She applied good principles to the rescue operation. Her demand for perfection provided those who did escape assurance of proper housing, proper upbringing. Henrietta met every single ward that came off the boat.

But the tragic fact is that in light of the history that followed, Jewish steps toward rescue were a classic World War II case of "too little and too late."

And what of the British? A nation that had the courage to snatch 360,000 men from the bombed beaches of Dunkirk in eight days grudgingly permitted Henrietta Szold to save less than five percent of that number in eleven years because of its morbid fear of Arab retribution. As Josef Mengele decided the fate of a Jew at Auschwitz with the wave of his hand to right or left, so a British civil servant in Jerusalem decided the fate of a Jew destined for Auschwitz by saying yes or no to the request for a permit. But the lack of permits cannot completely absolve world Jewry from dragging its feet. When, in March 1938, the Mandate government announced it would give "unrestricted" immigration certificates to students, Henrietta wrote in despair, "Unrestricted! On second thought – restricted not by Government, but by our limitations: available places and available funds."

And what of American Jewry? They held the richest pocketbook in the Jewish world. Millions of dollars were urgently needed from them but only thousands were given – sometimes with hesitancy. Such was the temper of American Jewry that in December 1936, when Hadassah petitioned the British to grant Youth Aliyah permits for young Jews from Poland, in addition to those from Germany, protests were heard. At best, American Jews were out of touch with the scene in Germany. The American Jewish Committee's *Historical Review* for 1936-1937 noted a tone of unconcern in words that today are chilling:

> For the first time since the Spring of 1933, when the present regime in Germany began, there were indications that although it is continuing to follow with lively attention the events of Jewish interest abroad, the Jewish community of the United States is again beginning to give the major part of its thought to domestic needs.

Hadassah never claimed perpetual control of Youth Aliyah in America. Finally, when Jewish Agency leaders thought of *aliyah* of youth in terms of 50,000 rather than 10,000 and budgets soared beyond the capacity of one organization, Hadassah took the initiative in relinquishing its monopoly. On November 29, 1943, Henrietta together with Kaplan and Landauer confirmed (in a cable, of course) that a coordinating committee suggested by Hadassah would now operate to collect money in America. Joining Hadassah in the fund-raising effort on an equal footing were the United Palestine Appeal, Mizrachi Women and Pioneer Women. Hadassah was permitted to retain the title of official agent for Youth Aliyah in America.

Hadassah's noteworthy achievement in the early years of the Hitler menace was to awaken masses of Americans to the needs of Europe's children. No other organization was sufficiently broad or more intrinsically suited to the task. There are no measurements to judge the accomplishment in human terms. In terms of money, the results achieved were impressive. The original contracted sum of $60,000 in two years was actually quadrupled. In the first eight years, Hadassah alone covered 75 percent of Youth Aliyah's requirements. At the beginning of 1960 when Hadassah's accumulated contribution was close to $40 million, Israel's director of Youth Aliyah Moshe Kol said, "Were it not for Hadassah, Youth Aliyah would have ceased to exist.

By the same token Hadassah benefited enormously from its involvement. Saving children worked like magic to attract members. Within one year after assuming responsibility for Youth Aliyah, the number of chapters rose from 272 to 375. Ex-President Judith Epstein remarked at the time that Youth Aliyah was a "turning point" in Hadassah's development. Bertha Schoolman, Henrietta's successor as mother of Youth Aliyah, regarded the association as "a humanizing force" in Hadassah's work in America. Gisela Warburg Wyzanski, a "lonely refugee" from Germany who charted the work in the war years, saw it forging a "maternal tie" between Hadassah and Israel.

However one characterized the effect of the Hadassah – Youth Aliyah union, in practical terms the results were long-lasting. After World War II tens of thousands of Jewish children were saved. Not all were Holocaust victims. During the 1950's and 60's orphans from Asian and Middle Eastern countries were cared for. When immigration slumped in the late 1970's, Youth Aliyah changed course, focusing on culturally-deprived children of large immigrant families born in transit camps (*ma'abarot*) who were doing badly both in school and in a western society in which they could not compete. Youth Aliyah came to the rescue. In the early 1980's there were 18,000 wards in its institutions, nearly all Israeli-born. Its thrust was to fit them into the jigsaw of Israeli life.

A two-year-obligation became a life-long partnership. Youth Aliyah saved lives; Hadassah paid most of the bill – to the tune of $135,000,000. More than 60 years old now, the contract has been honored many times over.

NAILS ON THE ROAD

After the Arab excesses of 1929, with few exceptions Palestine enjoyed seven years of truce. Then, in 1936, began the worst reign of Arab terror in living memory.

Exasperated by the flood of Jewish immigrants and frustrated because the British had not blocked the tide, extremist Arab nationalists demanded armed action. More moderate Arab leaders, meanwhile, were engaged in confidential but futile talks with David Ben-Gurion and other Zionists to seek an understanding. In one such conversation in August 1934, Ben-Gurion was asked to agree to restrict immigration so that in ten years the Jewish population would not top one million. Ben-Gurion replied negatively, even though the Jews in Palestine then numbered only 400,000. By 1936, Arab right-wingers had gained the upper hand; their three demands: stop Jewish immigration, stop land sales to Jews, make Palestine an Arab state now.

The British tried to coax both sides to accept a single, bi-national state and invited Arab leaders to confer on the subject. When the divided Arabs failed to agree on the make-up of their delegation, the British finally despaired of the proposal. That undermined the moderates further and by mid-April the Arab fanatics, riding high in the saddle, flashed the signal for a rebellion that flared intermittently until the eve of World War II and ended in a major, if short-lived, political victory for the Arab nationalist cause.

Evening, April 15, 1936, outside Nablus, the eye of the Arab nationalist hurricane. Ten trucks and cars are stalled in front of a barrier of barrels and rocks. An eyewitness recalled:

> We were proceeding from Haifa to Tel Aviv. Yehoshua Napchi, of Tel Aviv, stopped his car. Two Arabs appeared from the side of the road. They took Napchi to a lorry standing in front of us and they shot him, but he was only wounded. The shots killed Israel Khazan, 61, a Salonica Jew who was taking a load of chickens to the poultry market. They also wounded Zvi Tannenburg. A bullet went through his spine and he died later. One Jew identified himself as a German and he was not touched.

The leader of the gang was a feared highwayman, Sheikh Izz e-Din, who had marauded in the Samarian hills for years. Now he was mixing business with politics. He informed his victims before he shot them, "I am taking your money to buy arms for the holy cause."

Friday, April 17, was a day of public bereavement for the *yishuv*. Thousands attended Khazan's funeral and Tel Aviv Mayor Israel Rokach addressed the mourners, "Our innocent brother was murdered by people who wish to frighten us and stop our work. But the world will know that terrorist acts will not stop our work."

Someone in the assembly cried, "Revenge!"

Rokach replied: "Our revenge will be in creative work!" The policy of the *yishuv* throughout the riots was to be one of *havlaga* (self-restraint).

But the Jewish crowd marched to Magen David Square where they scuffled with British police. Flying stones, the traditional weapon in Palestine since the days of David, injured a few constables who finally dispersed the demonstrators with shots in the air.

Arab violence mounted by geometric proportions. A false rumor spread in Arab Jaffa that Tel Aviv Jews had murdered several Arabs. Arab gangs, some dressed in Boy Scout uniforms, smashed, knifed and clubbed their way through the Jewish Quarter on the border between the twin cities. Elsewhere, Jewish movie houses, clinics and ships were broken into and their occupants shot. Arab protest took many forms. At Kibbutz Ein Harod, Arabs uprooted five hundred citrus trees. Houses, barns, machinery and forests were scorched. Arabs returned eight times to burn groves near Mishmar Ha-emek. A children's home was set afire but doused before the 100 infants were singed. Crude bombs were thrown in market places. Snipers shot at cars on the road and at Jewish pedestrians. The terrorists poured lysol and kerosene on vegetables being delivered by Arab peasants to Jewish markets. Henrietta Szold commented wryly in a letter in the summer of 1936, "It is interesting that the typhoid record for these months is the best yet. The elimination of vegetables raised by Arabs in Palestine with their use of sewage for fertilizer has in turn eliminated typhoid." By the end of April, half of Jaffa's 18,000 Jews were refugees in Tel Aviv. Refugees filled synagogues in Jerusalem and Tiberias. As a result of the general strike called by the Supreme Arab Council, hundreds of Jews were unemployed because they feared to cross picket lines. No accurate count of the losses can be made, but the toll between April and October of 1936 is estimated at 700 persons dead, thousands wounded, 2,000 Jewish communities attacked, 100,000 trees destroyed and $15,000,000 in property damaged.

In an attempt to tame the tempest, the British dispatched an army to Palestine and promised to establish a Royal Commission that would probe the causes of the disturbances. After a long hot summer, the Arabs finally called off the strike in October, and in November a six-member commission arrived.

The people of Palestine were cynical about commissions. Moderates on both sides of the fence were doubtful that any third force could possibly solve Palestine's problems; left alone, Arabs and Jews might possibly work out a *modus vivendi* whether through arms or negotiations. But this was never to be; foreign noses would always be stuck, and stung, in the Palestine beehive. Even so, this latest commission, led by Lord Peel, managed to raise faint hopes that Jews, Arabs and British could together pave a new road to peace. In the end, the Peel Commission failed in its immediate mission, but it did succeed in introducing a new concept in the tiresome search for a settlement. From the Commission's sessions came the first concrete proposal to carve a Jewish and an Arab state out of Palestine. It was an idea that would be partly realized precisely eleven years later.

On their arrival in Jerusalem on November 11, 1936, the Commission members checked into the five-year-old King David Hotel and then drove straight to the British War Cemetery on Mt. Scopus for Armistice Day services. In Jerusalem, the Anglican bishop and the chief rabbi of the non-Zionist Agudat Israel issued appeals to pray for the success of the commission. But the Grand Mufti of Jerusalem did not consider such an appeal appropriate. The Arab leadership decided on a boycott and dramatized it in a bizarre fashion. On the day after their arrival in Jerusalem the Commission members were the guests of high commissioner Sir Arthur Wauchope at a gala reception held at the official residence on the Hill of Evil Counsel. On the way one car after another was put out of action. The Arabs had strewn nails on the road. Lord Peel got through unscathed, but one of his colleagues was immobilized three times by flats.

The Peel Commission opened its hearing in the rococo ballroom of the Palace Hotel on November 16. Sir Arthur was the first of many witnesses who would testify in 66 sessions over the coming two months and two days. The third witness was of special interest to Hadassah. He was Colonel George Heron, the director of Palestine's medical services, who told the commission: "The Arabs must rely on Government health services whereas the Jews have their own organizations." He noted that the government spent £180,000 a year on health work, while Jewish organizations spent nearly twice that much. "On the Jewish side there are very complete medical services," he stated. And he boasted that Palestine had one physician for every six hundred persons, compared with one for every eight hundred in the United States. That was one of the highest – if not the highest – ratio in the world. Nearly all the doctors were Jews, many of them newcomers.

The most poignant moment in the Commission's hearings was the appearance of Chaim Weizmann. Speaking in deep, measured tones, he traveled the history, hopes and fortunes of the Jewish people for more than two hours. He spoke prophetically and tragically of Jews in Europe "pent up in places where they are not wanted and for whom the world is divided into places where they cannot live and places which they may not enter." He flayed at the bugaboo of Palestine's "absorptive capacity" – the specious argument used by anti-Zionists to keep Jews out – when he recalled that Lord Passfield had once told him, "But Dr. Weizmann do you realize that there is not room to swing a cat in Palestine?" Weizmann could now tell the Commission, "Many a cat has been swung since then and the population of Palestine has increased since that talk with Lord Passfield by something like 200,000." The Zionists weighed in with forty more witnesses, among them David Ben-Gurion and Henrietta Szold.

So strong was the evidence on behalf of a Jewish state that the Arabs broke their boycott and testified. The Grand Mufti went first with a counter-balancing review of Arab history, hopes and broken promises, and of fears that the Jews were immigrating with the intention of reconstructing the Temple on the mount where now stood two of Islam's sacred shrines. Fourteen more Arab leaders followed and finally on January 19, 1937, the Commission members started for home to determine the fate of Palestine.

Of all the sessions, the most fateful was a closed meeting with Chaim Weizmann on January 8, 1937. One member of the group, Oxford University historian Reginald Coupland, asked Weizmann to comment on the possibility of partitioning Palestine into independent states. Within the British government the idea of establishing a Swiss-like cantonal system under a British federal government was being mooted at the time, but this was the first occasion that the idea of two independent states was broached officially to the Zionist leadership. Weizmann believed that he had finally arrived at the threshold of the Jewish state. He spoke with high enthusiasm to intimates; he was aware that the road ahead was burdened with obstacles, but he intuitively realized that somewhere at the end of the maze partition was the only way out. Aloud, he asked the members of the Commission for time to consult his colleagues. The story is told – although it may be apocryphal – that a few days later Weizmann met secretly with Professor Coupland in the cooperative farm village of Nahalal. There they stooped over maps to try to determine rational borders for the two new states. And when they emerged from their meeting place in a wooden shack Weizmann exclaimed to a group of inquisitive Jewish farmers, "Today, here in this place, we have laid the foundation for a Jewish state!"

Lord Peel published his report in July 1937, and died days later. He complimented the Zionists for their constructive work in Palestine and presciently noted that "there is no common ground" between Jews and Arabs. "Neither Arab nor Jew," he wrote, "has any sense of service to a *single* state." Thus partition was the only solution, because it alone would allow for the parallel development of national goals and cultures. Having come to that sensible conclusion and having noted that the country's 400,000 Jews made up 40 percent of the population, the Commission went on to recommend the creation of a Jewish state with only 20 percent of the territory. The much larger Arab state was to be united with Trans-Jordan. Jerusalem was to remain British – a captivating jewel in the imperial crown. These recommendations appeared in a White Paper issued by the British government almost simultaneously with the appearance of the Peel report.

The White Paper of 1937 angered the British administrators in Palestine who wanted to retain more control over the land and its people through a federated system. The Arabs, horrified at the prospect that Jews were about to be given a part of the Arab domain, reached again for their guns. The Jewish leadership, meeting at the Twentieth Zionist Congress on August 3, fought bitterly over the Peel report. The partition principle itself was acceptable to most, but the size of the state proposed by Peel was not. Favoring the map were Weizmann, Ben-Gurion and most Palestinian Jewish leaders. Opposed were the Americans led by Stephen Wise and Robert Szold, who were supported by Hadassah. Among the militant "maximalists," surprisingly, was Henrietta Szold who opposed Peel partly because he severed Jerusalem from the Jewish body. "How can one be with a Jewish state from which Jerusalem is excised," she wrote. "I don't like it." In whole or in part, neither did most Zionists.

Those in favor, however, made a strong argument that any small bit of sovereign territory was welcome now to provide a haven for masses of European refugees who had nowhere to go. "Territorial adjustments" could be made later, Weizmann said. "The Negev will not run away." The opponents argued that a state the size suggested by Peel was not viable. One speaker ridiculed the proposed state's dimensions: "We will call the new Jewish state 'England' because it is so small." The opponents' argument was that the Arabs would not resist the temptation to declare war on the state; it would be quickly overrun, thus destroying forever the dream of Jewish national renascence.

In the end, the Congress rejected Peel's proposals. The overwhelming majority of Hadassah's eighteen delegates, who were elected as a separate political entity for the first time, rejected partition on any terms. This stand was confirmed by a large vote at the Hadassah convention in Atlantic City two months later. But the Congress, having in mind the refugees and the first practical offer of Jewish sovereignty, did not close the door completely. It accepted the partition principle as a basis for negotiation.

As it turned out, the fight was academic since the Arabs were not ready to tolerate the most microscopic Jewish state in Palestine and the British were in no mood to buck Arab opposition. The Arab response to Peel was murder. After a congress of four hundred Arabs held at Bloudan, Syria, rejected the surrender of even an inch of Palestine to the Jews, they cranked up the rebellion. In October, one of the first victims was the popular district commissioner in Nazareth. That was enough to tame the British lion and in November the government pacified the Arabs by declaring that it was not bound to partition. But within three months the government formed a new commission, presided over by old India hand Sir John Woodhead. He was assigned the task of drawing up new partition borders. Woodhead presented two maps, both of which whittled down Peel's Jewish state to 400 square miles – the size of Hong Kong – or twenty times smaller than the state that came into being in 1948. No Jew could possibly have accepted such "a useless little ghetto," as it was described by historian Christopher Sykes. In the face of this new absurdity Britain, in November 1938, froze the idea altogether, announced that it was renewing its hold on the Mandate, called the Jews and Arabs to attend a negotiating conference in London and warned them that if they did not reach a settlement, one would be imposed.

February 1939. The mood of western Europe was appeasement. In March, Prime Minister Neville Chamberlain spoke foolhardily of "peace in our time" as Hitler devoured Czechoslovakia. The Arab delegation arrived at St. James's Palace in London for talks and promptly announced its refusal to sit in the same room with the Jews. As a consequence, Prime Minister Chamberlain ordered two ceremonial openings for the conference and for his pains gave the same speech twice. The London negotiations were stillborn: the Jews said that the Peel report was their basic minimum; the Arabs pushed their demands to stop immigration, stop land sales and declare an Arab state in all of Palestine. True to their ultimatum, the British tried to enforce a solution. Weizmann had some forewarning of what was coming after a long conversation with Lord Halifax, the foreign secretary, who suggested to Weizmann that he forget about the creation of an independent state. "Renounce your rights under the Mandate," Halifax advised. On May 17, 1939, the Chamberlain government issued a White Paper that will live in infamy in Zionist annals. On the same day the Nazis took Prague. With only four months to go before war would trap millions of Jews inside Hitler's bastion, the White Paper decreed a drastic reduction of Jewish immigration into Palestine (only 15,000 yearly for five years). It placed heavy restrictions on land sales to Jews. And it called for the establishment of a bi-national state within ten years. The limitation on immigration made it certain that the Arabs would rule Palestine. But even this proposal was utterly rejected by the Arabs: they demanded a state immediately, an absolute stop to immigration and a review of the status of all Jews who emigrated to Palestine since 1918.

Nullification! That word became the branding iron of enraged Zionist leaders, for with the White Paper of 1939 the British government nullified the Balfour Declaration. By their intransigence, the Arabs had won a major political victory.

Dejected, disheartened, Chaim Weizmann could only call the White Paper exactly what it was – "a sellout." But it was for a younger man of action, David Ben-Gurion, to utter a rallying cry. As chairman of the Jewish Agency he characteristically set a course of defiance: "This cruel blow will not subdue the Jewish people." But after the war against Hitler began, it did present a dilemma. Should Jews in Palestine fight a weakened, pre-occupied Britain for a Jewish state, or should they join Britain to fight the greater evil, Hitler? Ben-Gurion's reply was Solomonic. At a public gathering he declared the words that would be quoted for years to come: "We will fight together with Great Britain in this war as if there is no White Paper, and we will fight the White Paper as if there is no war."

Ben-Gurion sensed that the British had papered over the Balfour Declaration for reasons of expediency. With war imminent, Britain could not anger millions of Arabs into firing up the revolt again. But Ben-Gurion knew also that the Jews would pay a heavy price for that expediency: the lives of those masses who could not pass the locked gates of Palestine. For Ben-Gurion, there were now two supreme tasks: to build a Jewish army that would help fight Hitler and to build an organization that would bring in Europe's refugees despite the British lion and the German werewolf.

Now Jews were facing their darkest hour. Everyone seemed to be against them – Germans, British, Arabs. An unholy combination of forces had dashed their sweetest dreams. Isolated, the Jews of Palestine steeled to meet all comers.

Dark as the hour was, the *yishuv* did not give up faith. The Jews of Palestine continued to build, to train and to prepare. The concrete mixers churned and the hammers swung. In Jerusalem, morale lifted considerably only eight days before the White Paper was issued, when Hadassah opened for all creeds the Middle East's most modern healing, research and medical education center. The glistening hospital on Mt. Scopus in Jerusalem dominated much of the city. Not overlooked at the time was that this accomplishment of Zionist endeavor stood on the site from which the Roman Emperor Titus launched his attack on the Holy City nearly 1,900 years before.

MOUNT SCOPUS

For several days in October 1934, sound engineers of the Palestine Broadcasting System bustled in the turret office of the Hebrew University's chancellor on Mt. Scopus. They had a thousand problems. Not the least of them were the heavy echoes in the room and the field mice that nibbled away at the tangles of wire lying twisted on the floor. In preparation was the first live broadcast from the Middle East to New York through relay stations in Cairo and London. From the Manhattan studios of the National Broadcasting Company, the program was to be transmitted from coast to coast and piped specially into the grand ballroom of the Wardman Park Hotel in Washington, D.C. where 1,500 Hadassah delegates were assembled for their national convention.

H-Hour was four o'clock in the afternoon on Mt. Scopus, nine o'clock in the morning in Washington. The date: Tuesday, October 16, 1934. Seated uncomfortably in the office of Judah Magnes with a grand view of ancient Jerusalem were Henrietta Szold, Nahum Sokolow, Menachem Ussishkin, Hadassah Medical Organization Director Haim Yassky and Magnes. Ground-breaking ceremonies on Mt. Scopus, attended by 500, were over. In the Washington auditorium the delegates had been in their seats for many hours; some had gone without breakfast to make sure they were close to the loudspeakers. Across the hall was a banner: "We Will Build."

A few minutes after nine, Rose Jacobs read a cable from Jerusalem into a battery of NBC microphones that relayed the proceedings over a national hookup. The cable described the ceremonies that had just taken place on Mt. Scopus. At 9:28 a crackle of static filled the hall. The first words were those of Magnes's assistant Julian Meltzer: "This is Jerusalem calling from the Hebrew University on Mt. Scopus."

Then came Nahum Sokolow's voice: "...world Jewry celebrates..." The static allowed only a few words to get through. Magnes was heard to say, "it is but a few minutes' walk to the laboratories of the Hebrew University..." Third was Henrietta. The delegates were on the edge of their seats: "we celebrate today the culmination of an idea... the healing of my people." Dr. Yassky followed: "coordination and united effort will bridge the distance between us..." Radio was not sufficiently developed at that early stage for such broadcasts but that did not matter. The "Hadassah Newsletter" reporter wrote:

> The words are not clear. But that does not matter. Hadassah's founder is speaking to thousands of her colleagues and it was enough to hear her voice. On the platform and scattered throughout the hall are some who toiled with Miss Szold in the early days. Before them, in these seconds, must have flashed a quick kaleidoscope of those pioneer days. They could not restrain their tears. The audience is tense, electric, trying to catch every syllable. And when the 20-minute broadcast is ended the whole assembly rises to its feet, applauds and cheers and breaks into singing Hatikva. Women weep for joy and kiss and embrace one another.

The same exuberance burst forth at the Hadassah convention in Chicago the previous October when, the depression be damned, the delegates voted to raise $200,000 from Hadassah's 30,000 members to build a hospital in

Jerusalem. But it was on October 15, 1934, in Washington, that Hadassah formally voted to join the American Jewish Physicians Committee in the construction of a medical center on Mt. Scopus. With that act, Hadassah moved from an age of pioneering into an age of sophistication and voted itself a physical permanence in Palestine. It thus gave full expression to the idea that medicine – healing, teaching and research – was inextricably bound to the ultimate goals of the political Zionist movement.

The idea itself was not new. In 1920, the Zionist Organization in London probed the possibility of establishing medical and scientific institutes in Palestine. As a follow-up, Albert Einstein and Chaim Weizmann, on behalf of the Zionist Organization, sailed to America in 1921 to drum up support for the Hebrew University. While there they inspired the founding of the American Jewish Physicians Committee under Nathan Ratnoff. The committee raised $500,000 and in 1924 bought land on Mt. Scopus for a projected medical school. Later, more land was to be donated by the JNF and Mary Fels, the Philadelphia Zionist and soap heiress. In that same year – one year before the Hebrew University was to open – the first medical institute in microbiology was begun by Saul Adler, world-famous parasitologist.

In 1926, the malaria-fighter Israel Kligler, director of Hadassah laboratories and head of the University's Hygiene Department, urged the establishment of a medical center in Jerusalem. Henrietta Szold was four-square behind Kligler and drew in Chancellor Magnes. The first formal discussion of the joint project was held on April 23, 1927, with the American Jewish Physicians Committee acting as marriage-broker.

The medical center proposal took seven years to blossom and another five years to ripen. Countless meetings were held in New York and Jerusalem to clear the many obstacles posed by financing, planning and division of authority. One roadblock was Hadassah's budget. In 1930 it was cut for the first time owing to the depression. But on the other hand, with immigration beginning to soar in the new decade, hospital space rapidly became inadequate. At times, some departments of Hadassah's 150-bed institution were running at 120 percent capacity. Magnes spoke of the 80-year-old Rothschild building as "that rickety, dangerous structure." Finally in 1934, Hadassah and the Hebrew University reached a sensible agreement on the running of the medical center: the former would oversee its medical work while the latter would supervise its teaching aspects. A monumental debate, however, broke out over the site of the center. Magnes insisted that a medical center should be located close to a university and he maintained that the only plausible site was Mt. Scopus. The university was in general agreement on that point. But Hadassah was split. Dr. Ephraim Bluestone, who resigned as director in 1928, but continued as chief consultant in New York, fought a mighty battle to put the center where potential patients could get to it quickly. Bluestone claimed at the time that it was folly to site a vulnerable medical complex where it would be isolated from the rest of the Jewish population and surrounded by hostile Arab quarters and villages. To arguments that Scopus had the most beautiful view in the Jerusalem area, he answered, "It is more important for a patient to see a doctor than to see the landscape. Never place an obstacle between the patient and his doctor and remember that distance is an obstacle."

Magnes rebutted, somewhat illogically, that Montefiore Hospital in New York, of which Bluestone was then director, was far from the center of the people it served. What Magnes overlooked was that the Indians had for several hundred years ceased to be a danger to New York City. The primary difference between the two men was in outlook: Magnes, a pacifist and humanitarian, believed with all his heart that Jews and Arabs would soon live in peace and then could jointly enjoy the fruits of the university and center. He felt the medical center would hasten the peace process. Bluestone, a coldly analytical scientist and realist, was just as sure that the medical center would be a sitting duck for vengeful Arabs.

Bluestone received backing from many Hadassah physicians and leaders, some of whom were hoping that the center could be placed in what became Jerusalem's elite residential neighborhood – the Rehavia quarter.

Inter alia they also objected to the building of the center close to the World War I cemetery on Scopus. For political reasons the Jewish Agency sided with the University. It was interested in building up Scopus so that Jewish Jerusalem could then "reach out" to the ridge and encompass the neighboring Arabs.

Hadassah failed to support its chief consultant. Instead it sought more advice and sent to Palestine the director of New York's Hospital for Joint Diseases, Jacob Golub, and Dr. Nathan Ratnoff to examine all the possibilities. Hadassah agreed in advance that their decision on siting the center would be irrevocable. On July 23, 1934, Golub and Ratnoff cabled: **CONCLUSIVELY DETERMINED SCOPUS MOST SUITABLE SITE.**

Looking back many years later, Golub wrote that the clinching argument for Scopus was the fact that a medical school would one day be established there and it was only logical that it should be near the University. Even as late as 1947, Golub wrote: "The hilly landscape of Mt. Scopus will increasingly become a university and hospital campus for students and faculty."

But Golub wrote too soon. Within one year, a convoy of physicians, nurses, teachers and workers of Hadassah and the University would be ambushed by Arabs while passing through the Sheikh Jarrah Quarter of Jerusalem on its way up to Scopus and most would perish. Not long after the ambush, Scopus was abandoned for 19 years and for most of that time Jerusalem was to be without proper hospital and university facilities. It was a crippling blow and a mighty expensive price to pay.

What went wrong? "Two mistakes were made," says former President Rose Halprin, who served as Hadassah's liaison in Jerusalem in the 1930's. "The minute that our hospital went up, there should have been a Jewish community started near Scopus. That was our mistake. The second error was that of the Jewish Agency. They should, as they promised, have built settlements to close the gaps in the road."

In mid-1935, Golub reported to Hadassah that during the first half of the decade the number of physicians in the Jewish population had doubled.

One out of every 225 Jews in the country was an MD. Because of the immigration from Central Europe, there were proportionately four times more physicians in the Jewish area of Palestine than in the entire United States. Hadassah, in an attempt to cope with the integration problem, took in as many as 35 doctors at one time to prepare them for medical work in Palestine. But the organization soon realized that it must get on with the medical center if for no other reason than to build a bigger roof to house this vast treasury of brain power.

They now had Ludwig Halberstaedter, from the University of Berlin, one of the world's greatest authorities in cancer therapy. Refugee Halberstaedter arrived carrying one-fifth of a gram of radium, an enormous amount in those days, worth $15,000. With it he opened the first radium and X-ray institute in Palestine under Hadassah's auspices. So badly quartered was Hadassah at the time that the professor had to work with his precious radium in a converted stable. With him from Berlin came an equally noted cytologist, Leonid Doljansky. They worked in tandem, providing Palestine with its first effective treatment of cancer. Gynecologist Bernhard Zondek, a co-developer of the first quick, reliable test for pregnancy, known popularly as the A-Z test, was among the immigrants. Viennese surgeon Felix Mandel opened a second surgery department in Hadassah. Pediatrician Benno Gruenfelder and physiologist Ernst Wertheimer were familiar names in the Old World. But there were young men, too, who would soon make their mark. And most of them would work as volunteers. The volunteer doctor is a strange phenomenon in the annals of medicine, and in Palestine – rich in talent, poor in everything else – the profession was to bear voluntarism for years to come.

Some doctors had escaped Europe by the skin of their teeth. Aharon Yehuda Beller, born in a small town in Galicia, was 24 when he was arrested by the Nazis in Vienna. It was November 1938. "The [Vienna] Rothschild Hospital was closed. I was taken. My head was shaved and I was put on a bus to Dachau. En route we were turned around. There were no places left

for us in the death camp and for some unexplainable reason I was released."
Via Rumania, Beller reached Palestine.

> I started working under Dr. Joseph as a volunteer in the
> Department of Surgery. I was the seventeenth doctor – only
> one was paid. Dr. Yassky gave me a job as a translator. The
> German physicians had to lecture in Hebrew and they did not
> know the language so I translated their papers from German
> to Hebrew in Latin characters.

Professor Beller later served as Hadassah's Chief Neurosurgeon for many
years. He died in March, 1996.

Some became experts in other fields. Theodor David Ullmann was born
in Germany in 1908:

> Following my graduation from medical school in Würzburg,
> I came to Palestine in 1934. At that time it was very difficult
> for a young medical man to practice medicine so I went to
> work in a paint factory in Haifa. Gradually I advanced in this
> factory to the position of manager. There was a time when I
> was more experienced in making paint than treating the sick.

Professor Ullman, Hadassah's leading authority on kidney diseases, headed
the Nephrological Service until his death in 1975.

Hanoch Milwidsky, born in Berlin, arrived in Palestine in 1932:

> I saw there were sufficient doctors here so I started working
> for a fruit jobber. I also knew some car mechanics and found
> that helpful. In those days it was more of a *mitzvah* to go into
> agriculture and the trades than take up a profession. But my
> father insisted I return to Germany to complete my medical
> studies. When the Nazis came, I went to Strasbourg because
> I did not want a diploma with a Nazi signature. Then I
> returned to work in the only Jewish hospital in Berlin. When

the Germans got wind that I was also helping Jews leave the country illegally, I had to run away. In Jerusalem, there was no possibility of getting a job as a surgeon at Hadassah because the hospital was so small. I worked in pathology and as an anesthetist. I started as a volunteer but later received a salary of £1 a month. Dr. Yehuda Bromberg, the Hospital's red-headed administrator, told us volunteers when we asked for a proper salary, "It is a buyers' market. I am an economist and I work according to market conditions. If I can get doctors like oranges, why should I pay high salaries?"

Surgeon Milwidsky was the first to perform a heart operation in the Middle East. The operation, carried out against the opposition of hospital authorities, was successful. He had been warned by senior hospital officials not to go through with the operation because it would reflect on the medical reputation of Hadassah. It did, but in a positive way. The elderly patient's stenotic valves had become obstructed by scar tissue due to rheumatic heart disease and his only chance to live was through the radical new surgery that Milwidsky learned under the tutelage of American heart surgeon Charles Bailey. The procedure later became commonplace. Hanoch Milwidsky perished when a Swissair plane blew up in mid-air en route to Israel on February 21, 1970. The Arab Popular Front for the Liberation of Palestine proudly claimed responsibility.

Ino Sciaky was born in Salonika, spent his childhood in Turkey and studied dentistry in Switzerland when his parents moved to Bulgaria:

When I came to Jerusalem as a tourist in 1937, I declared my desire to settle but the British refused me permission. They said I could remain only if I were a capitalist. I went to Egypt, borrowed £1,000 – the minimum needed to be regarded as a capitalist – sent it to Palestine and followed soon thereafter. After I was accepted as an immigrant, I returned the money to my cousin. I was then a bona fide capitalist but without capital.

Professor of Oral Medicine Ino Sciaky was appointed the first dean of the School of Dentistry. He died in 1982.

One young doctor who received his education in Odessa left for Palestine before earning his degree. The closest job to medicine he could get from the British health authorities was that of sanitation inspector in Tel Aviv, for which he received £6 monthly. That was in 1919. After tiring of running after garbage men, he left for Geneva with his wife to continue his studies in eye diseases and public health. In 1921, with his framed degree on the wall, he joined Hadassah in Haifa as an assistant in the ophthalmology department. Three years later he headed that Hadassah department in Tel Aviv. It was there that this six-foot idealist caught the eye of Henrietta Szold. "Trachoma in the villages and settlements is appalling," he insisted. "I want to go out there." She agreed. And the lanky eye doctor, often traveling bareback on a donkey, his shoes scraping the ground, went as far as the Galilee, treating and operating on Arab and Jew alike. In 1927, that "lanky eye doctor" Haim Yassky, was called to Jerusalem to take over the department of ophthalmology.

After much soul-searching, Henrietta Szold named Yassky acting director of the Hadassah Medical Organization. In 1931, likewise after much soul-searching, the Hadassah National Board made the post permanent. Haim Yassky held his post until he was murdered in the Scopus convoy on April 13, 1948.

Yassky did not rise easily to the custodianship of Hadassah medicine in Palestine because he was not an American. Understandably, the Hadassah board in New York kept its faith with American medicine and administration and during the first decades its man in Jerusalem was an American citizen. In the early years of the 20th century, American medicine was avant-garde, lacking the tradition of Vienna, Berlin or Geneva. The New World's doctors were much more informal and its hospital administration was much less bureaucratic than that of the autocratic, status-conscious Old World. New Zealand surgeon Edward Joseph would soon find that "the German doctors considered themselves the top people.

They looked upon American-trained physicians as being beneath contempt. A director coming from America would also be considered beneath contempt and so there was always hostility between them." Russian-born Moshe Rachmilewitz, the noted heart specialist who arrived at Hadassah in 1931, was critical of "the German approach" even though he himself was trained in Germany. Not long after his arrival he went off to New York for 18 months of advanced study at Mt. Sinai Hospital where, he recalled later in life, "I was reborn medically. There had been a shifting of centers for me from the European Continent to America." The American approach was direct, simple, natural. Status did not decide which medical opinion should be accepted. An opinion was judged solely on its merits. A young man was able to express himself – he was free to speak up. That was distinctly different from the European approach.

The clashes of approach, the Babel of methods, the mixtures of nationalities had made it impossible for American directors to work in Jerusalem at the efficiency to which they were accustomed back home. Their problems were aggravated by Hadassah's requirement that policy and budget be controlled from New York. Thus decisions could not be made quickly. And where there were basic disagreements between these two ends of Hadassah's world, much time was lost as telegrams bounced back and forth over the seas. In the end, medical work was bound to suffer. Often, even Henrietta Szold found herself locking horns with Hadassah's centralized authority. The result was that, as she focused her interests more and more on local problems of social welfare, she began to urge Hadassah to become increasingly subservient to local Palestine Zionist authority. But Hadassah in New York understandably insisted on making its own policy to ensure maintenance of high American scientific standards in Palestine. The problem was to be a constant irritant. In time, the Hadassah Medical Organization would grow to undreamed of proportions with a budget comparable to that of a large American corporation. And with medicine becoming so complex, the lay leadership in New York could no longer cope. A number of remedies were attempted but none was satisfactory. Too much power in the hands of the Israel leadership became self-serving and did not always meet American Hadassah's needs. In 1996 a Solomonic solution was attempted: the HMO would be run by a 21-member management board consisting of equal numbers of independent experts, National Board Members and Israeli professionals. How it would work out was the question that might not be answered for a considerable period.

Henrietta's headaches with Hadassah directors began the moment she stepped into Jerusalem in 1920. The first formally appointed medical director, Dr. Rubinow, gave up after two attempts to juggle budgets and staff. Henrietta took over for a time, then asked Magnes to step in while she returned briefly to the United States. In November 1923, Simon Meshullam Tannenbaum, of New York's Beth David Hospital, went to Jerusalem, but left in October 1924. Henrietta then asked Alexander Salkind, chief of the department of Internal Diseases, to assume charge, but he had to quit after falling ill. The search for a permanent director ended, so it was thought, with the appointment of the assistant director of Mt. Sinai Hospital, Ephraim Michael Bluestone. Young, talented, idealistic, determined Bluestone was regarded by the Hadassah board as the answer to any organization's prayer. He came from a well-known Zionist family, was graduated with distinction from Columbia University's College of Physicians and Surgeons, served overseas in an American base hospital during the war and by the age of 35 was well known in hospital administration in New York City. He signed on for three years; Hadassah felt he would remain longer. But Bluestone was back home in America little more than two years after he arrived in Jerusalem in March 1926.

"Dr. Bluestone had a horrible time," according to one physician who served during the period. Henrietta Szold, who admired Bluestone's talent but found it difficult to work with him, once confided to Hadassah President Irma Lindheim, "I have been afraid of only two persons in my life. One was the maid that we had for very many years and the other is Bluestone." As strong-willed as Henrietta herself, Bluestone was hamstrung from the beginning – his sharp sense of humor, facile pen, ramrod sense of duty were to no avail. He had an early warning of what he might expect. On the ship to Palestine he met an elderly man who had taken ill. The doctor, loyal to his new employer, assured the gentleman that once he reached Jerusalem, he would see to it that the patient received perfect care. When they arrived in Jerusalem, little could be done for the old man because Hadassah's X-ray department was on strike. To Bluestone of Mt. Sinai this was anarchy. But that was only the start. Word had spread throughout the *yishuv* that the chief at Hadassah was receiving the absurdly high salary of $10,000 a year – about ten times the amount of a worker. That brought upon Bluestone the wrath of labor leaders as well as newspaper editors who singled him out in editorials. Doctors in Kupat Holim, the health fund of the budding Histadrut which Hadassah supported financially for a number of years as it teetered on bankruptcy, spread vicious rumors about Bluestone. The young doctor, unwilling to suffer these indignities, considered returning to civilized New York. But Henrietta, joined by Rose Jacobs and Irma Lindheim, urged him to remain.

Henrietta reported to the Hadassah board in June 1926, only a few months after Bluestone's arrival, that he was commendably "guided purely by professional considerations." But there were other considerations too, Zionist ones. She noted that he objected to Hadassah's participation in running hospital facilities in Tel Aviv and Haifa. He was not attuned to the consensus technique of arriving at decisions and he did not have time to train administrators. Bluestone complained that the *yishuv's* National Health Committee was "a serious menace to the independence of Hadassah." Henrietta wrote to New York, "If that means detachment from the Zionist movement, I am personally not interested in medical work in Palestine." She was firm that Zionist interests must transcend Hadassah's exclusive objectives. On that, Bluestone and Henrietta split. He resigned in February 1928.

This state of affairs could not last long. Henrietta concluded that Hadassah must have a director who was ready to cast his lot, physically and spiritually, with the *yishuv*. Bluestone wisely concurred. With Henrietta's acquiescence, he approached Haim Yassky. Yassky was reluctant but when Henrietta impressed upon him the importance of the task, he agreed. Bluestone left early in September 1928 and continued a long association with Hadassah as a consultant, becoming the first chairman of Hadassah's Medical Reference Board.

Dr. Yassky found that he was not alone at the top. Hadassah retained him as acting medical director, because he was still in his early thirties and he had no formal training in hospital administration. Reuven Katznelson was named acting business director. As they shared a stormy stewardship, Henrietta sensed that one permanent Palestine director with overall authority was the only answer to the Hadassah Medical Organization's problem:

> The time has come when the permanent Palestinian and not the elusive American should be considered for the directorship. We cannot go on paying salaries and we cannot go on paying apprenticeship monies to Americans who must adjust themselves, each one in succession, to the conditions of Palestinian life and who, no sooner adjusted, take flight. Whether we approve or disapprove of the conditions of Palestinian life, for better or worse, they are the conditions under which the country is being developed by the forces who are content to throw their lot in with the country.

In New York, Hadassah's board realized that a co-directorship could only be a stopgap solution. Finally, after several reappointments as acting director, Yassky was appointed director-general of the Hadassah Medical Organization in June 1931. And in 1932 under the board's auspices he spent six months in the United States studying administration. On his return, he set his compass in the direction of Mt. Scopus. There he was to achieve his greatest dream and his tragic end. His objectives were high: "To create a medical institution whose fame will extend far beyond the boundaries of Palestine is our national and human duty." Without Yassky on the spot, the Scopus institution would certainly not have been ready for

World War II. He was the engine that kept the project moving forward. It was he who created a pre-medical faculty that was to be the forerunner of the medical school which he never lived to see. Under his directorship new medical disciplines were introduced into Palestine – neurosurgery, occupational therapy, a medical record system. "The medical center," said Yassky's widow many years after his death, "was Dr. Yassky's entire life – his whole devotion."

After Mt. Scopus was finally agreed upon as the site of the center, Hadassah sent Dr. Golub on several trips abroad in connection with the plans. On one occasion he met in London with the exiled German architect Eric Mendelsohn who had taken up residence in Palestine and who was chosen to create the hospital complex on the stony ridge. Mendelsohn dreamed of the simple lines of Escorial and Assisi: "I want to create monumental austerity even though it will disappoint the layman who expects British baronial splendor or America's imposing verticals." He took as his guide the simple lines of the Arab village because he was seeking local harmony – of non-ornamental walls, of courtyards with fountains and pergolas. "This," he said, "must be built for the ages."

Mendelsohn had great problems in creating immortal architecture. The location was a narrow, knifelike ridge about one mile long, rising 150 feet above the city of Jerusalem. On the east there was a deep descent toward the Dead Sea, to the west a slope into the Kidron Valley facing the site of the Temple upon which Moslems had built the dominating golden Dome of the Rock. He had cold, rainy, windy winters of four months to cope with and dry, cool summers of eight months with parchment-dry days of spring and autumn sandwiched in between. Mendelsohn laid out three three-story buildings in an east-west pattern: the hospital connected by his beloved pergolas to the Henrietta Szold Nursing School and, opposite, the Nathan Ratnoff building for post-graduate studies. Like the surrounding Arab villages, the architect kept the profiles low.

First earth for the hospital and nurses school was turned in mid-November 1936. The buildings were completed in September 1938.

Construction of the post-graduate institute was started in January 1937 and was finished in April 1939. For the first time in Palestine's construction history, machine-cut white stone slabs were used to face the edifices rather than the traditional hand-fashioned stone. For greenery, Hadassah planted a grove of 1,500 pine trees in honor of Henrietta. The total cost was over $1,000,000 – the single most expensive project Hadassah had undertaken up to that time. Said Golub, "For the first time there will be an institution which combines teaching and research and the immediate care of the sick. The medical men of Palestine look forward to the new institution as a model not only for the medical work of that country but for the whole Near East."

On May 9, 1939, Chaim Weizmann rushed out of Palestine on an Ala Littoria plane from Haifa for London after hearing that in eight days the British White Paper was to nullify the Balfour Declaration. Berlin and Rome agreed on a pact that established the Axis and Japan said it was willing to join. In Germany, a quarter of a million Jews were waiting for visas to leave: 90 percent would never make it. On Mt. Scopus, Mendelsohn looked upon the completed work as though it were Shangri-La and said to a colleague, "It has the serenity of the greatest spiritual creations in this part of the world." The dedication was modest; it had to be because of the security situation. Haim Yassky was the chairman of the ceremony. Rose Jacobs spoke on behalf of 82,000 Hadassah members in America. Dr. Magnes spoke for the American Jewish Physicians Committee. Henrietta Szold, now 77, opened the ceremonies and accepted a silver key from Yassky. On the key was an inscription: "From Hadassah in Palestine to Hadassah in America with deep appreciation."

The ceremonies were hardly over when the move began from the old Rothschild Hospital on the Street of the Prophets in downtown Jerusalem. Even as the trucks lumbered up to Mt. Scopus doubts still lingered about the site. "I remember the morning when we moved to Scopus," Dr. Moshe Rachmilewitz said later. "There was an explosion. There was shooting throughout Jerusalem. There had been much discussion whether it was advisable to move the hospital to Scopus. I was not clear in my own mind about it." The move went on nonetheless and the old Rothschild building was put up for sale. Approval for the sale was given by the Rothschilds on condition that their family name be part of the new Scopus building. But the building was not sold and in the end was to serve Hadassah's educational needs for decades to come.

Scopus opened with modern lighting and 200 beds. It was later expanded by 80 and now is officially listed at that number. Nurses could effectively control an entire ward from their central stations. "It was a fine hospital from every point of view," said veteran surgeon Edward Joseph:

> The best in the Middle East. A very elaborate place. Of course, they made mistakes. For instance, the operating theaters had huge glass windows. The whole side was one field of glass. It looks very beautiful from the road but it was the unfortunate surgeon who had to operate there, for the sun came in after noontime making it difficult to work in that place. We tried not to operate in the afternoon. We used to sweat dreadfully. All the time our foreheads had to be wiped.*

By May 14, the Hadassah Medical Organization's offices were on Scopus and on Tuesday (a twice-blessed day, according to Jewish tradition), May 30, 1939, the hospital doors swung open for the public. Happily, the first case was maternity and on that first day two babies were born. In all, 120 patients, aged two to 70, were moved up to Scopus. The first *brit milah* was held on the second day with Chief Rabbi Isaac Halevy Herzog officiating. The infant was named Meir in honor of the founder of the Rothschild family.

Little more than three months later, the world was at war. Palestine was soon isolated and threatened. Scopus was set for battle.

---

* Surgeons at both Hadassah Hospitals have an easier time of it now. Scopus is fully air-conditioned; the air-conditioning at Ein Karem was gradually introduced.

A WORLD AT WAR

Fighting back the tears on that late August night in 1939, Chaim Weizmann bade the 1,500 delegates farewell knowing in his heart that by returning home many were going to their doom. Said Weizmann: "It would need the eloquence of a Jeremiah to picture the horrors of this new destruction of our people. We have none to comfort us."

That was the end of the most melancholy Zionist Congress in the history of the movement – the 21st or, as Weizmann had hopefully named it, the "Coming-of-Age Congress." In the midst of the sessions Berlin and Moscow announced their villainous pact. War was now certain. The general mood was one of frustration, helplessness. President Judith Epstein, heading the Hadassah delegation, observed, "The most horrible feeling in Geneva was that not a sound came out of the magnificent League of Nations building looking at us. I shall never forget the silence coming from those portals."

Most delegates were warned to leave Geneva immediately. Polish delegates were ordered to detour Germany through Yugoslavia and Hungary. German Zionists faced the horrible dilemma of remaining abroad or rejoining their families. Some Palestinian Jews brazenly crossed into Nazi Germany to try to organize escape routes. The delegates, having gone through the motions of condemning and rejecting the terms of the British White Paper, turned out the lights and scattered. Weizmann, who returned to England a few hours before the ceremonial closing, embraced his old colleague, Menachem Ussishkin, and despairingly whispered, "What kind of a world will it be when we meet again, Menachem?" Ussishkin shook his head gravely.

Back in London, Weizmann penned a letter to Neville Chamberlain politely asking the British government to permit Jewish manpower and resources in Palestine to join the war effort. Chamberlain demurred. Then, a few days later Hitler bombed Warsaw. For the next six years most of the world was aflame.

Palestine at war became a menagerie of paradoxes. Cut off, the country fell into economic chaos. Banks took a three-day holiday to prevent a run. Prices skyrocketed. The depression hit so fast and hard that Jews and Arabs cooperated economically to stave off ruin. Hardest hit was citrus, Palestine's largest export, in which both communities were engaged. As markets closed abroad, however, oranges soon came into demand locally as a source of acetone for making smokeless gunpowder. Soon, Palestine re-geared for a war economy and emerged from its financial doldrums.

The *yishuv* was trapped into simultaneously helping the British fight Hitler and fighting the British to save the refugees from Europe. Throughout the war the Mandate administration successfully parried attempts to create an independent Jewish army. The British constantly obstructed Haganah men who trained to meet a Nazi invasion, but at the same time British Intelligence used Haganah agents on dangerous missions behind enemy lines. Arab countries that had alliances with Britain either cooperated with the Nazis or remained neutral until victory was almost in sight.

Amid these seething cross-currents of conflicting interests, the *yishuv*, which begged like a neglected child for British recognition, struggled for its survival and for its goal of statehood. That it finally achieved national status, considering the odds against it, is one of the most breathtaking dramas in the long history of this ancient land and one in which Hadassah played a key role.

As the war took its toll of European nations, Nazi Field-Marshal Erwin Rommel crunched steadily eastward across the North African sands toward British Middle East Headquarters in Cairo. Anxiety gripped Palestine and the British army hurriedly began training the Haganah's strike force, the Palmach, to make a last-ditch stand on Mt. Carmel which was to be a modern version of Masada. It was feared that if Rommel broke through to Cairo, the entire Middle East would fall under the sign of the swastika. In the summer of 1942 it seemed that the world's fate – which was actually more critically at stake at Stalingrad – depended on whether the British could hold Cairo. Weizmann saw the dangers as early as mid-1940, after the Italians joined the Axis, and so renewed his pleas in London for a Palestine Jewish Army. Winston Churchill, now prime minister, supported the proposal and, in February 1941, even arranged that Weizmann meet the intended commander of the Jewish force, General Leonard Hawes. In the end a combination of the opposition of the anti-Zionist British in Palestine and a dearth of supplies prevented the establishment of the army.

Overnight Palestine turned into a war camp of Allied soldiers. In light of the peril the British put the country under virtual martial law Anticipating the worst and hoping that the British would agree to the mobilizing of a Jewish army, the Jewish Agency opened its own national service register ten days after war began. Within two weeks, 135,000 men and women – about 20 percent of the entire *yishuv* – had signed up. In Jerusalem, the recently vacated Rothschild-Hadassah Hospital served as registration headquarters. Haganah men began to drill but the British, fearful of Arab reaction, brought their heel down heavily and on one occasion arrested 43 men eager to move against the Nazis.

But still the *yishuv* prepared; the Haganah secretly worked up contingency plans for partisan warfare should the British pull out. Blackouts, air-raid warnings and drills, food rationing and controlled prices were part of the scene. Forty-eight hours before fighting began in Poland, the 19th class of nurses and the first on Scopus was graduated. Dr. Yassky called it the "Disturbances Class" because the girls had studied through three years of Arab riots and terror. Even in August 1939, three months after the Arabs had supposedly been appeased by the White Paper, 87 persons died in riots. Yassky cabled New York for emergency funds and immediately the National Board sent a first-aid grant of $60,000. The role Hadassah was to play in the war was described to Yassky by Tel Aviv Mayor Israel Rokach: "We turn to Hadassah in our need just as grown children turn to their mother when they are in distress."

Feverishly, the preparations to withstand an onslaught went on. Most feared was attack from the air. Patients and staff were given air-raid drills. On Mt. Scopus, a shelter was built with seven self-contained units for doctors, nurses and patients. By setting up emergency beds, Scopus was ready to care for 500 patients. The 20th class of nurses was accelerated by two months and all graduate nurses were called for refresher courses. Over the Palestine Broadcasting System, Hadassah dieticians gave instructions on how best to use rationed foods. Yassky offered the British Medical Corps and the families of all men in uniform the full use of Scopus's facilities. Henrietta Szold cabled New York from Jerusalem **"CRY OF THE HOUR TO FEED HUNGRY CHILDREN."** Hadassah put 25,000 children on an emergency feeding program in addition to serving 75,000 lunches daily in 600 schools. And apart from free medical services for men and their families in uniform, refugees received free medication and clothing.

In so doing, Hadassah was on a full war footing at least two years before the United States itself. In an Order of the Day sent to the national membership, President Tamar de Sola Pool wrote: "Our front line of defense lies in Zion as in Britain." Hadassah's Palestine Chairman Rose Halprin announced at a press conference that "Britain, America and Palestine are one fighting front.... The 500,000 Jewish inhabitants of Palestine are banded together as one man to aid England and protect democracy. The aggressor stands for everything which, both as Americans and Jews, we abhor. By helping Palestine defend itself we are helping the

Allies." Zionist objectives were thus immediately aimed at making Palestine part of the Allied war effort. At the same time, Hadassah did not neglect homefront duties – selling War Bonds, mobilizing members for Civil Defense, volunteering for auxiliary services – and, for its work, in December 1944, won the big E (for Excellence) award from the U.S. government. Hadassah could make this contribution to the war effort because of its ability to meet crises as they arose. In responding to the government representative at the presentation ceremony, President Judith Epstein said: "We are proud to receive this award; we would have been ashamed if we had failed to receive it."

As Britain's fortunes worsened on all war fronts, the Palestine administration began putting uniforms on Jewish volunteers. A Palestine Battalion was organized under the Union Jack and by March 1940 nearly 2,000 Jews were fighting. By June 1941, the number reached 8,900 and already 1,000 were missing in action and 1,200 were Nazi prisoners in the Greek campaign. Jewish soldiers fought in Libya, Greece and Syria. They served in the Royal Air Force. Haganah scouts opened the way for General Maitland Wilson's forces moving into Vichy-held Syria where Company Commander Moshe Dayan lost his left eye. Others parachuted into Europe on British intelligence missions. Bombs crashed into Palestine's cities. Haifa was hit most often from the air because it was a principal naval facility, but Tel Aviv suffered too. In September 1940, one air attack took the lives of 122 persons in the all-Jewish city.

While the Jews of Palestine were understandably jittery, the Arabs seemed sure of their future regardless of who won. In London, Weizmann heard that the Arabs of Palestine were preparing to divide the spoils once Hitler arrived. He noted in his memoirs, "Some of them are going about the streets of Tel Aviv and the colonies marking up the houses they expect to take over: one Arab, it was reported, has been killed in a quarrel over the loot assigned to him."

In June 1942, in one of the major tank battles of World War II, Rommel shattered the British defense at Tobruk, Libya, and took 33,000 British prisoners, including Palestinians. The fateful breakthrough left Egypt wide open. Churchill sailed secretly to Washington for a conference with Roosevelt. There he received a letter from Weizmann offering to raise three divisions of 32,000 men and a force of 40,000 home guard. "If we go down in Palestine, we are entitled to go down fighting," he pleaded. That and the apparent hopelessness of the situation persuaded the British to enlarge the Palestine Battalion to a regiment of about 2,000 men. It was still not a Jewish army nor could it stop the Nazis. But few as they were they acquitted themselves well enough to win Churchill's commendation.

For eight months before the fall of Tobruk, the transport company of the Palestine Battalion kept the British at the front supplied and after the defeat, transferred a New Zealand division from Syria to Egypt in a record six days. The engineers kept the bombed roads and ports repaired and paved the way for the fateful battle at El Alamein, where Rommel's advance faltered, one day's ride from Cairo. As the British moved westward pursuing Rommel, the Palestine regiment marched in the vanguard. In Tunis, where the chief rabbi welcomed the battalion as "messengers of peace," their commander, General Fred Kisch, a Jewish Agency Executive member in the 1920's who served as General Montgomery's chief engineer, was killed.

For the Allies in the Mediterranean area, the big headache was lack of supplies. Convoys had to pass mined waters and duck sorties of Axis bombers. Tens of thousand of tons of shipping went to the bottom. The civilian effort was likewise dependent on a constant supply of goods, medicines and equipment from abroad. Some did get through the Mediterranean; others had to be rerouted around the Cape of Good Hope to Basra on the Persian Gulf, then by truck over the desert to Palestine – a voyage of 18,000 miles. Like clockwork, 30 tons of supplies were shipped every month from Hadassah in New York to Hadassah in Jerusalem. Along with the new wonder sulfa drugs came surgical instruments, serums and vaccines, cod liver oil, clothing and X-ray film. On one ship there was a twelve-ton steel elevator for the Scopus medical center's underground shelter and an incubator. More than 1,000 Hadassah sewing groups in the United States sent hundreds of thousands of clothing items.

As a result of the need to get these vast quantities of scarce supplies through war zones, Hadassah became a familiar figure in high places in Washington. In 1939, foreseeing the need, the National Board appointed one of its new members, New Orleans-born Denise Tourover, to represent the organization in the nation's capital. Having lived in Washington since 1920, Denise soon became as familiar as the Washington Monument to political leaders. She moved among them with an easy informality but could, if necessary, be as determined as a bulldozer in removing bureaucratic roadblocks. At the beginning of the war, it was as yet possible to move money and supplies abroad since America was not at war. Because shipping was severely restricted, the White House set up a special board – the President's Advisory Committee on Foreign Voluntary Aid – to approve good causes. Hadassah became a member in 1949 and attended meetings for the next 34 years. Recalls Denise:

> We had to clear everything with the Board of Economic Warfare. To do that we had to have export licenses from Washington and import licenses from the British in Cairo. We did a great deal of work with both the British and the American boards. For example, if we needed quinine, which was in short supply, we would put our hands on the drug through various drug associations. Then we had to see the right people in the Board of Economic Warfare to get clearance. Very often we got the licenses, sometimes we did not. If after ten days we did not receive an affirmative reply from the British, we would assume the clearance was lost. We would send the article on and mark on the shipment **CLEARANCE LOST**. Somehow, they worked out the problem on the other side. It could be maddening work. I remember well a shipment of *milchig* and *fleishig* [dairy and

meat] dishes which had to be sent. When all was cleared we found that 24 dozen cups were left behind. I had no chance to get clearance and I felt the best thing to do was to take the cups to the top of the White House and throw them one by one down into the street. But the man who was helping me insisted we could get clearance. We succeeded but only after a long struggle.

Denise had her own peculiar techniques in snipping red tape. It helped that she represented a volunteer, humanitarian organization. At the time Washington was crawling with war profiteers and "ten percenters" – agents making fortunes on 10 percent commissions. In contrast, Hadassah was "clean'" and not one major Hadassah item was refused by the board during the entire war.

Of all the war years none was more crucial for Zionism than 1942. Annihilation seemed constantly imminent. The scare of invasion did not pass until November, but there was much more to be dreaded than Rommel's tanks. On January 20, subordinates of Hitler, meeting at Wannsee near Berlin, adopted a program of systematic genocide, euphemistically calling it the "Final Solution." The decision that led to the extermination of six million Jews would not reach the ears of world Jewry until autumn.

Even without knowing the specifics of Wannsee, Chaim Weizmann was sufficiently depressed by the turbulence thrashing world Jewry to call an extraordinary conference of Jewish leaders in New York City in May. He felt that without a united front in America – the only great bastion of free Jewry remaining – the hobbled Zionist effort could collapse. The assembly of about 650 delegates, among them Tamar de Sola Pool and Bertha Schoolman representing Hadassah, met at the Biltmore Hotel. Emerging from the deliberations was the first clear call by Zionists for the establishment of an independent political state in Palestine as distinct from the less precise "national home" of the Balfour Declaration. The Biltmore

Program also demanded unlimited Jewish immigration at a time when the British were limiting it to 15,000 a year. Biltmore put the derelict Zionist movement on a firm course. But it also served as the scene for a bitter fight between Chaim Weizmann and David Ben-Gurion. Shortly after the meeting ended, Ben-Gurion, who was now the Jews' shadow prime minister in Palestine, challenged Weizmann's leadership. At a painful meeting in the private study of Rabbi Stephen Wise, chairman of the conference, Ben-Gurion accused Weizmann of depending wholly on his own personal prestige to fulfill Zionist goals and thus, of failing to create a Jewish army. No one had ever addressed the eminent Zionist in terms so brutal and so frank. Weizmann could only reply that there was no answer to political assassination. Ben-Gurion went on to claim credit for the Biltmore Program although Weizmann had outlined its principle in an article in the January 1942 issue of *Foreign Affairs*. Whatever the source, the Biltmore Program was a Zionist milestone that brought the movement's blurred aims into sharp focus.

In a negative sense Biltmore spotlighted the widening gap between Diaspora and Palestine Zionism. Weizmann believed that an irreparable breach with Britain would be more injurious to the Jews than to Britain, that if America had to choose between Britain or Zionism she would ally herself with Britain. Ben-Gurion held that only two forces mattered – Palestine Jewry and American Jewry – and Weizmann would get nowhere because non-Jewish politicians would always act in their own national interests. Ben-Gurion's policy was radically new. It reflected a new spirit that had been born among the pioneers in Palestine, and Ben-Gurion was its spokesman. But at first it was not universally accepted. In 1942, Ben-Gurion, except to his disciples, was too raw and too brash for the more conservative American and British Zionists. The difference between the two men was the difference between the silk glove and the sledgehammer. Although both Weizmann and Ben-Gurion agreed on the Biltmore Program, they differed on how it was to be implemented.

Populist Ben-Gurion made the most of Biltmore. He used it as a rallying cry – to state forthright aims in simple terms, to excite the people into sounding trumpets and waving flags. In the process Ben-Gurion made many enemies; they called him "a wild man" and worse. His protagonists swore by him. But on whichever side one stood, all could acknowledge that a new force, a dynamic leader, forceful and single-minded, was abroad ready to lead his people to the ramparts. He had the pulse of his people at his fingertips and he knew they were ready to march.

The Biltmore Program achieved its goal of rallying American Zionists. At the 1942 convention held in New York City, Hadassah gave the program its whole-hearted support. For the National Board of Hadassah, however, a serious problem grew from the fact that the founder of Hadassah, Henrietta Szold, and the chairman of the Hadassah Emergency Committee, Judah Magnes, were among the founding members of Ichud (Unity), a new organization proposing the establishment of a bi-national state in which Arabs and Jews would share sovereignty. A bitter debate erupted within the leadership over a proposal to disassociate Hadassah from the stand of Dr. Magnes and Henrietta Szold, both closely identified in the public mind with Hadassah. At this critical stage in Zionist history Hadassah was in no mood for solutions such as bi-nationalism; it was now mature enough to say so and to put the organization four-square behind the concept of a Jewish commonwealth. That was a significant milestone in Hadassah history for it had taken a firm stand in political affairs. With a membership of around 150,000, Hadassah had grown enormously on the American scene which had been dominated by male leadership. That growth was irreversible and in time would make the organization the largest single Zionist group in the world.

In the mid-war years, Hadassah was so active in so many fields in Palestine that it could justifiably throw a little weight around. Scopus was the center of much of that activity. British army physicians took courses on tropical diseases from Saul Adler, a world authority. That led to a series of regular, formal medical conferences attended by British military doctors who were just out of medical school. "I don't know what we would do without you," the British army medical chief wrote Dr. Yassky. Hundreds of physicians attended lectures. In the labs, British army X-ray machines were repaired and its margarine was regularly tested for vitamin content. Hadassah supplied Britain's Royal Air Force in Egypt with medicines that it could not get from its own medical corps. Hadassah sent vaccine and supplies to the Russians, the Turks, the Free French, the Czechs and the Anglo-Iranian Petroleum Company; trained a lab technician for the Yugoslav partisans; sent eight nurses to care for war wounded at an Alexandria hospital directed by the personal physician of King Farouk of Egypt.

With the war came the fear of epidemics. By right, the health department of the Mandate government should have commanded the battle. But it was Hadassah that inoculated 70,000 school children against typhoid, furnished the department with anti-typhus vaccines, reduced the incidence of malaria to a point where it no longer posed a risk for troops, even set up small emergency field hospitals.

Then there was the regular regimen of work: combating tuberculosis brought in by immigrants (the anti-TB hospital in Safed maintained a 110 percent occupancy rate and Hadassah was planning a new hospital in Jerusalem, when new drugs practically eradicated the disease); establishing a home medical service to relieve overcrowding on Scopus; launching two major vocational education centers in Jerusalem and preparing the groundwork for a medical school; a medicine-producing pharmacological institute that would one day be turned into a school of pharmacy; helping found a soldiers welfare committee; setting up more kindergartens and playgrounds and supervising nutrition in 77 summer camps.

With it all, Hadassah's performance in medical work was impressive: 90 percent of all seriously war-wounded treated at Hadassah survived. And in Palestine, largely as a result of Hadassah's care of the young, the *yishuv* had the world's lowest child mortality rate – 27 per 1,000 (seven per 1,000 in 1996).

To keep the machinery well-oiled, Hadassah set up the Hadassah Emergency Committee. With the onset of war it was clear that the National Board, 6,000 miles away, could not keep its grip on the wheel. There was thus need for an independent field command with powers almost equal to that of the board. In 1940, Rose Jacobs, Hadassah trouble-shooter, asked Judah Magnes in Jerusalem to head an emergency committee that would, in fact, play the role of trustee for the National Board. The eloquent Magnes accepted the task "to imprint upon the community a Hadassah personality."

Hadassah always faced the problem of running affairs with its mind in New York and its heart in Jerusalem. Soon after non-medical projects were begun in the early 1920's a Palestine council coordinated activities. In 1924, Henrietta Szold urged the Central Committee (predecessor of the National Board) to appoint Nellie Straus Mochenson as its representative in Palestine. The council had an executive secretary, Yugoslav-born Shari Berger, who as a child had witnessed the assassination of Archduke Ferdinand at Sarajevo. After arriving in 1923 she helped Henrietta and Jessie Sampter set up the Hebrew Women's Organization which later became the World International Zionist Organization (WIZO). Rose Halprin went to Jerusalem in 1934 when Shari resigned and remained until 1939. During those years Rose kept a flood of reports flowing to New York.

Thus, the Emergency Committee had strong precedents on which to build. It kept firm control over expenditures and it negotiated for Hadassah with the government and the Jewish Agency. Its long-lasting importance was that it broke down the artificial barriers between the preventive and the curative services. Until 1939, the Hadassah Medical Organization was a power unto itself while the Palestine Council served as a cover for all other services. Now the Emergency Committee was responsible for all.

The Committee could pull down the barriers only because three persons of stature were in command: Magnes, Henrietta, and Julius Simon of the Palestine Economic Corporation. Later on, others were co-opted – Ethel Agron, Rose Viteles, Yassky himself, Yehuda Bromberg – and when the state was finally established, the Committee's successor, the Hadassah Council in Israel, would become a permanent feature of volunteer service in Jerusalem.*

One of the more piquant aspects of Scopus's personality during the war was the salutary relationship that existed between Jew and Arab. Feelings between the two communities improved enormously once the fear of invasion diminished. By 1943 Arabic was being taught in Hebrew schools, the League for Jewish-Arab Relations opened joint youth clubs; school children exchanged visits. Part of the reason for this era of goodwill was that some of the trouble-makers were out of the country. The Mufti of Jerusalem, who fled first to Iraq and then to Iran, consorted with the Nazis in Berlin where he worked out a plan with Hitler for the future of Palestine. In 1943 and 1944, there were no serious outbreaks between the two communities. On his discharge from Hadassah, the Emir Abdullah – the future King of the Hashemite Kingdom of Jordan – on the opening page of the Medical Center's visitors' book penned words of praise for Hadassah and invited Yassky to visit the palace in Amman. "More than half of our patients in the neurosurgery department were Arab," recalled Professor Aharon Beller.

Although Hadassah was to suffer deeply at the hands of Arab nationalists, no Arab was ever turned away. Abdullah himself – and King Hussein, his grandson – would be responsible for keeping Scopus a lifeless shell for 19 years after Israel's War of Independence. Yet they would not hesitate to allow Jordanians to be treated in Hadassah's wards when specialists were not available at home. Hadassah personnel were killed by Arabs in the 1920's while on mercy missions. Yet one of the prize documents in Hadassah's archives is a letter to Joseph Krimsky, dated November 1918, from the British military governor in Beersheba and signed by 27 Bedouin sheikhs, thanking him and his nurse for saving the eyesight of Bedouin patients.

---

* The Hadassah Council was absorbed into Hadassah-Israel in 1996, 12 years after its birth as the first unit in the Hadassah International family of organizations.

During World War II Arab royalty sought out Hadassah's doctors – among them King Feisal of Iraq who had reneged on his agreement with Chaim Weizmann in 1920, and a prince of Saudi Arabia, whose father, King Ibn Saud, would toward the war's end influence President Roosevelt to veer away from a Zionist policy. But it was in the summer of 1944, shortly before the Roosevelt-Ibn Saud meeting, that Saudi Prince Mansour insisted that his brother-in-law Prince Fahd be hospitalized at Hadassah. Ibn Saud objected to a Zionist state but not a Zionist hospital. Said Prince Mansour to Dr. Yassky: "When my brother-in-law fell ill there was a consultation of some 20 physicians in Cairo and it was suggested that he be flown to London. I said, 'Nonsense! Why should he be taken to London if there is Hadassah in Jerusalem?' Now nobody will go anywhere but to Jerusalem."

During the war years – even as the *yishuv* smoldered because of Britain's immigration policy – formal visits were made by the British high commissioner. On those occasions, the hospital would be on its toes as though an admiral were being piped aboard a destroyer. On one such occasion, Esther Passman Epstein, who served as a one-member Hadassah welcoming committee, took the high commissioner, who was a bachelor, into the maternity ward. "He was twirling his walking stick and looking at the infants when a sudden smile crossed his face. He lifted his hand and started waving to the babies. Lord Gort turned to me and said that they were lovely children. Without thinking, I replied, 'Yes, this is our internal immigration department.' He looked at me, his face red and gruff, cleared his throat and said, 'Yes, you have a point there.' Then we looked at each other and broke into laughter. The ice was cracked and after that we were all good friends." It was during Lord Gort's administration that a measure of peace between Arabs and Jews was possible, but he did not remain in Jerusalem for long.

Immigration was the issue on which the British, the Arabs and the Jews were ready to risk their future. The Arabs feared inundation. The British feared Arab retribution. The Jews feared neither and by a combination of audacity, terror, skill and sanguinity decided the issue. In the end the

British would take desperate departure of the land; the Arabs who sought to resolve the problem by arms would be defeated.

Even before Hitler rose to power, the refugee flood began to accumulate. Some could not wait for British certificates. The first known attempt of a large group to steal into Palestine was carried out successfully in 1934 by 300 Polish Zionists who landed in the night aboard a small hired Greek boat, the *Vellos*. Quickly they dispersed into the collective settlements where they took on new identities. The second attempt of the *Vellos* failed and no large-scale attempts were made for several years. Finally, in 1937, at a clandestine meeting in Tel Aviv a group of Haganah, labor and kibbutz leaders set up Mossad l'Aliyah Bet, the Institute for Immigration B, a euphemism for uncertified, or as the British called it "illegal," immigration. In 1938, Mossad agents were operating in Nazi Germany and Austria. They made contact with Adolph Eichmann, then head of the Central Bureau for Jewish Emigration, and won his agreement to help them establish training farms for Jews wishing to live in Palestine. Eichmann,* the fiend who transported millions of Jews to extermination camps, was certainly no lover of Jews. He implemented Hitler's genocidal policy to make Europe *judenrein*.

By mid-1939, many hundreds had managed to slip by the British. To show they were in earnest, the British callously returned refugees on three small ships to their ports of departure in Nazi Europe – a virtual verdict of death in each case. The resultant world-wide uproar prevented further repatriations. On the day war was declared, the Mossad ship *Tiger Hill*, carrying 1,205 refugees, settled in the sands south of Jaffa. As it approached the shore the British opened fire on it killing two passengers, one a

---

* In 1960, Mossad agents captured Eichmann, a fugitive living in Argentina under an assumed name, and flew him to Israel. He was tried and convicted in Jerusalem for crimes committed against the Jews and humanity. After the Supreme Court dismissed his appeal, and the President refused clemency, Eichmann was hanged in 1962. He remains the only criminal to be put to death by the State of Israel. Unknown documentation and evidence from survivors, submitted at the nine-month trial, awakened a horror-stricken world to the enormity and bestiality of Nazi crimes against the Jewish people.

physician. The senseless shooting was ordered by over-anxious officers who suspected that the Gestapo had planted Nazi agents among the immigrants. With the help of the Mossad about 7,000 others set sail but never reached Palestine's shores; leaking, rusted, rotten boats that should never have ventured on to a lake tried weathering heavy seas and, like the S.S. *Salvador* carrying 300 Bulgarian Jews, sank with everyone aboard.

The more the British tried to limit the entry of refugees the more the *yishuv*, directly and indirectly, tried to break through. Because of the unauthorized immigration, the Mandate government on July 12, 1939, proclaimed a ban on the entry of all Jews to Palestine for six months starting October 1. On January 5, 1940, the British decreed that fleeing refugees with German or Austrian passports would not be allowed to enter Palestine because they were "enemy aliens." In November 1940, refugees intercepted on their way to Palestine were transferred to the S.S. *Patria* in Haifa harbor. The *Patria* was to deport these 1,771 Jews to the Indian Ocean island of Mauritius where they were to be held for the duration and presumably repatriated after the war. But the *Patria* never made it out of Haifa harbor. On November 25, an explosion rocked the ship, killing 241 persons. In a misguided attempt to prevent the vessel from leaving port, a Haganah agent attempted to immobilize the engines, but the blast was heavier than planned and lives were lost. The surviving *Patria* refugees were held in detention at Atlit, an internment camp near Haifa, and finally released. But nearly 1,800 others were sent to Mauritius where they languished for the remainder of the war.

While the Jews were restricted, other refugees were permitted entry and colonies of non-Jewish Poles, Serbs, Greeks, Czechs and others began growing in Tel Aviv and Jerusalem. The British were effective to a greater degree than they might have hoped. On April 1, 1944, when the White Paper's quota restrictions on immigrants ran out, about 20,000 certificates were still unused. The British extended their validity, offering a visa to anyone who managed to reach Turkey. By the beginning of 1945 they were finally used up and simultaneously the British withdrew their agreement to grant visas automatically to Jews arriving in Turkey. With that the Turks no longer would grant transit rights to stateless Jews en route to Palestine. Knowing that the war would soon end, the Jewish Agency requested permits for 100,000 survivors in Europe. The reply, in February 1945, was that because of housing difficulties only 1,500 certificates would be available monthly. That was a slight improvement over the previous 15,000 yearly but not nearly enough to absorb the expected deluge.

One effect of relentless British efforts to restrict immigration was the rise of Jewish extremism. In 1942, two such groups appeared on the scene. One was the Fighters for the Freedom of Israel (known by its Hebrew acronym LEHI), or as the British called them, "the Stern Gang." The Sternists, smallest of the underground groups, were led by a young poet, Abraham Stern. One of their most notorious acts was to assassinate Churchill's Minister of State in Cairo, Lord Moyne, on November 2, 1944 (Balfour Day), only two days after Weizmann and Churchill had discussed the partitioning of Palestine. Many believe that Moyne's murder so angered Churchill that he temporarily set aside his pro-Zionist sympathies.

A much larger and older clandestine underground group was the Irgun Tzevai Leumi (National Military Organization) which broke away from the Haganah in 1937. Allied to the Revisionists and to Zev Jabotinsky, it was commanded by Menachem Begin, a Polish soldier who crossed into Palestine from Trans-Jordan in 1942. Although its terrorist character cannot be denied, it respected a truce for most of the war and allied itself with the Haganah in a number of operations toward the end of the war.

In Europe, Jews tried desperately to break out. Few succeeded. There were examples of incredible endurance such as the ill-fated flight of 1,200 Jews from Vienna, Danzig and Czechoslovakia who sailed down the Danube in three boats, were delayed on the Yugoslav frontier and were frozen in for three months. The British agreed to release certificates for 200 children on board and they found their way overland to Palestine. The corpses of the 1,000 adults who remained were discovered by the Serbian government after the war, fully dressed, their passports in their pockets. The Germans had caught up with them.

The most heartening tale, because it ended happily, was that of the Teheran children. Their saga began in the Russian-occupied part of Poland shortly after the fall of Warsaw. Hundreds of thousands of Poles, among them thousands of Jews, were deported to Siberia. There they worked in the forests and in labor camps. But when work became scarce, they began to move south toward warmer climes. They spent long days and nights traveling and trudging from village to village. Always their preoccupation was to find food. So scarce were provisions that they took to eating grass, dogs and fruit pits. Thousands died of malnutrition on the back roads of Russia. They trekked onward into the Asiatic republics and many found shelter in or near the kolkhozes. Nearly 1,000 children, either orphaned or separated from their parents, were among the ragged contingent of Poles (Christians and Jews, adults and children, civilians and army detachments) who struggled into Teheran in late summer, 1942. Henrietta Szold won permits for them and the Jewish Agency negotiated to have the children sent to Palestine through Iraq, but Baghdad refused. Neutral Turkey likewise denied the children passage.

Zionist leaders were incensed, particularly since Iraq was then receiving Allied aid. At that point Hadassah entered the picture in Washington. Denise Tourover had been keeping abreast of developments through her contacts in the State Department. This is her story:

> We called on the Turkish Ambassador but made no progress. We called on companies that had major oil interests in Iraq. That too failed and I was really incensed that a two-by-four government which was getting lend-lease from us should set its will against a humanitarian effort such as this. I went to the White House. The meeting there was arranged through Mrs. Henry Morgenthau [wife of the Secretary of the

Treasury]. A few days later the White House said that
nothing could move the Iraqis.

Together with Tamar de Sola Pool and Youth Aliyah Chairman Gisela
Warburg, Denise then called on Lord Halifax at the British embassy. It was
December 1942. The ambassador told them, "I am most sad that at this
time of the year when the world is about to celebrate the birth of Jesus that
I have not been able to do something on behalf of Jewish children. But I
will make one last effort."

A few days later Denise heard from British War Ministry chief John
McClay in Washington that, after having waited five months, the children
were to be shipped out within a short time. On January 2 1943, the first
group of 600 with 60 guardians left their special camp in Teheran, where
many had been waiting ten months, for the Iranian port of Ahwaz. They
sailed to Karachi, then to Bombay and after that across the seas to Port Said.
On the way, hostile planes scouted their vessel, but did not attack. At Port
Said they entrained for Palestine and arrived at Atlit on February 18 – a
voyage of nearly seven weeks. For Henrietta, who was there to meet them,
their safe arrival was one of her most ecstatic moments. The *yishuv* was
joyously delirious, for refugees had not been arriving in large numbers and
here at last was a large treasury of Jewish children snatched from sure
death. Wherever the train stopped on its way to Atlit, it was mobbed by
persons seeking their own children or relatives. They threw flowers and
pushed food and drink through the windows. The bewildered children
looked down wide-eyed, silent, from the windows, waving little white and
blue flags that they had been given in Port Said. At the clearance station in
Atlit one of the women guardians on the train fainted. In the crowd she had
recognized her husband, an officer in the Polish army who had been
transferred from Russia to the Middle East. And as fate would have it, one
woman among the greeters found her own child on the train – dazed and
sobbing.

"They nearly tore us apart when we landed," recalls one of the children, Yaacov Orr, who later fought Egyptians on the southern front in Israel's War of Independence. Orr was 13 when he arrived clutching the hands of his 11-year-old brother Ron and baby sister Leah. "Everyone fought over us. It was like a war. The *yishuv* thirsted for immigrants. Wherever we went we were showered with gifts. If we took in a movie and said we were from Teheran they refused to take money. If we went to a kiosk to buy a drink it was free. We came from Teheran."

Thus, the story ended happily. None was more elated than Denise Tourover, whose only gripe was that after the children arrived, she received a bill of $57.46 from the State Department for cables made on Hadassah's behalf. It was paid.

About a year after the first group of Teheran children arrived, rumors began reaching Palestine that Jews were walking out of the desert from remote sections of the Arabian peninsula and appearing in the British Crown Colony of Aden at the confluence of the Red and Arabian seas. The Joint Distribution Committee sent an old hand, Harry Viteles, off to Aden. He reported back that about 1,200 people were lying in the streets, in courtyards and in synagogues waiting for the fulfillment of the prophecy that they would be returned to the Promised Land. Medical help was urgently needed. Immediately Hadassah's malaria expert, Israel Kligler, was sent to do control work. In April 1944, German-born David Ullmann, the MD who worked in a Haifa paint factory before joining Hadassah, was sent to Aden by the Joint Distribution Committee. With nurses Zipporah Friedman, Yehudit Kepara and Rahel Mashat, he spent six months caring for the refugees.

Professor Ullmann's account:

> Many of the Yemenite Jews who found their way by donkey and by foot to Aden were puzzled that they needed a permit to enter Eretz Israel which they had not seen for the last 2,500 years. They came in groups of 15 and 20; it took them

weeks, even months to reach Aden. They knew Biblical Hebrew from their religious training and nurses started modern language instruction in the camp that was set up for them. They had many medical problems – relapsing fever, malaria, dysentery, diseases caused by the intense heat. I was their only doctor and they called me King David. I had brought along a microscope – an unheard of instrument there – and diagnosed relapsing fever. Before that, all fevers were said to be malaria.

Among them were Jews from Habban in southern Arabia, one of the most remote places in the world. These Jews (a desert people) lived completely isolated; compared to them the Yemenites were a highly sophisticated people. The men arrived in white flowing gowns, long beards and distinctive headgear. The women wore nets on their hair with jewelry around their heads and wide silver belts around their waists.

Within six months they were put on ships by the Aden administration and taken to Port Said where they went by rail to the Promised Land.

In February 1945, the war was drawing to its close. In a few weeks the newly organized Jewish Brigade of several thousand men fighting under their own flag would be moved to the front in northern Italy. The brigade would taste only five weeks of battle before V-E Day and would have no serious effect on the course of the war. But by war's end, 19,207 Palestinian Jews, including 2,000 women, would have fought with the British forces, and 3,000 with other Allied units. In Palestine itself, 7,300 served in police units. By the time the Axis collapsed, 30,000 men and women were in uniform, some of them hardened soldiers and all of them with good basic training. They made a fine cadre for more difficult battles to come.

In that same month of February, the British halted the five-year internment of Jewish refugees on the Indian Ocean island of Mauritius. They originally numbered 1,520. In July 1945, a Hadassah medical unit was permitted to go to the island to care for them since their return to Palestine was imminent. The Hadassah team shipped back with the refugees and at the end of August 1,320 landed in Haifa. While on the island, 128 had died, 268 joined the armed forces, and about 60 children were born.

February was also a sad month for Hadassah despite approaching victory. The organization was bigger, stronger and more energetic than ever and ready to face a new world of challenges. But in a way Hadassah was now orphaned, for on February 13, 1945, her frail heart no longer able to keep pace with her breathless energies, death came in the Mt. Scopus medical center to Henrietta Szold. She was 84.

In her last years Henrietta was grieved that children on arrival were put into detention camps along with adults. As a gift to her, Hadassah had decided to build a $400,000 reception and screening center that would serve Youth Aliyah exclusively. She did not live to see it, although she attended its dedication in 1944. On February 10, 1949, Ramat Hadassah Szold was opened amid the oak forests in the Hills of Ephraim behind Haifa, not far from Alonim, the first kibbutz to be founded by Youth Aliyah graduates. It was a site that Henrietta herself had chosen. Ramat Hadassah Szold, its title bearing two names that would live inseparably in the annals of Youth Aliyah, was perhaps the finest tribute she could have. But inevitably there would be others. Hadassah established the Henrietta Szold Award for Humanitarian Service and conferred the first on Eleanor Roosevelt. The nursing school was named for Henrietta, as was the scenic road that leads to the Ein Karem medical center which would be dedicated on August 3, 1960. So were a social research institute, a forest, a publishing house, a kibbutz, a Tel Aviv taxi company. Henrietta was buried on the Mount of Olives opposite the Old City. Later, the Jordanians obliterated the grave and its precise position was lost. But nothing could erase her spirit.

SIEGE!

Hitler was dead. So were most of Europe's Jews. Stateless and penniless, 400,000 survivors wandered the face of the continent and finally moved into displaced persons camps while political leaders disputed their fate. Hitler's Holocaust had reaped a dreadful harvest. But it had also begun to generate a terrific creative force among the remnant.

In 1945, Zionists faced a new set of world leaders and a new balance in the power struggle. Britain was shedding its empire; France and Italy, struggling for internal stability, fell to the second echelon in the world order; Germany was prostrate; the United States and the U.S.S.R. now called the turns. In Britain, Clement Attlee succeeded Winston Churchill as Prime Minister. Campaigning vigorously, Attlee recklessly promised all things to all peoples. To Jews, his party pledged not only a national home but even an unrealistic exchange of Arab and Jewish populations. In Washington, Harry Truman was President and his Congress was strongly pro-Zionist even though his administration was not.

At the end of July, an exuberant but untutored Truman flew to Potsdam, outside Berlin, for a summit conference. Genuinely concerned over the fate of European Jews, Truman asked Attlee and his boorish foreign secretary, Ernest Bevin, to permit the Nazis' victims to move to Palestine. By making the request, Truman unknowingly drew America, for the first time, into the Palestine question. When Attlee asked him to help Britain by providing troops for Palestine so that Jewish immigration could be facilitated without bloodshed, Truman refused.

On August 1, the day the Potsdam Conference closed, Zionists from around the world gathered in London. The scene could best be described as pathetic. Weizmann's fears of August 1939 had come true. The once great Jewish community of Poland could send only eight delegates, four of them partisan fighters. German Jewry had only the gaunt, noble figure of Rabbi Leo Baeck, a concentration camp survivor. "To be a Jew," he told a stunned conference, "means to be prepared for tragedy. Our people were the objects of a brutally-minded gang which developed cruelty into a system, ferocity into a science and bestiality into a philosophy. The question now is, what is to be done?"

Hadassah had four delegates in London. Two – President Judith Epstein and National Political Chairman Rose Halprin – would lead Hadassah on Zionism's political march in the three bitter years to come. From London, Rose reported, "We did not acclaim the victory of the Labor Party as a Zionist victory... but still everyone looked forward to an improvement over the Churchill administration which allowed the White Paper to strangle Jewish development."

In the debate, Weizmann and Ben-Gurion disagreed over how to deal with the British. Impulsively, Ben-Gurion sped off to the Colonial Office and there, mincing no words, demanded 100,000 immigration permits and a Jewish state forthwith. Aghast, the neophyte colonial secretary spluttered that it was too much to expect the Labour Party to change Palestine policy after being in power only two weeks. In Washington, President Truman received a report that most of the Jews in the displaced persons (DP) camps desired no other home than Palestine and he pressed openly for the acceptance of 100,000 by the Palestine Mandate government. In Britain, the ruling Labour Party split over the next step. One faction, led by Harold Laski, insisted that the pre-election pledges be honored. But the majority, led by Attlee and Bevin, feared an Arab uprising at a time Britain was trying to sign a treaty with Egypt. The Americans, too, were split. While the White House and Congress were four-square behind the Zionists, the State Department and the military pulled in the opposite direction.

In Europe, meanwhile, the Mossad was reactivating its agents to get the stateless Jews out of the camps by hook or by crook, legally or illegally, and on their way to Palestine. So chaotic was the picture at this time that a surreptitious organization like Mossad could work at maximum efficiency. "Aliyah Bet," a shortened form of the full name of the Mossad, became a rallying cry that stirred the *yishuv*. After the State was established, when immigration was unrestricted, the Mossad served as an intelligence agency, respected by Israel's allies and feared by its enemies.

In Palestine, both Jewish and Arab leaders knew that the British could not hold on for long. Forces in both camps organized for an underground struggle. As pressures grew for and against mass immigration from Europe, the united Jewish underground struck a first blow. In one coordinated operation the partisans freed two hundred Aliyah Bet immigrants from detention, wrecked railroad lines, damaged the British-run Haifa oil refinery and hit British naval craft. The struggle for Palestine was now joined.

Anxiously, Foreign Secretary Bevin asked America to help him out of a tight spot by undertaking a joint probe of the immigration problem. Washington agreed to participate in a 12-member Anglo-American commission. Overjoyed by his success, Ernest Bevin committed himself to accept the body's findings. The members visited the European refugee camps, Palestine, the Arab countries and Washington. On January 8, 1946, Hadassah President Judith Epstein appeared before the commission. She represented 200,000 American women now, but she spoke for all Zionists when she said, "The burning need of solving the Jewish problem, of creating a home where those Jews who needed or wanted to rebuild their lives in a Jewish land be given that opportunity, was what moved this large army of Jewish women in America to dedicate their lives to this cause."

After four months of travel and toil, the commission reported in April 1946 that a bi-national state was to be preferred to partition, that 100,000 immigration certificates be issued to Jews immediately, restrictions on land sales to Jews be dropped and the Mandate continued. A happy Truman applauded the immigration recommendation but a flabbergasted Ernest Bevin cried foul. He told Parliament that he would never agree to 100,000 Jews going to Palestine. Now, the magic figure of 100,000 became a *cause célèbre* in the world press.

A series of events then shook Palestine and turned the country into an armed camp. On a moonless night in mid-June 1946, the Haganah blew up eleven bridges, all of them connecting Palestine and the neighboring Arab countries. This was the *yishuv's* reply to Prime Minister Attlee for saying that he, like Bevin, could not go along with the 100,000 immigrants until all the underground forces disbanded. On "Black Saturday," June 24, the British over-reacted. They rounded up the top Jewish Agency and Haganah leaders in Palestine including "Foreign Minister" Moshe Shertok (later, Sharett) and 2,800 young Jews and sent them all to detention camps. Ben-Gurion was then in Paris and for the rest of the year ran the *yishuv's* affairs from the French capital.

Two weeks later, the Irgun after a forewarning blew up the southern wing of Jerusalem's King David Hotel, headquarters of the British army. More than 90 Englishmen, Jews and Arabs died in the blast. The commanding officer in Palestine, General Evelyn Barker, ordered a policy of "non-fraternization" with the Jews and made the unhappy statement that he would punish the Jews "in a way that race dislikes – by striking at their pockets." Barker was subsequently transferred. The *yishuv* now knew that it was fighting not only anti-Zionism in the British administration but the much deadlier poison of anti-Semitism as well.

Despite British opposition, immigrants were pouring on to the shores of Palestine from Mossad ships. Most were caught and sent to the Atlit detention camp south of Haifa but some made it safely inland and "lost" themselves with fake papers in the kibbutzim. In July 1946, to make it a bit easier for the ships to land, a Haganah commando platoon led by a young Yugoslav Jew named Haim Bar-Lev (later to be Israeli chief of staff) blew up a British radar station that was tracking the ships. The ships began coming with such frequency that on August 12, the British announced Operation Igloo; henceforth immigrants arriving without permits would no longer be sent to Atlit but deported to detention camps on the island of Cyprus from where they would be released at the rate of 1,500 monthly. That same day a ship with 543 on board arrived from a Greek port. It was the *Henrietta Szold*, one of 63 ships to be bought clandestinely for Aliyah Bet with funds quietly collected in the United States. The *Henrietta Szold's* passengers were the first to be sent to Cyprus. Nearly 40,000 more followed until the end of the Mandate.

Only ten days before the *Henrietta Szold* arrived, the Jewish Agency put Hadassah in charge of immigrants' health. At that time 2,500 were cooped up in Atlit. Within 24 hours, Yassky had a 60-bed emergency hospital staffed round the clock by a doctor and five nurses. After an inspection trip to immigrant ships in Haifa, Yassky angrily reported, "Beasts are not kept under such conditions."

The Jewish Agency was banned in Cyprus, so Jewish teams went in under the aegis of the American Joint Distribution Committee. To organize the welfare work, the JDC sent American-born Rose Viteles, a member of the Hadassah Council in Palestine who, unknown to most, was one of the early organizers of the Haganah in Jerusalem. Rose was soon followed by units of Hadassah physicians and nurses. Tamar de Sola Pool arranged for an entire educational foundation for children, including teachers and texts, to be moved from the Abraham Ruttenberg Foundation in Haifa to the camps. The last Hadassah team returned with the last immigrant on February 16, 1949, nine months after the birth of the state.

As more ships challenged the British navy and underground pressure increased to lower the gates, the British committed more troops to Palestine. Eventually they would number 100,000. But Bevin knew force could not settle anything and out of despair he called for a conference of

Jews and Arabs in London in September 1946. Neither Palestinian Arabs nor Jews would attend, so the British met with delegates of the newly-formed Arab League, a loose union of Arab nations formed with British encouragement. The Zionists stayed away because the British refused to put on the agenda a new plan drawn up by Ben-Gurion. The plan was visionary, for it suggested the partition of Palestine along lines that were almost identical with the map which would be drawn in 1949 following the War of Independence. The British recessed the conference after two months of getting nowhere, but Bevin carried on discussions with the two sides nonetheless. Just as he thought he was making some headway, President Truman took the wind out of Bevin's sails by announcing full support of the Ben-Gurion partition plan.

November 1946. Bevin tried for his second wind by releasing the imprisoned Jewish leaders and the 2,800 youths. In return, the Haganah severed its ties with the more extreme Irgun and Sternists. On December 9, the Zionist Congress returned to Basel for its first post-war meeting. It was to be known as the "Confused Congress," for the leadership was divided on how to move forward to independence. At Hadassah's 32nd national convention in Boston, held prior to the Zionist Congress, Ben-Gurion railed at the British and demanded an autonomous Jewish state. He continued his attacks at the Congress. But no one was clear on what to do next or how to do it. Should Zionists encourage a regime of terror to get the British out? The great-maned, booming-voiced orator from Cleveland, Rabbi Abba Hillel Silver, who was to lead Zionism's battles in the United States as the head of the American section of the Zionist Executive, encouraged revolt. The aging Weizmann stuck to the guns of moderation. The Congress had before it the British Morrison-Grady plan to divide Palestine into four cantons and Bevin's call for another Jewish-Arab conference to meet in London in January 1947. The Congress rejected both. The Morrison-Grady plan would have given the Jews only 17 percent of the country. The Congress called for the establishment of a Jewish commonwealth and unlimited immigration, renounced terror as a political weapon and rejected Bevin's suggestion for a five-year trusteeship. Hadassah had its own private triumph at the Congress. Its "foreign minister," Rose Halprin, was elected to the Jewish Agency Executive's American section, later became its chairman and for much of the next quarter of a century she would be its sole female representative.

Zionism may have been perplexed about what route to take but it was not confused about where it was going, nor was it hesitant to look to bolder captains to get it there. A depressed Weizmann resigned as President of the World Zionist Organization when the Congress rejected Bevin's proposal for the London conference. As a sign of respect the post of president was left vacant, and by default, leadership of the Zionist Organization fell to the aggressive David Ben-Gurion. Out of office, a man divested of position and a future, Chaim Weizmann would 16 months hence play a fateful role in the birth of the Jewish State. History would then reward him with the task of appealing at the 11th hour to the President of the United States for vital American support.

On February 15, 1947, seeing no possibility for a peaceful settlement, Bevin announced Britain's intention to give up the Palestine Mandate. In consequence, the United Nations Assembly met in special session on May 9 and set up an 11-nation special committee on Palestine (UNSCOP). The Arabs announced their refusal to cooperate with the committee. The British Foreign Ministry showed no interest, expecting that after UNSCOP's failure the General Assembly would call upon Britain to return to make order out of chaos. Both the United States and the Jewish Agency held high hopes for the committee and both backed it fully.

UNSCOP began its work in June 1947, as terrorism and British counter-terrorism reached heights of insanity. The British made one *faux pas* after another. While UNSCOP was in Palestine, Bevin committed the worst blunder when he ordered 4,554 refugees in the Aliyah Bet ship *Exodus* to return to Germany. That single act brought widespread sympathy for the Zionist cause, for it dramatized the homelessness of the victims of Nazism and the empty-headedness of British policy.

As UNSCOP met in Jerusalem, it heard much the same testimony as presented to the commissions that preceded it. The Hadassah Council in Palestine presented a memo on behalf of 218,000 members in 47 of the 48 U.S. states (only Idaho was not represented among the hundreds of chapters). Hadassah's Zionist effort, said the memo, had transferred $25,000,000 to Palestine since 1921. In that time infant mortality had been reduced dramatically, trachoma was no longer epidemic and all-in-all "Palestine is the most healthful area in the Middle East." The memo ended, "The Jewish women represented by Hadassah will continue their unremitting efforts to help re-create Palestine, the Jewish National Home, as a democratic Jewish Commonwealth." UNSCOP visited Scopus on June 27 and heard Dr. Yassky say, "Everyone is welcome here."

Back in New York on September 1, UNSCOP voted seven to three, with one abstention, for partition. Its plan was much less than that suggested to the British by Ben-Gurion, but it was by far the best ever offered the Jews. The UNSCOP map cut the country into six interlocking segments – three Arab and three Jewish – and made Jerusalem an international city.

In Zurich, the Zionist General Council, meeting in place of a Congress, accepted the plan. The Arabs announced they would go to war to kill the plan. The British said they would leave Palestine so the two sides could fight over the map. As it turned out, UNSCOP not only created two states but unintentionally drew borders that were battle lines for the inevitable war.

For the next two months the U.N. was a labyrinth of confusion. The battle to win sufficient votes in the General Assembly of the United Nations was fought by Jews on all continents. Jewish Agency representatives used every stratagem, every contact, every argument to get the necessary two-thirds majority. In the United States, the head of the Jewish Agency delegation, Moshe Shertok, had the help of a vast array of volunteers. Booming out over all else was the voice of Abba Hillel Silver. Working in every single state to turn public opinion were nearly 250,000 Hadassah members. "We had something no one else had – grass roots,"

President Judith Epstein said. "We were everywhere. I remember one period when I had a midnight call from the Hadassah president of Philadelphia. 'We are still in the office,' she said. 'What can we do? We don't want to go home if there is something we can do.' They had written personal letters to every member of Congress, phoned, sent telegrams and still they wanted to know what they could do!"

As if to anticipate the historic events that were now about to occur, Hadassah, meeting at its 33rd convention in Atlantic City in late October 1947, adopted a record budget – $4,070,000. Speaking to the convention, Guatemala's UNSCOP delegate Dr. Jorge Garcia-Granados, compared the opposing positions: "There is a fundamental reason why the Jewish case is stronger than the Arab case. It is not a question of nationalism fighting for a land or a territory. It is a question of giving thousands of human beings hope and a reason for living.... The human case is unanswerable."

Retiring President Epstein turned her office over to veteran political fighter Rose Halprin with a simple equation of Hadassah philosophy: "From the very beginning of Hadassah – whether it was the establishment of a playground or the introduction of new hospital methods – we have always had before us the compulsion of a great idea – The Jewish State."

One month later, on Saturday, November 29, 1947, the U.N. General Assembly firmly implanted the seeds of a Jewish state in Palestine by passing the partition resolution, 33 to 13, five more votes than the required two-thirds. Ten states abstained. The news hit Palestine late at night. Unrestrained joy splashed over the *yishuv* and over Jews everywhere. The Arabs called for a day of mourning and the Mufti, appearing on the scene like an evil genie, called a three-day strike.

After the rejoicing over the U.N. decision, individual survival became a matter of fortitude, luck and ingenuity. One Hadassah board member who saw the radical change on partition night was Palestine Committee Chairman Bertha Schoolman, who arrived only a week earlier to help plan a program for educating and settling 6,000 Youth Aliyah children about to be freed from the Cyprus camps. She wrote:

I went down the street from my hotel to the Jewish Agency building. There were thousands in the streets – the old, the young, even British Tommies. They were in a joyous mood. Laughing British soldiers drove Jewish boys and girls in their vehicles; they thought everything was over now and they would be going home. At 2:00 a.m. Golda Meir, the highest ranking Agency member in Jerusalem – Ben-Gurion was resting at the Dead Sea – came out of the building and spoke to the crowds about the possibility of peace with the Arabs.

On Mt. Scopus, life had been a pleasant routine until November 29. Rumanian-born pathologist Alexander Laufer, who had joined Hadassah as a volunteer in 1941, recalled how it was in the bachelor quarters:

We had a cozy, warm atmosphere. We became a closely-knit group. Our social life was limited, our contacts being primarily with the nurses or nursing students. Our lifeline to the city was Hamekasher's Number 9 bus which made its last trip up to Scopus at midnight. We had walks to the university buildings or strolled to the nearby Arab village where we drank coffee at the El Tur cafe. The Arab bus drivers knew us and would often stop to give us a lift. Then the tension began...

On November 30 a reign of terror erupted. An ambulance on the way to Scopus was fired on at Nashashibi Bend in the Sheikh Jarrah Quarter. Located between the Jewish part of the city and Scopus, a half-mile narrow roadway that wound through this Arab Quarter was to be the scene of high tragedy and to paralyze Scopus as a regional center of healing and education for two decades. The Nashashibi house, a colonnaded manor dwelling of a wealthy Arab family, was to serve as a focal point from which continual attacks were launched on traffic. Several hundred yards farther on, at an L-curve that led down into a valley at the bottom of Scopus, was another manor house set back from the road in a lovely garden that belonged to the Mufti. Rented by the well-known Arab nationalists George and Kate Antonius, the dwelling was known as the Antonius House and would be another key point for the tragedy to come.

Arab rioting, under the Mufti's orders, broke out elsewhere on that last day in November. Two buses were gunned down near Lydda Airport; one of the six killed was Hadassah pathologist Nehama Zelutovsky. That night Arabs began shooting at buses on Route 9 to Scopus. On the first day of the Arab general strike, frenzied young Arabs stormed out of Jerusalem's Jaffa Gate, targeted their attacks on workshops in the New Commercial Center where they looted, burned, stabbed and stoned, and then headed for the center of the city. British troops did not interfere until the mobs approached downtown. There, Haganah men stood ready to make their first open stand, but the British arrested 16 and only then moved to stop the mob. Major attacks were launched against Jewish neighborhoods and against isolated settlements in all sections of the country. A torch having struck tinder, the Jewish leadership ordered "a census" of all 17- to 25-year-olds for "public service." Eventually, men up to age 55 would be mobilized.

For the first five months of the war in Jerusalem, Scopus would remain open but would increasingly assume the role of a military hospital. Dr. Laufer recalled:

> It was distressing for us to see the wounded Haganah men being brought into hospital from the surrounding Jewish settlements of Atarot and Neve Ya'acov where they had been caught by the Arabs. I remember one day we had to watch from Scopus behind the hills as smoke came from one of the Haganah cars that had accompanied the bus on its routine trip to Scopus. A British officer came later with the bodies which had been mutilated.

Hadassah's local governing bodies – the Council in Palestine and the Medical Organization Board – met almost daily for the remainder of the crisis. Director Yassky was abroad from November until February to attend the national convention and to help plan Palestine's first medical school. That left the direction of Hadassah hospital activities to British-born Deputy Medical Director Eli Davis and Deputy Administrator Mendel Krupnik. Acting for the National Board, the Council in Palestine was chaired by Hebrew University Chancellor Magnes and in mid-1948 by Ethel Agronsky (Agron). Bertha Schoolman's presence in Jerusalem gave the Board an extra representative.

As fighting became certain, the legislature of the *yishuv* – the Va'ad Leumi – immediately urged Hadassah to prepare for the worst and appointed a national medical board on which Eli Davis was a representative.

Uppermost in the minds of the Hadassah people was the security of the road to Scopus. Within the week following the partition vote, Davis reported that all departments in the Medical Center had augmented emergency services. Although the Hadassah station wagon had a military escort through Sheikh Jarrah, only essential journeys were being made. On matters concerning Scopus, the University, represented by Administrator David Werner Senator, and Hadassah acted in unison. On December 8, Senator and Davis asked the police to station more guards at the hospital and to provide Hadassah's staff with arms. The request for more security was made the day after a bus, jammed with Scopus-bound workers, narrowly missed destruction when a grenade crashed through one window and went out another to explode on the ground. But 20 bullets hit the bus, wounding two doctors. Bus Number 9 windows were thenceforth screened with steel netting. One hundred staff members bedded down at Scopus rather than risk the ride. Patients went elsewhere for treatment. Despite the increase in war casualties, the number of admissions on Scopus declined in December. Davis judiciously set up an independent operating theater at Hadassah's downtown clinic.

Constant attacks indicated that the Arabs were intent on neutralizing Scopus to make an assault on Jewish Jerusalem that much easier. Before the year ended five doctors miraculously escaped injury when their car was set afire on the Scopus road. But 15 staff members were wounded in an attack on a bus and for the first time, on December 30, the magnificent foyer of the Medical Center was turned into a clearing station and shock treatment room. In one act of Arab terror, Szold Nursing School Professor Hugo Lehrs was murdered by three Arab gunmen at Jerusalem's Hospital for Contagious Diseases while walking in the compound with an Arab doctor and nurse. The Arabs asked them, "Which of you is a Jew?" and when the Arab doctor and nurse stepped aside, Lehrs was slain.

The year ended with another tragedy for Hadassah. On Friday, December 26, Bertha Schoolman and Youth Aliyah director Hans Beyth were returning to Jerusalem from the coast where they observed the arrival of children from camps in Cyprus. The long battle for control of a four-mile stretch of the road from Tel Aviv to Jerusalem was underway. As their convoy headed up the steep Judean Hills, past hostile Arab villages, the buses absorbed heavy Arab fire from the crests of the mountains on either side of the serpentine, two-lane highway.

Bertha was riding in a car with Golda Meir and two members of the Jewish Agency. She recalled: "Yitzhak Gruenbaum, one of the Agency men, had a small pistol and he kept shooting back through the window as we drove. Fifteen minutes from Jerusalem the bus ahead of us was hit. Hans was in the bus. He, too, had a gun and shot back. He was a good target when he stood and he was killed." From then on, Bertha shared the management of Youth Aliyah with Moshe Kol, who later joined the Israeli cabinet.

January 1948 began badly. Prospects for a military victory were dim. Arabs in Palestine outnumbered Jews 1,250,000 to 650,000. Arab armies had a two to one advantage (115,000 to 50,000). Although the Jews had a well-trained core of 20,000 who had fought in World War II, they had only one gun for every four men, no air force and no navy to speak of. The Arabs on the other hand, had planes, ships, tanks and heavy artillery.

They also had defense treaties with Britain and British officers serving in Abdullah's Arab Legion. The United States clamped an arms embargo on the Middle East in December; in January Britain announced it would supply arms to Egypt, Iraq and Jordan. Secretly, Ben-Gurion sent agents to Prague to buy weapons, but Arab agents were there doing the same and before the arms arrived the fighting could well be finished. The Zionists could not have been in a grimmer position. Their scattered forces were surrounded on three sides by hostile Arab nations and in the west by an unconcerned sea. Triumph would emerge out of tragedy nevertheless, but at a tremendous price in casualties: 10 percent of the entire Jewish population.

Aware of the looming struggle, Hadassah called an extraordinary meeting of the full National Board on January 4 in New York. Yassky informed the members that all 105 Hadassah doctors in Palestine were at the service of the *yishuv* and in fact 30 had donned uniform.

In response to the *yishuv*'s request that Hadassah coordinate all medical services for the emergency, the Board voted extra allocations including an immediate grant of $100,000 to help develop the central military hospital at Tel Litwinsky, near Tel Aviv. In so doing, Hadassah became a founder of the Israel Army Medical Corps. By the end of 1948 the extra disbursements would reach nearly $1,000,000.

The first heavy attack against a Jewish settlement outside the Jerusalem area was launched against Kfar Szold, a new kibbutz only 200 yards from the Syrian frontier. Nine hundred Arabs rushed the tiny outpost, but British armor drove off the attackers. Isolated settlements everywhere were pounded.

Battle-hardened by war, riot and plague, Hadassah was on the outlying front lines in two urban areas where the *yishuv* was most vulnerable – in Safed and in Jerusalem. In the mountain-top town of Safed, center of Jewish mystics for centuries, Hadassah's tuberculosis hospital lay between the Jewish and Arab quarters. Most of the TB patients were sent home as fighting began and the hospital, the only one in town, was used for casualties. Safed was a key to upper Galilee and the vital waters of the Jordan River. Arabs outnumbered Jews ten to one. As in Jerusalem, the Arabs began a war of attrition, blowing up houses, firing on traffic, encircling the Jewish area. The British left in April and turned over the main forts of the city to the Arabs. Before they left, an officer warned Hadassah's chief nurse, Russian-born, Pittsburgh-trained Nellie Helfand, a Safed veteran of 11 years, to run away. Nellie replied, "What would you think of a matron in London if she were advised to evacuate under similar circumstances and did so?"

The officer reddened and whispered, "My apologies."

Bitter fighting by the Palmach finally captured Safed on May 11. The hospital cared for 250 casualties.

In January, in the Jerusalem area, the war was rapidly moving in favor of the Arabs. Near Hebron, south of the capital, the four kibbutzim of the Kfar Etzion Bloc were under pressure from 1,000 Arabs. A rescue platoon of 35 men set out afoot to help the defenders but was massacred on the way. One of the 35 was an American volunteer, Moshe Pearlstein, son of Ella, a prominent Hadassah member in the Borough Park section of Brooklyn. The Kfar Etzion fighters held out until mid-May and by so doing relieved the pressure on Jerusalem.

In Jerusalem itself, the Arabs doggedly tried to stop the flow of traffic to Scopus. Davis reported to Yassky early in January that the staff no longer had confidence in British assurances of security. While Davis was writing a report to Yassky, he had to stop to read an urgent communication. Then he went back to writing: "We have just been informed... that a car with bullet-proof sides, with 25 of our personnel, an ambulance and a police escort going to Hadassah were attacked near St. George's Road. A bomb was thrown. Shots were fired and a bullet pierced the roof. A student nurse, class of '48, Hannah Gardi, was killed."

Hannah's death was followed by a three-hour battle between the Arabs and the Haganah during which all eight phone lines to the hospital went dead. Morale on Scopus plummeted. After prolonged pleading by Davis and

Magnes, the British finally replaced the police with army units on the road. Spirits rose, but not for long.

Rationing went into effect at the Medical Center. Nurses pitched in to carry out menial tasks because of the larger number of persons remaining on the hill. As the starkness of the situation became evident, Magnes brought up the possibility, for the first time, of moving off Scopus to downtown Jerusalem. The faint-hearted had begun whispering that it might be best to abandon Scopus. But the hospital's management committee at the time firmly decided to stand fast "even though absolute security is no longer possible." They anticipated Jewish Agency Chairman David Ben-Gurion who, one month later, appointed David Shaltiel as commander of Jerusalem and gave him orders not to surrender one inch of ground anywhere in Jerusalem. The possibility that the Arabs would launch a frontal attack to capture Scopus was real. With more than 700 persons, mostly civilians, on the hill, the decision to stay put was not a light one to take. But there is no doubt that it was the right one since it was instrumental in helping save most of Jerusalem for Israel. Wrote Davis to Hadassah Medical Organization Chairman Etta Rosensohn on January 20:

> The most important fact of all is that the hospital remains open, is carrying on much as usual... Were Mt. Scopus cut off, the Arabs would have a very much smaller Jewish area to besiege and against which to deploy their forces.

The role of the British in the quickly deteriorating situation in Jerusalem was ambiguous. Some were strongly pro-Arab, others – probably a minority – were pro-Jewish. The bureaucracy continued to function for the most part as though the crisis facing it was of no matter. Nothing was done to prepare an orderly transfer of government. The Mandate administration was interested only in safeguarding British interests until evacuation.

The British stoutly turned down pleas from the Hebrew University to remove an Arab Legion camp stationed a few hundred yards from the Medical Center or even to install a "hot line" to the camp from the

University. Even less comprehensible was the British refusal to permit the Jews to build a short $88,000 ring road – at Hadassah's expense – that would bypass the Sheikh Jarrah Quarter and Nashashibi Bend.

By the end of January the war in Jerusalem accounted for 300 Jewish casualties. Nearly all were treated at Hadassah. On the night of February 1, Hadassah itself became a casualty. Early in the day Eli Davis escorted a Red Cross delegation through the clinic in Hasolel Street (now Hahavatzelet) and through the Scopus hospital. They parted in high spirits; the delegation complimented Davis on the high level of excellence he had achieved under battle conditions. At 10:58 that night, a stolen British police truck that was parked outside the offices of *The Palestine Post*, the country's English language daily, exploded with tremendous force and laid waste to the building. The Hadassah clinic across the street was badly damaged as was the entire street. Two British deserters hired by the Mufti and an Arab accomplice were implicated. The explosion rattled windows two miles away. Three persons were killed and 50 were injured.

By February 3, Yassky had returned from America and was again at his post. Upset that his beautiful Medical Center had to be turned into an army base hospital, he recalled in a letter to Etta Rosensohn how British medical personnel had benefited from the hospital during theSecond World War and how British personnel "were now forced by a treacherous policy of their Government to take the road of treason." However, he added, "Mt. Scopus should not be abandoned." He gave orders to brick up operating theaters and halls, fortify windows, build blast walls, dig wells for water reservoirs and build storage huts for food stocks. Yassky was preparing for a siege – and none too soon. The Arabs intensified their attacks. No one was spared. They even exploded a mine under a truck escorting a funeral.

The Trojan Horse trick used against *The Palestine Post* was to be used twice more inside Jewish Jerusalem with devastating effect. Shortly after dawn on February 23, the British deserters were back with more Mufti agents. This time they planted three trucks, each loaded with one ton of TNT, in the middle of Ben Yehuda Street, the city's main shopping district.

The resulting detonation smashed the thoroughfare along its entire length, crumbled six-story buildings, killed at least 52 and wounded 123. Hadassah took the 70 most serious cases and while they were being treated, the hospital came under attack. A guard on the hospital roof was killed and a bullet narrowly missed Yassky's head as he worked at his desk.

In the home of *The Palestine Post* editor Gershon Agron,* who 30 years earlier had greeted AZMU in London, a secret Haganah listening post had been set up to monitor British police traffic. Among those on duty on the morning of the Ben Yehuda bombing were two members of Junior Hadassah. One, Betty Schoffman Levin, recorded the conversation between a patrol and headquarters in the wake of the Ben Yehuda bombing. When the officer at the scene asked for instructions, British HQ ordered, "Leave the scene."

On March 11, the World Zionist Organization headquarters in the center of Jerusalem was blown up when a car bomb exploded in the compound. The Arab driver of the U.S. Consulate had parked it there. Among the 13 killed was Leib Jaffe, a founder of Keren Hayesod, the financial arm of the WZO.

Mines on the roads and 25-pound shells causing heavy casualties moved Magnes and Davis to ask the Board in New York to request that the State Department intervene. The University's David Werner Senator addressed a confidential memo to Magnes saying that since the British were unwilling to provide adequate security, the presence of the attackers "makes active Jewish defense unfeasible." Again, the voice of alarm. Magnes turned to the British commander of Jerusalem, Brigadier C.P. Jones, with a new plea for help. Jones replied through a subordinate that nothing could be done about the Sheikh Jarrah Quarter and fatuously suggested that the Arab and Jewish medical associations should work out a deal. By the end of February,

---

* Agron, who had emigrated from the U.S., often hosted top British officials. The British never discovered the monitoring room located next to the luxurious living room where they sat drinking cocktails and discussing politics. Ethel, Agron's wife, was Hadassah Medical Organization chairman in Jerusalem.

Magnes cabled the National Board, "Road impassable." Hadassah replied reassuringly, "Preparing memorandum to present to State Department."

The road connecting Jerusalem with the rest of the country was made hazardous by Arab bands soon after the Partition Resolution was passed. By February the road was virtually closed. Occasionally a convoy from Tel Aviv managed to reach Jerusalem with supplies albeit with heavy casualties. On March 27, a convoy that tried to break through was decimated. With some exceptions the British, who were ostensibly responsible for security, gave the Arabs a free hand while restricting the Haganah.

A four-week truce saved the Jewish population on June 11 when only several days' food and water remained. Had it not been for the truce the 70,000 Jews of Jerusalem would have capitulated. Jerusalem had a longer ratio of casualties then any other place in the country, proportionately five times higher than the casualties suffered by London during the World War II blitz. Casualties were nearly 10 percent of the city's Jewish population.

With its makeshift facilities, Hadassah cared for 2,800 wounded up to May 15, 1948. Most were soldiers. They suffered wounds similar to the battle injuries of World War II: multiple bullet damage to chest and abdomen and ruptured organs. Only because Hadassah was well-equipped with the latest antibiotics, had excellent operating theaters and especially-trained physicians and nurses to staff them around the clock were most of the wounded saved.

In his detailed account of Jerusalem during the War of Independence, "The Faithful City," Military Governor Dov Joseph wrote, "At the center of the whole (health) effort was Hadassah... Hadassah's doctors, nurses and staff workers served Jerusalem with selfless devotion."

Zionist fortunes elsewhere had reached their nadir. At Lake Success, the United Nations grappled unsuccessfully with the Palestine problem. Now that partition was decided upon, the United Nations was at a loss to find a way to ensure its implementation. The State Department, never happy with the resolution, tried to convince the United Nations to retreat on partition.

U.S. delegate Warren Austin declared that the U.N. Charter did not empower the Security Council to enforce the resolution. One month later he suggested that statehood for Jews and Arabs be postponed and replaced by a temporary U.N. trusteeship. In Palestine, the fighting *yishuv* looked with disbelief over its shoulder at America's acrobatics.

Twice the United States would reverse its position on the question of trusteeship.

Fearing a political disaster at the very moment of triumph, Chaim Weizmann rushed to New York on February 4 hoping to see President Truman. But Truman, weary from constant pressure by Zionists, held Weizmann at bay. Then, in what is now a well-told tale, the latter finally got to the White House through the intervention of Truman's gutsy former haberdashery partner, Eddie Jacobson. On March 18, Weizmann, in the greatest performance of his career, convinced Truman of the urgent need for a Jewish state. The crunching argument was humanitarian. Multitudes in Europe were heading for Zion's gate and would go nowhere else, he said. The following day Austin put forth his trusteeship proposal. A double-cross? No, the State Department simply had not informed Truman of the change. The sky fell in on the Zionists. But in retrospect the State Department's action was fortunate, for it apparently sealed, once and for all, Truman's decision to take his own independent course. Spitting fire at the "striped-pants boys," Truman asked an aide how this could have happened after his assurance to Weizmann that he was for partition. The following month, during Passover, Weizmann was told secretly by the White House that Truman would stand by his promise. The elder statesman kept it to himself but advised the *yishuv's* leaders to go on with the planned declaration of the State come what may. Within eleven minutes after the State of Israel was established on May 14, the White House startled Washington and the world by announcing *de facto* recognition. America thus became the first nation to grant status to the Jewish nation.

THE CONVOY

At 2:05 p.m. on March 2, the operator at the Hadassah exchange in Jerusalem heard an Arab voice warn that the hospital would be blown up within 90 minutes. The warning was not carried out but it was a clear giveaway of Arab intentions. Two days later, Hadassah President Rose Halprin and Denise Tourover called on the State Department and the British embassy in Washington to secure Scopus, then followed up with strong protests to U.N. Secretary-General Trygve Lie and the International Red Cross. Shortly afterward, the commander of Palestine Arab forces, Abdul Kader Husseini, spoke on-the-record to correspondents: "Since Jews have been attacking us and blowing up our houses containing women and children from bases in Hadassah Hospital and Hebrew University, I have given orders to occupy or even demolish them." Showing he meant business he placed a cannon on the roof of the Rockefeller Museum of Archaeology opposite Mt. Scopus and began using armor-piercing ammunition and electrically-detonated mines against Scopus traffic. Surgeon Edward Joseph penned a note to Yassky that he could no longer take the responsibility of transferring cases to Scopus. Yassky replied sharply: "The time has not yet come to evacuate Mt. Scopus... There is no security anywhere."

But reality won out. Yassky carried on negotiations quietly for the use of the Anglican Mission Hospice a few blocks away from the Hasolel Street clinic that Hadassah ran in downtown Jerusalem. On March 15, ten beds were set up for maternity cases and the site became known as Hadassah "A." History had played another of its pranks. One hundred years earlier Jews in Jerusalem were running away from mission hospitals; now they were running back into them.

By mid-March, the Hadassah Emergency Committee resolved that supplies would no longer be concentrated on Scopus but would be dispersed in the center of town. A meeting held at the home of Myriam Granott, later chairman of the Hadassah Council in Israel, considered the possibility, never implemented, of returning to the old Rothschild building where Hadassah's vocational school was located. Magnes noted that the Red Cross had offered to put Scopus under its flag on condition that Hadassah and the University agreed to demilitarize the area. To Hadassah, the Red Cross banner was the white flag of surrender and its leaders persistently refused the proposal.

On March 22, a crucial meeting of the Hadassah Council was held in the living room of Ethel Agron's split-level home in Jerusalem. Topic A was the extent of Hadassah's evacuation of Scopus.

Ethel Agron warned: "There will be complaints against the transfer of casualties to Scopus if Hadassah opens departments in town."

Rose Viteles: "No other road has so far been given up by the *yishuv.* Hadassah cannot be first."

Deputy Administrator Krupnik: "After the British leave, even a partial transfer will be most difficult."

Magnes weakly held out hope that the new trusteeship proposal at Lake Success "might ease the situation."

Yassky asked Bertha Schoolman to take a confidential note to Jewish Agency Treasurer Eliezer Kaplan in Tel Aviv. Unless the Agency did something at once to secure the road to Scopus, the memo said, the hospital would have to cease operations.

Fatigue and stiffer rationing added weight to the arguments to move down from the hill, despite a determination to remain as long as possible. In Jewish Jerusalem the supply situation was so bad that Jews were reduced to scrounging in the fields for a weed called *khubeizeh* to supplement their diets, which now consisted of a few slices of bread, an occasional egg, a handful of noodles, some jam and an orange. On Scopus and in the Hasolel clinic, reported Davis, "Our surgeons have been on the job night and day since the end of November, and not one of them has had a weekend off since then." Dr. Laufer recalled life on Scopus, "In our little time off we listened to the news and the firing of bullets. One of our colleagues would read to us from Sholom Aleichem. All personnel put in their spell of guard duty." Magnes informed British Chief Secretary Sir Henry Gurney, "I am afraid our devoted doctors, nurses and patients are being subjected to a strain too great to bear."

Yassky prepared an evacuation plan. At a joint Hadassah-Hebrew University meeting with Golda Meir, she was told that unless a minimum of three convoys could safely pass daily, the hospital would close. The only alternative was to accept the Red Cross offer. Golda agreed to raise the subject of Scopus at a Zionist Executive meeting in Tel Aviv. Meanwhile, the Zionist General Council, popularly called the Actions Committee, was in session to debate the proclamation of the Jewish state and to authorize the formation of a cabinet and legislature for the new state's functioning. For that historic session, Hadassah had flown in a delegation from New York: President Rose Halprin, Judith Epstein, Tamar de Sola Pool and Rebecca Shulman. Rose asked Yassky to join them in Tel Aviv, but he was too anxious about Scopus's fate to leave. On April 10, Yassky replied:

> Much as I wanted to do it I thought I cannot leave my post for a few days. The situation in Jerusalem is very serious and that of Scopus much more so. I do not exaggerate when I say that 100,000 Jews of Jerusalem depend on Hadassah's functioning somehow, somewhere. I am very pessimistic

about Scopus... It is our duty to prepare emergency arrangements in the city. We will do our best to hang on.

To Bertha Schoolman, who was to leave for the United States on April 12, he reported:

> Transport to Scopus did not improve in spite of all the promises of B.G. [Ben-Gurion] and G.M. [Golda Meir]. At best we have one convoy a day. With the number of casualties in town, one convoy is an absurd situation. I am afraid we will not be able to continue to operate the Hospital very much longer... I hope that we will meet again in not a too distant future.

The hope was not to be. Three days later, Dr. Haim Yassky was dead, shot through the liver in an Arab ambush on the road that he and Hadassah's leaders had tried valiantly to make safe.

Five days earlier, on April 8, in the northern outskirts of Jerusalem, the Irgun attacked the Arab village of Deir Yassin, a base for Arab irregulars. As many as 250 Arabs, mostly civilians, were slain. The effect was not, as so many commentators have claimed, to encourage the Arabs to retaliate by hitting a civilian convoy to Scopus, because the Arabs had planned the ambush before Deir Yassin; but the massacre was cited to justify the Arab attack on the convoy. The Arab leadership had three goals in mind in planning the attack on the Mt. Scopus convoy: to strike a decisive blow that would force the Jews to abandon Scopus and make Jerusalem more vulnerable, to destroy the will of the Jews to resist an Arab invasion of the city proper and to deprive the Jews of their largest medical facility. And there was another factor. On April 8, in hand-to-hand fighting for control of Qastel Hill, which dominated the Tel Aviv-Jerusalem highway, the Arab hero and ace military commander, Abdul Kader Husseini, was killed by Meir Carmiel, a mobilized Hadassah worker. Shortly thereafter, Carmiel himself died in action.

Conditions for an ambush were ideal in the Sheikh Jarrah Quarter. Over a stretch of a few hundred yards between Nashashibi Bend and Antonius House, there were stone walls on either side of the narrow road. The convoy would be traveling slowly uphill at that point and ahead at Antonius House there was a 90-degree bend. Caught in that stretch of road, the vehicles would be tin ducks in a shooting gallery. The plan was as old as Thermopylae. Possible intervention could come only from the Haganah escort and from a small unit of Scots' Highland Light Infantry stationed in Antonius House. But the British there would not shoot unless they received orders to do so, a possibility that was remote.

On April 11, the British military commander in Jerusalem assured Magnes and a Jewish Agency man that the road was safe though, because of Deir Yassin, the general area was tense. Even as Jones spoke, the Arabs were consulting expert British officer friends on the logistics of the operation. Subsequent events indicate that the Arabs had an understanding whereby they would not be disturbed in their mission so long as they did not shoot at British soldiers. The Arabs could not – and would not – lose this one.

On April 12, Deputy Medical Director Eli Davis returned to town from Scopus. Wryly he commented, "It was not comfortable on the way down." Customarily Yassky and he took turns up on the hill, but on the evening of the 12th Yassky had a social engagement and did not go up in the morning. Gynecologist Yehuda Bromberg was with him that evening. "I was struck by the great depression which had overcome Dr. Yassky," Bromberg wrote three days later. "It was clear that his depression arose from his deep concern over the fate of our hospital. The dangers confronting the hospital because of the difficulties of transport were clear to him, as was the fear of the destruction of the hospital to which he dedicated his life."

On Tuesday, April 13, the largest Scopus convoy yet assembled was to take personnel, patients, visitors, workers and supplies up to the hospital and university. At 8:00 a.m. people began converging on the clinic in Hasolel Street where a University bus and a Hadassah bus, both lightly armored, waited. Three blocks away, outside Hadassah "A," two armored ambulances were parked. Haim and Fanny Yassky entered one of the ambulances, a converted Dodge truck, which only the day before had been painted a glaring white with a big red Star of David on the body.

Back at the clinic the buses quickly filled. Hadassah Social Director Esther Passman, her arms brimming over with magazines and sweets for the patients, was so determined to get to her wards that she left behind her beloved son, David, who had been injured while carrying out a school experiment. At the clinic, Esther met the noted cancer specialist Leonid Doljansky who urged Esther to sit beside him. Three weeks previously, she had become his "mascot" when she moved next to him on a bus in which, while riding, a bullet pierced her hat. Had he, the much taller of the two, been sitting in her place he would have died. But this day Esther was not permitted to board the bus and the ill-fated doctor would have to ride without his lucky mascot. Swearing under her breath, Esther ran three blocks to find a seat on one of the ambulances; she would live to tell about it.

Dr. Moshe Ben-David, administrator of the planned medical school, got a late start from home, hailed a cab, finally caught one of the buses and so sealed his own fate. Shelev Truck Company manager Moshe Lazar had a safe seat in the six-ton Brockway truck of veteran driver Benjamin Adin, but in a move that cost him his life, Lazar changed at the last moment to one of the buses.

By 9:00 o'clock the vehicles were on their way. Three trucks filled with supplies for the hospital and for fortifications joined the two Haganah escort cars, two ambulances and two buses. The exact number of people in the vehicles is not known because precise lists were not kept, but there were well over 100.

At the final checkpost outside Hadassah's Tipat Halav station, which served as a Haganah outpost, the convoy halted to await the customary order from the Haganah to proceed. At Tipat Halav, Haganah officer Moshe Hillman phoned British inspector Robert J. Webb, chief of the Mea Shearim police station, who said the road was safe. Webb was known as a friend to both Arabs and Jews and was said to be well-rewarded by both. One job Webb did for the Jews outside his official duties was to drive over the road to Scopus before a convoy left. Webb would stop at Nashashibi Bend, look around and sometimes wait there till the convoy passed. On this day, Hillman said, he called Webb as usual and Webb answered that the way was clear. But Webb did not station himself at Nashashibi Bend on April 13 and all efforts made by the Haganah to contact him throughout the day were fruitless.

Commander of the convoy was Jerusalem-born Lieutenant Asher "Zizi" Rahav, a British army sergeant during World War II. Now he was in Company Noam of the Jerusalem Haganah, the only Jewish unit in the city to wear uniforms and black berets. His assignment was to escort convoys in the Jerusalem area in an armored Ford truck.

It was 9:30 a.m. Rahav was in the lead in his escort vehicle with 10 men and two young Haganah hitchhikers. "When we proceeded a short way through Arab territory on Nablus Road, near a mosque, I had an odd feeling that something was wrong, because there was no traffic. I thought of turning back but instead I told my men to load their weapons and keep their eyes open."

The car had peepholes through which the gunners could shoot and a winged roof of meshed steel covered by canvas.

"Step on it," Rahav told his civilian driver. At the first turn in the road the Arab grocery shop was shuttered – another bad omen. The cars began to climb. Ahead Zizi saw Nashashibi Bend curving on itself like a snake. Rahav held his breath. Through his peephole, he spied the movements of Arabs wearing green Iraqi uniforms with bandoliers. To his left, Rahav noticed that the road was broken. The driver had to swing slightly right to miss it. It was 9:45 on Rahav's watch. Suddenly the Ford truck shook violently, throwing the men forward. A mine was electrically detonated five feet in front of them, creating a narrow four-foot-deep ditch. The car's front wheels nosed into the hole and the car settled at a steep angle. The mesh roof and canvas slid back, partly off the vehicle, obscuring the view of the rest of the convoy. Bullets pounded on the armored car. "Bullets came through the armor like bees swarming around us," Rahav recalled later. Zizi shot holes in the canvas to see what was happening to the convoy behind. He saw the last cars trying to turn around. At Nashashibi Bend, two British armored cars blocked the retreat. Rahav gave orders to his armorer, Baruch Nussbaum, to fire a few bursts at the British cars to get them to move out of the way. He did not know that in one of those cars, sitting as a spectator, was Lieutenant-General G.H.A. MacMillan, commander of all British forces in Palestine. MacMillan ordered his driver to move away from the convoy. Two days later, MacMillan would reply to a protest by University Chancellor Magnes in words that unintentionally admitted British neglect in the convoy tragedy:

> I myself motored through the area, passing under the fire of an automatic weapon in a Jewish armored car at 9:45 on my way to Kalandia [Jerusalem's airport]... I assumed that the situation was clearing up and my inference at the time was that it would have cleared up much quicker, had the Jewish armored car stopped firing.

Five vehicles managed to extricate themselves and get back to Jewish quarters. The Haganah escort car in the rear, its tires punctured, inexplicably turned tail and returned. Driving blindly with only a crack to see through, Benjamin Adin reversed, advanced, reversed, backed into the wall of the Nashashibi House and finally turned his six-ton Brockway toward the city. His foot brakes were gone, his tires were flat, the steering wheel worked only partially. On the floor of the cabin was a weeping male passenger who had hopped on at the last moment in an effort to see his wife and newly born son on Scopus. "I never shall see them again," he cried over and over. Adin pushed his pedal to the floor and arrived safely at Mandelbaum Gate where his passenger fell out of the cab in a deep faint.

The driver of the larger of the two ambulances, Yosef Levy, was wounded in the head. Surgeon Edward Joseph took a quick look, found it was only superficial and urged him to get moving toward Scopus. Reported Joseph, "We thought the driver was going on but instead he wisely turned the car around and returned. It was the first to get back." Dr. Joseph, who then crawled to join the Haganah men who were trying to edge close to the besieged convoy, reported:

> We were being attacked by a tremendous amount of shooting. It was impossible to lift one's head. The bullets were whizzing everywhere. I asked the soldier nearest me, 'Are these Arabs shooting at us?' He replied, 'No. They are English soldiers.' I knew it had to be true because it was the kind of shooting that only a proper army could do. They were shooting at the Haganah boys. If they had not, we could have reached the convoy.

The surgeon then joined a few men who had been in the Haganah vehicle that retreated and ran to the roof of the Tipat Halav station. Esther Epstein, who had been in Joseph's ambulance, joined the men. With his old pistol, Joseph ran from roof to roof trying to get close enough to get a clear shot. It was a hopeless act. As the ambush appeared to be succeeding, Arab volunteers from the region ran to the scene to get in on the kill. Esther could only sob at the end of the day, "It was horrible to see."

On the spot, blood was beginning to flow in Zizi Rahav's thinly armored escort car. Private Shlomo Mizrahi got two bullets in the stomach and fell on his commander. Rahav himself caught a steel splinter in the temple, his eye swelled and blood gushed. He kept shooting, aiming with his one good eye. Around noontime one of the hitchhiking Haganah young women, Shoshana Ben-Ari of Kibbutz Yagur, rose from the floor to help a wounded man, was hit in the mouth by a bullet and died shortly thereafter. At 12:15, Zizi dispatched his armorer, Baruch Nussbaum, to Antonius House about 200 yards farther on to get help from the Highland Light Infantry officers who were observing the battle, their heavy weapons silent. Baruch, who had a slight limp from a case of childhood polio, jumped into the deep ditch made by the mine and crawled along the wall. Baruch's body was later found in a wadi in Arab territory.

Back in Jerusalem proper at Haganah headquarters, Commander David Shaltiel called 21-year old Baruch Gilboa, who had arrived in Jerusalem early that morning from Tel Aviv. Gilboa was a commander of an armored unit that had escorted over 150 trucks of supplies to the city, following the capture of Qastel Hill on the city's outskirts. Shaltiel ordered him to take some men in his armored car to the Sheikh Jarrah Quarter and try to tow out the four vehicles that were under Arab fire.

"I don't know where Sheikh Jarrah is," said Gilboa.

"Take my operations officer with you," Shaltiel ordered.

It was obvious that Shaltiel's intelligence from the scene of battle was faulty; otherwise he would not have ordered a lone escort car into that trap. Gilboa and his men were fatigued from 14 hours on the road. His civilian driver, apparently shocked by the battle, saw the ditch made by the mine across the road, decided to try to drive over it, put on speed as he came up to the left of Zizi Rahav's embattled vehicle and landed with a thud in the ditch, injuring some of the men. Had he gone to the right of Rahav, he would have missed the ditch, gone on to Antonius House and the men could then have engaged Arabs who were firing at the convoy from a house across the street. Now, the two Haganah cars were stuck at the head of the convoy.

Close behind was Yassky's ambulance, its tires shot out, standing breadth-wise across the road where it had good protection from the two Haganah cars just ahead. About 50 yards behind were the two buses. They were the most open to attack from both sides of the road.

One attempt to extricate the buses was made by a British friend of the Haganah. Major Jack Churchill of the Highland Light Infantry, on his own initiative drove an open-fronted armored car to the scene and was about to put a tow-line on one of the buses when his driver was killed by a bullet in the neck. Churchill pulled in the tow and drove out of the area, but before doing so, banged on one bus and shouted to the occupants to risk getting out and returning with him. He later reported they refused to do so.

By early afternoon the two buses were sieves. Only one man from each vehicle survived. Shalom Nissan, a university student, jumped when the Arabs began lobbing grenades at his stricken bus. Miraculously, he dodged the rain of fire and ran all the way to Mt. Scopus where he was to provide the first on-scene account of events.

In the other bus was a guard, Nathan Sandowsky, who told a ghastly story that has since been verified. Nathan said that the driver was wounded from the initial fire and lost control. The second driver was lightly wounded but froze from fear and could not function. Nathan reported:

> The fire grew ever stronger. I heard the Arabs approaching with wild singing. In our car Yitzhak Berger had a Mauser pistol with eight bullets which at first did not work. We transferred all the suitcases to the rear of the car and tried to keep the shutter [of the peephole] in place. Dr. Ben-David held the shutter with all his strength but finally was overcome by the heat and asked to be relieved.

The bus had three lookouts inside. One was Nathan. Another was Dr. Avraham Freiman, lecturer in Jewish Law, and a third was University employee Zev Mariasin.

> From the rear opening I saw that all the time the British army passed in large convoys. They continued on their way. We shouted 'Help! We have wounded women and men!' But they did not stop. Armored cars of the police arrived and stood for a time without extending any help whatever and without even communicating with us. We were sure that at least they would not let the Arabs approach so close as to burn the vehicles.

From inside the buses could be heard clearly over and over again Arabs shouting, *Minshan Deir Yassin* (For Deir Yassin). Nathan reported that the arrival of Gilboa's armored car caused rejoicing in the bus. "We saw that our people were at last coming. But the Arabs derived courage from the fact that the police and army cars which passed did not raise a finger."

From the early hours on, bullets found their marks. Gas fumes began to seep in as the Arabs made ready to burn the bus. Molotov cocktails were being thrown. Some of the unhurt passengers tried to make a dash to safety. But the Arabs, only a few yards away, picked them off as they jumped out. As four men ran, a girl in the bus cried, "They are being killed." Nathan deliberated:

> I sat at the side of the opening of the bus with a scalpel – my only weapon. Fire started from the rear of the bus. There were cries, 'We are burning alive.' I dived. The blade of the scalpel broke. I ran the length of the road zigzag. I passed the ambulance and approached an escort car, waving the broken knife in my hand. I pounded on the door shouting, 'I am one of you.' The door opened. Inside all the men were dead or wounded.

It was now about 2:30 p.m. Inside Gilboa's armored car, Sandowsky saw Safed-born David Bar-Ner with a grenade in his hand. The pin was out and the grenade primed to explode. Recalls Bar-Ner:

> When Sandowsky climbed in we were waiting for the final assault. It was now a tradition in the Haganah not to be caught alive. We had five dead. Gilboa was paralyzed by a head wound. I had three bullets in my arm. I piled up the six grenades left in the car and pulled the pin on one to blow us up if the Arabs tried to take us prisoner. We had plenty of ammunition left but there was no one left to fire it. Then Sandowsky appeared. His face was blackened from the fire in

his bus. He grabbed the grenade from my hand and threw it outside where it went off. Then he took one of our two machine-guns and kept shooting short bursts. That kept the Arabs at bay since they knew we could still shoot back. He saved our lives, for soon after, the British picked us up.

One further feeble and futile attempt to save the convoy was made in the afternoon by the Haganah. Haganah Squad Sergeant Haim Kimron took an armored car to Sheikh Jarrah to tow out the vehicles. As Kimron entered the ambush he saw the buses burning. His vehicle stalled in a ditch. Almost immediately from the fire overhead two of the occupants were killed and three wounded. He wrote:

Hysterically, I ordered my driver to get the hell out of the ditch. He reversed and we went around to the right of the road, past the two armored cars and beat it up to Mt. Scopus. My tires were shot full of holes. When I reached Scopus I was so enraged, I ran to the top of one of the buildings and shot off my machine-gun in frustration and revenge at a nearby Arab village.

No one at this time knew what was happening in the white ambulance with the big red Magen David Adom. Its armor being the thickest of all the vehicles, this wagon was the safest place to be in that corridor of hell. Next to driver Zecharya Levitan sat Yassky. Behind him on the benches were Mrs. Yassky, six doctors, a nurse and a wounded soldier. The ambulance behind the two armored cars was a poor target for the Arabs and so it absorbed the least punishment. Yassky, who sat by the driver because he had a revolver and could more easily use it, concerned himself with appraising the situation by looking through the tiny window in the vehicle.

"Every time he opened the window," Yehuda Bromberg reported later, "a rain of shots was fired at him. At 2:00 p.m. Yassky informed us that everyone had been killed in the burning buses."

After the buses turned into pyres, Yassky announced, "Now our time has come. No escape from our fate is left. We must bid one another farewell."

Yassky took leave of his wife and, Bromberg reported, thanked her for the happy life which they had lived. At 2:30 Yassky was wounded in the liver by a bullet that must have ricocheted through the ambulance's engine.

"I'm hit," he said and then after a few minutes of continuous chatter, he whispered to Fanny, "Shalom, my beloved." He lost consciousness and was dead five minutes later. There was nothing the six physicians and one nurse in the ambulance could do. Ironically, there was not even a first-aid kit in the vehicle.

Pediatrician Yehuda Mattot, who sat on a bench behind Yassky, recalls: "Fanny Yassky took off her blouse and with it I bandaged Yassky. Only an immediate blood transfusion and an operation could have saved him."

Fanny remained strong. Someone began to weep. Fanny asked, "Why do you cry? Soon we shall follow him."

Zecharya, the driver, suddenly got up, opened the door and jumped out. He was shot dead a few yards away.

Dermatologist Haim Cohen asked gynecologist Bruno Berkovitz to join him in an attempt to run for it. But Dr. Ullmann said firmly, "Cohen, we have survived this together from nine o'clock. You can wait another few hours."

Mattot, who missed sure death by changing at the last minute from a bus to the ambulance, tried his luck a second time. He recalled:

> I thought that if I stayed put it would be the end. My wife
> later thought I did it because I could not stand to be without
> a cigarette. I jumped into the ditch and I began to crawl. The
> Arabs spotted me and began shooting. I got one bullet next
> to my spine. I kept going and got to Antonius House where
> the British troops welcomed me. Just opposite on the other
> side of the road were Arabs, apparently the leaders of the

whole thing. The British took me in and bandaged me. They were apologetic. They said they were a small unit and they could not do anything. They had been asking for reinforcements but could not get any. I was not able to convince the British to do anything for the convoy.

Throughout the day, pleas to intercede were directed to the British by the Jewish Agency, Haganah, Magnes, Davis and others. The British authorities suggested a truce to both sides and waited. The few troops at Antonius House were consistently refused permission to use their heavy machine-gun and bazookas; a few bursts from these weapons could have smothered the Arab initiative. Monitoring by Hadassah volunteers followed the British radio conversations throughout the day. This exchange was noted at a critical point:

Forward British observer: "The buses are burning. Someone has put out a white flag. Request permission to intercede."

British headquarters: "Reinforcements are on the way. Keep everything steady."

But reinforcements, which were only a few minutes away, took seven hours to get to the site.

Lieutenant-General MacMillan returned to the site at 4:30 p.m. Incredibly, he admitted to Magnes by letter that he had been uninformed all day about events in Sheikh Jarrah. Wrote MacMillan:

I was surprised... to find heavy firing in progress on the spot and my own car, which had been back to barracks and returned again to meet me, had been pierced by a bullet. On arrival once more on the spot, I found that Brigadier Jones had got the matter in hand and had persuaded the Arabs to stop firing but had not been able to achieve this until after he had been forced to fire heavily upon them and kill 15.

At about 4:00 p.m., Brigadier Jones had been given permission to open up with bazookas. Another army post fired off a few mortars. Then under a smokescreen, half-tracks were sent in to pick up the survivors. A British Intelligence captain, who had befriended the Jews, arrived under his own steam from military headquarters at the King David Hotel. Wounded Zizi Rahav was already in Antonius House. When he asked Zizi what he could do to help, the captain acceded to his request to return to the scene to bring back the weapons and secret operational papers on the body of one of the men. The captain did just that.

The captain would never forget the scene.

> It was grotesque. People were standing over the body of Dr. Yassky, screaming and yelling, while a little farther back beside the two burned-out buses the dead were piled in heaps. The corpses were burning and it was at least 20 minutes after the shooting finally stopped that someone thought to douse them with water.

Precisely how many were killed and wounded in the convoy? It is unlikely that anyone will ever know. A marble memorial bearing 76 names stands near Nashashibi Bend. A 77th is listed as "Unknown." Later, the number was set at 78. So badly burned were the bodies that remains were buried in a common grave in Jerusalem's Sanhedria Cemetery.

Three days after the attack, Hadassah handed the Red Cross a list of 30 persons whose bodies were identified and a list of 47 "still unaccounted for." In the mid-1970's an inquiry commission reportedly determined that only 25 of the bodies were buried in Sanhedria. Later, Yehoshua Levanon, son of victim Zvi Levanon,* located an Arab who claimed to have participated in the ambush. The Arab reportedly said that remains of the

---

* Palmach veteran Zvi Levanon, 25, the deputy commander of Mt. Scopus, was employed by Hadassah in the technical department. He was returning to his post after going home to celebrate Yehoshua's second birthday.

22 were buried in an Arab cemetery outside the Old City wall. But officials cast doubt on the veracity of the Arab's statement.

Late in 1996, the Israel Defense Ministry announced it was creating a genetic data base as a means of identifying the remains of those buried in Sanhedria. Whether the Ministry could inspect the alleged site in the Arab graveyard was questionable given the prevailing political antagonisms.

On the night before the massacre, Rose Halprin and Bertha Schoolman flew home and heard the news on their arrival in New York. Judith Epstein and Rebecca Shulman, who remained in Tel Aviv, were having dinner at their hotel when a newspaperman came up to their table: "I have terrible news for you. Yassky was killed today."

On her return to New York Rebecca told the Board in New York, "I doubt whether we will be able to use Scopus again soon. I recommend that we start building somewhere else."

To Ethel Agron and Eli Davis the Board cabled in May: "We dedicate ourselves to the task of maintaining services and rebuilding Hadassah."

The British reinforced Antonius House and warned both Jews and Arabs they could countenance no further military activity in Sheikh Jarrah. Nevertheless, on April 25, the Haganah under a young Palmach officer named Yitzhak Rabin, occupied Nashashibi House. But next day he was shelled out by the British. The Israelis would not return for good until 19 years later when, under Chief of Staff Yitzhak Rabin, they occupied all of the Arab sector of Jerusalem.

Shelling and sniping made life on Scopus impossible and the road impassable despite the British presence. Fresh food and water were near to vanishing point on the hill. Davis had to find a way to get the more than 700 people down. He contacted Major Jack Churchill. This is Davis's account:

> Major Churchill told me there was a slight chance of getting through to Mt. Scopus, because the Arabs saw the British meant business. He agreed to make the trip up to Scopus and

invited me along. The Major took a jeep and his driver. I sat while he stood in the jeep twirling his stick. He looked as though he were on parade in London. Nothing happened as we went through Sheikh Jarrah. On Scopus we were embraced. We had shown it was possible to get through.

Davis decided on the spot to risk a major evacuation because of the low morale. Ben-Gurion had told Hadassah and University representatives several days before the disaster that the hill was to be held at all costs. But Ahron Brezinsky, who was acting as medical director of the hospital, reported to Davis, "You cannot hold a front-line with sick people who do not want to stay. The atmosphere here is that of a refugee camp. With all the strategic importance of this place, we must get out with what we can."

Davis returned to town to organize the evacuation and to consult. A decision was taken to retain a 50-bed hospital on Scopus and thus demonstrate that the hospital was not being abandoned.

Davis scrounged the impoverished city for fuel for the partial evacuation. So empty was the city that he was reduced to collecting gasoline from private homes, institutions, friends – bottle by bottle. Four convoys made it. The last, on May 5, was the biggest because Churchill pleaded with Davis, "I've exceeded my orders. I am in trouble with my superiors." Brought into town were 200 patients, 100 student nurses and 300 staff members, as well as 600 tons of equipment and supplies. Not a shot was fired. Left behind were 150 persons, including eight student nurses who ran the kitchen and 40 patients. In the university buildings were another 150 men.

Now in charge of Hadassah's destiny were Davis and Ethel Agron, as chairwoman of the Council. Magnes, broken and sick, shattered by British nonchalance over the convoy ("This happened not out in the desert but in plain sight of Jerusalem," he wrote indignantly to General MacMillan), left Jerusalem for the United States where he died in October 1948.

On May 6, Haim Halevy, who administered the hospital, reported, "The hospital no longer exists for all practical purposes." Water and flour were sufficient for two weeks, power was rationed to only four hours daily and "soon there won't be refrigeration." Compounding the problem were intelligence reports that King Abdullah was about to shell Scopus preparatory to assaulting it.

By the beginning of May, Davis and the Hadassah Council in Jerusalem had managed to set up reasonably good facilities in Hadassah "A" and, two blocks down the street in St. Joseph's Convent, now known as Hadassah "B," but the accommodations were hardly luxurious. St. Joseph's, leased on April 29, had been a school for 600 Arab girls, run by French nuns. After shells hit the converted hospital, the top floor was evacuated and patients were removed to the dank basements where there was neither water nor electricity. Shelves that stored potatoes were cleaned and became emergency beds. Nurses knelt on the stone floor to change bandages and physicians sat on the floor to examine patients. Together with "A" and "B," the Straus Health Center and the Hasolel Street Clinic, Hadassah improvised 300 beds or nearly as many as it had on Scopus. Heroic volunteer work temporarily made up the difference. Nurse Madeline Lewin-Epstein, who had come with AZMU in 1918, turned her large apartment into a 20-bed hospital. She often braved snipers' bullets and mortars to pick up the wounded in the streets and pull them into her home. Hers was the first military hospital in Jerusalem and many of her patients were wounded underground soldiers who could go nowhere else. British police officials would be sitting in a chair in the dental clinic of her popular husband, Sam Lewin-Epstein, while in the living room only a few yards away from them were the men they were hunting.

At the height of all Hadassah's problems, the Old City of Jerusalem fell to the Arabs on May 28. Hadassah had staffed the hospital in the Old City's Jewish Quarter early in the fighting. But the position of the Jews had been hopeless against overwhelming numbers of Arabs. They fought until they were too few, too starved, too fatigued to go on. Avraham Laufer, one of the surgeons who was sent into the Jewish Quarter, reported a week before the surrender that the top floors of the hospital had been shelled and 70 patients had to share mattresses and wooden benches in a synagogue and in basements.

Laufer told of one young soldier who had shrapnel in an eye but refused to wait 15 minutes for an operation to remove it because the situation at his post was desperate. "An hour later they carried him back. His handsome face was blown away by a shell."

About 1,300 women and children were evacuated to the Jewish side of the city, while the men were taken to a prison camp in the Jordanian desert. Three among the POW's were Hadassah physicians: Egon Rys, Eli Peiser and Laufer. Two weeks later, while Rys was in the prison camp, his wife, Hava, a Hadassah nurse, was killed in the last pre-truce shelling of the city.

The refugees from the Old City were put up in the abandoned houses of the Katamon Quarter, a large neighborhood of Arab villas that was conquered in bloody fighting by the Haganah. There, Jerusalem's meager food supplies were tightly rationed by Hadassah volunteers, who themselves were now on starvation diets. Under the supervision of Sara Bavli, head of Hadassah Nutrition, these 1,300 and 20,000 others were given frugal daily meals in what was known as a "battle of the calories."

One of the Hadassah volunteers who cared for the Old City refugee mothers and children was Betty Levin. She was given charge of a three-room abandoned apartment in which each corner served as "home" for 10 refugees – 120 in all. Recalls Betty:

> At the end of the fighting in the Old City they fled to a synagogue where they huddled together until the Arab Legion found them. The Legion expelled them with only the nightgowns and slippers they wore. My job was to feed them. They got two slices of bread each and, for the children, four teaspoons of jam. One day, a distraught mother threw the

bread down and cried, 'My children are filthy: their heads are full of lice. I need soap.'

But there was no soap. Betty remembered that before the siege began her absentee landlady locked 10 large blocks of laundry soap in a room. Disregarding the mortars exploding around her, she traipsed back to her apartment, a kilometer distant, broke into the locked room and took the soap back to Katamon. There, she sliced each block into 16 squares. The lice were subdued and peace was restored to the apartment.

In the turbulence of siege, Friday, May 14, 1948, was no more than just another day of hunger and death in Jerusalem. No street celebrations marked David Ben-Gurion's proclamation of the State of Israel in the Tel Aviv Museum. Hardly anyone knew about it until the following day, for few in the city had electricity and news had to be passed by word of mouth. Only on Sunday, May 16, did *The Palestine Post* appear with its headline **STATE OF ISRAEL BORN.**

The highway to Tel Aviv had been cut again by the Arab armies. Daily rations were down to slow starvation level. The Holy City's only link with the outside world was a small one-engine plane that landed under fire in the Valley of the Cross. While great military advances were being made in the rest of the country, Jerusalem, at the end of May, appeared to be doomed. The last of the British had left Jerusalem on May 14 – except for those officers who remained behind to command Abdullah's Arab Legion. Residents of the city knew these officers were in command because the merciless shelling would stop precisely at 4:00 p.m. daily, so that the British officers could enjoy their tea. It was during that hour that most Israelis dared to go outside for their rations. Scopus was no exception to the bombardment. The buildings suffered badly, but casualties were few because the underground tunnel between the nursing school and the hospital served as a perfect shelter.

Born under fire was a new Hadassah service for Israel – orthopedic surgery. One of its pioneers was British-born Myer Makin, who had been a medical officer with the troops when they landed on the Normandy beach in 1944 during the Allied invasion of Nazi Europe. Soon after demobilization in 1946, he joined Hadassah as a surgeon. Battle casualties were nothing new to him. He wrote:

> We worked 24 hours on and 24 hours off. The main trouble was getting to work through the shelling. I would borrow my neighbor's bicycle and dash like hell through the streets. The shelling of Jerusalem was much worse than any I had gone through in France. In France we were at the front for three or four days and then were taken for a week's rest. Here it went on constantly. No let-up.

In mid-April, after a British effort was rejected by the Mufti, the U.N. Security Council authorized the Consuls-General of the United States, France and Belgium to try to arrange a truce in Jerusalem. At the same time, American Consul-General Thomas Wasson, the most congenial and effective diplomat in the city, worked to secure Mt. Scopus from attack. At the end of the month he was killed by Arab fire near his consulate. Hadassah doctors fought 12 hours in vain to save his life.

Immediately after May 15, the British established a consulate in Jerusalem proper and appointed two consuls to handle Arab and Israeli affairs. Consul John Guy Tempest Sheringham applied himself to the Scopus problem and on May 31, in a phone conversation with Hebrew University Administrator, Werner Senator, he advised Israel to surrender Scopus. Senator left a record of the talk:

> Sheringham: 'The best way to safeguard the University and Hadassah buildings would be to accept King Abdullah's offer to put them under the protection of the Arab Legion.'

> Senator: 'The best way it seems to me would be to advise King Abdullah not to shell the University and Hadassah.'

Sheringham: 'Your military situation is not very bright. You have not succeeded in driving the Arabs out of Jerusalem.'

Senator: 'The responsibility for the Legion's acts against the University and Hadassah lay with the British Government.'

In Washington, innumerable pleas were made to every imaginable source to help relieve Scopus. The State Department was helpful in one respect: Secretary of State George Marshall agreed that cables from the National Board be relayed through the consulate in Jerusalem to Davis and Ethel Agron.

In the end, an agreement was worked out by all parties whereby the United Nations would assume control of Scopus, over which it would fly its flag and provide observers to maintain the area as a demilitarized zone. Eighty-four Jewish police would guard installations at Hadassah and the Hebrew University while 40 Arabs would guard Arab property on Scopus. The United Nations agreed to supply and exchange the Jewish police in regular fortnightly convoys through the Arab Sheikh Jarrah Quarter. Hadassah and the University were evacuated on July 6 and demilitarization was completed on July 7, when the first police, who were Israeli soldiers in police uniform, went up.

Out of tragedy and fortitude had come triumph. While the price – an entire medical center and university – had been high, Mt. Scopus had not fallen into Arab hands and it would serve as a base for Israeli forces to win the entire city in 1967. On balance, Scopus was the pawn Hadassah sacrificed to save the queen.

Jewish Jerusalem was rescued at the 11th hour by a month-long truce that went into effect on June 11. In another 24 hours not another scrap of food would have been available. Battered and bloody, the city stood – most of it in Israeli hands. Looking back, Davis hardly knew how he had made it. Tetanus antitoxin was near the vanishing point and could no longer be given routinely; two wounded died for lack of the drug. X-ray film was short, morphine low; hypodermic needles, alcohol, adhesive plaster and catgut silk practically gone. "We were forced to keep one eye on stocks and one eye on the patient," Davis reported. He pleaded for help from the Red Cross but aid first came dramatically from New York due to the frantic efforts of the National Board.

Hadassah's Margaret Doniger set up blood plasma collection centers on America's east and west coasts. But the more immediate first aid act was the organization of an airlift of 15,675 pounds of medicines and supplies under the direction of Purchasing Committee Chairman Miriam Handler. The supplies were only a drop compared to the more than 2,000,000 pounds of supplies sent by Hadassah that year, but they arrived at a critical time.

On the plane was Lola Kramarsky, the first European-born leader to be elected Hadassah president (1960). Lola and Siegfried Kramarsky, both committed Zionists and close friends of the Weizmanns, arrived in the United States in 1940 as refugees from Hitler's Europe. Lola had been active in the Youth Aliyah movement and in 1935 was present with Henrietta Szold as she greeted the first group of Youth Aliyah children to reach Palestine. With Lola on the plane was Jeanette Leibel Lourie, Hadassah's meticulous executive director. It was now the beginning of July 1948, and the one-month truce was about to end. The chartered craft landed in Amsterdam where the supplies had to be reloaded on a C-54 cargo plane. At that time, Israel had no airfield that could take a larger craft. After long and harrowing hours in flight, during which the pilot of the plane had to radio several times for landing instructions, Lola, Jeanette and the supplies bumped down at Ein Shemer, south of Haifa. Appropriately the date was July 4. Forty Israeli soldiers rushed to the craft and began unloading. The scene was one of great relief and hilarity. Arthur Lourie, a South African-born diplomat, ran out in underwear to greet his wife; he had been bathing when he heard the plane land. Next day, the convoy of trucks arrived in Jerusalem, only four days before the resumption of war.

The next phase of the fighting lasted only ten days but it was sufficient for the Army of Israel, resupplied during the 30-day truce, to take the initiative. Jerusalem was no longer in danger although it was again being continuously shelled. Twenty-four hours before the war was renewed on July 9, Davis had completed a fully-equipped underground operating theater in St. Joseph's Convent – the first of its kind in the country. Forty-six direct hits were suffered by St. Joseph's. On the third day, Dr. Shlomo Gorfunkel, a Hadassah X-ray specialist who had organized the Vilna Ghetto uprising and served with the partisans in the Vilna forests, was killed by Arab fire in the streets of Jerusalem.

The fighting finally ended in Jerusalem on July 19, although sniping and occasional shelling would continue for several years. From the beginning of the shooting in December to July 19, Hadassah had treated most of the Jewish casualties in the city – a total of 3,550.

At the time, United Nations peace mediator Count Folke Bernadotte* was in Jerusalem offering compromise solutions – among them a considerable withdrawal by Israeli forces. On September 17 he and his French aide were fatally shot by members of LEHI. On arrival at Hadassah there was no hope for their lives. The provisional government of Israel under David Ben-Gurion abhorred the act. Three days after the assassination, the Mufti proclaimed a Palestine Arab state – one he could have had less than a year earlier without bloodshed – but now it was too late. King Abdullah outfoxed him and in October mobilized 5,000 notables to accept his sovereignty over all Arab Palestine. In another year he would annex the West Bank and East Jerusalem to his newly-named Kingdom of Jordan.

But the war was still not over. In mid-October, Israeli forces, now an organized army, moved south to take a Bedouin village called Beersheba. Hadassah would soon follow the troops to open a clinic there – the first in the Negev – as a memorial to Haim Yassky. And at October's end, the Israelis consolidated gains in Galilee.

---

* Bernadotte, who had arranged the month-long truce in June, proposed a peace settlement that would have given all of Jerusalem and the Negev to Jordan in exchange for western Galilee. Later fighting would, in any case, win all of Galilee for Israel.

The final campaign of Israel's War of Independence occurred as the year ended. Forces moved deep into the Negev and Sinai and on January 19, 1949, the shooting war came to an ironic end. Hours before the cease-fire went into effect, five British-piloted Spitfires flew from Egypt to determine whether the Israelis had, as agreed, withdrawn from Sinai. Mistaking the planes for Egyptians, the Israelis brought four of them down in air-to-air combat and one by ground fire. The word flashed around the world and for a few days it seemed as though the triumphant Israelis might have to fight the British. President Truman and others, including friendly British leaders scolded the Royal Air Force for having stuck its nose where it did not belong and the crisis subsided. In the Rehovot home of Chaim Weizmann, the soon-to-be President informed a British friend and Member of Parliament, Richard Crossman, of the incident. Crossman is said to have replied, "Don't worry. This means that you are now a state. Britain will recognize you within the month." On January 30, a chastised and humiliated British Foreign Secretary Bevin accorded de facto recognition to the State of Israel.

Succeeding Count Bernadotte, American mediator Ralph Bunche negotiated armistice agreements with Egypt, Lebanon, Jordan and Syria in the months of February, March, April and July. Iraq refused and removed its troops from the West Bank. While the armistice lines would be the frontiers of Israel for the next 19 years, the agreements were flimsy and did not, as hoped, lead to peace pacts. But they were a measure of the state's permanence and no one who had gone through the War of Independence in Israel now doubted that the incubating state would live.

Hadassah had been a midwife to the state all through its difficult birth. In recognition of that service, David Ben-Gurion, after becoming Prime Minister in the State's first elections held on January 25, 1949, said:

> The achievements of Hadassah in Zionism generally; its invaluable contribution to our war of liberation and independence; the work of its people here under fire on Mt. Scopus and on the fronts, will live in the history of our nation forever.

THE WEB AND THE WOOF

Israel, the State of the Jews, appeared so abruptly that it left the world breathless. Zionists and most other Jews could not immediately rationalize the event and, for years thereafter, would speak of the State in metaphysical terms – as the miraculous rebirth of the Jewish commonwealth or as the advent of the Messianic Age. Even some Christians greeted Israel as prophecy fulfilled and prepared for the coming of the Messiah.

Zionists could therefore be forgiven for not having realized that their political mission had now terminated and that their further participation on that level had diminished. Worse, they were confounded by abuse emanating from Israel. Angry that Zionist leaders did not rush to settle in Israel, Prime Minister Ben-Gurion would belittle those who remained abroad, referring to them merely as "friends of Israel." Great names in the movement gave up their roles like actors on closing night. The noble Chaim Weizmann was elected first president, a post that had no political power, and in 1952, almost 35 years to the day after the issuance of the Balfour Declaration, he died. Others, like Abba Hillel Silver, who waited in Cleveland for a summons from Jerusalem to join the cabinet, Stephen Wise, who died within a year of statehood and Louis Lipsky, the once powerful head of the Zionist Organization of America, would play no part in the political affairs of the state for which they had so valiantly fought.

To all this, Hadassah was an exception – and for good reason. Hadassah had been on the scene from the beginning. Through the years it adapted to and even thrived in the Middle East's wars and plagues. Henrietta Szold said in 1929, "Hadassah entered into the fabric of Palestinian life, into its web and woof." While other Zionist groups decreased in size or importance after 1948, Hadassah, because of its deep roots in the Land of Israel, would flourish. By the end of Israel's first quarter of a century, the membership of Hadassah would number 325,000 organized in 692 chapters.

None of this was yet evident on a searing August morning in 1948 when three board members – President Rose Halprin, Rebecca Shulman and Anna Tulin – met in Jerusalem with the Hadassah Council and the hospital administration to map a new course for the organization's work in Israel. The task was not easy since Israel itself, still taking form in the crucible of war, was embarked on an uncharted course.

For five days, under the chairmanship of Ethel Agron who headed Hadassah's Council in Israel, they tried to plan for an unpredictable future. Ethel posed some of the alternatives:

> Will we return to Scopus? Should Hadassah take over the health department of Jerusalem if the city is to be internationalized or should it now limit its work to preventive services? Should Hadassah expand outside Jerusalem? Does the Medical School have an absolute priority?

With the political destiny of the state uncertain, with masses of poor, ill, uneducated immigrants crowding into the country, Hadassah once again faced an old problem that repeatedly nagged Henrietta Szold – everything had to be done at once.

Some of the leaders meeting in Jerusalem insisted that Hadassah should concentrate on immigrant care. But Eli Davis spoke against Hadassah's providing across-the-board care for newcomers. That was now the Israeli government's task. Hadassah should do only what it knew best – provide service in specialized fields.

"Hadassah's duty is to administer the medical services for immigrants," retorted Rose Halprin.

"Whatever we do, we must not desert Jerusalem," said Rebecca Shulman.

A compromise solution came from Davis. "The best way to become a factor in Jerusalem and in the State is through the Medical School. The Medical School must get priority." And so it did.

The concept of a school of medicine in Palestine is almost as old as political Zionism itself. In 1913, the Zionist Congress accepted "as a matter of urgency" the establishment of a medical faculty at the projected Hebrew University. After World War I, the American Jewish Physicians Committee was organized to raise funds for the school. In the 1920's, a parasitology department under British-born Saul Adler and other medical research facilities opened at the University, but no serious thought could be entertained until Hadassah built the hospital center on Mt. Scopus. Preparing for that moment, a postgraduate teaching and research center for doctors developed and served physicians attached to the Allied armies during World War II. Clinical departments formed and the University granted status to heads of Hadassah departments. In December 1945, a $4,000,000 building fund took shape and as the exhausted world laid down its arms, the University and Hadassah finally looked forward to accepting the first students in 1947 or 1948. But these were crisis years. The new generation of physicians would wear uniforms of khaki rather than white.

Soon after World War II Director Haim Yassky, aware that a successful school depended on a corps of bright young physicians, initiated a fellowship program. He chose his best and sent them to the finest medical institutions in the United States. The first was Polish-born neurosurgeon Aharon Beller. He left on a troopship in April 1946 and returned to Jerusalem two years later because the country was without a neurosurgeon.

One of America's most prominent physicians, Johns Hopkins's Jonas Friedenwald, visited Jerusalem to assess the needs. In March 1946, he reported to Hadassah:

> Virtually the whole of European medicine has been wiped out. Work in Switzerland and the recovery of medical schools in Holland and Denmark are tiny oases in the desert. In short, there is no first class medical center east of London. Jerusalem is the obvious place. On Mt. Scopus there are enthusiasm, devotion and scientific maturity.

Friedenwald was only one of a few score physicians who, together with Hadassah women, labored to create the school. In the United States, Hadassah took counsel from its Medical Reference Board headed by Dr. E. M. Bluestone, who had gathered together some of the best-known physicians in American medicine: Duke University's William Perlzweig, the U.S. Public Health Service's Harry Eagle and Henry Makover, educator and author Abraham Wilinsky and Johns Hopkins's Abel Wolman. In Israel, there were Bernhard Zondek, Arieh Dostrovsky, Leonid Doljansky, Moshe Ben-David, Saul Adler, Arieh Feigenbaum. But above all there was Haim Yassky, of whom Eli Davis would say, "He had the vision of a great modern healing-teaching center. For that he worked always. Before his death he had been working on the blueprints of the school. It was the most natural thing in the world, when he had come down from Scopus, to carry on with the healing-teaching hospital idea."

But there was also one other who was only a distant relative of the Hadassah family. He was the first surgeon-general of the Israel Defense Forces; his name was Haim Sheba and he served as a catalyst.

As the head of the Haganah medical services in January 1948, Sheba wrote to all Palestinian Jewish students studying medicine abroad to return home. About 50 answered the call and immediately went into uniform. They were joined by medical students from Russia, Lithuania and Rumania who left their schools and emigrated to Israel. Recalled Sheba:

I suggested that we ask Hadassah not to wait with the medical school until they could begin with the first year but take the boys and girls who had already completed three years, give them a refresher course and proceed with the fourth year. Those who did not respond to the call to return would have to serve an extra year in uniform before they could receive their licenses so as not to give them an unfair advantage.

On September 10, 1948, Sheba formalized his suggestion in writing to Medical Director Davis.

"I felt when I wrote that letter," Sheba recalled later, "we would not only be creating a Medical School but we would also be saving Hadassah from losing some of its most valuable senior members who might not have had the stamina to remain in Jerusalem while the city was under fire. A few of them had made it clear that they could no longer continue after five months of continual siege."

Davis replied with a qualified approval saying that the students could begin in April 1949. But the students did not want to wait that long. Taking matters into their own hands, they went to Jerusalem to protest. They started a rumor that the army was about to begin a medical school since Hadassah and the University were dragging their feet. Sheba himself gave some credence to the rumor by forming a medical school preparatory unit in the army hospital in Jerusalem. He had ordered four senior officers to begin screening prospective students, but he had no intention of opening a school. The result was that Hadassah and University representatives quickly co-operated. One hundred and twenty candidates passed before the committee, a third were accepted and by November 1948, a three-month preparatory course began. In the meantime, Sheba had difficulty with the army. The Ministry of Defense only learned much later that Sheba, at his own initiative, had excused soldiers from regular duties to start studies. Not surprisingly, Sheba was soon in civilian clothes. He organized Israel's

Ministry of Health, set the foundations of the state's health services and co-opted three Hadassah senior administrators to assist him.

In February 1949, studies started informally. The scene for the official opening of the school, on May 17, 1949 – the holiday of Lag b'Omer in the Hebrew calendar – was foreboding. Claps of thunder and occasional streaks of lighting in an overcast sky interrupted the proceedings. Only a few hundred yards away, across the coils of barbed wire that delineated the divided city, King Abdullah's Arab Legion shot off a few rounds at the thick-walled, shell-pocked building which a year earlier served as the base for attacks against Arab positions. In one respect, this was a homecoming. Three decades previously, the building had been the Hotel de France – Hadassah's first official home in Jerusalem. In the municipal garden facing the school sat 2,000 guests. The 44 members of the first class were all in army uniform. David Ben-Gurion was the principal speaker and he spoke of a far-off day when the nation would be at peace. No medical school ever had an inauguration quite like it. At the end of 1949, a second class of 63 was formed with many Zionist medical students from Bulgaria, who needed only one year to receive their degrees. Thus, in premises on a hostile border, with students in military dress using texts in English, Polish, Russian and Bulgarian and listening to lectures in Hebrew, did the Medical School begin.

While most of the professors were European-trained, the influence of American medicine was strong because of the Hadassah Medical Reference Board. Polish-born Moshe Prywes, who spent five years as a prisoner-of-war in a Russian concentration camp in Siberia before emigrating to Israel, served as associate dean of the school until 1965. He considered the American-European synthesis beneficial and wrote:

> The American system brought a new informal approach that gave the students more freedom and produced better teamwork. Our curriculum was European – a six-year course which includes pre-medical sciences – but we applied the

American system of pre-selection. We did not, as did the
Europeans, allow everyone to enter and then permit only the
best to continue.

One innovation was wholly Israeli. The first graduating class on May 13,
1952, took the Oath of the Hebrew Physician. It was written for the
occasion by neurologist Lipmann Halpern, the school's fifth dean.
Addressed as "New Men of Medicine in Israel," the graduates were blessed
"to enhance the heritage of medicine in Israel." While the best of the
traditional Hippocratic oath was retained, the Greek gods played no part in
the Israeli doctor's obligation to his patients and to his profession.

After the graduation of the first class in 1952, undergraduate studies
were begun and since then the Medical School has provided the State of
Israel with 3,500 physicians, one eighth of the total number of its doctors.

Recalled dermatologist Arieh Dostrovsky, first dean of the Medical
School: "At the beginning we felt that the Medical School could only have
been established by Hadassah in Israel, for it was the only hospital that had
a standard of any significance."

The logical consequence of a functioning medical school was the
appearance soon thereafter of a school of dentistry. Veteran dental surgeon
Samuel Lewin-Epstein, who arrived with the American Medical Zionist
Unit, urged the creation of a school in the early 1930's. Finding little
interest, he contacted professional fraternities in the United States for
support. His determination won the backing of Alpha Omega, a large
American dental society. The first class of 15 students was opened in 1953.
Two years later, the faculty opened a clinic in the crowded Straus Health
Center where Hadassah ran a dental service for Jerusalem's school
children. It was then that Hadassah gave the school its own home and
equipment and joined hands with the Hebrew University to provide a
budget for staff and teaching facilities. Later on, Alpha Omega would top
its original contributions with a fund of $1,000,000 for a permanent site in
the new Medical Center complex at Ein Karem.

In that same year of 1953, an old dream of Akiva Kosviner came true. Akiva was born in Galilee in 1892, studied pharmacology in Beirut and after practicing briefly in Egypt, settled down on the eve of war in the Rothschild Hospital in Safed as pharmacist. When his Egyptian employer asked him why he was returning to "that desert" in Palestine, Kosviner replied, "Even though I will be making only half the salary, I feel I must contribute something of myself to that desert now."

During World War I, Kosviner spent much of his service at a small Turkish army hospital in a death hole called Tabuk in northern Saudi Arabia. Thankful to be back in Palestine after the war, Kosviner moved his family to Jerusalem and opened a pharmacy, the first in the city outside the ancient walls. Soon, Kosviner became Hadassah's chief pharmacist and began teaching at the Nursing School. But always he dreamed of a school of pharmacology. The school finally began in 1953 with Kosviner as executive secretary. Strictly speaking, it was not the first. Kosviner himself had rented a room in a hotel in the early 1920's and there gave a one-year course to Jews, Arabs and Christians.

Hadassah served as teacher and healer not only in Israel but also in underdeveloped lands far beyond, providing experts in many fields for the nation's foreign-aid program. Two of the most successful were in the fields of eye care and mental health. In 1959, much of black Africa had specialists in neither and many natives had only witch doctors to turn to for care. Hadassah's chief ophthalmologist, Scottish-born Isaac Chesar Michaelson, toured Africa's oldest republic, Liberia, and some of the newer ones. In the early 1960's, Michaelson sent 25 eye doctors to Africa to set up hospitals in urban areas and to organize clinics in the bush.

In October 1961, Hadassah psychiatrist Dan Hertz arrived in Monrovia to direct the black continent's first modern psychiatric hospital. He lived in Africa for three years introducing therapeutic methods in four countries. For his work in mental health, the Liberian president awarded Hertz the Star of Africa.

The Medical School's associate dean, Moshe Prywes, traveled widely advising on teaching programs – to Guatemala in 1959, to Singapore, Ceylon and India in 1960, to Argentina in 1961, to Ghana in 1964. Between 1960 and 1964 the Medical School brought French- and English-speaking Africans to study; 73 of them were graduated as physicians in Israel's capital. They returned to their home countries to teach other physicians and together with them, these Jerusalem alumni developed a fluency in the Hebrew language which they used to communicate with each other. Few medical schools have had such exotic alumni as those of the Jerusalem Medical School.

Dentistry's first dean, Ino Sciaky, was called to the island republic of Malagasy in 1964 and later to Senegal and Congo (Brazzaville), to teach his profession. His successor, Jacob Lewin-Epstein, would make numerous visits to Iran.

One unplanned visit of a Hadassah physician to Africa had an immediate political reward. In October 1961, heart specialist Moshe Rachmilewitz was on his way home from South Africa when his plane made an unscheduled stop at Addis Ababa. Israel's consul was there waiting for him and rushed the doctor to the palace of Emperor Haile Selassie, Lion of Judah, where the Empress lay ill. She was being treated by Jordanian and Yugoslav doctors but the medical complications were difficult. After Rachmilewitz put the Empress on the road to recovery, he was given a formal dinner at the palace. Rachmilewitz noted:

> The Emperor emphasized that the Jews and his people were related. On the floor I noticed a huge carpet with a large Magen David. We talked about many things, including politics, and after an hour's conversation he said to me, "I want to tell you something that will please you. Your country was not recognized *de jure* by us. You are leaving tomorrow. On your way to Israel, recognition by Ethiopia of Israel will

be announced – this will be in appreciation of the service you
gave my wife.

At home, there were tens of thousands of disadvantaged and culturally
deprived to care for. The immigrants brought with them their poverty and
their sicknesses, their superstitions and their illiteracy. First, they came
from the camps in Cyprus and from the displaced persons camps in Europe.
Then from Poland and Rumania. After that, they came from Yemen on the
wings of chartered eagles and from Iraq in an airlift named "Operation Ezra
and Nehemia" – 800,000 in all by the end of 1952.

Strict rationing went into effect throughout the country. So poor was
the nation that food and goods unloaded from ships went straight from the
docks to empty market stalls and shop counters. *Tzena* was the byword –
"austerity." Hadassah worried about getting large amounts of emergency
staples into the larders of the poorest of the poor; it provided healing to the
sickest of the sick immigrant children; it offered teenagers an opportunity
to take up a dignified vocation. It even arranged large loans for the
government. In the first years after independence, Israelis were
unashamedly and painfully hungry. In Washington, Hadassah
representative Denise Tourover, a member of the national board, was put
to work to get food from U.S. government warehouses to the Israeli
housewife. By virtue of its membership on the President's Advisory
Committee on Voluntary Foreign Aid, Hadassah had the right to receive
government surplus foods for free distribution. Immediately available at
the time, Denise learned, were tons of potatoes stored at Presque Isle,
Maine. Israel's embassy in Washington announced that it would gladly
accept them provided they were fumigated against the red potato bug.
Hadassah had them fumigated and sent shipload after shipload to Haifa
harbor. Meat followed. In 1953, Hadassah undertook Operation Reindeer –
a one-time project that provided $12,000,000 of kosher meat, dried fruits
and staples. They were placed into bags inscribed with American and
Hadassah insignia and distributed free. The U.S. government sent the

rations as a Christmas gift. Among the recipients were both Israeli Arabs and Jews. The project was something to ponder: an American Christmas gift distributed by a Zionist organization to Palestinian Arabs.

Butter followed meat, but here there was a major slip up. The Israeli government understood that it could sell the butter on the free market, but in fact the sales were a technical violation of the American law. One diplomat at the American embassy in Tel Aviv acknowledged later, "There had been some sort of agreement [with the Israeli government to sell the butter]." Whatever the case, visiting Congresswoman Frances Bolton noted that butter was fetching high prices in grocery stores and protested loudly when she returned home. Denise Tourover was called before the Foreign Aid Committee to explain. Fortunately, Denise was able to report that she had already mentioned the sales to the American embassy in Tel Aviv. The statement was accepted and Hadassah was cleared. But long negotiations between the two governments followed and finally, after demanding $6,000,000, the United States accepted $800,000 as compensation. The butter crisis was over and surplus foods continued to arrive. Until 1969, Hadassah channeled nearly $27,000,000 of food to hospitals and welfare institutions. The U.S. stopped the program when it became obvious that Israel no longer needed help to feed its people.

No less a problem for Israel was the lack of shelter. The government was determined that no one would sleep on the beaches under the open skies as immigrants did in the mid-1930's. The answer, provided by Jewish Agency official Levi Eshkol, was to set up transit camps. By the end of 1952, 250,000 persons were living in tent and shanty towns up and down the country. One of the largest, and in winter the muddiest, was set up east of Tel Aviv at Rosh Ha-ayin for the Yemenite immigrants. It was there in 1950 that Hadassah pediatricians Yehuda Mattot and Zvi Shamir headed a children's hospital, set up in an abandoned army camp. Shamir reported:

We were dealing with terribly ill children. Almost everyone who came to the hospital suffered badly from malnutrition and acute intestinal infection. These people had no natural immunity. On the way from Yemen to Aden they contracted a severe type of malaria. The youngsters needed care 24 hours a day. At the beginning the staff was enthusiastic; they were accustomed to dealing with sick children. But these were more dead than alive and after making the round each evening we found many dead in their beds. They died like flies. They had reached the point of no return. We soon became depressed.

Routine treatment of children in such conditions was to give large quantities of intravenous fluids. But the doctors realized from post-mortem examinations that these children were so exhausted and malnourished, their bodies could not absorb large amounts of nourishing fluids. Their enervated, overtaxed hearts simply gave out. The amounts of fluids were accordingly reduced and with the aid of antibiotics, the death rate plummeted from 50 to five percent. Other problems arose. Reported Mattot:

We could not keep them long in hospital because of the large numbers and we grudgingly sent them back to their huts where there was insufficient food and horrible living conditions. We tried distributing food to the families for the children but we soon learned that the fathers were taking it all. We set up a feeding center so that the kids could have at least one cooked meal a day. Then we found that the children had strict orders to throw the food over the fence for their fathers. We called in the police to stop it, but this started riots.

Accommodations for the medical staff were very bad, Shamir recalled:

The rats from a nearby stream crawled over us at night. We started a new sport – trying to kill them with shoes and brooms. The summers were unbearable. The heat and the lack of proper water facilities made work impossible. Diapers had to be washed by hand. Nurses covered the huts with sheets and poured water over them in an attempt to cool the huts which were steaming ovens.

Hadassah staffed the hospital for two years. Then, the state's health service was sufficiently organized to move in.

Talpiot camp, on the other side of the railroad tracks in southern Jerusalem, was even larger than Rosh Ha-ayin. Ten thousand would crowd into the wooded area. There, Hadassah was to do a job it knew well from start to finish – mother and child care. It was in Talpiot that an energetic young Jerusalem-born physician, Kalman Mann, medical deputy to Eli Davis, spoke up for a different approach to medicine. He said:

We usually emphasize disease in our hospital but as a medical organization we should emphasize health. Because we cater to disease, the emphasis is on diagnosis and treatment. It should be on prevention and promotion of health. Most of the illnesses we meet are really emotional and social – particularly among immigrant communities.

Mann urged the creation of a community health center to monitor all the families in the neighborhood. The family, not the individual, was to be considered the unit of care and all problems – not only medical – would come under the trained staff in the center. Thus began, in 1953, in Jerusalem's immigrant suburb of Kiryat Yovel, a unique experiment in social medicine.

A five-year study, carried out by Mann and the center's South African-born director, Jack Medalie, proved that the immigrant community – representing newcomers from 30 countries – achieved one of the lowest mortality rates in the country.

Other community health centers developed under Hadassah's planning. The community idea worked to such an extent that it spread to Arab communities and even to South America.

The newcomers needed only training and direction to become productive. Because Hadassah had faced the problem of vocational education nearly two decades earlier, it was ready for that task. In the early 1930's, Henrietta Szold worried much over the problem of wayward Jewish children who were sent by the British courts to dubious institutions housing delinquents of all communities. She believed that delinquent Jewish children should be cared for in Jewish homes. She was especially vexed about young Jewish prostitutes and the fact that many Eastern girls became child brides or servants. In 1940, she received $25,000 as an 80th birthday gift from Hadassah. With it she established the highly-successful home for disturbed, delinquent girls at Ein Vered, east of Tel Aviv. In her search for the right kind of institution, she also developed the idea of training girls for such vocations as preventive therapy.

On one of her Youth Aliyah trips to Haifa she met a robust, energetic home economics school principal named Helen Kittner. At the time Henrietta felt that Youth Aliyah children need not be sent only to farms but could also be integrated into urban life, providing they had a vocation. After consulting the Hadassah Council's first vocational education chairman, Rose Viteles, Henrietta dispatched a 15-page memo to the National Board suggesting the establishment of a vocational girls' school in Jerusalem. By coincidence the Board was then considering a memorial project for Henrietta's closest friend, Alice Seligsberg. The Board accepted the idea and Henrietta asked Helen Kittner to head the school. The official opening took place in two converted wards of the old Rothschild Hospital on October 14, 1942, the day that Hadassah met in national convention in New York City.

In 1944, the hospital compound also housed not only the Seligsberg School but a new vocational center named for Justice Brandeis and workshops for 160 boys and girls under the direction of an unsung pioneer of progressive education in Jerusalem, Deborah Kallen. But within eight years, Helen Kittner had taken over the entire building. The workshops were moved and Miss Kallen was retired.

Helen Kittner, who, at the age of four, was skilled at knitting stockings for her family, was often ahead of her time in later life, too. In 1949, when Jerusalem had no tourist trade, she opened a school to train hotel personnel. But in the early 1950's hotels were closing and the school had to be transferred to the government. Likewise, in 1949, when the country could not feed its burgeoning population properly, much less dress them in haute couture, Helen started a fashion school. It was discontinued after the graduation of the first class. Nevertheless, Seligsberg School was responsible for highly successful fashion shows that Hadassah sent to the United States to raise funds.

The Alice Seligsberg School outgrew its converted wards and 16 years later had a $1,000,000, five-story edifice. During its first 25 years the school graduated 2,200 girls. Henrietta Szold had said, "I see the school as a big school with every girl in a blue dress and every girl in a white apron... bringing honor to an apron." Helen Kittner fulfilled Henrietta's wish.

In 1944, three teenage boys were taken into a hut in the Rothschild Hospital compound under Hadassah's sponsorship and taught precision mechanics by German-born, Czech-trained Tunia Gladstein. Within three years, the Brandeis Training Center's 15 students and their teachers were turning out weapons and ammunition for the Haganah. They produced heads for the Haganah's secret weapon – a heavy, noisy mortar called the Davidka. They made hand grenades and mechanisms to set off mines. During the fighting early in 1948, Arab agents learned that Brandeis was the center of an arms workshop and directed shells against it from positions in the Old City. The Rothschild building's thick stone walls provided good protection and no one inside was hurt, but one student was killed on the street on the way to his bench. Conditions became impossible and the workshops moved first to a nearby cellar cafe, then farther away to the Bezalel Art School where the boys had their own electricity generator and could work in two 12-hour shifts.

Brandeis's technical designer Yitzhak Schneider invented a flame-thrower for which the boys made most of the parts. They also turned out muzzles for smoke bombs used to screen Jerusalem's lone landing strip from Arab gunners. With the battle raging around them, the school went on to produce more and more complicated products as the Haganah, cut off from supplies outside Jerusalem, made more and more demands. Schneider, together with handwork technician Yitzhak Moshieff, even put together binocular telescopes. When materials were difficult to obtain, one of the Brandeis men endangered his life by going to the Jerusalem railroad station under fire to rip up tracks for metal. The school, only a few years old, thus played a key part in the battle for Jerusalem.

Brandeis taught more than precision instruments. In 1949, the country's first printing school was begun. The school's director was French-born Henry Friedlander, who distinguished himself by designing a new Hebrew script after 30 years' research. He named the script Hadassah. It was the first original Hebrew type of modern times. Beautiful in its classic design, yet uncomplicated, Hadassah fonts were adopted for the Swiss-made Hermes typewriter and were widely used by the Israeli government printers and by public institutions.

With bequests from the Brandeis family, new quarters were built in northern Jerusalem in 1951. Then it became possible to introduce such sophisticated courses as industrial electronics under director Edgar Freund. On the eve of the Six-Day War, Brandeis could convert immediately to the production of complicated components for the Israel Defense Forces, among them vital parts used in the bombing of Egypt on June 5, 1967.

But by no means was the school a war factory. Characteristically Israeli, it was civilian but was subject to call-up at short notice. In civilian life Brandeis would not only teach but it would build instruments to measure avocado peels and sections of the heart-lung machine used by Hadassah for its first open-heart operations.

In 1969, Seligsberg and Brandeis amalgamated into a comprehensive high school. At the same time, the idea of a junior college was developed by Esther Gottesman, chairman of Hadassah's Israel Education Services. Precisely three decades after the Seligsberg School was founded, in November 1972, the nation's first junior college students were graduated. The school expanded rapidly. In 1977, a top-notch education administrator, Dr. Ya'acov Amidi, took over and a year later the name of the institution was changed to the Hadassah College of Technology. By 1996, having been accredited with academic status in some fields, the College of 900 students was offering four-year courses in a few selected departments.

While it was good that Hadassah provided vocational education to students who had no talent or desire to become scholars, it was another matter when young people could not decide what they wanted to do or what they could do. Research carried out among Jerusalem's high school seniors would show that only 25 percent knew their own inclinations regarding their education and future occupation. The others were in a state of indecision.

To test, to counsel, to direct students became the function of Hadassah's Vocational Guidance Bureau, founded in 1944. Its first director was Haim Ormian, one of the country's pioneer educators. Under Director Zev Sardi, the bureau branched out into counseling, teaching and research, and its name was then changed to the Hadassah Career Counseling Institute. Said Hadassah's former Education Services Chairman Esther Gottesman:

> We do the job that at least four agencies in America would do. The Department of Labor would put out statistical information and resource material. Psychological counseling would be done by another agency, personal assessment by a third and still another would be management consultant.

Testing and therapy for emotionally disturbed school children required an institution of its own. That need was filled in 1949 with the opening of the Lasker Mental Hygiene Clinic.

During the past 50 years, the Institute has had 535,000 clients. More than half were high school graduates for whom the Institute determined the most suitable occupation. Psychometric tests – 420 of them – are conducted in 12 languages.

Not merely a testing organization, the Institute has carried out 850 research projects and serves as a management consultant to Government and to hi-tech companies.

One of its research projects found that among young Israelis the most popular of 420 possible occupations was business administration. That was followed by mass communication, economics-accounting, design, law and psychology. The glamor and status appear to have faded from medicine (14th place). Physicians' incomes are lower than the preferred professions and today's Israeli youth, says Director Yitzhak Garty, are more practical and materialistic, less idealistic than previous generations.

Dr. Garty, who has led the Institute since 1984, now serves 40,000 persons annually. The Bureau began with 600. The number has grown, he believes, partly because young people have a harder time than ever making up their minds. "Never before have so many opportunities and specialties been open to them nor the competition so great," says Dr. Garty.

Important as its educational function was in the 1950's, Hadassah's main preoccupation was with the medical organization. With the end of the War of Independence, hospital facilities expanded in a makeshift way utilizing alphabetical names. Hadassah "A" and "B" were war-born, as we have seen. They were soon followed by "C" for tuberculosis patients; "D," in a derelict building that once housed the harem of the Turkish governor, served internal medicine patients; "E," in an old German Lutheran Hospital, took in surgical cases. One unlettered institution that Hadassah inherited as a result of the war was an Arab leprosarium. When the Arabs abandoned it, the dermatology department assumed responsibility and did notable work there in alleviating the pains of leprosy. By 1951, Hadassah was spread out in at least a dozen buildings over the face of the city.

All told Hadassah had put together places for 452 beds in Jerusalem in the 1950's, but if one included the hospitals in Beersheba, Safed and Rosh Ha-ayin, they numbered 700. Occupancy at one point, reported the statisticians, was an unbelievable 298.4 percent.

Without Scopus, however, Hadassah was bereft of its crown. Rebecca Shulman had said at the August 1948 meeting in Jerusalem, "We will have to build anew." The loss of Scopus was too fresh to begin rebuilding immediately, but by 1951 the shock had eased and Hadassah leaders began to plan for a new medical center.

One had only to visit the scattered premises to appreciate the need. Working conditions were almost laughable. So cramped were the facilities at the mission, now called Hadassah "A," that they expanded into the private quarters of Canon Jones, the mission's director. The delivery room was put into his bathroom and an expensive cobalt unit for cancer therapy was set up in a room the Reverend used for prayer meetings. In a small kitchen next door, Hadassah opened Israel's first medical isotope center. Down in the damp basements, the walls covered with fungi, were the X-ray labs.

The time had now come not only for a new center but for new management. Eli Davis, the British-born physician who had gone to Jerusalem on a promise from Yassky that he would be able to keep in touch with medicine while serving as deputy administrator, found that administration at Hadassah was a 20-hour-a-day job. Eli Davis had worn Yassky's mantle with great fortitude at Hadassah's most trying hour. Davis was a man who spoke directly, plainly and rarely wavered. If these characteristics sometimes brought him into head-on collision with the Hadassah leadership, they also brought him the Board's deep respect; so much so that when in 1950 he decided that, the war being over, he could now return to his first love – medicine – Hadassah dispatched President Rose Halprin and incoming President Etta Rosensohn to Jerusalem to change his mind. Throughout a snowy night in the winter of 1950, even their considerable powers of persuasion failed. Davis, fortified by his wife's resolution and support, had made up his mind and that was that.

Hadassah was now left without Scopus and without a director. Fortunately for the deputy director, the task at that moment looked like an impossible one because few qualified men in American medicine would entertain moving to poverty-stricken Israel to take over a hospital dispersed in dilapidated buildings. And so the directorship fell to Davis's deputy Kalman Jacob Mann, son of the city's first Jewish building contractor, seventh generation Jerusalemite, born in the year Hadassah was founded. The house he lived in as a child also served Ray Landy and Rose Kaplan as an eye care station in 1914. Mann himself had been treated for trachoma. ("I used to run away because of the painful treatment and they would run after me, catch me and drag me back. This did not endear the nurse or the physician to me. But it did cure me.") He was graduated from a teachers' college at 19, went off to England to study medicine with the aim of entering psychiatry. Instead, he took four degrees in medicine, a diploma in tropical medicine and specialized in chest diseases. During the war he served as a resuscitation officer at Hendon airfield in charge of chest cases. It was an experience that would prove useful in the Six-Day War.

Mann returned to Jerusalem in 1948 on the promise of a position at Hadassah. But by the time he arrived, Scopus was lost and Eli Davis told him, "It's a shame you came. We have no job for you now." Mann was about to leave to establish a group practice when one day, as he crossed the Street of the Prophets, he met Rebecca Shulman who spent much of Israel's first year in Jerusalem and Haifa.

"How are you getting along at Hadassah?" she asked.

"I'm not."

Under St. Joseph's galvanized roof they sat and they talked. A week later Kalman Mann began as Davis's deputy. He explained: "My mother thought it was an honor and Rebecca Shulman kept after me. Dr. Davis was a good teacher and I felt a partnership growing in the building of Hadassah."

Hadassah sent Mann to the United States under its fellowship program, to study hospital administration under Dr. E. M. Bluestone. While he was in Rochester, New York, in 1950, Mann received word from Davis that he was about to resign. So it was that at 38 years of age Kalman Mann became Hadassah's eighth director. He was the first to come from native soil and he would serve much longer than any of his predecessors. Under Kalman Mann's steady hand, the Hadassah Medical Organization would build a new home and keep faith with an old one.

...he undersigned, in consultation with other women Zionists in ...ew York City, have reached the conclusion that the time is ripe for ...large organization of women Zionists, and they desire to invite you ...attend a meeting for the purpose of discussing the feasibility of ...orming an organization which shall have for its purpose the promo-...ion of Jewish institutions and enterprises in Palestine, and the foster-...ng of Jewish ideals.

The meeting will be held Saturday, February 24th, at eight P.M., in the Vestry Rooms of Temple Emanu-El, Fifth Avenue and Forty-Third Street.

SOPHIA BERGER,
GERTRUDE GOLDSMITH,
EMMA GOTTHEIL (Mrs. Richard),
LOTTA LEVENSON,
ROSALIE S. PHILLIPS (Mrs. N. Taylor),
MATHILDE SCHECHTER (Mrs. S.),
HENRIETTA SZOLD.

New York, February 14, 1912

February 14, 1912. Temple Emanu-el, meeting place of Daughters of Zion. There, on Purim, Henrietta Szold proposed the creation of Hadassah.

1913. First American nurses sent by Hadassah to Jerusalem: Rose Kaplan, left, and Rachel Landy, right, with Eva Leon, a member of New York chapter, outside original Hadassah welfare station.

Hadassah's "Drop of Milk" Campaign brought homogenized milk to Palestine for the first time and was delivered to mothers via donkey "express".

1918. First American Zionist Medical Unit on eve of departure with Central Committee of Hadassah, front row, right to left: Henrietta Szold, Alice L. Seligsberg, Dora Lefkowitz (Dorothy Leffert), Ruth Fromenson, Emma Gottheil, Bertha Weinheim, Ida Danziger, Libby Oppenheimer.

1918. Doctors, sanitarians and other medical personnel. During World War I, Palestine and Egypt were under the British Middle East Command.

November 3, 1918. British Army hands over the keys to the Rothschild Hospital in Jerusalem to the AZMU, whose 44 members became the "founding fathers and mothers" of the Hadassah Medical Organization. Standing, center, James de Rothschild. After the Rothschild- Hadassah Hospital on Mt. Scopus opened in 1939, the original building later housed the Alice L. Seligsberg Trade School for Girls. Today, it houses the Hadassah College of Technology.

1922. Henrietta Szold with administrative staff at Rothschild Hadassah Hospital.

1926. Henrietta Szold and staff of Safed Hosital, whose specialty was the care of patients with Tuberculosis.

1927. Nathan Straus lays the cornerstone for the Nathan and Lina Straus Health Center in Jerusalem. Today the building houses Hadassah Youth Services, Hadassah-Israel and Hadassah International offices, Career Counseling Institute and several clinics of the Hadassah Medical Organization.

1930. Henrietta Szold with members of Junior Hadassah, which merged with Young Judaea in 1967. Hadassah assumed sole sponsorship for the expanded American Zionist youth movement Hashachar, comprising young, intermediate and senior Judaea, and college-level Hamagshimim.

1930. Hadassah's school hygiene program was part of its systematic, coordinated effort to wipe out trachoma and other endemic diseases.

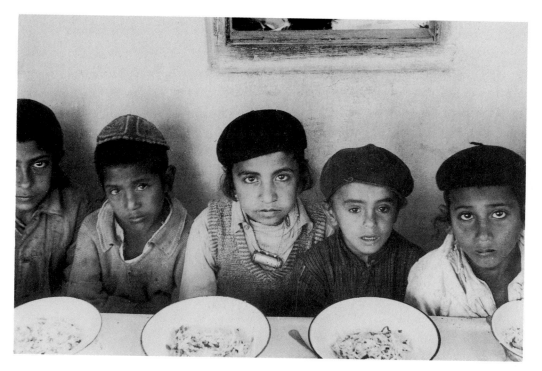

1930. The school lunch program taught hygiene and good nutrition to thousands of children who, in turn, helped change the eating habits in their homes.

1933. Nurses on Hadassah Infant Welfare Day.

*1936. Henrietta Szold swinging an ax at the groundbreaking ceremony
for the Rothschild Hadassah University Hospital on Mt. Scopus.*

*Before 1948, Militia guard the Hospital and School of Nursing on Mt. Scopus. From 1948 to
1967 the road to Mt. Scopus was in Jordanian hands and Hadassah continued its work in
five scattered buildings in Jerusalem. After the Six-Day War in 1967, all of Scopus was
restored to Israel.*

1941. Henrietta Szold, first director of Youth Aliyah, dancing with Youth Aliyah teenagers.

1943. Malnourished "Teheran children" arrive in Palestine after wandering across war-torn Europe.

1959. Eleanor Roosevelt, world patron of Youth Aliyah, during one of several visits to a children's village in Israel.

May 14, 1948. Chaim Weizmann inaugurated as first President of the newly proclaimed State of Israel.

April 13, 1948. Hadassah convoy with supplies and medical personnel is ambushed at Shiekh Jarrah Quarter on road to Mt. Scopus Hospital. 76 doctors, nurses and staff were killed, including Dr. Haim Yassky, HMO Director General.

May 17, 1949. Rose Halprin speaking at dedication of the Medical School. Seated, right: David Ben-Gurion, Prime Minister of Israel, and James G. McDonald, American Ambassador to Israel.

1949. The first class of The Hebrew University – Hadassah Medical School opened with 70 veterans still in the uniforms of the Israel Defense Forces.

1952. Groundbreaking ceremony for the Hadassah Medical Center at Ein Karem. Dr. Kalman Mann, Director-General, speaking. Dr. Miriam Freund Rosenthal to his right; Etta Rosensohn, Prime Minister David Ben-Gurion and Rebecca Shulman to his left.

1961. Patients are moved from temporary Hadassah hospital buildings in Jerusalem to the new Medical Center at Ein Karem.

1962. Marc Chagall, at left, studies installation of his world-famous 12 stained-glass windows in the hospital synagogue with the Medical Center's architect, Joseph Neufeld.

1967. Hadassah's staff is overjoyed when they learn that Mt. Scopus has been liberated in the Six-Day War.

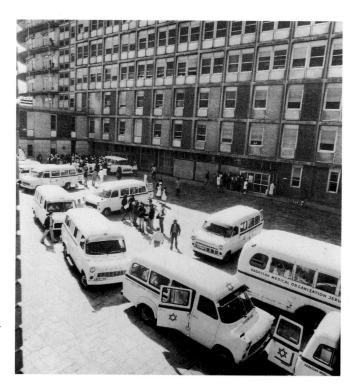

1976. Ambulances at Ein Karem prepare to move patients to Hadassah's rebuilt hospital on Mt. Scopus.

1954. Hadassah Study Circle meets in National Office to learn Hebrew.

May 17, 1949. Hadassah participates in Solidarity Day March in New York City.

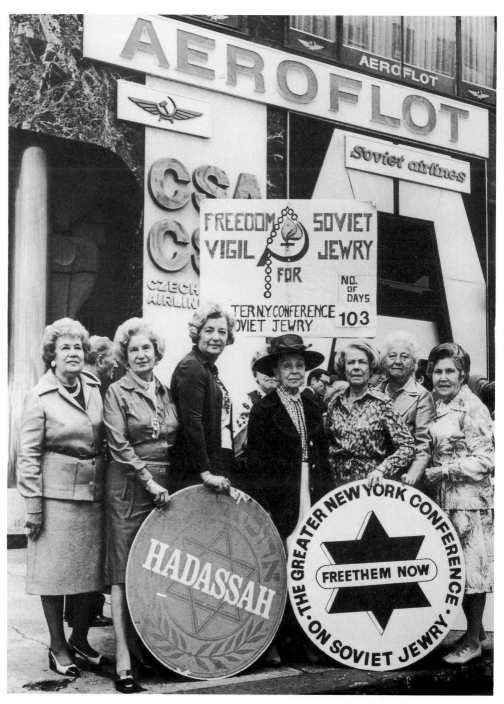

May 31, 1977. Hadassah participates in Soviet Jewry Vigil in New York City. From left: Charlotte Jacobson, Bernice S. Tannenbaum, Rose E. Matzkin, Rose Halprin, Dorothy Brill, Bess Katz and unidentified woman.

EIN KAREM

"You are crazy, Mann!"

With that, the distinguished rector of the Hebrew University turned on his heels and tramped down the slope to the parked jeep. He had been invited to the top of the mountain by Hadassah's enthusiastic medical director. Spread out before the two men in a majestic panorama was the Valley of Sorek, the lair where Delilah snared Samson. It was here that the Philistines planned to break through to subdue Judea and, not far away, the youthful David foiled them by slaying Goliath. Peaceful, even primeval, the blue-tinted Judean Hills were ideal for quiet study and research. Kalman Mann had explained to the rector that Jerusalem, lying five miles to the north, had nowhere to grow but southward. A broad highway from Tel Aviv would one day be cut through the valley and this spot would be the city's grand new entrance. What could be more fitting, he suggested, than to build fortresses of healing and teaching on opposite hills to guard the gateway to the City of Peace.

The realistic rector was unimpressed. This place was good for goats or Philistines or even for prophets but definitely not for serious students who had to rush to jobs in the city after classes or for sick people in urgent need of a specialist.

Disconsolate, Mann began feeling a little silly that he had supported this site as the successor to Mt. Scopus. But before he would surrender to goats and Philistines, he was determined to get one last opinion and that from a latter-day prophet.

The year was 1951 and by then the loss of Scopus lay as heavy as a dirge on the soul of Jerusalem's physicians and professors. No one doubted any longer that the Hebrew University and Hadassah must build anew. The problem was where. Jerusalem offered no easy locations. Fashioned by nature in the shape of an outstretched hand – of ridges and valleys – the city was further limited for reasons of security. Jewish Jerusalem was the end of a salient that began in the Judean foothills to the west and stuck out like a thumb, in the gut of the heavily populated sections of Arab Palestine that had been annexed by Jordan. Arab military positions dominated the city from high points to the south and north. On the eastern border, which cut through the middle of Jerusalem's commercial section, Jordanian sentries sat perched on rooftops. Few sites anywhere were at that time beyond the effective range of Arab guns. Ein Karem was one.

Hadassah and the University considered four sites. For Hadassah each had its disadvantage: one was too small for expansion, another was out of the mainstream of the developing city and a third was needed for an airport. That left Ein Karem – distant but enticing. Ein Karem – the Well of the Vineyard – is a quaint village snugly held in the Valley of Sorek, an artist's dream of statuesque cypresses, crooked lanes and stone-walled churches. Tradition has it that St. John the Baptist was born there.

Long, hard-fought sessions between Hadassah and Hebrew University representatives over sharing the new site came to naught. Always before the University was the specter of the ill-fated Scopus convoy trapped on hostile ground between the city and the campus. Hadassah was torn between the desire to remain with the University inside urban Jerusalem and to strike out independently on the edge of a wilderness where it could expand without limit. The final decision was put in the hands of David

Ben-Gurion, Israel's political seer. At the site, the security-minded prime minister turned to his Hadassah escort and said, "Magnificent! Build here."

From that moment Hadassah and the University went their separate ways. Not even a compromise worked out later by Defense Minister Pinhas Lavon, who suggested that the University's science faculties remain at Ein Karem, could bridge the gap. In the end, the Medical School and the schools of Dentistry and Pharmacy as well as the Microbiology and Biochemistry departments voted to stay with Hadassah. The University itself built its campus on the Givat Ram ridge, which soon became the geographical center of Jerusalem.

The issue having been decided, Hadassah received 315 acres above Ein Karem through the Jewish National Fund. The first problem was to carve a road to the site. Working with primitive equipment, the state's Public Works Department set out bravely. But on the way the workers ran into a political barrier that could not be budged with TNT. Part of the land belonged to the Russian Orthodox Church, which took its orders from the vicars in the Kremlin. Israel could not then afford diplomatic crises with major powers, so it agreed to stop the work while lawyers fought the issue.

In the autumn of 1956, everyone expected Israel to launch an attack against Jordan. Repeated Arab raids against Israeli towns and farms on the frontiers had made life there unbearable. The crisis peaked on October 25 when Jordan joined Syria and Egypt in a military alliance against Israel. On October 29, the Israeli army struck deep into Sinai in an attack that was coordinated with Britain and France. In 100 hours, Israel occupied the entire peninsula, broke Nasser's blockade of Eilat and smashed Nasser's army. Militarily, Israel's operation was a resounding success. Politically, it was a failure. President Eisenhower condemned the action and forced Israel's withdrawal.

Hadassah had prepared for heavy military casualties, but when the front opened in Sinai rather than in Jordan, the hospitals in Jerusalem were not needed. Most of the wounded were taken to Beersheba where Hadassah organized and staffed a field hospital.

Golda Meir was then foreign minister. After the Russians broke relations with Israel because of the war, Mrs. Meir told Hadassah, "Finish the road quickly. Our relations with the Russians could hardly be worse." Before Moscow could return to Israel, the Henrietta Szold Road was completed to the plateau. And there, four years later, at the southernmost limit of Jerusalem, the Medical Center complex stood.

Not all Hadassah's expectations were fulfilled. The projected highway through the Valley of Sorek that was to open a new gateway to Jerusalem turned out to be a seldom-used secondary two-lane road. Down in the valley an agricultural school was built, a far cry from a university. And near the site that the University rejected, the city fathers dumped and burned Jerusalem's garbage. These shortcomings, however, had no effect on the development of the center. And, as Ben-Gurion had promised, the city did indeed grow toward Ein Karem and even beyond.

The Ein Karem site inspired grandiose dreams among department chiefs that would have required an 800-bed hospital, a 450-student medical school, a 120-student dental school, four acres of space to teach basic sciences and an out-patient clinic to handle 1,000 patients a day.

In New York, the National Board was stunned by these proposals. To build a medical center of such proportions went far beyond anything Hadassah had ever attempted. The shock was not so much over the expanse as over the expense. The original building budget amounted to nearly $8,000,000 with an additional $2,500,000 to be provided by the University for the professional schools. What Jerusalem was requesting would, at prices current then, have amounted to three times that sum. As it developed, soaring costs and needs did force Hadassah to spend an astronomical $30,000,000 by 1971, a decade after the Medical Center was opened, in addition to $6,000,000 provided by the University.

Hadassah turned to its Medical Advisory Board to study Jerusalem's program for the Center. Dr. Harry Eagle, an advocate of modest medical centers, was sent to Jerusalem. His presence there stirred a hornet's nest among Hadassah's equally distinguished physicians. Men such as gynecologist Bernhard Zondek, pathologist Henry Ungar and others protested indignantly that their concepts were questioned.

Sandwiched in the middle was Kalman Mann. On the one hand, New York complained that Jerusalem's doctors were "building personal empires." On the other, his staff insisted that Jerusalem's Medical Center must be large enough to stand on its own with the best in modern medicine. Permission for an agreed-upon program was finally accepted by the National Board and architect Joseph Neufeld was given the green light to prepare blueprints for actual construction.

Both sides had grudgingly compromised. Mann had scaled his staff's demands down to a 540-bed hospital. But that clashed with the Board's insistence on 350 beds. The center finally opened with 420. Yet within a decade the number had risen to 690, the maximum licensed by the Health Ministry. But because of the heavy demand for Hadassah's services, some departments were working at 120 percent occupancy. Four-bed wards often had to accommodate five. When they were filled, the corridors were used. At any one time the hospital might have as many as 750 beds occupied.

In New York, a vigorous building-fund campaign was begun. To raise the money for the single largest project in Hadassah's history, the Medical Center was "sold" in bits and pieces. Donors could buy a brick or square foot in the Center or could be listed as a Founder for $10,000. Out of the Founder's program emerged Hadassah's Major Gifts project ($5,000 and up) which became an important source of funds. The largest single gift until then, $1,000,000, came from Siegfried and Irma Ullmann of New York, for the establishment of Hadassah's 60-bed oncology institute. Named for Moshe Sharett, Israel's second prime minister who died of cancer, the Institute under the late Avraham Hochman was designed to launch a new era of medical science for Hadassah. Built in 1980, it stocked an arsenal of cancer-fighting weapons: 50 cytotoxic drugs, two supra-modern accelerators, units for psycho-oncology and adolescent oncology. By the end of the 1990's the Institute, under Director Tamar Peretz, was treating 10,000 patients yearly, of whom 45 percent were disease-free after five years.

From the cornerstone laying of the Ein Karem center on June 5, 1952, to the projected completion of the Sharett Institute in 1975, Hadassah leaped into a new age of medical care.

To design the Center, Hadassah chose Vienna-educated Neufeld. It had long been realized that the accepted shoe-box form of most hospitals was inefficient, dismal and hard on nurses' feet. Neufeld substituted a semicircular shape which he called "radial." Thus, the distinguishing feature of the Medical Center became the 11-floor radial unit. Inside, on each floor, the nurses' station was located in the center of the half-circle and from there, nurses and attendants were within easy reach of all the wards. To eliminate the gloom of the ordinary hospital, Neufeld put the corridors in the adjoining recovery wings on the outside – one facing north and one facing south. In summer, the north corridor, opposite the picturesque Sorek Valley and the village of Ein Karem, became a lounge. In winter, when the north side was buffeted by wind and rain, the sunlit south corridor became the lounge. Neufeld prescribed red and white bricks and pink Jerusalem stone for the building's exterior to blend with the constantly changing colors of Jerusalem's landscape. The overall cheerful effect and the awesome view caused Rebecca Shulman to remark, "This center has been designed so that people will be able to enjoy their bad health."

Neufeld was beset with unusual problems. One was to secure the building against war damage. Surgery, for example, had to be located two floors above ground – high enough to minimize the effect of near-misses of shells and bombs and low enough to be insulated from a direct hit. Three floors, built underground with connecting tunnels, could be converted into emergency wards.

Inevitably, mistakes would be made in the planning. Large windows facing east and south were sun collectors. In the Mediterranean, where the light is blinding during hot dry summers, planners have learned to use small windows. Neufeld assumed that the hospital would be air-conditioned, but in 1957 a decision was taken to save $1,000,000 by eliminating artificial cooling. The result was that, until air conditioners were finally installed, staff and patients suffered during hot spells.

Jerusalem's water, heavy with sedimentation, wreaked havoc on the American-engineered boilers and pipes. Medical Center Building Chairman Pauline Mack commented on the problem, "I spent long sleepless nights because of Jerusalem's water. We had to spend enormous amounts of money on retubing, reconditioning and cleaning the boilers. Finally, we put in a whole new water system."

But no problem was so ticklish as that which involved the pathologists and rabbis. Religious law forbids *kohanim* (men belonging to the priestly class) from entering a building in which a corpse is lying. Since pathology was an integral part of the Center and it was the only hospital in Jerusalem to dare open a pathology department, Director Mann took the problem to Chief Rabbi of Israel Isaac Nissim and received a facile reply, "Erect a separate building for pathology." Mann blanched; he did not have the extra $5,000,000. Like a patient seeking a more effective cure, he went off to consult another sage (without telling Nissim). The consultant was the Chief Rabbi of Jerusalem, who suggested that if the post-mortem room had electronic doors that opened when one approached and closed before others opened, then the pathology department would be sealed off as though it were not part of the rest of the building.

Happily, Mann went back and ordered electronic doors for the hospital. But the cure failed. Staff and visitors who did not have the patience to wait until one door closed as the other opened even broke the equipment. Mann was left with the problem of how to make the hospital on-bounds for observant *kohanim*. The solution was deceptively simple – revolving doors were installed.

Problems notwithstanding, the Medical Center slowly took shape as the 1950's ended. When it was completed, even the critics could agree that no similar institution existed in the Middle East.

One day in the spring of 1959, as construction moved forward, Hadassah President Miriam Freund sat with Neufeld in her New York office discussing the shape of a small synagogue to be built at the Center. She commented that just that week she had read a newspaper item that Marc Chagall had done some windows for a French cathedral. "Both Neufeld and I had the thought at once that it would be a wonderful thing if Chagall would do windows for our synagogue. I took the idea to the Board."

On the plane to Paris to negotiate with Chagall, Miriam met violinist Isaac Stern and she asked him to accompany Neufeld and her. In Chagall's apartment near Notre Dame the trio tried to convince Chagall in Yiddish, Russian and French. Miriam related:

> While the men were studying the plans for the synagogue, I spoke with Marc's wife. She said, 'Chagall is unhappy that the whole world has come to him but not the Jewish people.' In my broken Yiddish I went over to Chagall and said, 'I have come on behalf of the Jewish people.' I took a deep breath and plunged on, 'We could never repay you enough for doing these windows. I cannot even ask you what your price is since all I can spend is $100,000. That has to cover everything. I know this is no fee for you... but you will be shaping the art history of a new country. All young Israelis are interested in art. You will be their lodestar.' He listened intently, but his only reply was, 'I shall see.'

That was in June 1959. The following December, Miriam and Neufeld flew to Chagall's home in Vence. There they saw already completed drawings for 12 windows: each bore the name of an ancient tribe of Israel and its symbol. Subsequently, the windows were painted in striking blues, greens, yellows and reds. The glass was made at the Simone atelier of Charles and Brigitte Marq in Rheims. Says Miriam: "When the windows were finished, it was much more than we had ever bargained for. They were so beautiful that France's Minister of Culture André Malraux insisted on showing them in the garden of the Louvre. After that we put them on display at the Museum of Modern Art [New York City]." That was in November 1961.

Hundreds of thousands packed the museum to see the hit art show of the season. Then the windows were packed and for security flown on three planes to Israel. The windows arrived in Jerusalem in perfect shape; the replacement pieces were shattered. They became one of Israel's most valuable art treasures and one of the greatest tourist attractions, drawing several million tourists to the Medical Center.

The tiny synagogue which houses them is a modest structure and critics carped that it was much too modest to wear so priceless a diadem. Chagall himself was patently disturbed when he attended the dedication ceremony in 1962. The artist from Vitebsk should have remembered that some of Italy's greatest art works repose in far shabbier churches, but he suggested that they be transferred to the Israel Museum, Chagall promised to replace them with other windows. He had a few supporters, Miriam Freund among them, but the National Board rejected the idea and they remained at the Center.

The dedication of the Ein Karem Medical Center took place on August 3, 1960. The day began routinely for Hadassah's 254 physicians, 514 nurses and 1,352 staff. In Ophthalmology, red-haired Professor Walter Kornblueth operated on three cross-eyed children. A housewife from Athens began to receive massive doses of steroids in Dermatology to fight an advanced case of pemphigus, which had been a fatal disease until the early 1950's. "Cancer patients who are incurable are never hopeless," Oncology Department Chief Hochman told his students that day. "We can always add time to their lives." Then carrying his pipe, which he had stopped filling with tobacco for the last month, he went on to check patients whose tumors were being bombarded by cobalt. Orthopedic surgeon Myer Makin removed a torn cartilage from the knee of a football player. Then he turned the leg of a club-footed boy. Green-uniformed nurse Haya Dorit, a 35-year veteran who directed one of Hadassah's 14 Tipat Halav mother-and-infant welfare stations, reassured Hassida Frumkin. Hassida was eight months pregnant with her first child and suffered from swollen legs. In the Kiryat Yovel Community Health Center, Dr. Charlotte Hopp spent part of the morning reviewing the case of 15-year old Rahamim, a hemophiliac who had lately developed asthma.

Thus was Hadassah occupied on August 3. In the late afternoon nearly all workers left their stations to troop out to the plateau above Ein Karem. There, they joined Israeli notables and 400 overseas guests on the red flagstone plaza. President Freund began with a prayer in which she noted that Hadassah had entered into "a partnership with Him in the healing of the sick, in the rescuing of the homeless and in the mothering of the motherless." A Freedom Bell, shaped like the Liberty Bell, on which was inscribed "Proclaim Ye Healing Throughout the Land," was ceremoniously rung by Fanny Cohen, former Medical Center chairman. American Ambassador Ogden Reid began speaking in correct, if halting, Hebrew, then switched to English so that the American guests could understand him. He noted that $100,000 was provided by the U.S. government to build the premature baby wards.

Prime Minister Ben-Gurion, the featured speaker, complained that he was asked to speak English whereas the non-Jewish ambassador could get away with Hebrew. "I have two wishes," said Ben-Gurion. "One is that I hope we go back to Scopus. And the other is that I hope Hadassah women learn the Hebrew language." He went on to chide American Jews for not sending their children to settle in Israel, but more to the point, he paid tribute to Hadassah's founder:

> Henrietta Szold, who was not only the greatest woman America has yet produced, but undoubtedly one of the noblest personalities of our generation, had two great qualities: her profound knowledge of the Hebrew language and culture and her great desire to work in Israel... May the memory and life's work of Henrietta Szold be a light to guide your path. She gave herself to our country.

Ben-Gurion sat down to polite applause. The dedication was over.

Moving Day followed on June 6, 1961. In May, advance parties had transferred the administration and 250,000 individual records, the huge cobalt therapy unit and medical stores. The army provided 20 ambulances to shuttle 300 patients. Director Mann remembers the day with something less than glee:

> I knew we were not completely ready. I was asked to postpone the operation but Hadassah chapters were celebrating the day. We simply had to go. Top administrative people actually shook me and if others had not interfered I might have been mauled. I was accused of 'killing them,' of 'sucking blood' from them. This was a great psychological crisis in the life of our people because so many changes were involved.

Mann frankly admitted that he had not properly prepared his staff. In the United States, hospital directors trained for such moves for up to two years. He explained, "We could not afford the time." A few were indeed sent abroad to learn how to use new equipment. But even the head of the kitchen, who was thoroughly trained, had a revolt on her hands over a new belt system. But finally when the day was over, Mann cabled New York:

> Proudly report superbly successful completion operation M-Day. 6:00 a.m. nurses prepared patients transfer. 7:30 Hadassah flags unfurled at Medical Center; Mrs. Perlman cut ribbon to admit first convoy of army ambulances bedecked with chapter flags. First came worst cases to avoid the midday heat. Medical corpsmen closing in tenderly to transfer stretcher and transfusion cases to previously designated beds under supervision of doctors and nurses. Next came children, some jumping with excitement; babies in arms of girl soldiers, Ya'al volunteers. 45 minutes after leaving town,

patients comfortably settled in flower-decked wards, admiring breath-taking view, reciting benedictions.

As convoy followed convoy, department after department resumed normal working, treatments, X-rays, examinations – as kitchen prosaically prepared meatballs. 1:00 p.m. army had transferred 300 patients, half stretcher cases, completing this stage of move. Impossible express boundless joy, gratitude of staff, patients to every member of Hadassah who made this great day possible.

In Hadassah's first century this event had made such an indelible imprint that, in the ensuing years, the name "Hadassah" became associated in the public mind mainly with the Ein Karem Medical Center, to the neglect of its many other activities and achievements.

Three hundred thousand members had been preparing for M-Day by raising an additional $300,000 to meet the extra cost. Each chapter undertook to contribute a share of the total and this effort was symbolized by a blue satin pennant on which the name of the chapter was stamped in gold. A duplicate of each banner had been sent to Jerusalem to be affixed to the army trucks transporting the patients. At the 1961 national convention in Denver, the hall was darkened and the pennants distributed to the achieving chapters. As the lights went on, the hall was a sea of pennants.

For the chapters there was an additional reward, for the film *Fifty Miracle Minutes* picturing the move was shown at the evening meeting and there, projected on the screen, they saw the flags flying atop the army trucks as they moved from the town of Jerusalem to the hills. Arthur Goldberg, then U.S. Secretary of Labor, was a guest of the Hadassah convention. He watched in the darkened room and caught something electric, unique, from the assemblage in that hall. When the lights went up and the women cheered and wept, he too was visibly moved.

In Jerusalem, once the jitters of moving passed and everyone became accustomed to the elephantine elevators, the intercom systems and the push buttons, Hadassah settled down to its primary tasks of healing, teaching and research. The years to mid-1967 were relatively calm and richly productive. Hadassah physicians were doing 90 percent of all medical research carried out in Israel. Much of it was too technically complex for laymen to grasp, but some of the projects did manage to fascinate them.

Gynecologist Bernhard Zondek worked toward the development of a new contraceptive. He had already produced a series of pregnancy tests, a urine analysis to determine whether a fetus was alive and a test to find the dominant sex in hermaphrodites. Now he and his associates had found that when an alarm clock was rung regularly within the hearing of mice during their mating sessions, they became temporarily sterile. Zondek achieved the same results with a supersonic device. The obvious continuation was to develop an audio-contraceptive for humans, but Zondek died before achieving his aim.

Zondek's student and successor, Wolfe Polishuk, concentrated on the most serious problem facing gynecology in the Middle East – sterility. In one aspect of the work he and his colleagues found a way to replace a non-functioning fallopian tube with the appendix.

Heart Surgeon Joseph Borman's cardiac surgery unit developed an electronic defibrillator that controlled irregular heart beats during open chest operations.

Neurologist Lipman Halpern did major experimentation into color medicine. In a rare sickness which he called unilateral disequilibrium, a condition in which patients see abnormally on the affected side of the brain, Halpern found that red-colored glasses aggravated the symptoms while green or blue glasses corrected them. The result of a blow on the head or sclerosis, the disease made patients stumble while walking or see pictures tilted on walls.

Orthopedic surgeon Myer Makin, who won a British medical medal for introducing bone formation through bladder transplants, developed a procedure to lengthen shortened legs by as much as two and one-half inches.

Dental School Dean Jacob Lewin-Epstein, together with pharmacologist Edward Superstine, pioneered the use of a pre-anesthetic suppository for children undergoing dental surgery. Children fall asleep and wake up without any recollection of undergoing an unhappy experience.

Dermatologist Jacob Sheskin prescribed the drug Thalidomide, which had been responsible for causing deformed babies, to help lepers. He found that while Thalidomide did not cure leprosy it did alleviate pain, skin eruptions and fevers to such an extent that at least half of the patients could be released from hospital.

Former Medical Director Eli Davis and ophthalmologist Jacob Landau reported on a method to diagnose such ills as arteriosclerosis, hypertension, diabetes and rheumatic fever by placing a patient's fingertip under a microscope. Called clinical capillary microscopy, the test became routine at Hadassah for the first time anywhere.

Ringworm, which was usually treated by first shaving heads, affected about 20,000 persons in the late 1950's. Then, dermatology chief Felix Sagher discovered a new remedy that eliminated the shaving and the disease.

In the chest disease department, Professor Joseph Rakower reported that if one had to smoke, the safest of all was an old-fashioned narghileh, the water pipe of the Arabs.

Hadassah was back on the job and ready for the new challenges that were sure to come.

SIX DAYS IN JUNE

In June 1967, Israel was again at war and, as usual, the unexpected happened. The bitterest fighting and the heaviest casualties occurred in the City of Peace. Until the latter part of May, Hadassah did not anticipate a war in Jerusalem any more than anyone else, but like the entire nation it was prepared for what it did not expect.

As early as December 1964, in conjunction with the army, Hadassah administrators drew up a confidential manual that detailed Hadassah's aid requirements in time of national emergency down to the last safety pin. Periodic drills tested the manual's instructions. Unexpectedly, hospital chiefs would receive a call from an army officer: "In a few minutes you will be receiving 50 wounded soldiers." A short while later, 50 serious-faced school children would be brought up in ambulances, each wearing a tag describing his imaginary wounds. Medical Deputy Director Jack Karpas, satisfied with the lessons of the drill would say, "We are ready."

On May 15, 1967, Israel celebrated its 19th anniversary with a military show in Jerusalem. In Egypt, soldiers began to march too, but not in parade. They were headed for Sinai. By May 26, war appeared inevitable. On that day the Hadassah hospital pharmacy, under the direction of Detroit-born Edward Superstine, began preparing massive amounts of sterile solutions, analgesics and antibiotics. Reported Superstine, "Our 20-member staff worked 20 hours a day. In our storerooms we kept 5,000 different types of pharmaceuticals. Drug trucks were fitted out to be sent to other areas in case the war went on for a long time and we could not accommodate all the wounded."

Military intelligence passed the word that the Egyptians might use gas as they had done in the Yemen war. (Gas installations later captured in Sinai justified the report.) Superstine had quantities of one antidote, atropin, on hand, but it was useless against nerve gas. Cables were sent to Gladys Zales, in charge of purchasing supplies, to buy large quantities of the effective antidote. Gladys said, "We were told everywhere it simply was not available. The Red Cross told us to try the military. We called the Pentagon, but they said that we must first get permission from the inventor in Paris. We got a call from the FBI wanting to know why we wanted this antigas medicine. In the end we failed." But on June 4, one day before war began, a supply sufficient for about 5,000 casualties arrived at Ein Karem. The supposedly secret formula was produced by scientists of the Weizmann Institute of Science in Rehovot. Fortunately it was never needed.

The weekend before the storm broke was unusually quiet. In synagogues the portion of the Law to be read that Sabbath was the beginning of the Book of Numbers wherein Moses is commanded by God to take a census of all military-aged men fit to fight for the Promised Land. Not everyone was in synagogue. Large numbers of soldiers, who had been given leave to confuse the enemy, spent their time on the Mediterranean beaches. In Tel Aviv, Prime Minister Levi Eshkol's cabinet determined that Big Power intervention against Nasser's blockade of Israeli shipping through the Tiran Straits was not in the cards and that the 100,000 battle-ready Egyptians poised in the Sinai desert were a death threat to the State of Israel. It authorized Eshkol and the new defense minister, Moshe Dayan, to resolve the problem at their own discretion. In effect, that was the green light for a preemptive attack against Egypt.

In Jerusalem on Sunday, June 4, some householders busied themselves filling sandbags, preparing air-raid shelters and taping up windows. At Ein Karem, Director Mann and Deputy Director Karpas had 2,000 windowpanes to worry about. Workers and student volunteers labored throughout the day and night filling sacks and hanging blackout material. Said Mann,

> The day before the war, I asked all personnel to volunteer to work an additional two hours. The Workers Committee complained that I was creating panic. This is one of the times I thought I would have a heart attack. I blew up. 'Don't you see a war is coming?' I shouted. The head of the committee replied there was no war and I was only getting panicky. But they finally agreed to work the extra hours... At the end of the week the committee came to drink *l'hayyim* and to apologize.

Of particular concern were the Chagall windows. To extricate them without damaging the glass was difficult. Mann cabled Charles Marq in Rheims to fly to Israel to remove them. He arrived on Saturday night, June 3. On Sunday, Marq and Jerusalem architect Dan Ben-Dor studied the problem. Each of the 12 windows was divided into 12 sections. Each section was made up of between 40 and 50 individual pieces of glass. The glass in the center was held fast by putty but around the frames, where the glass was set in concrete, they were reinforced with cement. Ben-Dor carefully tried a dentist's drill with no success. He tried other types of saws with little result. That night, Mann visited Marq at the King David Hotel. The only other tourist in the city's largest hotel was former Hadassah president Rebecca Shulman who had been on the way to the airport to fly home when her son Paul informed her that war was imminent. She turned back on the spot.

Mann recalls, "Marq felt we were all doomed. I tried to assure him that we would survive but he did not believe me. I left the hotel with a heavy heart and he departed next morning on the last plane. Rebecca remained throughout the war."

That same sense of doom pervaded the Western world. Marc Chagall cabled Hadassah, "I am not worried about the windows, only about the safety of Israel. Let Israel be safe and I will make you better windows."

To some extent the threat to Israel's survival was illusory for the nation was sufficiently strong militarily to withstand the onslaught of all its hostile neighbors. The unanswerable question for Israelis on June 4, 1967, was not whether they would fall but how badly they would bleed.

In New York, Hadassah reacted to the crisis on two levels – the political and the material. President Charlotte Jacobson set up an operations room at National Hadassah headquarters on 52nd Street. Says Charlotte:

> We went to Washington at the end of May and we came away with a sense of frustration. We saw every senator and congressman. Everyone said that he would never let Israel down. They all made beautiful speeches. When we pressed them, they admitted that the United States would not act alone but in concert with the United Nations. We came away with a terrible feeling. Although no one doubted American friendship, nothing moved. This gave us the sense of urgency. We had to see to it that everything was well-prepared in Israel.

If the leadership in Washington could do nothing to prevent the war, the alerted American citizen did everything to ensure its outcome. The staff and volunteers at Hadassah's New York headquarters worked 24-hour days for two weeks. Medical institutions and personnel throughout the country called Hadassah to offer supplies and volunteers. An additional switchboard operating night and day in Hadassah headquarters was swamped with calls. During the crisis Treasurer Faye Schenk did not have to spend an extra cent from the normal budget. "Everything," she said, "was contributed." After hostilities ended, Dr. Mann reported that not one of the thousands of items required by physicians to treat the casualties was missing except for the single exception of a Number 7 cannula needed for insertion into a soldier's windpipe. "The surgeon managed with a larger size," Mann reassured Gladys Zales, Hadassah's purchasing chairman. For one operation ophthalmologist Michaelson needed a pair of human eyes and got them. One morning during the war, Gladys was startled by a call from the executive director of the International Eye Foundation in Washington.

"Mrs. Zales," he said, "I have two fresh eyes to send to Jerusalem. They must be there within 24 hours."

A National Board member was assigned to meet an Eastern airlines flight from Washington, pick up the seven-pound vacuum jug containing the eyes and put it on an El Al flight. The transfer was accomplished and the eyes were in Michaelson's hands with little time to spare.

Johnson and Johnson, the pharmaceutical firm, like many others, donated supplies. Upon receiving Hadassah's thanks for the 1,200 cases of surgical dressings, the firm said it planned to make a gift for Israel a yearly event. (True to its word, America's largest medical supply company continued the donation until 1988). An El Al spokesman assured Hadassah that next to ammunition, Hadassah had top priority to move its supplies. TWA and KLM topped that by taking freight free of charge.

The stories of giving and helping during the war are now part of American-Jewish folklore. Some Jews signed their Social Security checks over to Hadassah. One man said: "If Israel loses, I won't need it. If Israel wins, I am sure to get it back."

Treasurer and later President, Faye Schenk received a total of $1,200,000 in cash. One envelope arrived with a $100 bill and a newspaper clipping from The New York Times advertising the opening of Peter Ustinov's play, An Unknown Soldier and His Wife. A check for $250 was sent by the Fifth Avenue Presbyterian Church with a simple message: "We want to help." From Chicago, an eight-year-old girl sent in several dollars with an apologetic note, "This is all the cash I have on hand."

A young man appeared at Hadassah headquarters on June 5 saying he had just finished medical school. He organized 30 young doctors to help determine priorities for shipping medicines. There were humorous sidelights, like the man who sent in a huge consignment of pajamas with pop art flowers emblazoned on them. He thought they would help cheer up soldier patients. One late afternoon toward the end of the war, Gladys received a call from S. Klein, a New York department store.

"I understand you need linens," said the Klein official.

Wearily, Gladys replied, "Yes, yes. Send them right over."

"They will be there in one hour," he replied blandly.

An hour later a truck driver interrupted Gladys. "Ma'am, I have some linens for you."

"Fine," she smiled mechanically. "Just put them there on the right of the receiving area."

The driver looked perturbed. "Lady, I don't want to bother you but I think maybe you better come outside and have a look."

Gladys, somewhat annoyed at the interruption, stepped outside. "I nearly fainted," she said. There before her was parked a 50-foot trailer filled to the roof with 7,500 sheets, 4,500 pillow cases and 1,200 blankets. She asked the driver to take them to a garage and the following week they were on a ship to Israel.

In Israel, three weeks of escalating tensions broke in a crescendo of violence at the breakfast hour on June 5. At 08:10, the Voice of Israel gave a terse report that fighting had broken out on the southern front. At that very moment the first wave of Israeli jets screeching precariously low over the Mediterranean had surprised the Egyptian air force and by the end of the morning would smash it out of existence. At about 09:00 hours, the Israeli Army Chief Medical Officer called Deputy Director Karpas: "Fighting has broken out in the Negev. Prepare to receive wounded." This time it was no exercise. Hadassah was put immediately into a Phase IV emergency, the highest state of preparedness provided for in its manual.

Outside the synagogue Dan Ben-Dor and an assistant had been busy with buzz saws carefully grinding away at the cement. Slowly they lifted the small pieces of glass from the Chagall windows and placed them in the original packing cases which had been brought up from the storerooms. Dan began work on the north side because he feared that the first shelling would come from Jordanian positions on Nebi Samwil in the north.

Director Mann arrived at the hospital early that morning.

> I gazed from my window and could see the sandbags being filled. I heard the bells pealing from the churches of Ein Karem. The picture seemed serene. When I saw tanks crossing the road in the distance, I gave the order to bring the patients down. Then I saw shells begin to fall in the valley, first near the Agricultural School and then inching toward the hospital. I could not believe my eyes. It was as though I was watching a movie. I could not believe they were aiming at us. But they were.

As Ben-Dor buzzed away with the saw out in the open, a tremendous blast shook the synagogue on the east side. The shells – probably mortars – had come not from Nebi Samwil but from Beit Jala to the southeast of Jerusalem, near Bethlehem. "If I had started on the windows on the east side I would not have been here today," Ben-Dor said later. Fragments of shells ricocheted from the paving stones and punctured five of Chagall's windows. But the damage was not serious. Altogether six shells hit the medical center. Ben-Dor took cover till the shelling stoppped, then returned to his work. By Wednesday, working night and day, he removed nine whole windows. At that point, he realized there was no longer need to continue. All Jerusalem was in Israeli hands.

In Pediatrics, department chief Alex Russell was sitting in his chair by the window when a mortar shell burst outside. Shrapnel sprayed through the aluminum blind. "Over my desk," he recalls, "a beam of light shone.

That was the window crashing through." Russell rushed off to the maternity pavilion. He reported:

> Windows were shattered on both sides. The last of the babies had been evacuated within minutes before we were hit. Their empty cots were full of splintered glass. All the children were taken to shelters just in time, except for three children having blood transfusions. None was hurt.

In that long day at Hadassah, five normal births would be registered and three circumcisions performed.

After the sixth shell had fallen, all was quiet. The Jordanians now concentrated on the center of the city. Mann and his emergency staff had to determine whether to evacuate the hospital of its civilian patients. War casualties would soon be arriving. According to plan, they had to leave, but with the shelling going on in the city could he risk sending them away? He did. The time chosen, in mid-afternoon, could not have been better. A lull in the firing had occurred as the buses and private cars moved out of the Ein Karem compound. Not one of the 300 evacuees was hurt. About 150 who could not be moved were left behind.

Nine teams of surgeons were ready when the first war casualties from the fighting in southern Jerusalem were hurried in. All told, 1,200 beds were available at Hadassah and 17 operating theaters stood by, eight of them underground. During peacetime, the hospital had room for less than 700 patients and ran nine operating theaters. Pediatricians, psychiatrists, dentists, biochemists, not normally needed for casualty work, were pressed into service as assistants to surgeons and as anesthetists. All had taken special courses for emergency work.

The casualties were rushed to the out-patient department, which had been turned into a receiving station. There, two of Hadassah's most senior surgeons – Nathan Saltz and Nathan Rabinowitz – personally examined them and made the basic decisions for their care while, at the same time, they were registered. Says Karpas, "The fact that we had these senior men in charge saved many lives because a patient who is properly prepared for an operation stands a much greater chance of survival."

What concerned the surgeons most was shock. Physical shock is the result of severe tissue injury or heavy loss of blood and can be fatal. During shock, blood pressure falls and because of the insufficiency of blood to carry oxygen to the tissue, it dies. Physicians were hard put to know clinically when shock was no longer reversible or what caused the condition to be halted.

But they did know that in many cases of shock, infusions of blood plasma could make a difference. At Hadassah during the Six-Day War, surgeons made much greater use of another fluid called Hartman's Solution. Says chief surgeon Saltz: "Before the war we learned that tissue destruction resulted from the contraction of a certain amount of the actual tissue fluids in the spaces of the body, not in the bloodstream. In addition to the bloodstream there was a contraction of fluid that surrounds the cells."

Twelve thousand bottles of Hartman's Solution, a modified salt formula containing lactate, had been prepared in the hospital's pharmacy. Ten thousand bottles were used on the 927 cases who were admitted within three days. On the other hand, only 1,000 bottles of blood were used. The result was phenomenal. Says Saltz, "No patient who came to our hospital without an absolute mortal wound was lost in shock."

In the first day of fighting, Hadassah received 86 casualties. They were well-spaced and Saltz thought that the hospital would have no trouble coping from then on. But he did not know that during the first day in the Jerusalem area the troops were only organizing for the big confrontation.

Jordan had four full brigades ready to do battle. Facing them in Jerusalem, Israel had a brigade of reservists, many of them middle-aged, with orders not to shoot unless they were shot at and not to escalate the firing. The big action was expected in the south; Sinai was the objective. Jordan was not thought likely to become involved and so Jerusalem, lightly held, became a calculated risk. Prime Minister Eshkol made repeated attempts to assure King Hussein that he need not worry about an Israeli attack on the Jordan front. But Hussein, who had signed a defense pact with Nasser and had put his forces under an Egyptian commander, was receiving enthusiastic messages from Nasser that the Egyptians were bombing Israel into submission. Thus, Hussein agreed that the front be opened in the east and the Jordanian shelling of Jerusalem began at about 10:15 on the morning of June 5. A brigade of Israeli paratroopers under Colonel Mordecai "Motta" Gur was brought up hastily from the Southern Command and thrown into the battle which did not begin in earnest until early on the morning of June 6. That day was a grievously memorable one. Savage hand-to-hand fighting at such places as Ammunition Hill, Mivtar Hill and the Police School were among the most bitter actions in Israeli history. Companies of men were decimated on both sides. At the end of the day, however, Sheikh Jarrah was taken and the road up to Mt. Scopus was opened. Fate gave the victory to Jerusalem-born Chief of Staff Yitzhak Rabin, who 19 years earlier had been forced by the British to abandon Sheikh Jarrah and Mt. Scopus.

Recalls Saltz:

> On that Tuesday morning, the wounded suddenly started pouring in and by afternoon we had every single hall of the first and second floors filled with casualties – Jordanians among them. I remember looking over some that I had not managed to get to and I was in despair. I wondered how we were ever going to manage. But we did and everything was ready. No one was lost.

Operations went on around the clock – 310 in three days. And some lasted four hours. Says Saltz, "I never believed it was possible to go three days without sleep but I proved it to myself."

Neurosurgeon Aharon Beller was abroad when the wars began in 1948 and 1956. He was in Madrid for a meeting of neurosurgeons when the Tiran Straits were closed. "I packed up and returned fast this time and arrived less than two weeks before it broke out. We did not have as much work as in 1948 but it was so concentrated we had to work day and night. I operated non-stop for 50 hours. We had 40 head and 10 spinal cases."

Ear-nose-throat chief Moshe Feinmesser's team worked on 50 soldiers with ruptured ear drums and inner ear damage. Only five percent were left with severe handicaps. Ophthalmologist Michaelson and his colleagues had 50 major eye operations in four days, about 25 of them to remove foreign bodies.

Good as the results were, bottlenecks developed. One of the most difficult to handle was the appearance at Ein Karem of about 1,200 volunteers. Karpas reported, "All our well-prepared plans were nearly spoiled because there were so many volunteers. We had to put a special person on duty to direct them." Ya'al (Hebrew acronym for 'A Helping Hand to the Ill'), an organization of white-smocked Israeli women, during the war cleaned floors and cupboards, made bandages, assisted mothers in the maternity hospital to move into shelter, worked in the emergency wards and ran the cafeterias. Over 500 members were registered at Hadassah. Other hospitals adopted the idea and now there are altogether more than 3,000 Ya'al volunteers throughout Israel.

A strange story of one volunteer is told by orthopedic surgeon Makin. He rushed back to Jerusalem from New York, where he had been on sabbatical, arriving on Thursday, June 7. He found that most of the casualties needed orthopedic attention and that his colleague, Gordon Robin, had worked continuously for more than two days. Two members of an orthopedic team were so fatigued they were sleeping on the floor.

> First thing I did was to take Robin off and start work. After about 12 hours, a Canadian Gentile appeared and said, 'My name is John Hall. Can I lend a hand?' He had been a professor of orthopedic surgery in Saigon during the war and was just the person we needed. He had been back in Toronto only a week and when he heard the war was on, he boarded

the first plane.... When he was no longer needed, he left and we never heard from him again.

On Wednesday, June 7, heavy fighting ended in Jerusalem. Israeli troops crashed through Lions Gate of the ancient walled city and ran toward the Western Wall as Jordan's troops fled back across the Jordan River. When the battle-weary Israelis reached the Wall, they wept. Some prayed for the first time in their lives. Later, they had difficulty in explaining their reactions. But they did acknowledge that their arrival at the Wall was for them a transcendental moment that bridged two millennia of Jewish history.

With the dwindling of fighting in the Jerusalem theater of operations, the inflow of casualties slackened. By the end of the sixth day, Hadassah had treated one-third of the nation's casualties.

On the seventh day, Israelis rejoiced and much of the world rejoiced with them. In Washington, recalls Hadassah's 15th president, Rose Matzkin, "Jews from every walk of life – from the *hasidim* to the most assimilated – felt very much involved. It was a kind of spontaneous uproar of joy, of dancing and praying, all outbursts of great emotion and relief."

At Ein Karem, Prime Minister Eshkol addressed the doctors, nurses and staff:

> I wish to thank you from the bottom of my heart for all that you have done and are doing to treat the wounded and to return them to a productive life, and I am speaking for the families of the wounded Arab soldiers, too.
>
> God knows that in our hearts we have no hatred for the Arabs and I hope that we can work out some system of peaceful coexistence for the benefit of both peoples. The proof of the lack of hatred is the extreme care that is being given to these Arab prisoners of war here at Hadassah. I am sure that the

same spirit can prevail and be extended to all our relations in peacetime.

The Six-Day War offered Hadassah and the Hebrew University a special prize – Mt. Scopus. After 19 years in limbo, the mount was once again part of Jewish Jerusalem.

For Israel and for Hadassah, 1967 was a watershed year.

In Judea, Samaria and the Gaza Strip, Hadassah extended its medical consultative services to Arab institutions. Until more Arab hospitals could be built and staffed in what were now officially referred to as "the Administered Territories," Arabs would crowd to Ein Karem for medical care. That meant that the first order of Hadassah's priorities in Israel would be the revival of Mt. Scopus.

The astounding victory of June 1967 had finally convinced a skeptical world that Israel was a permanent geopolitical fact. On the home front, the pre-war economic depression ended abruptly as the nation prospered. Israelis moved into the territories to found new settlements on barren soil. Within the neighboring Arab world, revolutionary forces formed and under the leadership of Yasser Arafat, Palestinians went on the rampage for liberation from Israeli occupation.

Still, the euphoric Israelis were hoping for peace. Prime Minister Eshkol offered a treaty based on the return of captured lands. But the revolutionary groups turned to acts of terror. And the Egyptians resumed hostilities even though they held only one bank of the Suez Canal and the Israeli hinterland was well beyond the range of their artillery. For its part, Israel felt more secure and invincible than ever.

Nasser retained faith in ultimate victory through a combination of massive retaliation and Big Power politics. Negotiation with Israel was for him tantamount to surrender. In answer to Eshkol's offer, Nasser declared at an Arab summit in Khartoum that there would be no negotiation, no peace and no recognition. Israel replied: no negotiation – no peace.

The result was deadlock and more fighting. Concurrent with vain attempts by Arab irregulars to terrorize Israel to its knees, Nasser declared a war of attrition along the Suez Canal in 1969 with the aim of exhausting Israeli forces through constant shelling and eventually taking back Sinai by direct assault. Against these threats, Israel built an electronic fence on the eastern and northern borders. In the south, it constructed a massive earth fortification: the Bar-Lev line, named for Chief of Staff Haim Bar-Lev.

For 18 months the line withstood murderous night-and-day cannonading that came to be known as the War of Attrition

No attempt was made to conceal the bloodletting from the public. Hourly, the state radio broadcast names of the fallen soldiers. Citizens worked with transistors held to their ears. In shops, restaurants and in parlors conversation stopped every hour on the hour. In Jerusalem, all eyes lifted skyward when a military helicopter appeared heading southward toward Hadassah. The city then knew a battle was in progress. On Yom Kippur 1969, the service in one synagogue was halted when a helicopter was heard overhead, so that prayers for the wounded it bore could be recited. The military established a liaison office in the hospital at Ein Karem to alert the staff of incoming casualties. A helicopter pad was built on the western flank to receive them. Half of all the casualties were taken to Hadassah. Fifteen teams of physicians and nurses remained constantly prepared as the hospital built up its capacity to treat as many as 1,800 in case of total emergency. Partly because of the wars, Hadassah built up its orthopedic and rehabilitation departments and instituted units for intensive care.

In 1970, when the Russians began to intervene directly on Egypt's side, the Americans stepped in and forced a cease-fire. This, the fourth of Israel's wars, was the most enervating of all to date. Casualties were higher than those in the Six-Day War: 552 dead and 1,761 wounded.

Still smarting from their humiliating defeats, Egypt and Syria quietly trained to take revenge. It came when Israel least expected – on Yom Kippur, Saturday, October 6, 1973. The unprepared, over-confident Israeli forces were taken by surprise and suffered heavily. But in the end they scored a military triumph that would lead to peace with Egypt. At the same time the "victory" created political upheaval at home and sent the population into a long, deep depression.

These wars, interlaced with acts of terrorism, would place heavy burdens on Hadassah and the entire medical establishment. It was some comfort, however, that the "daughter of my people" was on hand to provide a reply to the 2,600-year-old lament of the Prophet Jeremiah:

> Is there no balm in Gilead?
> Is there no physician there?
> Why then is not the health
> Of the daughter of my people restored?*

---

* Jeremiah 8; 22.

SCOPUS REVIVED

On the morning of Sunday, April 25, 1976, eight freshly-painted blue and white ambulances from the Ein Karem Medical Center moved in single file toward Mt. Scopus. In the ambulances sat the first contingent of patients to be transferred to the rebuilt and refurbished building that had lain desolate for 28 years.

As the convoy approached Sheikh Jarrah, the site of the 1948 ambush, the vehicles halted and those patients who were mobile joined staff to stand by the modest stone memorial. Wearing roses on their hospital gowns, they laid a wreath on the monument and then continued their journey to the top of the mountain.

The hospital had been rededicated six months earlier, well before it was finished, on October 21, 1975. In the presence of political leaders and 2,000 Hadassah members, Benjamin Adin, the now 74-year-old truck driver who had survived the convoy massacre, hoisted the flag.

Prime Minister Yitzhak Rabin, who fought for Mt. Scopus as a soldier in 1948 and as Chief of Staff in 1967, remembered how for 19 years Israelis would look across the hills "and recall the majesty of this great hospital and the tragedy that had befallen it. Its name will forever be linked with the agonizing battles for freedom and for the reunification of Jerusalem."

U.S. Ambassador Malcolm Toon praised Hadassah for opening the hospital "to people who had previously fought on opposite sides."

Nine years earlier soldiers fighting their way to the Old City of Jerusalem and the Western Wall overran all of Mt. Scopus. They found the hospital and the University derelict. Moving in the wake of the troops, the city's intrepid Mayor Teddy Kollek stopped at an Arab hotel in the eastern part of the city to put a call through to HMO Director-General Kalman Mann.

"If you want your hospital," Teddy called in his typically direct manner, "come and get it."

Mann knew the day before that Scopus had fallen into Israeli hands and he sent a cable to Hadassah headquarters in New York: **"SCOPUS REGAINED."**

On the morning of June 9, 1967, Hebrew University President Eliahu Elath and Mann set off with their parties for Scopus in seven cars. With Mann were Hadassah's former President Rebecca Shulman* and his predecessor, Eli Davis. Despite occasional sniper fire from Arab quarters, the vehicles paused in the Sheikh Jarrah quarter to stand at the site of the 1948 convoy ambush while Mann recited *kaddish* for the victims.

They then traveled the extra mile to the crest of Scopus where they were welcomed by the 120 guards who a few days earlier withstood a 36-hour Jordan Army bombardment. While Israeli jets circled the sky, flags were raised on the roofs of the Hospital and the University. Inside the buildings of both institutions the bulletin boards still bore notices dating to 1947.

On his return to Ein Karem workers hoisted Mann on their shoulders as though he were the groom at a traditional Jewish wedding. Tears of joy flowed when he reported that Hadassah's flag again flew over Scopus.

---

* Rebecca Shulman, who in the early 1950's pledged that Hadassah would return to Scopus, was present during all of Israel's early wars. During the 1948 War of Independence she was Hadassah's representative in Israel. Her late son, Paul, a volunteer with the Israel Defense Forces, was the first chief of the Israel Navy.

Speaking over an intercom to those assembled in the dining room of the new hospital at Ein Karem, Mann said, "This flag symbolizes an unusual type of war – the war against disease and ignorance. It is a flag of peace."

Later, Mann would write in his *Reflections*:

> It was an example of the general state of elation, relief and almost hysterical happiness that gripped the entire nation. We will build those who were slain in the convoy a glorious monument.

President Charlotte Jacobson arrived in Israel shortly after the war. She, together with former president Lola Kramarsky, had received special permission from the State Department to fly into the forbidden zone. Prime Minister Levi Eshkol invited her to his office where he told her that it was essential for Hadassah to reopen the hospital because it would help in the reunification of the city. He explained that large housing projects were about to be built in the area.

Before Charlotte visited the hospital building she went with Kalman Mann to the Mount of Olives and there, with the help of several rabbis searched for the grave of Henrietta Szold. They found that the Jordanians had built a road over the graves of Judaism's oldest cemetery, Henrietta's included. Some stone markers were obliterated, others were reported to have been used as flooring for Jordanian military barracks. Using a cemetery chart and counting the indentations in the ground they identified the site. It was rebuilt and in a formal ceremony a new stone was put up.

Israeli soldiers escorted Charlotte's party to Scopus* past minefields and the debris of war. When Charlotte entered the building she saw devastation. It was immediately clear that what Hadassah received on returning was not so much a hospital building as a ruin.

---

* The Jordan-Israel Armistice Agreement that ended the 1948-49 war provided free access to the Western Wall, Hospital and University even though the Arab Legion controlled the area. Jordan ignored the provisions even though Scopus was supposedly demilitarized. Every two weeks, a U.N.-supervised convoy supplied and relieved the Israeli guards at the Hospital and the University buildings.

"I'll never forget the weed-choked paths, the areas of waste and loneliness," Charlotte later recalled.

Walls were broken and defaced by shell holes. Woodwork was rotted. Medical equipment and beds were rusted. Winds tore through shattered windows and howled down corridors in what had once been wards and nurses stations. Henrietta Szold's carefully tended garden was overgrown with weeds. Weeping, the visitors read aloud a message scribbled on a wall by an Israeli guard who had stood lonely watch under the U.N. flag during those 19 years:

> If the day comes and this building is filled again with patients, let them remember those who watched over this place during difficult years.

Charlotte Jacobson returned to her quarters and overcome with emotion addressed a letter to Hadassah leaders throughout the U.S. She quoted one severely wounded soldier at Ein Karem who told her with a wan smile, "When we entered Hadassah we knew we were in good hands."

She related what she saw on Scopus and described her first pilgrimage to the Western Wall where, like thousands of others, she could hardly believe she was not dreaming.

"Verily," she wrote, "the age of miracles is not over. This is indeed an age of renaissance for the Jewish people."

On the national level, Israel's leadership had learned from the siege of 1948 and the war of 1967 that to protect its capital, it must build well in the north, east and south where the city faced Arab armies. In the north, as the Romans had known 2,000 years earlier, Scopus was the key to the city. And on that hill the Hospital and the University would be rebuilt as fortresses both above and below ground, thus serving a dual purpose – institutions for both peace and war.

For the government it was politically vital to have the hospital in operation quickly because satellite communities were rising. Planned in a semi-circle around what was then the border of Jerusalem, thousands of stone-faced apartment buildings appeared on the map bearing names such as Ramot, French Hill, Ramat Eshkol, Neve Ya'acov, Talpiot East, Gilo. In effect they formed a *cordon sanitaire* for Jerusalem's Jewish population.

The Arab community fussed and fumed over the construction, claiming that Israel thereby changed the status quo of the city, and appealed to the U.N. There, diplomats condemned the residences as a danger to peace.

Jerusalem's mayor had plans of his own. In 28 years in office, he outdid Herod the Great. He garbed the city with gardens and parks. He initiated museums and a fine center for the performing arts. He provided the Arab population with new housing, schools and cultural institutions. Under his hand the city received a reliable water supply; sewage disappeared from the streets; tourists flocked to artistically-lit sites. In municipal elections held after the war, unprecedented numbers of non-Israeli Arabs flocked to the polls to vote for Teddy Kollek. Jerusalem had never been so grand or expansive.

Now that the hulk of a once statuesque edifice was in Hadassah's hands, what was to be done with it? Doubts were at first expressed about the necessity of reopening the hospital. On paper, the idea was not attractive. Hadassah now had the larger Medical Center at Ein Karem and the expense of building would be enormous. The late President Faye Schenk (1968-1972) who oversaw the building campaign laid any doubts to rest. She wrote,

"When Hadassah descended from Mt. Scopus in 1948, a silent vow was made that some day we would return." And for Hadassah, a vow could not be broken.

Hadassah National Board's Mid-Winter Conference of 1968 was the first to be held in Jerusalem and a pilgrimage was made to Scopus. Relates former President Ruth Popkin: "We gathered on a cold, miserable day. We literally froze but we were standing on the mosaic floor with Hadassah's symbol still there. We were warmed because we were back on our 'Hill of Healing.'"

The controversy over the character of the hospital absorbed the leadership for more than a year. Kalman Mann sought to have a general hospital built to serve the surrounding mixed community of Jews and Arabs. Others were more interested in specialist medical centers. Among them: a cancer center, a Mayo-type clinic, psychiatric hospital, institutes for brain research and tropical diseases.

A gift of one million pounds sterling was received from a Swiss Jew whose child was handicapped. But there was a string attached to the money: build a children's hospital. The gift was returned.

While Hadassah debated, cadres of young Israeli volunteers joined by youth from countries as distant as Australia, India and the U.S., began cleaning up. They cleared debris, painted walls, laid floors, removed rust from plumbing and built internal walls. That done, the builders could begin.

Charlotte Jacobson, who as HMO chairperson would preside over the reconstruction after completing her tenure as President in 1968, favored reopening the hospital immediately. Dr. Mann suggested that in view of the many war injuries a physical rehabilitation department with 120 beds be the first priority.

The medical board advising Hadassah had met to deliberate the question one day after the end of the Six-Day War. Working its way through a maze of complications, bureaucratic and otherwise, the National Board decided in August 1968 to reopen Scopus as a general community hospital to serve both Arabs and Jews. It would have one of the finest rehabilitation centers in the region.

The population in the vicinity of Scopus would reach 150,000 toward the end of the century. It was that population that the hospital was expected to serve. In the end, its reputation as a fine, clean, quiet institution grew rapidly and attracted Jewish and Arab patients from the entire Jerusalem region.

Politically, a community hospital was the right way to go. Hadassah lay at a strategic juncture between Arab and Jewish sides of the city. There were no general hospitals of Hadassah's caliber serving the Arabs. In a major sense, opening an all-purpose hospital was a goodwill gesture. Prime Minister Eshkol assured Charlotte Jacobson, "It will help ensure the unification of Jerusalem."

The dynamic Charlotte Jacobson moved to Jerusalem for an extended period to supervise: "I used to go to the site every day to ensure that the contractor played fair with us. I counted the number of workers who turned up daily and I checked the way they worked. If things looked crooked to me, I'd make them redo it!"

In America, Hadassah's largest money-raising drive ever was launched. Practically everything that would go into rebuilding Scopus was made available for naming, whether it be a bed or a brick, a ward or a washroom. Someone could have his or her name on it – for a donation. In the end more than $30,000,000 was raised.*

Tel Aviv architect Ya'akov Rechter was chosen to plot the layout. He would retain Eric Mendelsohn's external "design-for-the ages" Bauhaus architecture. Commented Rechter, "It would have been easier to raze the site and start again but the original building was classical and had been declared a national monument."

The exterior was saved but the interior was reconstructed from scratch. The revived hospital's first medical director, Uri Khassis, described the scene as construction got underway:

"A labyrinth of wires, pipes, ducts and cables was built to bring air conditioning, gas, demineralized water, soft water, sterile water, oxygen and vacuum, monitoring units for intensive care."

Over the years the Scopus hospital became a melting pot. At few other sites in the mixed city would Jew and Arab meet in such accepting

---

* The U.S. government contributed an initial grant of $5,000,000 toward reconstruction. Yearly, Hadassah has applied for and received grants under the American program to help schools and hospitals abroad (ASHA). Grants ranging between $300,000 and $3,000,000 have been used for everything from buying equipment in America to training African doctors. ASHA grants for Hadassah have amounted to nearly $40 million.

conditions.* In the pediatric departments alone, Arabs made up about 50 percent of the patients.

"While there are two Arab hospitals in the immediate area," says Scopus Medical Director Jacques Michel, "they [the patients] come to us probably because of Hadassah's name and tradition."

Staffs were integrated with Arabs serving at every level from medicine to maintenance. Dr. Najah Husseini, a relative of the late Grand Mufti of Jerusalem, was accepted as an orthopedic surgeon in 1976 at the age of 34. He recalls that when he decided to go to work at Hadassah his father cautioned, "Take the job but remember that there are people who won't like it. You may be endangering your life."

The threats did not materialize. Says Najah: On the contrary, the Arab community respects me because I work at Hadassah.

> As a member of an old and prominent family stretching back
> 700 years, it [working at Hadassah] was not an easy decision
> because of its Zionist enterprise. As an orthopedic surgeon,
> I need a big hospital to work in and Hadassah is quite simply
> the best. I'm not a political man, I am a doctor. My interest is
> in the physical health of my patients, not their souls.

Because he thought it would be wrong for him to work only in a Jewish hospital, he sought the administration's permission to serve as a consultant on Fridays and Saturdays in Arab towns and villages.

Apart from the usual departments found in a general hospital, Scopus boasts of the only 35-bed rehabilitation center in Israel. "There's nothing that is not done here," says Michel, "from road accidents to burns, children to the elderly." Its neonatal intensive care unit serves both Hadassah hospitals, as does its hospice for terminal patients.

---

* One poignant example: in 1989 Hadassah surgeons at the Ein Karem Medical Center transplanted the heart of an Israeli soldier killed by Palestinians in Gaza to save the life of a 54-year-old Jerusalem Arab.

Death is not a favored subject of conversation in hospitals. Much less so in the Ina and Jack Kay Hospice for the terminally Ill. With its panoramic view of the Judean Hills, the hospice is a scenic spot in which to live out one's last days.

Ruth Shahal Gassner, who at 32 became the institution's first director, is a nurse by training. She maintains that an occasional unorthodox treatment is beneficial and that a break from conventional treatment will do a patient more good than drugs.

"Hospitals are not the best place for dying," she says. "Terminally ill patients need dignity and tranquillity. They must be assured that they are still people who matter, not nuisances for busy staffs. And they need those around them to be attentive to their non-medical needs."

Still, about 80 percent of Americans and 70 percent of Israelis die in hospitals every year. Hospital treatment often deprives patients of their dignity and humanity, complications are common and increase as people age, according to the American Geriatrics Society.

The 14-bed Scopus hospice, unique in Jerusalem, has a staff of 45 nurses, social workers, physical and occupational therapists working in an integrated system. Thirty volunteers from half a dozen countries help out. About 10 applicants are available for every bed. But not every dying person can enter. A patient must be conscious, within months of dying and must have come to terms with his or her fate.

Despite its 100 percent mortality rate, the hospice has successfully escaped the air of a morgue. The decor of the carpeted, curtained lounge is one of tranquillity with its enormous oil painting of golden Jerusalem, book-lined shelves and classical music. On Friday nights candles are lit. Patients have access to the kitchen for a between-meal snack and visitors are never restricted. "The hospice is a home, not a hospital," says Shahal.

Pain is outlawed. Says HMO Director-General Shmuel Penchas, "Pain is an unnecessary curse. We can ensure that patients in the last stages of incurable disease do not suffer dehumanizing pain." For that alone the hospice fulfills the words of Dame Cicely Saunders who founded modern hospice care in London in 1977: "We'll do all we can not only to help you die peacefully but also to help you live until you die."

On Scopus, Adam Friedmann stands at the beginning of the life cycle. An Israeli-born scientist, he is among those at Hadassah who are plumbing the mysteries of life's source – the gene. It is a promising field of research seeking *inter alia* to ensure that embryos will grow into healthy humans and live long lives insulated from today's life-threatening diseases.

In 1985, Friedmann was a professor of neurology at Stanford University when Shmuel Penchas invited him to begin work on gene therapy. In 1988, Friedmann established the Middle East's first department in Molecular Diagnostics on Mt. Scopus.

Penchas was convinced that one day, perhaps in another 50 years, it would be possible to do genetic analysis on one of the first four cells that developed following conception, correct any abnormalities that appear and return the gene to the mother. It is generally accepted that susceptibility to disease, perhaps mental illness, results from a defective gene. By correcting a lame gene, scientists could assure babies long, healthy lives free from the dangers of life-threatening illnesses. So protected, they could be assured of reaching the traditional 120 years with ease and probably pass it.

"Preventive medicine for the 21st century," one researcher calls it. "Future generations will look on medicinal drugs the way we look at *Kame'as* and talismans."

"We are definitely on the road to that," says Penchas.

"The embryo is certainly one target for gene therapy," says Friedmann. "It is much easier to correct the gene in an embryo than in the whole body. We do it in animals. We could do it in humans but ethics are holding it up."

The technology is already being used to remove a fertile egg from a woman's ovary, fertilize it in a test tube and then return it to the womb, allowing a prospective mother to conceive a healthy baby. On November 1, 1983, Hadassah doctors succeeded in inducing a normal birth in a 35-year old 'high risk' woman after they had developed an embryonic cell in a test tube and implanted it in her womb. It was the first "test tube" baby born in Israel.

Scientists have taken the technology a step further in the lab to do gene repair. Explains Friedmann: "Once you change the DNA in an embryo, you change it for generations. We don't know how many human genes there are. We predict about 100,000; now we only know a couple of thousands."

One Hadassah unit is testing families' for cancer genes on a community basis. But once found, little can be done about preventing a cancer from occurring since doctors are not yet permitted to correct the defective gene.

Says Friedmann: "It can be done in a test tube, in mice. But were we to introduce a gene into a human we might knock out other genes at the same time and create much more of a problem than we had at the beginning. The ultimate gene therapy would be to target a gene to the right place and replace it with a good gene. We're far from achieving that but human minds are ingenious. No one else in Israel is doing what we are doing."

Still, the research has produced results. Using molecular diagnostics, Friedmann's Department of Genetics identified the chromosome that carries the gene for a crippling degenerative disease of muscles common among Persian Jews (inclusion body myopathy). A test is being established to determine in advance whether families carry the chromosome. Similar type testing can be made for some types of breast and colon cancer, cystic fibrosis, Gaucher's disease.

Hadassah's new gene therapy unit is inter-disciplinary and includes virologists, molecular biologists and physicians from hematology, neurology, surgery and the liver group.

"When you think about gene therapy," says Friedmann, "the ultimate thing we all want is immortality. And genes that cause death are known. We carry a lot of genes that mutate during our lives. We could repair all that."

For a university teaching hospital, research is essential to survive. Small as it is, Scopus carries an exceptional number of research programs. Among the researchers and their work:

Internists Drori Ben-Yishay and Michael Brusztyn: the relationship between insulin resistance and the development of high blood pressure;

Nephrologist Meir Brezis: the causes, prevention and treatment of kidney failure;

Neurologist Menachem Hanani: the physiology of the autonomic nervous system and of the smooth muscle system;

Gynecologist Neri Laufer: infertility in men.

As the renewal of Scopus reaches its third decade, the hospital's managers feel as though they are in a compression chamber. The number of beds permitted by the Ministry of Health is less than 300 (compared with the Ein Karem Medical Center's 750), but they are occupied 100 percent year round.

"From time to time our occupancy rate is over 200 percent. We have 50,000 visits to our emergency room every year," says Director Michel.

With Jerusalem's population bursting at the seams, Michel is troubled about Scopus's future. "I'm concerned about what will happen to this hospital in the next 10 years when there will be an increase of up to 100,000 population. We will not be able to cope for long with the same number of beds," says a worried Michel.*

Meanwhile, day-care surgery has helped cut the average number of days a patient spends at Scopus: overall 4.4 days compared with 5.4 at the Ein Karem Medical Center. Day-care units were developed to cut further the demand for beds. In 1995, 40 percent of operations took place in day-care units.

With Israel well into middle age, the country's population has grown older on the average. In Jerusalem, one out of every 13 residents is over the age of 65. Degenerative diseases are on the rise.

One innovative program has been to treat the aged at home. It not only cuts costs and frees beds but provides a better environment for the patient.

---

* Israel has one bed for every 117 persons, Australia 199, the U.S. 218, Egypt 504. It lags behind France, 81, and Uzbekistan, 83.

In 1991, Hadassah, together with Kupat Holim Clalit, was the first to develop the idea of treating the aged at home under Dr. Yohanan Stressman.

Should Scopus expand?

Being small has its advantages, admits Michel. "I know about the behavior of every physician. A proper doctor-patient relationship is a very important asset in this hospital and I don't want to give it up. My principal concern is the patient and his family. For me, treatment isn't only the technical aspect. It's also the environment, the human relationships, the way you address people. And for that I feel we have a tremendous advantage on Mt. Scopus, because this is a very congenial hospital. There is a tradition of good humane behavior here."

To preserve that tradition, Director Michel once had to resort to extreme measures. He dismissed a physician who struck a hospital guard. The physician went on to become a prominent personality in Palestinian politics.

If Scopus, and most hospitals in Israel, are to cope with the 21st century, they have little option but to expand. "For that we do not have the money," says Michel. "However, if we do not plan, all the good features of this hospital will disappear progressively as the result of overcrowding."

For Hadassah the conundrum of the immediate future is that expansion may well have the same result.

Twenty years of inactivity following the War of Independence turned the hospital into a "fossil," Kalman Mann once said. "Time and science passed it by. There was a lot of catching up to do. We left behind 14,000 square meters of building. When we finally returned we had 45,000 square meters."

Now, even that was not sufficient. Twenty years after the return, there was still some catching up to do.

WAR AND PEACE

Israelis were returning home from synagogue for a rest after one o'clock on the afternoon of October 6, 1973, when across the nation sirens wailed. It could not possibly be a drill. A startled public had never heard an alert on a Saturday, certainly not on Yom Kippur, the holiest day of the year.

In Jerusalem, residents were equally shocked to see heavy vehicles rolling through the streets on the only day when traffic always came to a standstill. The radio, silent on the Day of Atonement, went back on the air to broadcast coded phrases that sent reservists racing to join their units.

The "War of Atonement" was underway. Israel's leadership had been caught off guard and the nation would pay dearly. At the Suez Canal, Egyptian forces broke through the lightly defended Bar-Lev line and quickly overran the bunkers. On the Golan Heights, brigades of Syrian tanks ruptured Israel's defenses and nearly forced their way into populated areas of Galilee. Only a small force of Israeli tanks heroically held them at bay until reinforcements could arrive.

It would be 18 days before the Israeli forces surrounded an entire Egyptian army and headed toward Cairo. In the north, on the Golan Heights, they threatened to march to Damascus, visible in the distance.

Jerusalem was deceptively quiet that fateful morning. In the absence of Prof. Mann, his deputy director was startled by a red alert: war would break out within a matter of hours. He set into motion the hospital's battle-rehearsed emergency plan. Immediately, 270 patients were sent home. Another 220 were transferred to the top floors. The hospital was ready for 700 military cases and, if need be, could treat 1,200.

Within an hour of the outbreak, 95 of Hadassah's 250 staff physicians joined other reservist staff members in rushing to their units.

Nearly 2,000 local volunteers took their places while others from overseas joined them later. In New York alone, about 100 physicians called Hadassah to offer their services. A man-and-wife team of radiologists from Philadelphia took off so hastily that they had to send back the following instructions to their eldest son: "Don't drive too fast. You'll find pocket money for everyone in the cookie jar."

On October 8, President Rose Matzkin hastily summoned a National Board meeting. She reported that as of 1:30 p.m. that day a tour of 21 Hadassah members was due to leave for Israel. Rose read a cable from Hadassah's tourist agent in Israel who said that the tour was important for local morale. She added that the members might yet get to visit the Golan Heights "since the Israel army is well on its way to Damacus." In fact, the opposite was true. The Syrian army was at that moment on its way into Upper Galilee.

Rose reported that the national office switchboard was inundated with phone calls. Members wanted to know how best they could help. Chapters around the country collected cash and blood.

Back in Israel, 80 percent of the doctors in military field hospitals were Hadassah graduates. Not only were their trained skills needed but so were their inventiveness and their nerve. In one reported case, a Hadassah physician serving in Sinai improvised a collar from local sand and water to provide traction for a spinal injury. The soldier was thus saved from total paralysis. Another MD, working under fire successfully grafted a soldier's severed arm – a delicate procedure even under optimum conditions.

The Ein Karem Medical Center did not come under fire as it had in the Six-Day War. Fortunately for Israel, this time King Hussein of Jordan kept his nation out of the fray. Three years earlier, in September 1970, Israel had saved him by sending tanks to the Syrian border when the Syrians and the Palestinians threatened to overthrow his regime. Although Hussein may not have consciously thought he was returning the favor, in actual fact he was.

Hadassah's role during this war was to handle the most difficult cases, especially in surgery and rehabilitation. All told, 527 critically wounded soldiers were treated. Half were orthopedic cases. Only eight could not be saved.

Egyptian shoulder-held rockets set Israeli tanks afire and caused severe burns. Using porcine skin and silver sulfadiazene, Hadassah had an effective treatment available. Plastic surgeons could thus save most men from horrible disfigurement and loss of limbs.

Ophthalmologists used a new radiation detector to search out metal splinters lodged in eyes. For the first time the psychiatric and social services treated the men and their families simultaneously. Mobile battery-operated X-ray machines had pictures ready in minutes.

The Arabs had achieved complete tactical surprise. Despite threats from Arab capitals and hostile maneuvering, Sinai and Golan were being defended as though Israel were at peace: small and ineffective formations were in position when the Arab forces moved.

Shortages of ammunition and faulty equipment hindered the defense; Israeli planes and tanks fell easy prey to Egypt's Russian-supplied rockets and missiles.

It was 1967 in reverse. As Egyptian forces moved dangerously close to Israel's border and the Syrians reached the entrance to Galilee, panic-stricken Defense Minister Moshe Dayan observed to Golda Meir that the Arabs were about to destroy the Jewish State.

Prime Minister Golda Meir got on the phone to Washington. She repeated appeals to President Nixon and Secretary of State Kissinger to restock Israel's depleted armories. Should the Arab forces threaten Israel's existence, she said, Israel would use every means at its disposal to defend itself. The possible use of Israel's undeclared atomic resources could not be ignored. Nixon lost no time. He ordered supplies rushed to Israel forthwith from America's European warehouses. They arrived none too soon. The Russians were reported to have dispatched a nuclear ship in the direction of Alexandria harbor. Little did the world know how close it was to nuclear war.

Despite heavy casualties and the loss of enormous quantities of materiel, the Israel forces turned the tide in less than three weeks. But the human price for Israel was high: 2,600 dead, 7,300 wounded. The fact that the number of Arab dead was many times that number gave the Israelis no satisfaction. Despite their trouncing, Egyptians under Anwar Sadat claimed a moral victory. Their national honor was restored.

Although Israel could justifiably celebrate its military achievement, the "victory" had deep traumatic repercussions. The Six-Day War triumph led the nation to believe in its invincibility. But the tragic number of casualties and the diplomatic isolation of 1973 destroyed that illusion.

By 1974, Israel agreed to pull back from the Suez Canal in Sinai and from forward positions on the Golan. A depressed Golda Meir left office in April 1974, after encouraging her ambassador to the U.S., former Chief of Staff Yitzhak Rabin, to replace her. He would be Israel's first sabra prime minister.

In the national elections of 1977, disaffection with nearly three decades of Labor Party rule became evident. The public called on veteran right-wing statesman Menachem Begin to run its affairs. Dayan, who escaped official responsibility for the 1973 war's initial failures, became foreign minister in a national unity government.

Begin was in power only five months when, on November 15, 1977, he sent an invitation to Egyptian President Sadat to visit Israel. Five evenings later, Sadat thrilled the entire world by flying into Israel. In an address to the Knesset the following afternoon he declared, "No more war."

Sixteen months of arduous negotiations followed, capped by talks between the principals at Camp David, Maryland, where President Jimmy Carter took charge. Begin agreed to hand back all of Sinai to Egypt, uproot the existing Jewish settlements there and offer the Palestinian Arabs autonomy in lands occupied since 1967. Ransom having been paid, Egypt, the world's largest Arab nation, made peace with Israel.

In Washington, on March 26, 1979, a distinguished crowd of 1,200 gathered on the north lawn of the White House to watch a smiling Sadat and Begin* sign the peace documents, with President Carter as witness. In Tel Aviv, 100,000 people gathered to celebrate. In the capitals of extremist Moslem nations, the people mourned and demonstrated.

Hadassah President Bernice Tannenbaum was present for the historic event as she was in 1977 when Sadat made his precedent-shattering visit to Jerusalem. At a peace banquet in a striped tent on the White House lawn, Bernice met Sadat and his wife Jehan and was welcomed by Menachem Begin and his wife Aliza. Subsequently, Bernice headed a six-member group of Hadassah leaders, including former President Rose Matzkin, to Cairo where they and Jehan considered how special education in Egypt could benefit from Hadassah's services, notably in vocational training. Nothing concrete emerged from the meeting because of the cold peace that followed Sadat's initiative. Nevertheless, with this tentative proposal Hadassah had entered the field of international affairs.

Says Bernice, "The peace opened a new vista of possibilities for Israel and for Hadassah."

---

* For their efforts, Anwar Sadat and Menachem Begin shared the Nobel Peace Prize of 1978. But the treaty eventually cost Sadat his life. He was assassinated on October 6, 1981, while watching a parade in Cairo. His successor, former Air Force Chief Hosni Mubarak, honored the peace accord.

Thirty-one years had passed since Israel was founded. The pity – or stupidity – of it was that the bloodshed, displacement of peoples and squandered resources could have been avoided if the Arabs had accepted the 1947 U.N. decision to partition Palestine into Jewish and Arab states.

The Arab world had in the meantime created the Palestine Liberation Organization under Yasser Arafat. The stated aim was to regain all of Palestine and set up a "democratic" Arab state in which Jews would have minority rights. No match for the Israel army in battle, the PLO chose terror as the weapon to achieve its ends.

Terror was taken to new lengths as airplanes and civilian buses were hijacked, schools attacked and children killed, bombs sent through the mail and settlements in Galilee rocketed. Headquartered in Beirut and the refugee camps of Lebanon, the PLO targeted Israeli and Jewish institutions overseas. Israel's toleration finally broke when its ambassador in London, Shlomo Argov, was gunned down by a terrorist. One of Israel's most brilliant Foreign Service career officers, Argov remains completely helpless, a paraplegic, in Hadassah hospital on Mt. Scopus to this day.

Shortly thereafter, on June 6, 1982, Prime Minister Menachem Begin launched the Peace for Galilee campaign, ostensibly to protect Israel's northern frontier. In reality, the objective was to destroy the PLO's infrastructure. Eighty-five thousand Israeli troops invaded PLO strongholds in Lebanon, a nation already torn by civil war and controlled by Syria. The Israeli forces temporarily occupied Beirut and destroyed the PLO's ability to operate. After the ground forces left, the Air Force carried out heavy bombings of the city and finally forced Arafat and his cadres to leave the country. They continued fighting Israel from Tunisia and elsewhere in the Arab world.

Israel evacuated most of its troops from Lebanon by August 1985, but set up an 860-square-kilometer security zone in the south of the country to prevent the Iranian-backed Hizballah and other fundamentalist groups from attacking settlements in Galilee. The fighting on Lebanese soil, in which Israel also engaged Syrian troops, was costly. From the beginning of the Peace for Galilee campaign until the end of 1996, 713 young Israeli men were killed on Lebanese soil and at least 2,300 more were wounded.

While Israel was simultaneously making both peace and war with its neighbors, Hadassah became engaged on a completely different front. In the U.S. women were demanding entitlements long denied them. As it began to question its relevance to the assertive American woman, Hadassah saw that its "new vista" was at hand. It had to take up "issues." And none too soon.

THE JEWISH WOMAN

The '80's were the "Decade of Women." In the U.S. women were marching out of their homes to battle for their rightful place in society. Although Hadassah under Henrietta Szold had shown the way in the 1920's, it was only in the latter half of the 20th century that the feminist movement gathered enough momentum to move women out of the lonely drudgery of the home into the glamorous drudgery of a career. In the '60's and '70's the American woman organized to challenge a male-dominated world. She was joining the army, founding corporations, directing banks, preaching from pulpits, running for high office.

Many Jewish women were in the vanguard. A Hadassah-sponsored study of the period showed that 46 percent worked full-time outside the home. That had serious implications. More than ever before, marriage as a formal religious rite was put on hold and single parenthood became respectable. Marriage of Jew and Gentile was no longer an oddity. Increasing numbers of Jewish women were working as volunteers for non-Jewish organizations.

With the changes, Hadassah began a period of soul-searching in the 1980's. Says Hadassah President Marlene Post, "We continued with all our projects but we asked ourselves whether we really were relevant to people in America, in Israel. We got down into the trenches."

Surveys conducted by Hadassah showed that half of the 300,000-plus membership belonged to 100 of the organization's 1,374 chapters.* Most members were aged 55 or over. New York and California, America's largest Jewish centers, were under-represented. The typical member was married, not single, and led a traditional, conservative lifestyle. Membership was dropping. It was easy to get new members but difficult to retain them. Young women joined the ranks when they had time on their hands, quit when they took up careers.

Board Member Leah Silverstein, former President of the 4,000-member Chicago Chapter, describes the Jewish community as "more apathetic. Young people never knew a world where Israel did not exist. Even though we included Israel and Zionism in most of our programs, young women were looking for something to do in their own communities."

Former President Carmela Kalmanson painted the picture more starkly: "We faced the danger of eroding knowledge of and commitment to Jewish life and Israel."

It became obvious that if Hadassah were to remain afloat on a Zionist keel in American waters, it would have to change course to one closer to that set by the feminist movement. Hadassah fixed its bearings on two parallel directions: "action" and "issues." "restructuring" and "strategic planning" were the compass points by which Hadassah would find its way. Greater emphasis was placed on issues not necessarily connected with Judaism, Zionism or Israel. Studies were commissioned.

In 1987, President Kalmanson ordered the first five-year restructuring plan and set up a strategic planning committee under the leadership of Sue Mizrahi and Jane Zolot. In 1993, it was followed by a second committee, headed by Karen Venezky, that was to extend its reach to the year 2000.

---

* The largest chapter: Philadelphia with 7,868 members; the smallest Montana with 14. There were chapters in all 50 states and Puerto Rico.

Professionals were called in to guide the volunteer leadership. By the mid-1990's, the staff in Hadassah House numbered 229, half of them in executive or managerial positions. The Executive Committee allocated $2,500,000 to revitalize Hadassah chapters in many communities. Enhancement grants were given out. The result was larger membership, better fund-raising, new ventures.

In keeping with the new look, Marlene Post asked, "Are we addressing the bottom line?" Clearly, Hadassah was shedding its clubby character and adopting a business approach more akin to that of a corporation.*

Essential for any big business is a consistent, determined drive to raise new capital. So it was for the National Board.

"We changed the way we do business," says HMO chairman Bonnie Lipton, formerly in charge of fund-raising. "In days gone by our major funds came from the grass roots. We would wait until they came to us. Now we aggressively look for gifts, bequests and annuities. We set up task forces, make appointments to see prospective donors, explain our work and we try to provide them with the opportunity to be recognized while they are still alive."

Still, some donations drop into Hadassah's lap.

One such largess appeared in the wake of a phone call to Hadassah House in 1992. On the line was an aged resident of Los Angeles. Her question was simply put: "What can I get if I leave you money?"

"Like many others," says Bonnie, "this lady was shopping."

Nothing happened until the spring of 1996 when out of the blue another phone call came from Los Angeles. An attorney declared that he had a prospective donor with a considerable amount of money.

Bonnie recalls that the lawyer described the donor as a secretary who retired in 1947 and had never married. She was a modest woman, now about 90, who still lived alone in her own house and took care of herself.

---

* With 262 women on its National Board, Hadassah has one of the largest boards of directors of any institution, or corporation, in the U.S.

In a matter-of-fact tone the attorney went on, "She wants to leave Hadassah $5,000,000."

"A retired secretary with that much money?"

"She made it in the stock market. I believe she owns the first shares issued by American Telephone and Telegraph. If you extrapolate all the income she gets from this, it would blow your mind – and that is not her entire estate."

Bonnie Lipton flew to Los Angeles in June 1996 to suggest a number of projects that could bear the donor's name. Out of that meeting came the concept, suggested by HMO Director-General Penchas, of the Goldyne Savad Institute for Gene Therapy.*

She made a condition. "I want my name in marble," she said. Bonnie recorded a video tape showing her name at the site of the Institute and took the video to Los Angeles. "To see the video we had to go to the house of her nephew who is a retired doctor and trustee of the estate. She did not own a VCR."

With Hadassah's membership aging, it is reaping millions of dollars from wills. Says Bonnie, "A large percentage of the money comes from non-members. Some of them say that they are giving to Hadassah because they had a neighbor who spent a lot of time with the organization and who was nice to them."

Hadassah receives gifts in the form of bequests, even works of art. A male chemist who had been blinded in a factory accident and collected a large sum of money offered $5,000,000 on condition that a hospital be built in the Negev in his name. "We don't plan building another hospital in the Negev," says Bonnie. "But until such time as we do we can use the interest for our hospital in Jerusalem."

Another woman walked into the office with a gift of $1,500,000 for the Orthopedics Department at Ein Karem. She traveled by bus, refusing to take a cab. Bonnie held a lunch for her at Hadassah House. The grateful

---

* For gene therapy alone Hadassah has raised more than $20,000,000. Of that, $2,500,000 has come from a project launched by the small community of Greensboro, NC.

donor admitted to Bonnie, "This is the first time I've had a meal with company in 20 years." Bonnie nearly cried. "It broke my heart."

On another occasion an altruistic angel dropped in to Hadassah House in connection with an estate of which she was a trustee. Bonnie befriended the smartly-dressed woman and when the woman completed her business she recounted her own heartwarming life story. As Bonnie tells it:

"Her name was Ida Goldwurm, the second wife of a wealthy movie theater owner who had recently died. Goldwurm and his first wife, Jula, who was a prominent opera singer in Europe in the 1930's, were Holocaust survivors from Holland. He had no children from either marriage."

Ida and Jula had become fast friends and were companions for many years. When Jula died, Ida married the widower. Bonnie says Ida told her, "My husband was a generous man. He gave me beautiful jewels. Nothing was too expensive. I used to plead with him to do something in Jula's memory and he replied, 'One day you will have all the money. Then you will do something.' He did not know how to give it away. I don't understand why people deny themselves that pleasure."

After telling her story, Ida said, "I really want to do something important for Jula. They did not have children and I'd like to do something with children."

Nine months went by. Ida declined every suggestion – an offer to name a hospital room for $50,000 or labor and delivery rooms for several hundred thousand. She kept saying, "I want to do something big and special."

Taking the cue, Bonnie went all out. "Ida, would you consider naming the maternity pavilion in the new Mother and Child Center for Jula?" She did – at a cost of $2,500,000.

"I was overwhelmed," says Bonnie. "When I thanked her she replied, 'You shouldn't thank me. It wasn't my money: I didn't earn it. I've seen the hospital. I should offer to wash its floors. That's how impressed I was.'"

Bonnie offered to put Ida's name on the $1,000,000 wall in Hadassah House. Ida refused saying, "I don't want any recognition." She did accept an offer of Life Membership.

Ida's rejection of public credit was in the best tradition of Jewish charity. Then, almost as an afterthought, Ida told Bonnie, "I'm not Jewish."

Bonnie says she thought at the time, "I never met a woman who wanted to do something for her husband's first wife!"

Hadassah's full-fledged entry into the women's movement aptly came on an issue that challenged its Zionist identity. The subject was "Zionism is Racism." It was first brought up by Palestine Liberation Organization delegates at the First International U.N. Decade of Women Conference held in Mexico City in 1975. "Until that time we were standoffish about women's issues," says Bernice Tannenbaum.

Helplessly, Israel and Diaspora delegates watched the PLO resolution equating Zionism with racism pass. Only the U.S. and Denmark joined Israel in opposition. Hadassah had sent a delegation to help in the fight but could do little to change the anti-Israel attitude.

Later that year, 75 nations were mustered by the PLO from among the Arab, Russian and Afro-Asian blocs to steer a similar resolution through the United Nations General Assembly. Many nations, overcoming their better judgment, abstained out of fear of retribution by the Arab states. The 1973 war and the 1974 oil embargo were still in their minds.

United Nations Resolution 3379 equating Zionism with racism was the PLO's greatest political victory. Israel's Ambassador to the U.N. Chaim Herzog tore up the resolution in front of the members and the Australian Parliament condemned the U.N.'s action, but the resolution remained on the books as a tool for vilification of Israel for many years.

That put Hadassah, along with world Jewry, into a fighting mood.

What followed was more outreach to other women's organizations, more awareness of its potential strength as America's largest Jewish women's organization.

After its baptism of fire in Mexico City, Hadassah began to take positions on the status of women. A large delegation went to the 1980 U.N.-sponsored conference in Copenhagen* to struggle, in vain, against the anti-Zionist resolution. And in 1985 Hadassah leaders faced the critical meeting in Nairobi ending the Decade of Women.

What started out in Mexico City as a disaster for Zionism turned into a triumph in Nairobi. But the victory did not come easily. Ex-President Bernice Tannenbaum, then head of the American section of the World Zionist Organization, joined forces with Uzi Narkiss, information head of the WZO in Jerusalem, to initiate a campaign to nullify the U.N. resolution.

Their first goal was to expunge the resolution adopted at Mexico City from a document the Nairobi conference planned to adopt to sum up a decade of accomplishments. Toward that end a women's caucus was created. The WZO enlisted the support of the World Jewish Congress and Bn'ai Brith.

Once the anti-resolution forces were mobilized, a delegation of five women leaders, led by Bernice, headed for the White House on the morning of August 16, 1984. A smiling, charming President Ronald Reagan sat between Bernice and Barbara Mandel, and served tea, coffee and cookies. For 40 minutes he listened as they articulated the case. Unknown to them at the time, Reagan's daughter Maureen was chosen to head the U.S. delegation in Nairobi.

At the end of the meeting Reagan's advisor, Ed Meese, told him, "You should do something to please these women."** Before leaving the White House, Bernice asked Reagan to repudiate the U.N. resolution publicly. He agreed. In addition, he promised that the U.S. delegation would walk out

---

*   At Copenhagen, Bernice attended as a journalist, accredited to *Hadassah Magazine*. With her press card she slipped into a PLO meeting, but once recognized was ejected.
** The five-member delegation included three former Hadassah Presidents: Tannenbaum, Charlotte Jacobson as JNF President, and Frieda Lewis as Chairman, World Jewish Congress, American Section. The other two: Barbara Mandel, President, National Council of Women, and Midge Decter, Director, Committee for the Free World.

of the Nairobi conference if the resolution were included in the final declaration. The President's statement bristled with four strongly-worded paragraphs saying the United States would "oppose any agenda item at the Nairobi Conference which associates Zionism with racism."

A year-long campaign followed. AIPAC's Esther Kurtz, Bernice and others lobbied U.S. senators to support a resolution of condemnation that would call on the U.N. to repeal the invidious 3379. Tannenbaum remained in the U.S. as the preliminary women's forum began in Nairobi. After the Senate passed resolution 98 calling for the revocation of 3379, Bernice rushed to the airport where she hopped on a plane to Nairobi. With the issue about to be raised there, she did not wait for the final text of the Senate resolution.

With only a draft in hand, Bernice went straight from Nairobi airport to call on Ambassador Alan Keyes, State Department adviser to the American delegation. When she informed him that the resolution had passed the Senate he replied, "If that's so, our course of action is clear." He indicated publicly that the United States delegation, the largest at the conference, would walk out if a Zionism/racism motion were adopted. Until the last day the matter was touch and go.

PLO speakers received wild ovations. Eritrean women demanded independence for Eritrea but challenged Israel's right to statehood. With the exception of Egypt and Jordan, Arab representatives staged a noisy walkout, shouting as they went, when Israeli delegation head Sara Doron rose to speak.

The U.S. held the key. Each time an anti-Zionist proposal was made, Maureen spoke up loud and strong. The threat to make good on her father's pledge straightened the backs of Western European and Latin American countries. After much all-night deliberation, a compromise proposal by Kenya was finally accepted by the U.S.S.R., the PLO and then the conference: Zionism would be omitted from the final document. That rang a death knell for the entire issue.

A few months following Nairobi, the House of Representatives joined the Senate in overwhelmingly passing the same resolution. Six years later, U.S. President George Bush, following Reagan's lead, admonished the U.N. Assembly: "Zionism is not a policy, it is the idea that led to the creation of a home for the Jewish People... To equate Zionism with racism is to reject Israel itself, a member of good standing." On December 16, 1991, the United Nations finally cleansed its books of the smudge by a vote of 111 to 25, with 13 abstentions. Egypt, ostensibly at peace with Israel, was one of the 25.

At the next world conference of women held outside Beijing in 1995, Hadassah could address other critical problems. Zionism was no longer anyone's scapegoat.

Hadassah volunteers have always been active in Washington. That was particularly so during both World Wars. But then its concerns were narrowly focused on Zionist problems. It was not until the 1980's that the organization began to shoulder a breathtaking spectrum of issues ranging from welfare reform to religious freedom.

"I am a professional volunteer," says Hadassah veteran Shirley Blumberg. Like Denise Tourover before her, Shirley pounded the pavements from 1983 to 1991 as Hadassah's Washington representative. For the next five years she ran "Washington Programs," a project that yearly brought 800 members to the nation's capital for briefings in the Pentagon, State, Justice and Health Departments, in Congress and at the Israel Embassy. By the time they went home, says Shirley, "They were changed women, ready to campaign on behalf of Hadassah's concerns." Local legislators, the media and the public received clear messages from them on where Hadassah stood on the issues.

To get the message to its members Hadassah sells multicolored, nine-by-four inch "issue cards" for a penny a piece.* Each one navigates

---

* Hadassah has had other penny campaigns. Seven decades earlier it asked American school children to donate a penny to provide lunches for needy children in Jerusalem. Pennies arrived at the Hadassah office by the basketful.

members into action. One card, appropriately colored grass green, proclaims "Protect the Earth:"

"Because of abuse by humans, nearly every community on earth faces environmental destruction....

"**HADASSAH ACTS:**

"Collaborating with the Jewish National Fund to plant trees, conserve water resources, curtail soil erosion, preserve wildlife, and restore polluted rivers in Israel....

"**YOU CAN ACT:**

"Recycle and reuse products and materials whenever possible...."*

Black cards declare "Stop Terrorism," yellow "Stop Domestic Violence," purple "Promote Voter Registration and Participation." A bookmark informs the membership that more than 40,000,000 Americans aged 16 and over do not have a high school degree. It suggests, "Support nationwide reading and writing initiatives with coalition partners including Pizza Hut, Marvel Comics, National Association of Elementary School Principals."

Members are urged to mail the cards to Congress and "give them to a baby-sitter and college student." The issues are those on which there is a consensus among American women: free speech, domestic violence, ecology, equal opportunity, child abuse. One card addresses a specific concern of Jewish women: "Free the *Agunah*."** Women are advised to publicize the need for prenuptial agreements, work with the International Coalition for *Agunah* Rights, "shun men who refuse their wives a *get*."

As an issue, women's health was a natural for Hadassah. In 1992, President Deborah Kaplan took nearly 1,500 members to Washington to participate in the "March for Women's Lives." Their banners proclaimed a

---

* Hadassah-Israel launched nationwide campaigns to teach its members how best to recycle items. Empty paper towel rolls were used to make dolls and plastic bottles to hold string.

** An *agunah* (a "chained woman") is one whose husband refuses to grant her a Jewish bill of divorcement (a *get*) without which she cannot remarry under Jewish law. Women whose husbands abandoned them or disappeared without witnesses likewise are *agunot*. In Israel, men who refused court orders to give their wives divorces have been jailed until they did.

woman's right to make her own choice as regards her body. While eschewing the term "abortion" out of consideration for the views of the Orthodox community, Hadassah is clearly a pro-choice group. That was clear when outside the Republican and Democratic presidential conventions of 1996, Hadassah members held placards proclaiming "Pro-Faith, Pro-Family, Pro-Choice."

One of Hadassah's more original initiatives is the attempt to stop insurance companies from discriminating against women who are genetically disposed to cancer. Nearly 10 percent of all cases of breast and ovarian cancers are inherited. Insurance firms use genetic information to limit, deny or even cancel coverage – or to increase premiums. The result is that many women avoid being tested.

In Washington, after Rep. Louise Slaughter, (Dem.), co-sponsored legislation in the 104th Session to forbid the discrimination, a Hadassah task force began an information campaign among legislators. It deluged chapters with "talking points" to inform representatives in their home bailiwicks why they should vote for Slaughter's bill. The campaign was partially successful: the bill passed the House but was roadblocked in the Senate. In the 105th Session of 1997, Hadassah's task force was again back on the hustings stumping for the legislation.

Probably the best example of Hadassah's recent health work centers on illnesses specific to women – notably osteoporosis* and breast cancer – and afflictions such as heart disease not generally considered "women's disease."

Outside the New York office on 58th Street, curbside mammography examinations were made available to passersby. Mobile testing units were supervised by technicians of the Memorial Sloane Kettering Cancer Institute. The practice was later adopted by chapters throughout the

---

* Twenty-five million American women, and more than half of all women over 65, suffer the bone-thinning disease. In Jerusalem, Hadassah helped finance the Osteoporosis Center and undertook studies into causes and cures at its Minerva Bone & Calcium Research Center.

United States. The new Health Education Department ran "Hadassah Cares" cancer awareness programs for high school girls under the rubric "Check It Out" and for adult women ("Buddy Check Buddy").

Heart disease – America's #1 killer – rises among post-menopausal women faster than among men. But it is probably the most negelected of all women's illnesses. Says one American heart specialist, "Women go to the doctor less frequently than men; they complain less but they do die of heart disease. Research, however, concentrates on men." The famed Framingham, (Massachusetts) report that revealed the evils of high cholesterol was based on a statistical study involving males.

"Fewer angiograms are performed on women. Doctors hesitate to do them because women's blood vessels are narrower, so the test carries greater risk," says this specialist. To overcome the problem, Hadassah went to Washington in 1995 to help push legislation that established a women's division for health at the National Institutes of Health.

Non-health offensives occupied other task forces: violence against women ("That legislation was immediately accepted by Senators and Representatives," comments Shirley Blumberg); foreign aid and continuing support for Hadassah medical and educational institutions in Israel through the American Schools and Hospitals Abroad (ASHA) program.

A non-partisan campaign to get Hadassah members to register to vote was launched during the 1996 presidential campaign. "Shockingly the Jewish vote is on the decline," Hadassah informed its members. "A pool of 4,000,000 eligible Jewish voters are not registered...."

Hadassah made its voice heard on other issues:

– On immigration reform. Working with the Council of Jewish Federations, Hadassah helped tone down harsher aspects before the bill was passed.

– On a balanced budget. The organization spoke in opposition because it objected to anticipated cuts in human services.

– On funding private religious schools. Hadassah was firmly opposed. "We think it's wrong because it weakens the public school system. Jewish communities should support Jewish day schools," says Blumberg.

– On the environment. Hadassah has joined a Jewish consortium of organizations to preserve nature.

"These projects enabled us to involve many young women whose primary interests may not necessarily be Israel but who want to give service in the U.S.," says ex-President Deborah Kaplan.

Hadassah states emphatically that it is in Washington to educate and to inform but not to lobby. The Washington task force receives its marching orders from the American Affairs office in New York, which daily watches political events. This offer is headed by vice-presedent, Judith Palkovitz and Amy Rutkin, director.

Hadassah does not labor alone. It builds or joins coalitions for each new campaign. On the law to restore religious freedom to individuals (for Jewish men, the coalition secured the right to wear a skullcap in the army), Hadassah worked with groups as diverse as Baptist and Orthodox Jewish action agencies. Professional Marla Gilson and the six-member volunteer task force frequently labor 12-hour days out of their one-room Silver Springs, Maryland, office. For the swearing-in ceremonies of the 105th Congress the force was on the go in the Capitol from 9:00 a.m. to 9:00 p.m. meeting new legislators.

It was January 7, 1997. "We were doing a lot of partying," recalls Shirley. With Marla she spent part of the time talking in the corridors with Rep. Sander Levin and his brother, Sen. Carl Levin, both Democrats from Michigan. Overhearing them, Connecticut Sen. Joseph Lieberman feigned annoyance and interrupted, "Did I hear you taking my wife's name in vain?" Everyone laughed. They already knew that her first name was... Hadassah.

None of Hadassah's contacts in Washington, however, could help free Jonathan Pollard, the Naval intelligence officer who was sentenced in 1986 to life in prison for passing secret information to Israel. During her presidency Deborah Kaplan put the issue to the National Board. "We had reason to believe the sentence was unduly harsh," she said. In 1994, the Board wrote President Bill Clinton requesting that he commute Pollard's severe sentence. But its appeal, like all others, was rejected. As of the beginning of 1997 Pollard still languished behind bars.

More successful was Hadassah's participation in a large group of 1,200 Jewish leaders who went to Washington in September 1991 to support Israel's request for the Administration's guarantees of $10 billion in bank loans. An angry President Bush attacked the "powerful political forces" arrayed against him. He characterized himself as "one lonely little guy down here" who, by objecting to the loan guarantees, was presumably protecting the peace process.

After Jewish leaders expressed indignation at the remarks, Bush hurried to mend fences. He called in a small select circle of Jewish leaders to assure them of his support for Israel and his desire to avoid confrontation. Deborah Kaplan was one of two women in the group. In the end Israel received the loan guarantees.

For all its other concerns, it was not until late in the century that Hadassah targeted problems specific to the Jewish woman. For much too long had Jewish females been denigrated as *yentas*, matriarchs and JAP's. Wrote *Lilith* Editor Susan Weidman Schneider, "The *yenta* has gotten a bad press."

Henrietta Szold and Golda Meir were exceptions in a society where the image of the Jewish woman had become fixed in literature and in men's minds as a specialist in cooking chicken soup, matchmaking and spoiling her children.

One of the first attempts to tackle problems facing the Jewish woman arose during the 72nd national convention held in Miami Beach in August, 1986. Projects were initiated to address the increase in non-conventional family units. Hadassah began to reach out to young singles, single parents and career women.

In 1989, Hadassah provided its members with a handbook on "Jewish Marital Status," 43 sweeping essays on marriage and the family, edited by

National Director of Education Carol Diament. It revealed that one-third of Jews in the latter part of the 20th century were single, divorced, widowed, childless or homosexual. The traditional Jewish family as an underpinning of Jewish survival was obviously in trouble.

As Hadassah entered the '90's the situation had improved little, if at all. In 1994, it dealt with the problem by creating the 23-member National Commission on American Jewish Women to study their problems and to determine ways to bring greater Jewish meaning into their lives. One year later, the NCAJW published *Voices for Change: Future Directions for American Jewish Women*. Largely based on existing individual studies, it brought to light upsetting revelations:

- Childbearing appeared to be going out of fashion. Jewish families were having fewer than two children on average.
- More than one-fourth of young Jewish women were intermarried.
- Many younger Jewish women support causes, yet the numbers of those supporting Jewish organizations was decreasing.
- Most Jewish women were not affiliated with synagogues or Jewish organizations.

The picture was not completely bleak, *Voices* reported.

"This generation of Jewish women is the most educated in history and perhaps the most thirsty for a richer, deeper engagement with Jewish tradition."

Voices indicated that insufficient research existed on the American Jewish woman. One outcome was the joint funding by Hadassah and Brandeis University in 1996 of the International Research Institute on Jewish Women. The Institute was set up at Brandeis University under the leadership of Shulamit Reinharz, Director of Women's Studies. Brandeis, a non-denominational university in Waltham, Massachusetts, is an ideal center for the Institute since it is the only university with a graduate program in Jewish Women's Studies.

Remodeling the organization was not confined to the United States. In 1996, a new HMO board, with power to make decisions, would direct its medical centers. In a break with the past, the National President has only one of 21 votes on matters affecting the centers. Co-opted to the medical board were experts like Prof. Paul Marks, chairman of the board of Memorial Sloane Kettering, and Harvard University's Philip Leder, a board member of Massachusetts General Hospital. At the same time an Israel projects task force, headed by Treasurer Barbara Tirschwell and Bernice Tannenbaum, was established to see whether Hadassah's projects in Israel were answering Israel's present-day needs and its own contemporary needs.

A study of existing projects by Dr. Daniel Elazar's Jerusalem Center for Public Affairs found that on a national scale Hadassah could best serve by enhancing research and development. For Jerusalem, he suggested an education program to give job training to the *haredi* (extreme religious) community. Elazar predicted that by Hadassah's centennial year, 2012, the ultra-Orthodox would account for 38 percent of the city's Jewish population. He believed that had implications for Hadassah.

The monopoly of the Orthodox community on matters of personal status such as marriage and divorce is one of the most sensitive Israeli issues facing Diaspora organizations. On advocating religious pluralism, Hadassah maintained a consistently positive policy.

In 1980, Orthodox and secular Jews in the Knesset debated an amendment to the constitutional Law of Return.* The amendment would have recognized only Orthodox conversions to Judaism. Some American Jews, feeling threatened, considered withholding financial support for Israel. Hadassah could not stand by without taking a position.

"Our position was unequivocal," says Carmela Kalmanson. "We expressed strong feelings to the President of Israel and Members of the

---

* Israel has no written constitution but it does pass basic laws which are, in effect, the same. The Law of Return, one of the first to be adopted in Israel, gives all Jews – whether born to a Jewish mother or converted – the automatic right to immigrate to Israel and to citizenship.

Knesset. We stood with the majority of Israelis in rejecting the amendment."

Periodically, the issue returns to the Knesset but Hadassah administrations have not always expressed opposition so strongly as in 1980. The HMO leadership has usually obliged the medical demands of the Orthodox community in Jerusalem. In the U.S., most Hadassah members are affiliated with either the liberal or conservative wings of Judaism, both of which advocate pluralism in Israel.

While Hadassah favors equal rights for all denominations, it has interests in all camps and seeks to avoid confrontation. As Marlene Post puts it, "We are not looking to become a partner with any single grouping."

No matter how the city's demographic character changes, Hadassah and Jerusalem are firmly linked. The National Board made this clear at festivities marking the organization's 85th birthday year held in the Knesset in January 1997. It gave former Mayor Teddy Kollek a standing ovation when he remarked:

"Nobody has been as faithful to Jerusalem as Hadassah."

UNIVERSITY WITHOUT WALLS

It was 8 o'clock on a hot Monday morning in July 1996, when nearly 2,000 Hadassah women attending the 82nd national convention gathered in the ballroom of Miami's Fontainbleau Hotel.

Fourteen feet above the stage of the grand ballroom hung the longest prayer shawl ever made. Concocted of 48 embroidered, hand-painted patches, the quilted *tallit* measured 123 inches by 95 inches.* Its fringes (*tzitzit*) were an outsized six feet.

The setting was ready for America's largest bat mitzvah ceremony. One hundred and twenty-two women, ranging from Sara Leah Schuval, 12, to Gertrude Kussner, 86, recited the blessings over the Torah scrolls that lay open on four tables. At four lecterns, 12 celebrants took turns reading the portion of the week: Deuteronomy I ("...Go in and possess the land...," Moses exhorted).

The ceremony was a far cry from the first in America. In 1922, Judith Kaplan, daughter of philosopher Mordecai Kaplan,** celebrated her bat

---

* The numerical equivalent in Hebrew letters (*gamatria*) of 123 and 95 spelled the words *oneg malka* or "a queen's delight."
** In an address to Hadassah in 1936, Rabbi Kaplan urged its leaders to start a movement that would establish women's equality under Jewish law. Judith, who married Reconstructionist Rabbi Ira Eisenstein, died in 1996.

mitzvah in a modest Friday night service at the Society for the Advancement of Judaism in New York, which her father had founded.

In 1982, Hadassah conducted a small bat mitzvah ceremony at the Western Wall in Jerusalem to the hisses and boos of ultra-Orthodox women. At the Miami convention, some women wore phylacteries (*tefillin*) during the morning service. Nearly half wrapped themselves in *tallitoth*.

Convention Chairman Barbara Goldstein officiated. A yeshiva graduate, Barbara says, "Women can do everything men can do in synagogue."

"It used to be that boys got bar mitzvahs and girls had a sweet 16 party," added celebrant Fern Baum, 38, of Sunrise, Florida. "No more."

"The idea behind the bat mitzvah program," said Barbara Spack, National Education Chairman who served as cantor, "is to empower women with a knowledge of Judaism so they can teach others. It will deepen their spiritual involvement and their connection to the Jewish community."

Says Leah Reicin, co-chairman of convention, who conceived the program, "It has changed the lives of 122 women."

Each woman who was called to the Torah had completed a six-month course in Judaism, Hebrew language and observance. At the end of the courses, they were required to write a *drash* (commentary). All 122 did, some in verse. Hadassah later published them in a blue-bound volume.

One, from the pen of Gertrude Kussner, was short but profound. She wrote of her studies:

"I am 86 years old and a firm believer in God. He is my refuge and fortress, in whom I trust. I learned how God chose Israel because it is the center of the world, and Jerusalem is the center of Israel and the Temple is the center of Jerusalem."

Making the quilted prayer shawl was in itself an educational exercise for Hadassah members. Those who wove the fringes first studied the regulations given in the Talmud. Most of the swatch designs featured Jewish or Israeli subjects. One pattern based on the Hadassah-International logo was made by Bernice Tannenbaum. A swatch was sewn by

Ethiopian women in Israel. Nonagenarian Annabelle Argand, of Madison, Wisconsin, crafted another.

A "Bat Mitzvah Royale," the Fort Lauderdale *Sun Sentinel* called it. The ceremony has all the marks of becoming a convention tradition. For the 83rd convention in 1997, Spack offered courses to all of Hadassah's 30 regions and 158 women registered. Meanwhile, the *tallit* was in storage, waiting to be hung again.

The scope of Hadassah's education effort would do justice to the curriculum of any fine American university. Consider some of the subjects available: medicine and health, religion and ethics, Bible study, Hebrew language and culture, Middle East politics and American affairs, Jewish history, literature, family relations, group work, feminism, technology, and vocations from computers to cooking.

The roots of Hadassah's education efforts are long and deep, going back to the end of the 19th century when Henrietta Szold and her mother initiated study groups solely for women. Many American universities began similar study groups in the late 1800's but for men only. From its beginnings, Hadassah never neglected educating its members. In 1922, a "School for Zionism" was founded by Henrietta's friends, Jessie Sampter and Alice Seligsberg. They saw it as a prerequisite for the founding of a Hadassah group. The School was later transformed into an education department headed by a professional educator.

"By educating women," says Education Director Carol Diament,* "we create leadership and by doing so we interest them in Israel."

Says Carmela Kalmanson, "The more we know and the richer we are Jewishly, the more we can enrich the Jewish family." In the search for their Jewishness, Hadassah chapters formed education courses. In Westchester, N.Y., women became "taxi" drivers taking members to year-long courses in New York City. One of Hadassah's earliest publications was a guide for

---

* Dr. Diament, Hadassah's education professional, is the first and only woman to receive a Ph.D. in Jewish studies from New York's Yeshiva University.

teaching, "Great Ages and Ideas of the Jewish People." Adopted by universities, it was the brain child of Esther Gottesman, then Education Chairman.

In the late '50s, Hadassah joined the World Bible Society. Hadassah's Education Department, then chaired by Frieda Lewis, promoted self-led Bible study groups with guides prepared by American scholars. Because of the guides' comprehensive approach to the Book of Books, the study program's chairman, Rose Goldman, was able to announce after four years that more than 350 groups existed throughout the country. The guides were so popular that they were used by a diverse group of educators and institutions, and by WIZO in Switzerland and Australia. A request for them even arrived from the librarian of Alcatraz. When Hadassah President Judith Epstein heard that inmates of the California state prison were interested, she remarked, "Of course. They have time to study."

With the program's success, Frieda integrated Bible study and Hebrew language into the department's program. She was later elected 17th Hadassah President (1980-1984). One of Hadassah's erudite leaders, she passed away in 1996.

In the 1980's, the eroding commitments to Jewish life and Israel spurred new efforts. When Carol Diament took over the Education Department in 1985, she sought to raise education to a high academic level as a remedy for the serious demographic problem affecting Jewish women: late marriages or none at all, homosexuality, single parenthood.

On a trip to Kimberly, Texas, Carol visited a Hadassah weekend retreat where the topic centered on the issues discussed in "Jewish Marital Status." The president of the group, a divorcee, related to Carol how she rescued her self-image by climbing to the top of the local leadership ladder. "I now feel better about myself. Hadassah has really given me back my life."

Out of that experience, Hadassah developed Vanguard, a singles' project to bring together single Jewish men and women.

One of the more invidious threats poised at the Jewish family came from Christian evangelists who wore the mantle of Jews and referred to themselves as "Jews for Jesus" and "Messianic Jews."* One manual on conversion techniques distributed by the Chosen People Ministries, a missionary group, instructed its followers to "Build bridges, not walls" to Jews.

Some disciples crossed those bridges to join Hadassah.

Since the 1970's the problem has surfaced in all sections of the U.S. but principally in the southern Bible Belt. In San Antonio, Texas, a member of a messianic congregation reached a leadership position in Hadassah before her identity was discovered. Another woman, who requested permission to distribute missionary material, was cautioned and never returned. One Christ-believing Jew invited all the chapter members to her son's "Bar Mitzvah."

Christians, married to Jews, have been among Hadassah's most loyal members. But missionaries were another matter. One prospective Hadassah member in Texas was so miffed by the possible presence of missionaries among the membership that she refused to join the chapter. "They didn't say they were Messianic Jews when they joined. I felt betrayed," she commented to a reporter.

"The problem goes to the heart of the Christian-Jewish relationship in the U.S.," wrote Carol Diament in *Textures*, Hadassah's Jewish studies bulletin in May 1995. "The Christian use of Judaism and Zionism – both metaphorically and literally – continues to thrive. Evangelical Christians today support the state of Israel, yet... they have never shed their desire to convert Jews."

On the national level Hadassah was slow in coming to grips with the question since its constitution has no religious restrictions.

"A national policy is being developed," says President Post. "To be a Hadassah member you must accept Jewish values and Zionist principles."

---

* Israel's Supreme Court ruled on a 1962 petition submitted by a Jewish-born priest that a person could not at the same time claim to be a Jew and practice another religion. The priest, Oswald Rufeisen, had claimed Israeli citizenship as a born Jew under the Law of Return. His petition was denied.

How to triangulate Jewish values with Christian messianism posed a dilemma of Sisyphean proportions.

Assimilation, intermarriage and apathy were other perils to Jewish life. The reply, proclaimed American Jewish educators, was "Jewish continuity." To help stem the downhill slide, Hadassah developed a family learning program.

In the spring of 1993, Hadassah invited the Whizin Institute for Jewish Family Life at the University of Judaism in Los Angeles to help develop a project that would tune in to the need. The result was "Training Wheels: Cycling Through the Jewish Year with Hadassah," geared for children aged two to eight. In 1996, the project published a 484-page canary-yellow, loose-leaf manual that had as its logo a teddy bear riding a tricycle, emblazoned with the Star of David on the wheels. It was meant for use by Hadassah volunteer teachers and guides.

Popularly referred to in Hebrew as *Al Galgalim*, the aim was to reach the young Jewish family by teaching the children how to celebrate the Sabbath, Jewish holidays and customs.

"Training Wheels," a metaphor for learning, offered parents, grandparents and their young children a series of play experiences where fun and learning went hand in hand, while mothers and fathers discussed parenting.

The volume's coverage is encyclopedic. It provides instructions for activities from making *cholent* in a pumpkin to fashioning a simulated Torah scroll out of paper towel rolls. It instructs parents and teachers how the children should be taught to kiss a *mezzuzah*: "(1) Touch *mezzuzah*, (2) touch fingers to lips, (3) feel good."

It handles sensitive problems. Christmas, for one:

> Teach your children to appreciate, respect and even feel comfortable around your Christian neighbor's ...trees – but do not have a Christmas tree yourself. We can visit

Christmas... but we don't celebrate Christmas ourselves. In all likelihood there will be some tears.

At an academic level, courses and seminars were initiated on college campuses. So far, 2,500 women have participated in the seminars in what Carol Diament calls "a university without walls." The idea originated as a remedy for falling attendance at spring regional conferences.

In 1994, Carole Curtis, then president of the New Rochelle group, convinced the state university at Purchase, N.Y., to sponsor a joint program with Hadassah. Professors from the university staff volunteered to teach 28 workshops. So successful was the program that 14 more were begun on such campuses as Yale, Brandeis, Stanford and Memphis.

In Richmond, Virginia, Roberta Neblett, a retired Comparative Languages professor, began teaching a group of 60 women twice monthly. With her daughter she created a young study group that met with the older women and named the joint group "Bubbies and Babes." They used as their text 17 fictional short stories commissioned by Hadassah from Israeli women authors. The title, *Ribcage,* was a reference to Adam's rib, because, as Carol puts it, "The writers came out of their inner world to write about their lives."

Richmond was so enlivened and enriched after Prof. Neblett took over that it met its fund-raising quota for the first time. The group spawned five others in the area. By the end of 1996, there were 400 throughout the country. Enrolled in Hadassah's education programs are an estimated 30,000 led by a cadre of 4,000 peers.

Carol muses, "We should do a degree in Jewish-Zionist education." The idea is not that far-fetched. Hadassah already sponsors a successful degree college in Israel. Considering the popularity and breadth of its academic programs, it would come as no surprise were Hadassah one day to sponsor a college **with** walls in America.

The Hadassah College of Technology,* on the premises of the former Rothschild Hospital in downtown Jerusalem, is a success story by any standard. For one, it has the highest ratio of immediate graduate employment in Israel – 92 percent.

"That is because we teach and train only those skills the country needs," says Ya'acov Amidi, director since 1978. Soon after Amidi took command, he closed the electronics department. "I found that there were three other similar courses being given in Jerusalem."

A Ph.D. in Education Management, Amidi braved critical educators when he insisted that applied courses be taught by professionals in the field rather than by licensed instructors. "People worried that the standard of teaching would drop," says Amidi. "Here the pros get brief teaching courses before they enter a classroom."

Out of the College and into the marketplace flow a steady supply of optometrists, printers, chefs and concierges, computer programmers and engineers, dental technicians, video and X-ray technologists, aerial and underwater photographers.

HCT runs special courses in computers for the legally blind. Seven of the 850 students in 1997 were sightless. One blind graduate became so proficient at his work that he was put in charge of computers at a police headquarters.

A special one-year course was provided for Ethiopian immigrant students who had attended high school in Addis Ababa, but were unable to pass Israel's matriculation tests, required for university entrance. When all passed the rigorous examinations after the first year, the course became a fixture.

Among the student body are Israelis, Arabs, Druse and Europeans. More than half are women. One woman from Australia applied but Amidi had his doubts. She was the mother of four young children and the expense

---

* In 1988, Hadassah's Alice Seligsberg High School was transferred to the Jerusalem Municipality. In the following year, the name of the Community College was changed to College of Technology so as not to be confused with lower level prep schools in the U.S.

was high. She replied, "What's a husband for? I worked for him. Now he can work for me." After graduation from printing technology, she opened a graphics business. Reports Amidi, "Now her husband is studying so that he can help in the business."

Despite annual tuition of $3,000 (high, for Israel), the College is so popular it can only accept one-quarter of the applicants. Still, only 15 percent of the running budget is derived from fees. Hadassah covers 70 percent and certain Government Ministries the remaining 15 percent.

"Gradually," says Amidi, "we will upgrade all our programs to grant a bachelor's degree and we will be introducing courses to help women return to the work force."

Amidi stands by famed educator Alfred North Whitehead whose words were adopted as a beacon when the College was founded: "Education should turn out the pupil with something he knows well. And something he can **DO** well."

With so many opportunities available to young people, it is little wonder that many pupils are confused in choosing careers. Uncertainty frequently causes adolescent crises. The stories of Leah and Amir (fictitious names of real people) are common.

At 15, everything began to fall apart for Leah. Sensitive, artistically-inclined she began to eat obsessively, put on weight. "Eat carrots, not candy bars," her mother would beg her. But Leah could not stop. She felt the pressures of moving away from her old neighborhood and changing schools. Her parents wanted the best high school for her but, says she, "I felt I was not good enough, terrified I'd mess up my tests, had crying fits, a sense of foreboding. I was panic-stricken."

Her parents took Leah to the Hadassah Career Counseling Institute in Jerusalem where she met Nira Poliakin. "Leah's psychometric results were excellent," says Nira. "I'm a career counselor not a psychologist but I tried to find out why a youngster who was so bright had such an unrealistically low self-image."

"Nira talked to me," says Leah, "adult to adult. I poured out my heart to her, everything that had been on my mind. She listened intently and began putting things into perspective."

Nira singled out reasonable options for Leah. "There's a price to be paid for everything. You must set priorities. You don't have to do it all. Learn to live with who you are. It's OK if you're not superwoman," she would say.

Leah took Nira's advice to heart and by the time she moved to a new school was able to adjust. Some things did not change. She still rushed around town to voice training, dancing, choir singing, still competed hard. But, says Leah, she no longer felt guilty about things she could not do.

Three years later Leah was following a successful career in an army entertainment group. On completing her service, she intended to study theater, hopefully in London or New York.

Amir at 15 was having a horrible time in school. His grades were poor. His teachers reported "behavioral problems." Amir admits it: "I concentrated on being bad." No high school would accept him and he did not know what to do. His parents, he said, "dragged" him to the Counseling Institute.

There he, too, met Nira. "I entered with my 'don't-care-snarl.' Nira surprised me. She said tests showed I was very bright." But he was shaken when she told him that the tests also revealed low motivation.

"She showed me I could do things differently, that there were alternatives if the high schools would not take me because of my behavior record."

Amir found a good technological high school in Jerusalem which accepted him. There, Nira convinced him, he could be top of the class. "Why not be in the top of the class in a good school rather than at the bottom in a top school?" she asked. Amir agreed.

Amir did well enough to make "outstanding student" for several semesters, worked at electronics in the army, had a steady girlfriend and was confident that with his training he would find a good job in civilian life.

Since 1957, Hadassah has financed another "university without walls" in Jerusalem.

Founded in 1909 by Jewish students to further the goals of Zionism and foster traditional Jewish values, Young Judaea was sponsored by the Zionist Organization of America. Henrietta Szold edited its first journal, the *Young Judaean*. The first American Zionists to settle in Palestine during World War I were Judaeans. In 1927 it became affiliated with the scout movement in Palestine and many of its clubs thereafter took on the name *Tzofim* (Scouts).

In 1941, Hadassah joined the ZOA to set up a Youth Commission that took responsibility for Young Judaea. Its first venture was an experimental summer Zionist Camp Institute held in July 1941 outside Amherst, New Hampshire. Hadassah-ZOA scholarships brought together 50 outstanding Young Judaeans from 16 states. For one month the campers, who were known as the *Rishonim* (the First), attended seminars conducted by leading Zionists in the U.S. and Palestine, among them former Hadassah presidents. At the close of the Institute they voted unanimously to make the camp project a permanent feature of Zionist life in America and out of the experiment there developed the popular Brandeis camps.

Seven years later Young Judaea membership hit its all-time peak of 30,000, but then began slowly to decline along with that of other Zionist groups in the U.S. No longer able to bear its half of the budget, the ZOA opted out in 1967. Hadassah, under Charlotte Jacobson, assumed complete responsibility, built a headquarters for Young Judaea on the Hebrew University campus, sharing it with Hadassah's School for Occupational Therapy.

The building resonated with Zionist nostalgia. During World War II it served as the residence of Hadassah nurses and it was there that Henrietta Szold had an office and lived her last years.

Named for corporate magnate Meshulam Riklis who financed the building's reconstruction, Beit Riklis opened in 1969. Since 1956, Young Judaea had wandered from place to place around the city, running one-year courses for overseas youth. Now it had a home in an academic environment. Today, it serves as dormitory, dining room, library and classroom.

With new vitality injected into the organization by Hadassah, Young Judaea's membership gradually increased and its programs expanded.

In 1967 a group of Young Judaean graduates in the U.S. joined to form a cooperative settlement in Israel. While Hadassah's policy then was to remain neutral on the question of immigration, President Faye Schenk made sure the group had a "Hadassah flavor." Aliyah chairman Rose Goldman "kicked the doors open for us," says founding member Hinda Gross. In 1970, 62 families arrived to spend four years in an integration center outside Jerusalem while negotiating with the Jewish Agency for land.

At Passover 1974, 33 families from the original group moved to their new home on a strategically-located Judean Hills prominence above Abu Ghosh village at the entrance to the capital. Unlike other settlements, Neve Ilan was based on light industry – electronics and computers – and social services rather than on agriculture. Later, the settlement included kiwi and citrus culture as well as the raising of turkeys. Most successful of all has been a resort hotel that opened in 1977. Neve Ilan's population today: 55 families.

In 1973, Young Judaeans established a kibbutz at Ketura and thereby achieved one of the supreme goals of Zionism. Charlotte Jacobson assisted in negotiating for the land as she had done for Neve Ilan. The kibbutz (pop.: 300), located in the Rift Valley (Arava) north of Eilat, specialized in introducing exotic fruits to Israel. Its open society within a traditionally religious community is unusual for Israel, so unusual that the Knesset awarded Ketura a prize for tolerance.

In 1997, the number participating in one of five Young Judaea programs in Israel approached 550. American and British high school students attend a summer leadership training course. Or they join Israel Discovery groups for what Beit Riklis Director Dan Krakow calls "a positive exposure to Israel." A third group comprises young people sent by their home communities. On returning home they are engaged in local Jewish community work.

Post-high school pupils join Hamagshimim ("the Fulfillers") for continued study and travel in Israel. Often some are aged 30 and over. In 1996, Hadassah transformed one of its old buildings in Jerusalem's German Colony to serve Hamagshimim as a community and integration center for new immigrants from English-speaking countries. Among the Hamagshimim was a group of talented U.S. and South African actors whose first production was *Steel Magnolias* by Robert Harling.

Most scholastic of all Young Judaean activities is the 10-month program for high school graduates. Accredited through the University of Judaism in Los Angeles, it focuses on Jewish studies, the Hebrew language and Israel. The year of study is enriched, says Krakow, by months of work on a kibbutz.

"That's what makes the program special," says Krakow. "The living experiences really connect our students to the people and to the country. Every other year we have a Young Judaea contingent joining the March of the Living. They go to Auschwitz and other Nazi camps and ghettos in Europe. Those who go on the March must make a commitment to attend the year-long program. For us, the visit to Poland is part of an educational process."

In the U.S., Young Judaea conducts six camps – five junior camps for ages eight to 15. The sixth, Tel Yehuda, is Hadassah's youth flagship located in Barryville, N.Y. It serves as a national leadership center for those who return from their summers in Jerusalem and for those no longer eligible for one of the junior camps. All told, 1,200 attend every summer.

The benefits of these programs are evident. Krakow estimates that about 20 percent of the youth who attend the all-year program eventually settle in Israel. "The second end product," he adds, "is that they become actively committed Jews. We know that the rate of intermarriage among

them is lower – 20 percent vs. 52 percent for the general Jewish population.
At the same time they show a higher rate of affiliation with Jewish and
Zionist institutions." And they have a stronger attachment to Jewish ritual:

92% of graduates regularly attend a Passover seder vs. 62%.

85% light Chanukah candles vs. 60%.

A 1993 continuity study* of Young Judaean graduates was revealing:

- 64% are involved in a Jewish organization.
- 41% have done volunteer work.
- 59% have taught in religious schools.
- 66% demonstrate a strong affinity for Israel or 25% higher than their
  peers.

In 1996, 14 motivated Hamagshimim graduates enlisted in the Israel
Defense Forces. Before that Young Judaeans on programs in Israel showed
their true mettle by remaining during one of Israel's most threatening
crises – the Gulf War of 1991.

---

* The telephone study was made of 200 parents and Young Judaea graduates in August-
September 1993 by Alan Ganapol of marketQuest, Inc.

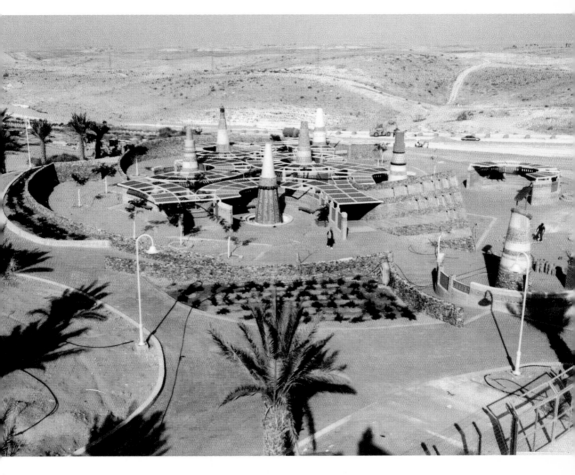

6. Hadassah Park. Since 1926, Hadassah and the Jewish National Fund worked together on projects to
beautify and strengthen Israel. Their latest joint project is Hadassah Park, at the northern entrance to Be'er
Sheva, to provide playgrounds and park facilities.

1996. Hadassah International delegates from more than 25 countries meeting in New York as members of the President's Advisory Council.

1996. 122 Hadassah members, ranging in age from 12 to 91, celebrate their B'not Mitzvah at the National Convention.

The Mandolin Orchestra, composed of teenagers from Youth Aliyah installations across Israel, performs throughout Israel and Europe.

1996. The Hadassah College of Technology's Hotel Management School - student chefs prepare a meal. Other departments include: Dental Technology, Professional Photography, Computer Science and Optometry.

*1996. The Hadassah Medical Center
at Mt. Scopus.*

*1996. Ein Karem - aerial view of the Hadassah Medical Center
with new Mother and Child Center on left.*

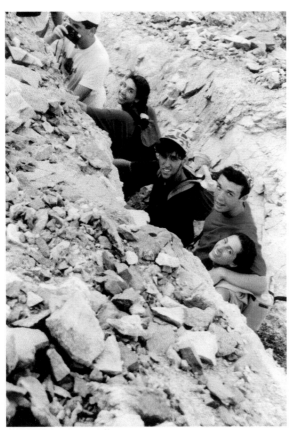

1996. Young Judaea hikers participate in a summer program in Israel. This Zionist youth movement, sponsored by Hadassah, provides programs in Israel and the U.S. designed for second graders through college and beyond, to promote strong Jewish identification and dedication to the State of Israel.

1992. Hadassah members marching in the Pro-Choice rally in Washington, DC. Deborah B. Kaplan in center.

1996. The entrance to the newly opened Mother and Child Center at Ein Karem.

February 6, 1997. Executive Committee. (photo copyright: Jennifer Weisbord)

Seated left to right: *Maureen Schulman, Vice President; June Walker, Vice President; Bernice S. Tannenbaum, Honorary Vice President; Marlene Post, President; Charlotte Jacobson, Honorary Vice President; Sue Mizrahi, Secretary; Annette Meskin, Recording Secretary; Judith Saxe, Vice President.*

Standing left to right: *Renee Albert, Karen Venezky, Marcie Natan, Bonnie Lipton, Jane Zolot, Mona Wood, Helene Karpa, Belle Simon, Beth Wohlgelernter, Executive Director, Joyce Rabin, Ruth B. Hurwitz.*

Absent: *Ruth G. Cole, Vice President; Barbara Goldstein, Diane Issenberg, Vice President; Carmela Kalmanson, Honorary Vice President; Deborah B. Kaplan, Honorary Vice President; Rose E. Matzkin, Honorary Vice President; Molly Novak, Vice President; Tobey Olken, Esq., Vice President; Judith L. Palkovitz, Vice President; Ruth W. Popkin, Honorary Vice President; Dr. Miriam Freund Rosenthal, Honorary Vice President; Barbara Tirschwell, Treasurer; Elaine Winograd; Susan Zimmerman.*

THE EXPLOSIVE NINETIES

Code-named "Desert Storm," the Allied attack against Iraq began at 2:40 a.m. on January 17, 1991. Since the previous July, Iraq had occupied the oil emirate of Kuwait. Fearing that the vast oil wealth of Saudi Arabia was next on dictator Saddam Hussein's list of conquests, the U.S. marched at the head of a coalition of nations to stifle the threat.

Geographically, Israel was far from the conflict. Located at the western side of the Middle East land mass that bridged Asia and Africa, Israel expected the worst from Iraq, and with good reason. Saddam had publicly threatened that he would char half of Israel with chemical weapons should the U.S. attack Iraq.

It was well known that Hussein had large stores of poison gas and bacteriological weapons and that he could deliver them in the warheads of Soviet-made Scud missiles. As a precaution, every Israeli resident received a protective kit containing a gas mask and a syringe to inject atropine, an antidote. Dread of unconventional warfare enveloped Israel. The fright was exacerberated when the Shamir government, at the insistence of the U.S., kept Israel's mighty air force out of the battle.*

---

* Israel was nonetheless at the Iraqi front by proxy. The U.S. Navy in the Gulf used Israeli-made drones – remote guided aircraft – to pinpoint Iraqi targets for its gunners.

To reassure Israelis, the U.S. sent teams with Patriot anti-missile missiles to intercept the Scuds. That was a precedent because never before had Israel depended on foreign soldiers to defend it. Over Iraq, the U.S. Air Force hunted down Scud launching pads. But the Patriots did not effectively stop the missiles and many of the launching pads that the Air Force bombed were dummies.

In anticipation of gas attacks, the Ein Karem Medical Center in Jerusalem installed a triage unit to treat victims on the plaza outside the hospital. With an emergency Hadassah appropriation of $1,000,000, the Center provided doctors with protective suits, arranged long rows of showers and tents, stocked up on anti-gas inoculations. One nurse commented at the time :

> I can just imagine what would have happened had dozens of
> naked, panic-stricken people gathered under cold showers on
> the windy plaza. Fortunately the installation was not used.

As a military weapon, the Scuds were duds. To reach Israel the Iraqis had doubled the range of the original Soviet-made weapon to 300 miles. In so doing they halved its payload to 160 pounds, a mosquito bite by military standards. Without accurate guidance systems, the Scuds often fell within several miles of their planned targets. But they were of some short-lived value in creating havoc among the civilian population. Believing correctly that Saddam Hussein would aim his missiles at the Tel Aviv and Haifa areas, tens of thousands of residents fled their homes. Many went to the resort town of Eilat which was thereby saved from a disastrous tourist season.

The first missile crashed into the Tel Aviv area before dawn on January 17. Six missiles followed within 24 hours. The army calculated that 32 more hit in the 37 days that followed, most of them aiming for vital installations in Tel Aviv, and at the port and refineries in Haifa. Some missiles fell into the Mediterranean, others near Arab villages.

In February 1997, the official Baghdad newspaper, *Qadissiya,* reported that of a total of 93 Iraqi missiles fired during the war, 43 were aimed at Israel, of which five were targetting the Dimona atomic reactor. Israel refused to confirm it but a map published in the Israeli press at war's end pointed to three missile hits in the general area of the reactor.

Earlier on, the military determined that Saddam Hussein was not arming the missiles with gas or germs. As a cautionary measure, Israelis were warned to remain in sealed rooms rather than move to underground shelters during attacks. In retrospect, that may have been an error since shelters would have provided better protection from the widespread damage that ensued.

Israelis went about their daily affairs with anti-gas kits slung over their shoulders similar to Londoners during the World War II blitz. Fashion-minded women in Tel Aviv made carrying cases for the kits to match their clothes. At the sound of a siren, everyone rushed to a sealed room, donned masks and waited anxiously for the all-clear or watched TV for word that the threat was over.

On the evening of February 23, sirens interrupted an Israel Philharmonic Orchestra concert in Jerusalem conducted by Zubin Mehta. Violinist Isaac Stern stopped in the middle of a Mozart concerto and walked off the stage with the orchestra as 3,300 persons in the audience put on their masks. Seconds later Stern walked back on stage, smiled at his ghostly-looking audience and began playing a Bach adagio – without his mask. He received a standing ovation.

Wholesale cancellation by American-Jewish tour groups created a strong feeling of annoyance among Israelis. The continued presence of German and Japanese tourists only heightened that feeling.

Hadassah snubbed the Scud menace and changed the location of its Mid-Winter Board meeting from Washington, D.C., to Jerusalem. Forty members arrived, a relatively large turnout for such meetings even in normal times. The timing was exquisite – it was the first day of the war.

Says Board member Ruth Cole, "We voted to go in order to show our solidarity." Apart from a group of French Jews, the members were the only guests in their Jerusalem hotel. Bernice Tannenbaum was one of two Americans who attended a Jewish Agency Executive meeting that deliberated in gas masks.

The war had its lighter side for the Hadassah leaders. Deborah Kaplan recalls that when the first Scuds fell, she was dining in a Chinese restaurant in Tel Aviv with a few Hadassah companions.

"A Chinese waiter calmly escorted us to a shelter where we were helped on with our gas masks. The two dogs in the shelter were not required to wear them," she recalls. But one of the group had a problem. She could not put on the mask without removing her wig. After a brief moment of hesitation she good-naturedly went about doing so, to everyone's approval."

On Mt. Scopus, most Young Judaeans in the one-year program remained at their work. Other youth groups suffered a high rate of attrition with most of their number leaving for home at the first opportunity. One Young Judaean said that the entreaties of his parents in the U.S. to return were more difficult to face than the Scuds.

Says Director Dan Krakow, "There was a feeling that the Diaspora was not really with us during the war. That is why the fact that most of our students remained made a big impact."

Amazingly, the 39 Scuds killed only two Israelis, one a volunteer in the defense effort. They wounded 223, most of them lightly. Twelve died indirectly, eight from needlessly injecting themselves with atropine and four from asphyxiation after they put on their masks incorrectly. A large number of deaths due to heart attacks was recorded during the period. Some of those might have been brought on by shock from missile explosions.

More than 4,000 buildings were damaged and 1,644 families were evacuated. The Blagin family, immigrants who had arrived from Riga on

December 13, suffered the loss of their home when a Scud demolished it on January 18.

Finally, at the end of February the terror was over. It was Purim day and across the country, children could safely go to parties. Some used masks of Saddam Hussein as the modern-day Haman.

While American forces were mobilizing for war in the Gulf region, the build-up for peace in the Middle East was likewise moving along. In October-November 1991, Israel and its Arab neighbors were brought together by the U.S. and the Soviet Union* for a six-day meeting in the Spanish Royal Palace in Madrid.

At the Conference's opening, President Bush pressed for "a real peace." But that was not going to be easy to achieve. Arabs and Israelis used the presence of the world's TV cameras to trade verbal blows and make impossible demands. Syria's foreign minister called Prime Minister Yitzhak Shamir a "terrorist" and Shamir denounced Syria as tyrannical. The Palestinians called for a two-state solution that they knew Israel would not even consider.

Behind doors, Israel and the Palestinians outlined principles for a five-year period of autonomy in the West Bank and Gaza to be followed by a final settlement. Syria foreclosed on a quick agreement by demanding that Israel agree to give up the Golan Heights even before talks began. Lebanon parroted Syria.

Beyond Israel's neighborhood there was a noticeable relaxation of tensions. The Gulf War had put Israel temporarily in the same camp with all anti-Iraqi forces, including Saudi Arabia. The fact that Israel had refrained from joining the battle played well in Riyadh. That, together with the Madrid Conference, signaled the Third World that it could now end its diplomatic isolation of the Jewish State.

---

* The Madrid Conference was the last major diplomatic move made by the Soviet Union before it broke into 15 nations.

In 1992, Israel was officially recognized by nearly one-half of the world's population when China and India established full diplomatic relations. In a gush of enthusiasm other nations followed suit, including most states in Black Africa and the Vatican. In the ensuing years, Gulf state potentates traded visits with Israeli leaders and, together with Morocco and Tunisia, opened offices in Tel Aviv.

The Madrid Conference had some value in that it had brought former enemies together to talk face-to-face, something that Israeli governments had sought for decades. Secretive Israel-PLO talks followed in 1993 in Oslo where a program was drawn up for Israel's gradual withdrawal from urban areas of the Gaza Strip and West Bank.

Oslo I, as it became known, was signed on the White House lawn as the world watched. It was then that Prime Minister Yitzhak Rabin, who had succeeded Yitzhak Shamir after the 1992 elections, reluctantly shook hands with PLO Chairman Yasser Arafat, but only after considerable nudging by President Bill Clinton. The picture of the hand-shake became a journalistic icon.

In September 1995, Oslo II continued the process. By the beginning of 1997 Israeli troops had redeployed out of all Gaza Strip and West Bank cities after making security arrangements for Jewish settlements.

All the while that peace with the Palestinians crawled forward, insurgent activities continued unabated. In December 1987, a traffic accident in Gaza involving an Israeli and a Palestinian sparked a six-year-long uprising. Known as the *intifada,** the Arabs refined and improved on the methods they used in the 1936-39 riots. Demonstrations led by Arab women and children were supplemented by youngsters throwing rocks at Israeli vehicles traveling on West Bank roads and at Israeli soldiers trying to contain the rioters. Nails and oil slicks placed on highways, tire-burning, Molotov cocktails, hostage-taking, shooting, bus bombings and finally

---

* The Arabic word *intifada*, literally translated as "shaking off," is taken from the shaking of a camel after sexual intercourse. In the case of the Palestinians, the intention was to "shake off" the Israeli occupation.

suicide bombs on public transport and in public places in Israel proper became commonplace. For protection, civilians traveling in the administered territories carried firearms and installed plastic windows in their vehicles.

With the signing of the first Oslo agreement the PLO no longer participated in the intifada. The extreme Islamic fundamentalist group, Hamas, fearing peace was at hand, continued with greater intensity to try and rid the area of the Jewish state.

The dimensions of the Israel-Arab conflict in the West Bank and Gaza were not generally appreciated because of the sporadic nature of the hostilities. In the period from the beginning of the intifada in 1987 until the end of 1996, official figures show that 159 Israelis were killed and 8,169 were wounded. The uprising cost the Palestinians 1,123 in dead and more than 18,000 wounded. Property damage, particularly in burned buses and damaged civilian cars, was considerable.

Throughout this period of peace-making, Hizballah attacks from Lebanon continued at a rapidly increasing pace. Most often hit was Galilee and, in particular, the border town of Kiryat Shemona. Ultimately, as residents threatened to leave Galilee, the Israeli military was forced to carry out two major operations into Lebanon.

In July 1993, Yitzhak Rabin ordered the armed forces to launch "Operation Accountability." Declared an angry Rabin, "If there is no quiet here, it will not be quiet for residents in southern Lebanon."

With that, Israel bombarded 70 villages from land, sea and air, forcing 300,000 to flee toward Beirut. On the Israeli side, half the residents of Galilee moved south, including hundreds of children. The operation ended after Secretary of State Warren Christopher brokered a verbal agreement between Israel and Hizballah to limit clashes. But the agreement was often violated and, in the latter part of April 1996, the Israeli army was back in Lebanon with greater force to punish Hizballah and Lebanon.

"This is war," Chief of Staff Amnon Lipkin-Shahak told a reporter. For 17 days Israeli guns, planes and ships rained terror on Lebanon in

"Operation Grapes of Wrath." The objective was to make attacks on Galilee too painful and costly to repeat.

During the fighting, Hizballah fired 700 Katyusha rockets into Galilee, nearly 20 times the number of missiles fired at all of Israel by Iraq in the Gulf War. Kiryat Shemona residents spent most of its time in stifling shelters but no one was killed, although 127 were wounded. Nearly all the 1,400 homes destroyed or damaged in Galilee from the rocketing were in Kiryat Shemona. More than half of the population of 20,000 fled for the duration.

Lebanon suffered more as 400,000 residents in the south fled from their homes. Most of Beirut was blacked out when Israeli planes hit a power station. On one sorrowful day Israeli artillery, responding to a Hizballah mortar attack, fired back at the source. Less than 350 yards away was a U.N. post where, unbeknown to the Israeli unit, Arab civilians had sought refuge. Several shells overshot the mark and killed 96 of the refugees.

"It is no accident that Hizballah fires close to U.N. posts, knowing that we will be cautious about replying," commented General Lipkin-Shahak.

The end of the fighting came after a week-long effort by Secretary of State Warren Christopher to arrange a cease-fire – this time, by way of a written agreement. To ensure that no further attacks would be launched against civilians, a monitoring group was set up consisting of Israeli, Syrian, Lebanese, American and French military. Few believed that the agreement would long endure.

The Hashemite Kingdom of Jordan had maintained friendly relations with Israel since 1970. In July 1994, the two countries began to formalize their cordial relationship. After three years of quiet negotiation, King Hussein and Prime Minister Rabin signed a declaration at a White House lawn ceremony ending their 46-year state of war. The two men had become personal friends and when they shook hands at the White House, it was sincere. Four months later, in October, with President Clinton again in attendance, the two met on the barren border between Eilat and Akaba to sign a formal peace treaty.* Those two acts brought peace officially to Israel's longest border.

Six months later, tragedy struck. On Saturday night, November 4, as he left a peace rally in front of Tel Aviv city hall, Prime Minister Yitzhak Rabin was assassinated by a law student, Yigal Amir.** The murderer's stated motive was to stop what he regarded as the surrender of Israel's birthright to the Arabs. Thus came to an inglorious end the life of an Israeli who was respected around the world as a patriot, soldier and statesman. His funeral on Mt. Herzl in Jerusalem was attended by world statesmen, among them President Clinton who ended an emotional eulogy with the words, "*Shalom, haver*" (Goodbye, buddy).

Rabin was succeeded by Foreign Minister Shimon Peres, who stepped up the peace process, much to the chagrin of a large segment of the population. A majority of the electorate was in no mood for what it began to regard as Israel's non-stop surrendering of Jewish territories to the Palestinians without reciprocal reductions in tension. If anything, violence increased in ferocity as both sides came closer to a final settlement.

In one macabre week at the beginning of 1996, Arab terrorists carried out five bloody onslaughts against civilians. Suicide killers blew up two buses in Jerusalem and a shopping center in Tel Aviv, and drove into queues at bus stops in Ashkelon and Jerusalem. Total Israeli dead were 58, injured 222.

Despite the sharp tensions that developed between Israelis and Arabs during these years of hostilities, physicians at Hadassah hospitals treated victims from both sides with dispassionate devotion to duty. One doctor reported to Hadassah at the height of the uprising:

> Our Palestinian physicians, nurses and auxiliary staff are
> continuing in their jobs. Our Palestinian patients continue

---

* At the White House ceremonies and in the Arava, Hadassah delegations were present.
** Amir was sentenced to life imprisonment by the Tel Aviv District Court. An accomplice received a similar sentence.

seeking Hadassah's help, sitting side by side with Israelis in clinics, lying side by side with them in our wards.

We are treating badly burned soldiers and civilians, trapped in the flames of vehicles set alight by Molotov cocktails and bombs. We are operating on gunshot wounds and on people with serious orthopedic and neurological injuries caused by hurled stones.

Angry at the Arab response to Israel's peace moves, the country went to the polls in May 1994. The results were close but when the final ballots were counted, the electorate had sent Peres and his Labor Party into opposition with a clear message: the Labor Party had given the Arabs too much, too fast for too little. Into office came Massachusetts Institute of Technology alumnus and former U.N. Ambassador Binyamin Netanyahu, a popular spokesman for conservative causes. President Bill Clinton's transparent support for Peres during the election campaign had been of no help.

Netanyahu, as leader of the right-wing Likud Bloc, slowed down, but did not stop, the peace process. The PLO understood the electorate's message and began to crack down on its extremist wings. The result was that during Netanyahu's first year Israelis no longer feared to step on a bus.

In that same month of May, talks began on the final status between Israel and the Palestinians. As the PLO under Arafat established a shadow government to run the Palestinian Authority, there was good reason for Israelis to believe that by the time the negotiations on the final status of the Palestine political entity were scheduled to end in 1999, the Palestinians would declare an independent state in the West Bank and Gaza. The most sensitive and divisive question was the sovereignty of Jerusalem, with Israel adamant against its division and the Palestinians demanding the eastern section for their intended capital. Over Jerusalem there would be acrimonious debate and bloodshed, before agreement, if any, would be reached.

These momentous events were paralleled by population explosions. Two nations – the Soviet Union and Ethiopia – that were poles apart geographically and culturally, inundated Israel with immigrants. The Soviet Union was by far the larger of the two sources and its captive Jews were more in the public eye.

Sympathy and support for the Jews of the Soviet Union began to be organized on a worldwide scale in the early 1960's. Among the most active in the U.S. on their behalf was Hadassah. In 1966, a delegation of 25 Hadassah leaders travelled to the U.S.S.R. where they met the "Jews of Silence."

"We all wore large Magen David pins on our lapels so people would know who we were," says Charlotte Jacobson who as President led the group. "And we were the first to visit Babi Yar."*

"The Hadassah women were like an army," said Nobel Laureate Elie Wiesel who was in Moscow at the time.

In the early 1970's when Charlotte was chairman of the American Section of the World Zionist Organization, the Israel Government asked her to promote the cause of Russian Jewry who were trapped in a country that would not recognize them as a nationality but would not let them leave. The issue was then being handled without too much enthusiasm by the Conference of Presidents of Major Jewish Organizations. Charlotte was instrumental in urging the recalcitrant Conference to support a separate organization. Thus was born the National Conference for Soviet Jewry.

From the beginning, Hadassah worked energetically within the NCSJ. It sponsored and participated in demonstrations, published literature, retrained and hired immigrant Soviet doctors and nurses in Israel as waves of mass immigration in the 1970's brought nearly 100,000 to Israel. But in a few short years the flow was stopped by the Soviet dictatorship.

---

* Babi Yar, celebrated in a poem by Yevgeni Yevtushenko, is the ravine near Kiev where in two days in September 1941, a Nazi *Sonderkommando* (SS unit), supported by Ukrainian militia, murdered 33,771 Jews with machine guns.

There then followed years of repression. Jews who applied for visas to emigrate to Israel immediately lost their jobs even though their chances of being permitted to leave were slim. A few brave men and women defied the Soviet authorities to campaign for free emigration. They quickly found themselves in gulags or incarcerated in KGB prisons.

In August 1984, on the eve of the Hadassah convention in San Francisco, President Frieda Lewis addressed a message on behalf of Soviet Jews to the Kremlin through the local consul-general. Requesting a renewal of exit visas she said: "We only ask that what has been done for other ethnic groups be done for Jews.... We ask that you grant the Jews the full nurture of their cultural and religious heritage." She appealed especially on behalf of Ida Nudel, "a lonely, isolated person to join her sister in Israel." Ida was released three years later.

When Mikhail Gorbachev lowered the gates in 1989, a tidal wave of nearly 700,000 engulfed Israel. Including the immigration of the 1970's, Israel became the recipient of nearly 800,000 Soviet Jews – the largest single ethnic group in Israel. Most noted among them was Prisoner of Zion Natan Sharansky who had spent 3,255 days in prison, arrived in 1986 and ten years later returned to Moscow on an official visit as an Israeli cabinet minister.

To organize a smooth flow of immigrants to Israel was a logistical headache. Under Jewish Agency direction, immigrants would entrain from Moscow for Vienna or Rome where they would remain in transit centers and choose their final destinations. Most opted for Israel but much to the chagrin of the Israeli government a significant number went to the U.S. and other countries. Hadassah pressed for a system that would encourage immigrants to decide their destinations in Moscow and then fly directly to Tel Aviv if that was the choice.

"Transit camps were eating up the resources that could be used for integrating immigrants in Israel," said President Carmela Kalmanson. "The primary focus of Jewish communal efforts and funding should be for resettlement in Israel."

In 1990, Hadassah allocated $1,000,000 to train newly-arrived former Soviet Jews in Israel. The Hadassah College of Technology was the first institution to propose a program of training and retraining. Special courses were mapped out in four fields. A large number of physicians arrived, 250 in one two-week period. Hadassah retrained more than 1,000 doctors, dentists and dental assistants, nurses and radiology therapists, thereby raising their skills to Western standards. So many doctors, nurses, dentists and technologists flooded the hospitals that Russian became the second language heard in the corridors. In a few years, about one-seventh of all employees working at Hadassah were recent arrivals from the former Soviet Union, including more than 200 nurses and 100 physicians.

In the U.S., Hadassah sent Soviet Jewish children to Young Judaea camps. The Atlanta, Georgia, chapter of Hadassah set up a screening clinic staffed entirely by volunteers. More than 100 of the area's Jewish doctors responded to help the arrivals integrate. In Israel, Young Judaeans formed welcoming committees to greet the Russians with flowers as they stepped off the plane. Volunteer Hadassah-Israel members successfully tutored Russian students at the Hadassah Ne'urim boarding school near Netanya. Their students received the highest marks in the state matriculation exams.

Russian immigration lavished a rich human harvest on the country. Engineers, mathematicians, surveyors, scientists, musicians, researchers in a myriad of specialties were among them; athletes with Russian names represented Israel on scoreboards the world over – Smashnova (tennis), Krasnov (swimming), Shmerkin (ice-skating). So many musicians came that cities never before endowed with symphony orchestras found themselves enhanced with virtuoso music played by artistes from the best conservatories in the Soviet Union. A popular quip at the time had it that whoever stepped off the plane from Russia not carrying a violin case must be a pianist.

No less rich culturally but totally different were the 25,000 Ethiopian Jews who emigrated to Israel. They arrived over brief periods in two large waves. When they first arrived, Israelis were impressed by these beautiful brown-skinned men and women with delicate features, aquiline noses and lithe figures. They spoke a native language called Ge'ez as well as Amharic and – those from the cities – English. Some knew Hebrew.

Their lineage extended back to the First Temple period in the ancient kingdom of Kush, homeland of the Queen of Sheba. Legend relates that Sheba's son, Menelik, fathered by Solomon, took Judaic customs to Ethiopia. Judaism was widespread in Ethiopia until the country was converted to Christianity in the fourth century.

Persecuted, many Jews retreated into the mountainous area around Lake Tana on the Blue Nile and into the Gondar region. They lived in their own communities, isolated from their fellow-Jews until the 20th century. But even in the wilderness they retained a traditional way of life linked closely to the laws laid down in the Torah. The Torah was taught to them in their native Ge'ez by a *kes* (priest) and his assistants. But even though they strictly followed the Mosaic laws of purity, the Sabbath and marriage, their Judaism was open to question in the West.

After much deliberation in the 1970's, the Chief Rabbinate declared that the *Falashas*, a derogatory name by which the Ethiopians were then commonly known, were indeed Jews. In 1984, the government of Menachem Begin decided upon an unpublicized and complex mission to take the Ethiopians to Israel from under the noses of a hostile regime that did not want to release them. Secretly, an Israeli airlift flew 10,000 of them into Israel during Operation Moses at the end of 1984.

When they arrived, they told stories of great adversity in heading out for the Land of Israel. Their families were broken asunder, they endured illness, brigands and murderers as they walked weeks on end to transit camps set up in Sudan. The story of Moshe Beruk, 38, is typical:

> I am one of ten children and we come from a village in the Gondar region of Ethiopia where we were 100 Jewish families. With my parents, our family numbered 64 in all. My brothers were farmers. I trained as a teacher and worked for

the government. Because of my status, my wife and I decided to travel separately with our two children so as not to endanger the others.

We bought a donkey and sold everything we owned, then headed into the forest. After five days we met other escaping Jews and joined them. Two nights later we were attacked by bandits. They stole everything we had – our donkeys, our money and food, even our water.

Traveling only at night, hiding during the day, they stuffed rags into the mouths of their children to keep them from crying as strangers came near.

When people began to die we were too afraid to stop to bury them. In February 1984, after walking 25 days, we reached the Sudanese border. We told the authorities we were Christians fleeing the famine and they let us into a refugee camp – a crowded, hungry place where dozens died every day.

In the camp Moshe found out that 59 members of his family had been caught five days from the village and sent back. They were dispossessed of their land, cows and donkeys, and imprisoned for one month. Nine months later, in November 1984, Moshe and his family were taken to Khartoum and flown to Israel as part of Operation Moses.

In Israel, says Moshe, "Every aspect of life had changed for us and we needed help to re-learn it." After three months in an integration center, they received an apartment and Moshe began his training as a social service worker.

By 1991, a government friendly to Israel ruled in Addis Ababa. At the urging of the Bush administration in Washington, the government permitted the emigration of its Jews. In a record 33-hour airlift, Operation Solomon took 14,000 Ethiopians from Addis Ababa on the last leg of their journey.

An 86-year-old *kes*, Menashe Zimru, arrived with 224 Ethiopians during the Gulf War. As he deplaned, he asked incredulously, "Are we really in Israel?"

A difficult period of re-education quickly began for most. As Moshe Beruk described it:

> We were weakened by the journey and very confused. We found that 'home' was an unfamiliar place. Everything about it had to be learned – its culture, customs, language, shops, food, services and opportunities.

Of the thousands of children who arrived in Israel during Operation Moses, 60 percent had lost one or both parents. Many had diseases no longer seen in the West. Some were HIV positive. Youth Aliyah Director Eli Amir recalls one child who told him, "Before I came to Israel, I thought God was black. Now, I think maybe he is white."

Says Amir, "Ninety percent of those we took in had never been to school and could neither read nor write any language. None of our textbooks was appropriate."

The Education Ministry could not help Eli. It did not have the necessary $1,000,000 for new books. So he called on Hadassah President Ruth Popkin. It was only one week before the national convention but she managed to squeeze the issue into the already completed agenda.

Pleading for eight minutes in a hoarse voice before the pre-convention Board meeting in Miami, Eli convinced the members. The Board voted to give him two-thirds of the sum. After the meeting, Ruth Popkin asked him, "How did you do it? We have a budget deficit of $2,5000,000 and you just increased it."

Replied Eli, "What the Board saw was not the Youth Aliyah director but the 14-year-old boy that I was when I went to Israel and was taken in by Youth Aliyah. That was who convinced them."

One of Hadassah's more innovative programs to help the Ethiopians was begun by the School of Dentistry. When requested by the Joint

Distribution Committee to help the community integrate, Community Dentistry Department head Jonathan Mann met with young Ethiopian women. Says Mann:

> They told their stories, in Amharic through an interpreter. All were about 18 and all had walked from Ethiopia to Sudan and many were without family. Rachel Yalu had a brother sitting in jail in Ethiopia. He lost his gun while he was in the army and he would remain in prison until the money for the gun was paid. Rachel's first imperative was to find the money and send it to him.

To help the women, the dental faculty opened a one-year dental assistant course in 1985 for 21 women like Rachel. Says Mann:

> There were vast cultural gaps that we didn't know how to bridge. We felt inadequate trying to explain things that were so simple for us. A filling, for example, is not something that needs explaining to Israelis but the Ethiopians never heard of it. Language was a barrier. Cut off from families, almost all the students had traumatic pasts and overwhelming personal problems.

Educators were brought in to help devise new ways to teach. The staff had to reduce the pace of teaching and become more aware of cultural differences. The one-year program was expanded to two years and in 1987, 18 of the students received Israel National Board licenses. After Operation Solomon, a second course was begun and in 1994, 18 more completed it.

By 1995, Ethiopians could join Israelis in a mixed course, and study was reduced to 16 months. Says Mann, "It was a major challenge for both the Ethiopians and for us. Both of us profited."

Netanya, one of seven cities with large Ethiopian populations, was the scene of a totally different effort on their behalf. Hadassah-Israel members in Netanya tutored at the Rashi elementary school where 470 of the 750 pupils were Ethiopian immigrants. For four days a week, four hours a day, the Hadassah members taught 100 pupils weekly.

"Our job was not only to teach children but to help them integrate," says Zillah Goldstein, 75, a psychologist who emigrated to Israel from South Africa in 1961. Zillah initiated the program in Netanya. "They are all bright kids but they have no cognitive skills. They learned to read and write but did not know what they were reading or writing."

Zillah and 35 other Hadassah members attended lectures on the culture and history of the Ethiopian Jews. They understood that much of the work being done for the pupils was wasted and the children, 11- and 12-year-olds, were dropping out of school because they could not cope. They were headed for the underworld.

"We began," says Zillah "by helping in the school luncheon club where meals were served to children who were not getting a good meal at home. From there we went to tutoring. Now we get letters from their teachers telling us how much better the kids are coping."

Rashi school principal Meir Reuven, an Ethiopian, once asked the children how they felt about a group of old ladies fussing over them. One answered for the group, "We feel we are worth something."

Twenty-five volunteers from the U.S. on Hadassah's two-month WIN (Winter in Netanya)* project tutored high school pupils, Ethiopians among them, at the Sinai School. Said Shirley Gladstone of Amherst, Massachusetts, "We had the satisfaction of doing good in a school that was wonderfully integrated." Shirley's husband, Saul, a retired assistant principal and teacher of industrial arts, accompanied her. While Shirley was tutoring, Saul was repairing doors and beds, fixing broken toilets and light switches in Netanya's Laniado Hospital.

As the historic events of the 1990's unfolded, Hadassah played a supporting role both in the U.S. and in Israel. When in 1990, the National

---

* National Hadassah also sponsors a yearly, one-month long volunteer work program in Netanya in the spring (SPIN).

Board decided to hold its mid-winter conference in Israel and later its national convention in the wake of the Gulf War, a grateful Mayor Teddy Kollek wrote President Kalmanson, "The economic damage to our Jerusalem [from the absence of tourists] is great but beyond that it is terribly demoralizing. With this hanging over us, your announcement was a silver lining."

A tradition of periodically assembling in convention more than 6,000 miles from home base was begun by Hadassah in 1978, the year that Begin and Sadat were locked in negotiations with President Jimmy Carter at Camp David. Hadassah took its 66th annual convention to Israel. Chairman Rose Goldman and co-Chairman Ruth Popkin worked out the logistics of transporting 2,600 delegates and guests to Israel. The largest group of visitors to arrive at one time, they occupied every hotel room in Jerusalem and the surrounding area.

"The ruby red taillights of 65 buses winding through the desert," recalls Ruth Popkin, "is one image that will always stay with me. You couldn't miss us."

On Purim 1987, Hadassah assembled 2,500 in Jerusalem for a 75th birthday party. President Popkin decided to include the entire city in the celebration by staging a parade. Her story:

> I wanted marchers and floats. Mayor Teddy Kollek agreed to close the streets. Kibbutzim made floats. The regions brought their banners with them. It rained the entire week before and everyone was telling me to cancel. But I was determined. I love a parade.
>
> Fortunately, the rain stopped on the morning of the parade. It was cold and bright when we set out and I rode down King George Street with Teddy in a flower-covered, horse-drawn carriage pulled by two horses. We had a ball. When the parade finished, the rain resumed. Next day's *Jerusalem Post*

commented, 'We knew Hadassah had clout; we did not know it had that much clout!'

Ex-President Kaplan, in 1991 the first to be elected in Jerusalem, states, "Our coming to Jerusalem demonstrated that Hadassah's heart is in Jerusalem – the place where Presidents take office." Adds Carmela Kalmanson,* "We had something to say about Hadassah's proper place, and the best way to say it was to go to Jerusalem."

Four years later, in 1995, at the 81st national convention, Marlene Post was likewise elected in Jerusalem.

During this same dynamic decade, the Hadassah Medical Organization was marching forward. In the wake of a change of guard in the leadership, a long list of "firsts" was achieved. Among them: state-of-the-art radio beam surgery, simultaneous transplanting of five human organs, a heart-lung transplant on an Arab mother of 10 and a liver transplant on an Ethiopian child. A rapid response trauma unit and a regional AIDS testing center were established. But of all the impressive accomplishments nothing on the Ein Karem campus caught the eye or captured the heart as much as the child-friendly new Mother and Child Center.

In the meantime, Hadassah's reach had become global. From its very beginning the organization had not seen the oceans as a barrier to its creativity. Until the establishment of the State of Israel it had concentrated, however, on the Jewish community in Palestine. Then, as the young State extended its help to the Third World under Foreign Minister Golda Meir, Hadassah sent its experts from Jerusalem to remote places in Asia and Africa. Their aid saved many lives and improved the quality of life of many unfortunates, but their presence was only temporary.

In 1983, acting on an inspiration from its HMO head, Hadassah gave birth to a worldwide organization that would become known as Hadassah International.

---

* Carmela Kalmanson was the first President (1988-1991) since 1956 to opt for a three-year term rather than four.

HADASSAH GOES GLOBAL

The 1970's were a decade of dedications for Hadassah. Some Hadassah veterans called President Rose Matzkin (1972-1976) "the President of Dedications" because few periods in Hadassah's history had seen so much ado.

In Israel, Hadassah staffs fought in the Yom Kippur War, reopened the Scopus Medical Center with its unique rehabilitation pavilion, established its first kibbutz, opened the state-of-science Sharett Institute of Oncology, graduated its first college class, and began the retraining program for Russian immigrant professionals.

In the U.S., Rose moved Hadassah House from its cramped quarters into a new home on New York's 58th Street and congratulated Hadassah's 100,000th Life Member. There was much more, not the least of which was a Tel Aviv Youth Aliyah day center opened in 1976 in the name of...Rose Matzkin.

This decade of "do" was appropriately capped by the birth of a totally new concept: Hadassah as a universal organization. The idea began hatching toward the end of the 1970's when Bernice Tannenbaum (1976-1980) was National President.

New projects and demands for high technology instrumentation created a need for bigger budgets within the Hadassah Medical Organization. At about the same time, large numbers of Jews, among them members of the World International Zionist Organization,* began moving from Canada to the U.S. WIZO members formed study groups in Florida, Texas and other states, causing unrest among local Hadassah leaders. A clash between the world's two largest Zionist organizations seemed to be unavoidable.

WIZO's infiltration into Hadassah territory was put by President Frieda Lewis before the pre-convention National Board meeting on August 6, 1981.

"Snowbirds are a phenomenon of Canada as well as the United States," she said with a touch of irony. "These women come to Florida and other sun belt areas and do not understand that they are not part of our organization and demand service from our chapters. They even bear the name Hadassah in their title... Canadian Hadassah WIZO."

WIZO, she said, was advertising in the Florida press, recruiting "people of great means" among the immigrants from South America and Iran. Frieda also recalled that WIZO was not bound by any formal contract but "there has been an understanding for many years that they would not organize in the United States and we would not organize outside of the United States."

She asked her Board, "How shall we deal with this?"

The answer came quickly. Hadassah would go global.

No longer bound by the unwritten understanding, Hadassah felt freed of its obligation to remain within the borders of the 50 states. HMO head Tannenbaum set objectives that would, within little more than a decade, put Hadassah into its global orbit and establish it permanently on five continents with medical relief associations. Members overseas would include men, women, Jews and non-Jews.

---

* Henrietta Szold created WIZO in Canada in 1929. An unwritten, long honored agreement with Hadassah held that WIZO would not canvas for membership in the U.S. while Hadassah would organize only in the U.S.

"I felt that overseas there could be a role for non-Jews," says Bernice. "Medicine has a universal appeal and instead of creating little Zionist or Jewish groups which would compete with existing organizations, we would appeal to everyone. This organization would be another arm of Hadassah, organized as a separate corporation."

The green light to move abroad was turned on at the August 1983 national convention in Washington, DC. The delegates, by acclamation, formally established the Hadassah Medical Relief Association, later to be known as Hadassah International. Bernice had already laid the groundwork. Hadassah abroad would be different. For one thing, men would be accepted* as members to raise money for medical work. Members did not have to subscribe to Zionist ideology. Functions would be held solely to benefit the projects of the Hadassah Medical Organization and to build relationships between the members and Israel.

To test the waters, Israel would be the first site for Hadassah International. There, Hadassah members who had gone on aliyah had jumped the gun.

Shortly after the 1967 war members who had emigrated to Israel believed that, since Hadassah had a presence in Israel, they would continue the same organizational and social activities in their adopted country. They were wrong. There was no structure within which they could function as they did at home. Life Members found themselves listed in Hadassah House as members of their American chapters.

Hadassah Council in Israel** Chairman Vera Tzur, called on one of the American immigrants, former Upper Midwest Regional President Barbara Schermer, to form some kind of organization that would give a home to the Hadassah alumnae. Barbara had arrived on aliyah in 1969 and by 1970 had put together *Olot Hadassah* (Hadassah immigrants). Around a nucleus of

---

* In the U.S., men could only be Hadassah Associates and 30,000 have done so. To grant men equal status in even an associate organization such as HMRA was revolutionary. It may well serve as a precedent for the U.S. organization in the 21st century.
** The HCI served as a liaison to the National Board in New York. It was dissolved in 1996. The HMO Israel Committee, a public advisory body, was still functioning in 1997.

HCI members, there gathered 200 members in Jerusalem. Later, Olot was extended to Tel Aviv.

Unrecognized by Hadassah in New York, *Olot* nevertheless kept busy. The members welcomed tourist groups, sponsored symposiums, held luncheons, assisted with the 1978 and 1982 national conventions in Jerusalem. But without backing from New York, *Olot* eventually collapsed.

A few years later, Hadassah Council President Sylvia Shapiro, a National Board member living in Israel, moved into the vacuum. She was convinced that with the Hadassah-WIZO agreement on its way out, the time had come to form a group with national support. Rose Joshua, a former regional president from Minneapolis, and Sylvia used former *Olot* members as the nucleus and started a unit at the conclusion of the 1982 national convention.

Recalls Rose, "We decided to give it six months to see whether we could convince New York during that time."

In January 1983, the ruling came through from the National Board: the understanding with WIZO was finished. It was during this period that Hadassah House was studying the feasibility of establishing HMRA.

In February, although not yet a recognized group, Hadassah-Israel began its activities with a Mediscope meeting at the Ein Karem Medical Center. The turnout of 150 members was larger than expected. With that conference they indicated that the incipient Hadassah-Israel, at least, would be more than a fund-raising organization. Thus, a pattern was set.

On Purim 1983, Hadassah-Israel was officially established. It was Hadassah's 71st birthday. The founding meeting was held around an oval table in Rose Joshua's living room in Jerusalem. Present were eight Hadassah members. Bernice Tannenbaum was there to supervise the birth. In the Fall, Hadassah-Israel held its first membership meeting and Rose Joshua was elected President.

Although the beginning was not easy, Hadassah-Israel passed the test for the leadership in New York. The already-existing natural constituency was American and their language was English, not Hebrew. At first, says

Rose Joshua, "We made the error of working like Americans. What we had to do was adapt."

Rose initiated yearly Mediscope programs whereby members gathered for an entire day to be briefed by Hadassah staff on a specific subject such as medical ethics or new developments.

During the term of office of Rose's successor, Annabelle Bienenfeld Yuval,* the organization began a nationwide health awareness program targeted at women, with emphasis on cancer prevention.

The third President Sylvia Mehlman, a former Baltimore chapter vice-president, bridged the language gap by introducing simultaneous Hebrew-English translations both at the Mediscope meetings and at the national conferences.

"At the beginning we were mainly English speakers, but the translations served to bring in more Hebrew-speaking Israelis and united us." It was also during Sylvia's tenure that Hadassah Israel's fund-raising reached major proportions. Its gift to HMO, an echo doppler for cardiograms, was bought for $200,000.

In 1992, Hadassah-Israel elected its first native-born Israeli as President, Ora Sela. She made it a priority to attract non-American Israelis. Hebrew-speaking groups were founded and with that the adaptation to the Israeli scene had succeeded.

Under the dynamic leadership of Hinda Gross, a Gratz College graduate from Philadelphia, Hadassah-Israel's projected membership by the end of 1997 grew to 2,000, organized in 16 chapters, representing women from 40 cities, kibbutzim and moshavim. Half the units were English-speaking and half Hebrew-speaking.

Says Hinda, "We are women who do not want to sit at meetings. We want to do things."

---

* Annabelle, who has held many leadership positions in Hadassah, emigrated to Israel in 1952, and married David Yuval who from 1980 to 1989 served as HMO international auditor and the HWZOA Representative in Israel. David died in 1989.

And they did. The cancer detection campaign expanded over the years, saving lives and improving the quality of life for many Israeli women. Apart from fund-raising events, Hadassah-Israel has instituted health workshops and campaigns to encourage the use of bicycle helmets. Senior citizens have been taught how to move about in Israel's horrendous traffic.

With Hadassah now established in Israel, the rest of the world was ready to be mobilized.

The second nation to join the Hadassah family was France. Instrumental in its beginning was Beatrice Birnbaum, formerly of Baltimore, now resident in Paris. Bea was vice-president of the new entity. After serving as a volunteer for several years, she was pressed into professional service as the International Directrice, based in Paris but serving Europe. There a cooperation agreement was concluded in 1989 between the Ein Karem Medical Center in Jerusalem and the Curie Institute in Paris. That made available expertise from the noted Institute's advanced research on cancer therapy. It also opened the door to future agreements with other scientific institutions throughout the world. The latest cooperative ventures are in Turkey with the Baskent University Medical School and with Hacettepe University Faculty of Medicine.

From France, Hadassah set up shop in Argentina. It began when a Jewish businessman offered his chalet on the snow-covered Andes at San Carlos de Bariloche for a medical conference for public health practitioners. Twenty-five Hadassah-Argentina members attended together with about 100 physicians from Brazil and Argentina.

Bernice exclaimed, "We were not yet viable in Argentina, but we dared to mount a medical conference in a world new to us. For many of those who attended it served as an introduction to the name Hadassah. Shmuel Penchas came to lecture and he was wonderful. From that little beginning we created a strong group of men and women, Jews and non-Jews, who became a force for Hadassah in the country."

Subsequently, Hadassah-Argentina, now headed by Dr. Enrique Pener, rolled up a membership of 350. In 1996, it held a symposium on trauma nursing organized by Barbara Sabin, Hadassah-International liaison, in which Hadassah nurses participated, and a medical symposium at the prestigious National Academy of Medicine.

Until 1995, with few exceptions, the Academy was closed to Jewish physicians, according to Beatriz Wolf Cheja, secretary of the group.

With Argentina established, Hadassah spread to other countries in South and Central America. Two groups were founded in Brazil and others in Chile, Colombia, Ecuador, Honduras, Uruguay, Venezuela and Mexico.

In Havana, Rosa Behar Hasday organized 60 Jews and non-Jews under the banner of Hadassah-Cuba. The group provides dental and ophthalmological services to schools. The Hadassah Pharmacy sorts and distributes medications to the community and to children in summer camps.

Rosa, who founded the Gastroenterology Department at General Calixto Garcia University Hospital, conducted a medical census of Havana's Jewish community of 500 families and found that hypertension was their main problem. The group then went to work to supply information on how to control the ailment. In conducting the census, Rosa discovered that Jews were living in all of Cuba's 14 provinces.

Hadassah-Cuba has alerted the women of Havana to the dangers of breast cancer. At one meeting on prevention, a woman in the audience stood up and said, "I am alive today because of what you taught me." Over and beyond the medical objectives of the group, there is a bond that ties the Cuban Jewish community to Hadassah.

Says Rosa, "Hadassah has helped us bring Cuba's Jews together. We not only learn about Israel and Israeli medicine, but it makes us more conscious of our Judaism."

Dr. Sergio Daniel Simon, president of Hadassah-Brazil, organized Hadassah-Sao Paulo, Brazil, in 1994. An oncologist with the Albert Einstein Hospital in Sao Paulo, his objective is to "disseminate the work of Hadassah among the whole Brazilian population (population: 160,737,489) in order to counteract Arab propaganda."

After a visit to Vienna by Bernice, Suzanne Shaked, retired fashion shop proprietor, mobilized 50 professionals and lay people to form Hadassah-Austria. She organized a project to raise funds for the adolescent psycho-oncology unit at Hadassah Ein Karem. During an earlier visit to Vienna, Bernice met with a prospective contributor whose interest was improving relations with the Arabs. Over lunch, she suggested that he meet the HMO Director-General. The result of the meeting with "Sami" Penchas was a substantial annual gift for scholarships for the training of Arab physicians at Hadassah.

Young Hadassah groups have been organized in Paris, Lyon, Luxembourg, Dusseldorf, Vienna and Caracas. Underway are young Hadassah groups in London and Buenos Aires. Hadassah-Germany's members have initiated projects oriented to helping the Palestinians. Munich, scene of Hitler's beer hall putsch, now has a Jewish community of 4,000. Reports Hadassah International's Sylvie Sullerot, of the Paris office, "This community is living with the eternal paradox of being Jews in Germany and that's why they raise their children with a close connection with Israel."

On the other side of the globe, Hadassah has targeted the two geographical extremities of China.

In Hong Kong, Karen Burgman, a marriage and family counselor from Chicago, moved to the British colony to "redefine my roots." Hong Kong, Chinese from 1997 on, opens for her Hadassah group a vast potential. "Health care is deficient in the provinces," she says.

In Beijing, the Jewish community is made up of expatriates who are there on business. One is Elyse Beth Silverberg, who has been in China since 1982. During the International Women's Conference in August 1996, Hadassah International's Eva Silberman invited Elyse to create a unit. Elyse agreed, hoping to direct the community's young couples to develop joint medical projects between institutions in China and the HMO.

On the North American continent, Hadassah and WIZO have joined hands in Canada. There, Canadian Hadassah WIZO has supported HMO's Scandiplan, a system that permits pinpointing of body areas for for radiation therapy. In 1995, Hadassah-WIZO hosted Hadassah International's Ninth Annual Congress in Montreal.

Apart from its scientific and cultural activities, Hadassah International has succeeded in its goal to raise significant amounts of money for the HMO. The largest gift to date was a total of $7,000,000 for the PET and Cyclotron unit given after a visit to Paris by Bernice and Prof. Henri Atlan, head of the Nuclear Medicine Department. The funds created the Human Biology Research Center on the Ein Karem campus. Hadassah-France also contributed $250,000 to buy the lithotripter, and large additional sums for the Mother and Child Center and the dialysis day care unit.

For fund-raising, the groups use the usual techniques: concerts, dinners, galas. Then there are events like these:

A debutante's ball in Italy.

An antiques furniture sale in Venezuela.

A "Jerusalem Grand Prix" at the Vincennes, France, race track which harvested a sizable sum by donating the "lost" bets to the Mother and Child Center.

An art sale and classical music concerts organized by the Hadassah-Sweden president, Psychiatrist Jan Martel, was used to support a pediatric oncologist resident training at Ein Karem.

The creation of Hadassah International has gone beyond fund-raising for HMO and creating good ties with Israel. In nearly every overseas group Jewish members freely explain that Hadassah is a splendid anchor for securing one's identity. And non-Jewish members generally use their Hadassah affiliation to improve Christian-Jewish relations.

Vienna's Suzanne "Suzi" Shaked, although not Jewish, reports that she was recently told by a non-Jewish member of her Board that she knew nothing about Jewish customs and ceremonies. "I took her to the Jewish community center," Suzi says. "There I explained Jewish ceremonies, like Havdalah. It took away a little of the frightening aspect of a different religion."

During its second decade, Hadassah International has been in the hands of former President Deborah Kaplan as coordinator. Deborah and a team of talented volunteers have kept up the momentum with new groups and new relationships with medical institutions. For the first time a European conference was held in Paris and a Pan-American conference in Buenos Aires.

Hadassah's grasp of the globe, excluding Israel, began decades ago when it shared its expertise with health care workers from abroad and began sending its people on temporary missions to Asia and Africa. Since then, more than 10,000 Hadassah experts have gone to over 100 countries. More than 28,000 trainees from 112 nations have come to Hadassah for courses. A map of the world where Hadassah has a presence or made an impact would extend from Fiji to Canada and from Denmark to Chile – 78 states in all.

By way of example a few of their exploits bear retelling.

First, there were the nurses and the civil war in Yugoslavia. As Hadassah sent Rose Kaplan and Rachel Landy to Palestine in 1912, so it sent nurses into Bosnia and Herzegovina in 1995 and 1996.

When Board Member Nancy Falchuk, initiator of the nurses councils, paid a visit to St. Louis she was approached by the council President Elsie

Shemin-Roth, R.N., who asked that something be done for the innocent victims of ravaged Bosnia and Herzegovina. In August 1994, Elsie was dispatched to Sarajevo to assess the needs of two hospitals. With her went Kathryn Bauschard of St. Louis, Deanna Perlmutter of Boston, and Charlotte Franklin of Santa Barbara, California, all registered nurses.

"The two hospitals we visited have been bombed and shelled, and anti-aircraft weaponry are currently pointed directed at the hospitals," Elsie reported. "Electricity to run the generators is limited and there is running water for two hours a day."

The hospitals needed everything from dialysis and I.V. solutions to cereal for babies and back packs for public health nurses. The result: a five-month campaign, launched by the Nurses Councils, amassed 33 tons of supplies valued at $3,500,000.

On February 22, 1995, Elsie and Sherry Hahn of Arlington, Massachusetts, arrived in Sarajevo. They "sneaked in," according to Elsie, under the banner of the U.N. High Commissioner for Refugees. For the following seven days they distributed supplies, among them a defibrillator and over 100 prosthetics to replace feet, legs and knees. They were assisted by La Benevolencija, the 102-year-old Jewish aid society.

In July 1995, Elsie was back, this time to help transfer four children and two adults to the Ein Karem Medical Center in Jerusalem. Some suffered from severe phosphorous grenade burns and could not be treated in the war zone. "These people had no future without Hadassah's help," Elsie said. On the way to Jerusalem the patients were attended by Hadassah surgeon Ahmed Eid and a surgical nurse.

By early 1996, the condition in war-torn Sarajevo had become desperate and Elsie,* 65, returned for a fourth time. In March, she left for the war zone accompanied by Sherry Hahn and a Bosnian anesthesiology nurse,

---

* Elsie was a homemaker until she began studying nursing. At 54 she became the oldest North American to receive a nursing degree. A mother of five and a grandmother of three she worked with immigrants in Israel after caring for Jews in Ethiopia. For her courage, *TIME*, the weekly newsmagazine, cited Elsie as a local hero (Special Report, June 17, 1996).

Safeta (Sada) Ovcina. Through the intervention of Defense Secretary William Perry and Democratic Party leader Richard Gephardt, the supplies were shipped on the S.S. Inspiration to Rotterdam. From there they went by rail to Lublijana, Slovenia, and then by truck to Split, Croatia. Each of the 8,000 cartons had to clear customs before they were allowed to continue to Sarajevo.

Elsie reported on arrival in the Bosnian capital:

> It has been 43 months since the war began and the people are freezing, hungry and emotionally exhausted. We are bringing the tools to help them survive, build a sense of self, and gain the confidence to start living again.

Hadassah's second shipment to Bosnia amounted to 75 tons, valued at $10,000,000. Contributed by more than 100 communities across the U.S, there were 35 hand-made quilts from California and hand-knitted hats and mittens from senior citizens in Florida. A Bar Mitzvah boy from upstate New York spent $500.00 of his gift money to contribute a package of medicines.

Some of the supplies were given to children in the Isak Samokovlija elementary school. Named for a Jewish physician and poet, the non-sectarian school of 1,200 pupils was hit by 5,000 shells. Thirty-three pupils were killed outside the school, 84 orphaned.

"There are no words in my language to say how grateful I am to Hadassah for giving me the chance to return to Bosnia to help my people," said Sada. The mission meant she could be reunited with her family.

The team spent Passover in Sarajevo where La Benevolencija arranged seders. In attendance for the ecumenical seder on the second night, apart from Jews of a Sarajevo suburb, were the Archbishop of Bosnia, leaders of the Serbian Orthodox church, representatives of the Moslem community and three American soldiers.

The saga of Elsie and her team was duly registered in the Congressional Record by Senator Barbara Mikulski, Democrat of Maryland, a life member of Hadassah.

Then there is the tale of the doctors and the earthquake of December 7, 1988 that took the lives of more than 55,000, entombed three cities, destroyed scores of villages and made tens of thousands homeless in northwest Armenia. Four days later, a call from Jacques Michel, medical director of the Scopus Medical Center, came through to Yoel Donchin, currently head of the Critical Care Transport Unit at Ein Karem. CCTU is a medical rapid response squad that answers emergency calls for help anywhere in the world.

It had its beginnings with the Armenian earthquake. Michel asked Donchin whether he would go. Donchin was the right man; he eagerly accepted, enlisted nephrologist Ze'ev Katzir, pediatrician Yaron Dagani and neurologist Alexander Lussus and emergency services chief Samuel Hyman. Supplies and equipment for two weeks were packed and sent to the airport labeled, "A Gift to the Russian People."

Part of a 19-man medical team under the supervision of the Israel army, the four Hadassah doctors did not arrive in Tbilisi, Georgia, until nine days after the quake had hit. Bad weather had delayed them. From the Georgian capital, their mobile hospital was transported in a convoy of trucks 100 miles through treacherous snow-covered mountains to Kirovakan. They were 20 miles from the epicenter.

The quake had left Kirovakan in the dead of winter without hospital facilities. Donchin's team was set up in a covered sports stadium that they divided with plastic sheets. They set up trauma and general medicine in one area and hospitalization in another. A tent became an operating theater.

"We saw about 350 patients a day for two weeks," says Donchin. "The first patients arrived in great pain from unset fractures and untreated infections. When word got about that the Israelis had arrived with a hospital, the doctors were inundated with Armenians complaining of everything from chronic ailments to headaches."

Donchin recalls, "People came from all over when they heard an Israeli hospital was available. Nobody was turned away. Our presence gave the people moral support. Some patients cried when they left us. They gave us fresh fruit to supplement our combat rations."

They came from as far as Tbilisi. All told, the MD's handled 2,400 cases, including non-quake illnesses such as tonsillitis and appendicitis.

So appreciative were the townspeople that shopkeepers refused to take money from the doctors. They were invited to private homes. Dressed in Israel army uniforms they walked arm in arm with Red Army soldiers. "Everywhere we turned, we were welcomed with outstretched arms," reports Donchin. Once hospitals became operative, they picked up their equipment and returned home. They had been away 14 days.

For Yoel Donchin flying out of the country to save lives is a common occurrence. His team of doctors makes up to 100 trips abroad yearly. "We can leave at a moment's notice." He can receive a call at 2 a.m. to go to Eilat to transport a 19-year-old girl, unconscious from a traffic accident, and transport her by helicopter to Beersheba. He can be off to Beijing bringing home a vacationing Israeli who has developed a hematological problem. Or he can send one of his team to India to transport home a young Israeli whose brain was damaged and legs broken from a motorcycle accident in the Himalayas.

Donchin says he likes the work although he is frequently on duty around the clock. "I am restless and I need quick rewards. Saving a life is my profession."

In the mid-'80's, Shmuel Penchas and the National Board considered projects to help African nations. One of the proposals was to staff a hospital in Sudan to serve Ethiopian Jews who reached the Sudan on their way to Israel. The hospital was to have been built by the U.S. Agency for

International Development (A.I.D.) but, as Penchas puts it, "someone got cold feet and it never went through."

Hadassah, however, was committed and on a suggestion from A.I.D., it was agreed that the organization would oversee the construction in Kinshasa, Zaire, of a "model hospital," as then President Ruth Popkin put it. Penchas turned over direct responsibility for the project to an old hand, his deputy in Ein Karem, Zvi Stern. The two went to Kinshasa in 1984 and 1985 to see the site and work out the overall project with the Government.

Stern told *Hadassah Magazine*, "The U.S. Government selected Hadassah for this project because it knows from experience that without the involvement of a private voluntary organization, A.I.D. money disappears and the project will fail. It did not fail and only one-third of the allocated money was spent."

Egyptian-born Eli Mor, administrator of the Scopus hospital, arrived in Kinshasa in January 1987. He remained for 30 months and supervised the construction of the hospital which consisted of eight single-story buildings. The site chosen was the poor Kimbanseke suburb of the capital, Kinshasa, the locality of a Christian sect known as the Kimbangists.*

A five-member team came next. It included Moshe Harel, head of the Scopus medical supply department, and Eli's 26-year-old daughter Astar, a designer, who laid out the interior. By serving as architect and contractor, Eli spent only $500,000 of the estimated $1,500,000 allotment.

Once the buildings were up, the first of Hadassah's specialists arrived for a two-month period to train the Zairean staffs. There was pediatrician Dan Engelhard, specialist in infectious diseases and immunology, who had already worked in the refugee camps of Cambodia. There was head ophthalmological operating theater nurse Zippora Sharon, who set up sterilization rooms and guided the nurses. Also in the group was veteran housekeeping services head, Sema Levy, who was part of the team that

---

* The Kimbangist Christians are followers of Joseph Kimbageh, a Belgian, jailed because of treasonous utterances. After dying in prison, his millions of followers regarded him as a prophet. They worked in the hospital as volunteers.

supervised the cleaning of the Scopus hospital after its return in 1967. Now, with a team of nine she was cleaning up the mess the builders left behind. Working in heat that reached 120 degrees, Sema introduced cleaning routines and taught the Zaireans how to use mechanical scrubbers. Before she left, the appreciative locals present her with a gift – a monkey. Sema politely declined.

In 1989, the Zairean staff took over and Hadassah retired from the scene to the plaudits of the A.I.D. administration. Penchas received a letter from Administrator, Peter McPherson who called the Kinshasa enterprise the "best project" ever launched by A.I.D. in Africa.

HMO has dispatched not only its experts but its ideas as well. One of those is a concept of health-care delivery. The concept holds that a community should receive its health services in relation to its measured needs.

It was in the Kiryat Hayovel suburb of Jerusalem that the idea was formed into a scientific model and tested. The experiment was initiated by Sidney Kark, a public health specialist who trained in Johannesburg and practiced in rural Natal and Durban. He could not test his concept in South African because the apartheid government at the time did not approve of it. Some of his South African colleagues left South Africa and went to live in Israel.

Kalman Mann had ideas similar to those of Kark and lectured on them at an international congress of Jewish physicians held in Jerusalem in 1952. He insisted against considerable professional opposition in Hadassah on establishing a public health program and staffing social workers for the hospital. In fact, Mann had made it a condition on taking his position that he open a community health center. He won out and in 1956 he opened the Kiryat Hayovel center primarily as a comprehensive family medicine practice.

When Mann heard Kark's lecture on a similar subject, he exclaimed, "I was most eager to get the Kiryat Hayovel project started." He said he lost no time in contacting Kark and his colleagues who worked with him in

South Africa. Kark began working at Hadassah in 1959 as head of the Social Medicine Department* and the Kiryat Hayovel community health project until his retirement in 1981.

In 1965, Mann hired Greta Fischer to head social services.**

When the Jewish Agency began to shut down the immigrant transit camps in the 1960's, large numbers of immigrants with tuberculosis were transferred to the Kiryat Hayovel suburb of Jerusalem. Many were Yemenites who had no immunity to the disease.

"Such a large number of cases is no longer an individual problem, but a problem of the whole community," Mann insisted at the time.

The Kiryat Hayovel community was multi-ethnic, coming from East Europe, North Africa and Yemen, and a small number of indigenous Israeli-born. The project found differences in the growth of babies. There were differences, too, in intellectual achievements and that led to variations in health standards.

Teams working out of the community center tailored health programs to fit the community's needs. To determine the needs, Hadassah public health nurses spent two years going from door to door in the suburb. They interviewed 12,000 persons. They focused on mothers and babies while other adults were questioned about coronary heart disease.

Using that as a base, Hadassah's public health staff began a care and prevention program which has continued since 1970. One of the longest running community health projects anywhere, the idea slowly took hold outside Israel.

---

* The Department of Social Medicine was begun in 1949 and headed by Theodore Grushka. In 1962, the Hebrew University combined the Department with Hadassah's Department of Community Health Services into a Department of Social Medicine which offered a Master of Public Health degree. In 1980, the School of Public Health and Community Medicine was founded.

** According to Mann, Greta made a strong impression on the medical board after a professor challenged her. "Public health is talk, talk," he said. She replied, "Professor, can you cure brain tumors or ascending myelitis? It's all talk you are doing." She was hired, said Mann, "and she was marvelous."

"There has been a tremendous spread of the gospel, if I can call it that," says Leon Epstein, Social Medicine Department Director. "The interesting thing is that in the U.S. today, with the move to managed care, Americans have concluded that this community orientation is critical to the future success of managed care. They realize they have to know what the health problems are and treat them as early as possible in order not to be faced with excessive costs later on."

Third World countries have taken up the concepts through students who have studied at the School. They have come from Myanmar and Belize, Canada and West Germany, Japan and Australia – nearly 60 countries.

"Our students have gone back to Africa, Asia, South America with these concepts and are developing programs," says Epstein. "We conducted workshops and seminars in the boondocks of South Africa."

Epstein and his colleagues took the concept to five areas in South Africa. They traveled to Tsingwalo in the northeastern Transvaal and to a Zulu locale in Natal.

"The important thing is that something that was developed in Kiryat Hayovel is having an impact in primary health-care services in many parts of the world. South Africans came to Israel to develop the idea and then we went back there with it 40 years later."

The community health idea was used throughout Israel. In the United Kingdom it was adapted to British general practice.

In 1971, the first international course in social medicine was begun in the department with the support of Israel's Foreign Ministry. More than 500 students from abroad have studied in the year-long course now given at the School. On returning to their native lands, most graduates occupy senior positions in public health.

Hadassah globe-girdling experts have gone everywhere physically except to countries hostile to Israel, meaning of course Israel's Arab neighbors. Ideas, however, do not need bodies. They merely have to be transmitted and radio is one good way to achieve that. Regularly since 1973, Israel

Broadcasting Authority staff member Ilana Basri has been reading medical advice provided by Hadassah physicians to radio listeners throughout the Arabic-speaking world.

Ilana was born in Iraq and made aliyah at the age of 18 in 1950. Soon afterward, she was employed as assistant director of IBA's Arabic Service.

In 1971, she entered Hadassah's new cardiac unit for tests. While there she was impressed with what she saw.

"I was so impressed, I decided to tell our Arab listeners about it," she recalls. In 1973 she began "Doctor Behind the Microphone" on a regular basis.

So popular was the program that she began getting requests by mail from listeners in Lybia and Iraq with which Israel has no relations and no postal service. Listeners would post their letters through neutral countries. The mail became so heavy that Ilana arranged for a post office box to be opened by IBA in Switzerland. Once the letters were in hand, Ilana would translate the questions into Hebrew and refer them to Hadassah physicians.

"No matter how busy the senior doctors are they always get back to me within two weeks," says Ilana. Ilana would read the replies in Arabic on the radio. On many occasions the patients would ask Ilana whether she could arrange Israeli visas for them so that they could be treated at Hadassah. In nearly every case she could.

The flow of Arabs from countries still at war with Israel grew to such proportions that Ilana went to Ben-Gurion Airport to meet the arrivals late at night. She received no overtime for her effort. One summer day, 12 patients arrived simultaneously, eight of them to be treated for eye problems.

"I am constantly deluged with problems from a dozen Arab countries, says Ilana. One psychosomatic skin problem was raised by a man in an extremely bellicose nation, whose identity Ilana refuses to divulge. The ailment was such that the patient had to be seen personally by the physician. The patient, who could not go to Israel for political reasons, asked that the physician, the late Ya'acov Shanon, meet him in Europe. Prof. Shanon, who at one time headed the unit at Hadassah Ein Karem dealing with the problem, agreed to go without a fee but only if Ilana accompanied him as translator.

Ilana and the professor set out and spent ten days abroad. She paid her own expenses and refused to accept the patient's offer of a refund. "The patient went home cured," Ilana reported.

A large number of Ilana's listeners complain of eye problems. Many ask for second opinions. A mother in Arab oil-rich state of Qatar wrote to Ilana that doctors in Europe refused to treat her three-year-old blind baby because the chance of success was low. Ilana consulted Shaul Merin, Ophthalmology Unit head at the Scopus Medical Center, who agreed to examine the child. His examination confirmed an unusual congenital vitreous disease which had kept the baby sightless since birth. He operated successfully and after a short recovery, the mother and her seeing child went home elated and full of praise for Israel, Hadassah and Prof. Merin.*

By the time Ilana reached the mandatory retirement age of 65 in April 1997, she was doing a five-minute spot six days a week, one live 55-minute call-in program on Sundays, and a half-hour show on Thursdays. When her listeners heard she was about to retire, Ilana was inundated with letters from all over the Arab world to continue. Her bosses agreed and so has Ilana.

"I will go on working even though officially I am retired," Ilana says, and adds with a laugh, "There are crazy people in this world and I am one of them."

---

* Hadassah Ophthalmologist Shmuel Levinger traveled to Tashkent, Uzbekistan, in 1995 to help open an eye hospital. He headed a team of 10 local doctors and 15 nurses. In three weeks, he examined 350 patients, did 49 operations on patients with cataracts and glaucoma, and gave 40 hours of lectures. In 1996, he returned and in one week he operated on 63 patients, half of whom were blind. All saw afterwards. "I kept busy," he says.

FOR THE LOVE OF PEOPLE

Most people have some natural, inner strength or
characteristic that helps express their personality.
For me, it has been a love of people.

– *Kalman Jacob Mann in "Reflections on a Life in Health Care"*

Changing of the Hadassah Medical Organization guard in Jerusalem took place on September 1, 1981.

It was on that day that HMO Director-General Kalman Jacob Mann, preeminent among the nation's medical managers, retired and made way for Shmuel "Sami" Penchas, a specialist in internal medicine and health administration. It was then that Hadassah moved into a new world of medicine where high technology and cost effectiveness took on paramount importance.

Kalman Mann had served as director-general for 30 years under ten Hadassah Presidents. No one in his position had ruled the roost longer. Under Kalman Mann's guiding hand, the hospital changed from a fragmented institution improvising to meet critical needs into an imposing university teaching medical center of world esteem.

Four of Ein Karem's five professional schools were founded during Mann's tenure – pharmacology, dentistry, occupational therapy and public health. He opened Ein Karem and reopened Mt. Scopus, and multiplied the number of beds at these institutions from 100 to 1,100 and the staff from several hundred to 4,250. During his tenure the budget increased over 40 times from $2,300,000 to $93,000,000.*

Specialization began on an organized scale, research programs were organized. Ten services magnified to 75. Acute care units were introduced as were academic nursing, social service and dentistry for geriatric patients. Hadassah became the first anywhere to start family medicine as a specialty.

But more significant than these, Mann had impressed the entire organization with the need to put heart and soul into HMO's bricks and mortar. He had brought to Hadassah new generations of physicians and nurses. His most difficult battle was against the explosive health costs that began in the mid-1960's. For him, a humanitarian and a healer, costs were secondary. His primary consideration was the doctor's need to provide the best in medical care to the most who could benefit. If a new building were vital to the community, he would begin in the spirit of Henrietta Szold, never sure where the money would come from to finish the job. Somehow the price tag would be covered. The economic philosophy underlying the principle was in keeping with the overall expansive, creative spirit of the new Jewish nation that was erupting with energy. Mann and Hadassah went right along.

Kalman Mann's peers and students remember him for his lectures on the overriding importance of people and spirit. A typical Mann lecture to students would contain lines like these:

> If your point of departure is always money, you will destroy
> the institution in no time. You take millions of dollars to
> build a hospital, millions of dollars to equip it and millions
> of dollars to maintain the physical part. If you don't have
> millions of dollars to create the people in it who will later on

---

* In 1997, HMO's operating budget in Israel topped $300,000,000. Hadassah bears all of HMO's development costs.

produce the *neshoma* (soul, spirit), then you have done very little.

In his soft, genteel tone, he would urge Hadassah directors:

> The human heart suffers as a result of the enormous expense on bricks and mortar. While they are important, you should allocate exactly the same sum of money for the spirit.

It was a tribute to his inspired leadership that of the 500 doctors he sent abroad to train in the U.S. and Europe only four did not return. In the end, he did not win the battle of the budget but he had set an example and a standard. After retirement, he continued his humanitarian work, caring for tens of thousands of Israelis by guiding the fortunes of Yad Sarah, a nationwide benevolent institution that provides free medical equipment and assistance to patients.

Born in 1912, the same year as Hadassah, Kalman Jacob Mann suffered fatal injuries in a traffic accident and died on March 14, 1997 in the Ein Karem Medical Center that he helped to create. The cherubic smile that reassured was gone except in the memories of hundreds of thousands of men, women and children the world over who had benefited from his care and concern.

Mann's deputy director, "Sami" Penchas, the new Director General, was the first to have been graduated from the Hebrew University-Hadassah Medical School. He took over the helm at a time when fast-changing sophisticated technology was rocketing western medicine into astronomical costs. Fortunately for Hadassah, he was well trained for the battle to contain costs.

Penchas had been the Army's medical director in Jerusalem during the Yom Kippur War. One of Mann's specialists in the practice of family medicine, he prepared himself for the new age that was dawning in the world of computers and high technology. He joined the world cybernetics revolution, first by studying electrical engineering at the Haifa Technion and then by two years' post-graduate work in medical engineering at London University.

That was followed by a period of computer science research in medicine at Harvard and Massachusetts General Hospital. On his return from Harvard, he was appointed second-in-command. He took up the title of HMO Director-General in 1981. Mann had prepared Hadassah well with a successor who could cope with the new age.

Penchas began by streamlining management and instituting strict control procedures. His operating style was new. No longer was the director-general's door open to all. Where once department heads burst unannounced into Kalman Mann's office, now they were forced to go through channels, reporting to the hospital director who in turn reported to Penchas.

"I installed an electrical door and after a few of them broke their noses against it, they stopped barging into my office. One was the chairman of the workers committee," says Penchas with barely disguised glee.

Penchas went after costs with a vengeance. His eye rarely left the budget or the bottom line. Cost-cutting and cost-effectiveness became his guideposts. He would oppose accepting an endowment for a building unless maintenance money came with it. With the purchase of a big piece of expensive machinery, he demanded that an additional 12 percent be set aside for maintenance.

His efforts sometimes reaped bitter fruit. In April 1997, the Israel Medical Association authorized rare work sanctions for Hadassah's 700 physicians. They protested, *inter alia*, against Hadassah management's cost-cutting measures calling for either a four percent reduction in pay or the dismissal of 80 doctors.

Penchas's deputy, Shlomo Mor-Yosef, explained that neither Hadassah management nor the physicians were responsible for the HMO's accumulated deficit of over $50,000,000. The blame for the strike was to be laid at the door of the Government which took upon itself the responsibility for a health system it would not or could not finance. Besides, the Government fixed fees and growth rates unrealistically. Hadassah is reimbursed for some services by as much as six or seven times less than the actual cost, says Mor-Yosef.

Personally, Penchas is spartan. On a typical day he is up at 7. He brews his own coffee on an Espresso machine. He exercises together with his wife, does not eat lunch unless ceremony requires it. He keeps a regular work regimen of 8 to 5, occasionally until 7. He keeps track of meetings on small slips of paper and limits meetings to 30 minutes.

At heart a family physician, he still treats a few patients. On the way to work in a Hadassah-provided car, he will periodically look in on a patient ill with a rare autoimmune disorder called "Wild Man Syndrome" (Wegener's granulomatosis). He described the usually fatal disease, characterized by red, peeling skin and restlessness, in the distinguished British journal *Lancet*.

"I learned that when we have a disease like this one where we do not know the etiology, we call it idiopathic – the patients are pathetic and the doctors are idiots," says Penchas.

Penchas is well aware that his style is not to everyone's liking. "A lot of people in this hospital will tell you I am a tyrant and run this place tyrannically. Actually this place is run by consensual decision-making bodies, by committees. There are umpteen committees for everything – obstetrics, mortality, morbidity, budget, university, general management, et cetera, et cetera and I am ex-officio on all of them. But I don't always go."

During the day, he steals time to keep *au courant* by reading the medical journals and surfing the Internet web. His demanding schedule, including monthly trips overseas for medical conferences and Hadassah meetings, takes its toll. He has been known to begin dozing in the middle of a conversation, often the result of accumulated jet lag.

Although he may have an autocratic reputation with his staff, he is understanding of their foibles. "Mistakes? No bedside manner? You have an environment here where 1,500 live. There are 15,000 visits a day. Mistakes are made because humans make errors," he says.

Penchas sees the most dramatic changes of the last quarter of a century in the soaring cost of medicine and in rapidly changing technology.

Costs have run so high that even wealthy states have found it difficult to cover the health bill. For medical practitioners, the ethical and moral problems that evolve can be horrendous. Doctors and nurses at Ein Karem's general intensive care unit* face these questions daily.

One patient arrived at the unit recently suffering the last stages of leukemia. After examination, the unit refused to receive him since it was obvious that he had only days to live. Comments the doctor who was then on duty, "He was about to die. I could have put him on a respiratory machine but I would not be prolonging his life, I would be prolonging his suffering. In this unit, unfortunately, we have to choose. The ethical problems are much sharper here than the medical."

General intensive care is a losing proposition financially. Each of the unit's 10 beds costs the hospital $1,000 a day to run. One nurse is assigned to each patient. A doctor can tend to no more than three or four patients. Patients need copious quantities of blood infusions, expensive antibiotics. Normally they remain in ICU three to four days although there have been exceptions. One patient remained 110 days.

In few other areas of the hospital does cost-effectiveness play so vital a role as in intensive care. Says Dr. Yoel Donchin, "If I have ten beds and 15 patients, some patients cannot be accepted. Every day we have to choose who is to be treated and who not. It is a matter of mathematical

---

* The medical center has special intensive care units for anesthesiology, neurology, burns, pediatrics, cardiology, cardiothoracic surgery, neonatology, and special diseases. Surgical cases are directed to general intensive care.

percentages. Overall, five percent are rejected. If they complain, they are right but there are limited resources."

The unit is well equipped and the quality of care good but physical conditions are below world standards. The unit consists of two small rooms and there is always the fear of contamination.

"Adding only two more beds in our unit means hiring six more nurses and that is a lot of money," says Dolchin.

In dollar and cents terms, the conclusion for a hospital manager is that more can be made by investing available funds in other units. Despite the problems and the conditions, the highly skilled ICU teams manage to save 80 percent of their patients – a high rate for acute care.

Donchin says the answer to the economic dilemma lies in prevention. "What we need today in medicine is more public health, more prevention," he states.

But there is a cost effectiveness to prevention as well.

"Not all prevention is cheap," says Leon Epstein, director of the Social Medicine Department of the School of Public Health School. "If I treat a person with hypertension and he does not get a stroke at 60 but lives to age 85, the cost of that extra 25 years has got to be weighed, in economic terms, against the prevention of the stroke and the cost of that stroke to society. With cost, it is not a one-to-one relationship."

The issue has its cultural and political dimensions. In 1978, a World Health Organization conference held in Alma Ata, Kazakhstan, took up the question of health for all. It was resolved there that governments in a free society have a responsibility for the health of their populations.

Says Epstein, "No country in the world can provide everything that everybody needs. In the U.S., that concept is accepted at the governmental level but there are 40,000,000 Americans without health insurance. Many people in the U.S. believe that health is a private commodity that people can buy if they have the money."

HMO Director Penchas, carrying millions of dollars of unpaid bills on his books, agrees that the State cannot be responsible for the health of everyone and that for most, health should be a private matter.

Says Epstein, "We know that the most expensive part of a person's life in terms of health care is the last six to 12 months. What is the right of an elderly person as compared with a young person? Many of us in this Public Health School are grappling with the question."

To provide the best possible care, a tertiary care hospital like Hadassah must acquire state-of-the-art technology. The new equipment in turn creates more sub-specializations which require numerous and expensive tests. Some examinations are not always needed for diagnosis but rather to protect physicians from the public's growing penchant for law suits.

"If you want to be in the forefront of medicine and to be a really good modern hospital with answers for many illnesses and have available the latest in diagnostic procedures, you must invest a lot of money. Otherwise people will not come to you," says hospital director Zvi Stern.*

As costs mushroomed, doctors developed group practices partly to pay for the heavy insurance they had to carry. Large sections of the population demanded more comprehensive medical insurance so that they could obtain the best medicine available. Health insurers ran into trouble when the law forcing everyone to join a fund also set the fees. The State tried to rescue the insurers through the national social security program. In so doing, the Government piled up a health debt of billions of shekels that it would not, or could not, pay. The result: a national health crisis in which top-notch hospitals like Hadassah have been left with stacks of IOU's.

"In the field of imaging, for example," says Penchas, "we have gone from Dr. Roentgen's simple X-ray tube to CT scans, MRI's and now the

---

* Dr. Stern is a Hadassah "product". He was born in Hadassah hospital on Mt. Scopus, studied medicine in the Hebrew University-Hadassah Medical School, trained there and now directs the Ein Karem hospital.

$4,000,000 Positron Emission Tomography (PET)* and isotope-producing Cyclotron." Lasers, nuclear medicine, cobalt guns, linear accelerators, automated labs, a lithotripter to crush kidney stones are part of Hadassah's inventory of equipment valued at $45,000,000.

Because of the cost issue, more medicine is practiced outside the hospital than in the past. Says Penchas, "Hospitals are slowly being transformed into huge intensive care units. Most non-intensive care is ambulatory or done in day-care units." And hospitalization periods have been cut. Where once mothers remained in hospital for up to one week after giving birth, they are now released from Hadassah within 48 hours.

At the same time, specialization has brought Hadassah an impressive list of Israeli "firsts": a bone bank, a skin bank to treat burns, a trauma unit. Shimon Slavin's Bone Marrow Transplantation Department was one of the first to carry out the procedure successfully. Like saplings from mother trees, new departments have sprouted from sub-specialties such as hematology, gastroenterology, nephrology, vascular surgery.

Zvi Stern wryly comments that specialization is a progressively intricate process in a professional's career: "You get your MD on a human being. You get your senior lectureship on a tissue. You become a professor on a cell, an expert on a molecule, and a world authority on a gene."

Not everything about the Ein Karem campus is cost containment, miracle-making machines or sophisticated specialties. It is also a world where pink kangaroos and yellow elephants exist with red rabbits and blue lions. This wonderland where Oz-like creatures delight the child's eye is located on the main plaza of the Ein Karem campus and is referred to by adults as the Mother and Child Center.

---

* PET is a research and diagnostic tool that goes one step beyond the images of a CT Scan and an MRI. It identifies the metabolism of a tissue, which is especially useful in treating tumors. It can show functioning of the brain in real time. Hadassah is first with it in the Middle East and among the first anywhere to use it. A French friend of Hadassah donated and his foundation maintains it.

Dedicated during the national convention in Jerusalem in September, 1995 as "child-friendly", the Center's Julia Goldwurm Maternity Pavilion opened the following June. On the 16th, the Center's first baby was born to Devorah Asulin by Caesarean section. He was named Israel.

The Sir Isaac Wolfson Children's Pavilion received its first patients on September 9, 1996. And four days later, for its official opening, the six-story building was tied like a gift package with 745 feet of cherry-red, polyester ribbon. "A gift from Hadassah to the people of Jerusalem," said President Kaplan. While she spoke, a donkey with milk cans suspended from its side, grazed the grounds during the ceremony. Veterans present liked to believe it was descended from the beasts who carried Hadassah's Milk Express some seven generations previously.

The building's entrance is an invitation to play. Architect Arthur Spector* designed an arched gateway for the $27,000,000 doll house with a decorative green cube on the corner of either side and a blue ball balancing a red triangle in the center. On the triangle, a smiling yellow kangaroo with an infant in her pouch greets everyone into the miracle building where sick children become well and mothers have babies. The marsupial mammal and its infant became the Center's logo.

Director-General Penchas set the tone for the building when he approached the National Board with a request that "we do something for the children". The concept of providing a Road to Recovery was that of the late Blanche Shukow, a national Vice-President known for her imagination and creativity. Says HMO Chairman Bonnie Lipton, "It was her idea that everything – sheets, towels, pajamas, ceilings, walls – be adorned with children's figures."

"To help a child find its way around," says Spector, "we identified each floor with its own color and an animal as well as a number." Oddly missing from the Maternity Pavilion's pictorial menagerie is a stork. Cars, trucks, boats, computer games, music room, kindergarten, glass elevator framed

---

* Arthur Spector's late mother, Dorothy, of Brookline, Massachusetts, was a member of the National Board and, later, a member for life of Hadassah's Honorary Council.

by towers and turrets – here was a world familiar to children. For them, the medical aspect could be a mere afterthought. What better place for the children to play doctor.

Wherever the kids turn, there is fantasy land. Smiling green-faced trash cans with round yellow tummies open to accept their chewing gum wrappers when they grab the trash man's nose. *Mezzuzot* are shaped like rockets with blue bodies and red-pointed tops. Two white hands clasp them. "Children like to grab," explains a guide escorting visitors.

Says Bonnie Lipton, "If someone gave us a $1,000,000 gift, their enamel plaque is designed with turrets and towers and magic hands. The motif is carried throughout."

The 50 maternity and 78 pediatric beds are in semi-private rooms, each equipped with Futon beds for parents to sleep overnight. Thirty-six cradles hold the newborn. Designed to serve Jerusalem's 200,000 children, the Center was so crowded during its first week that women had their babies in the corridors. Six delivery rooms* were insufficient.

Teachers tutor hospitalized school children and the children stay in touch with their schools via e-mail. Anorexia and bulimia patients attend cookery classes under the direction of a dietitian. A child recovering from brain surgery kneads dough. Choice of menu makes the hospital stay a happier experience especially when junior can choose lunch from a menu of hamburgers, schnitzel and hot dogs or pizza and French fries with cake and chocolate milk for dessert. Why go home?

Little wonder that Spector says confidently, "This building speaks a different language to a different generation."

But does it speed the healing? Some parents are certain that it does. Says Ahuva Shachar, mother of 18-month-old Rivka, who was moved to the new pavilion, "We'd been hearing about the move for a long time. I can't say I was particularly interested in luxury. All I wanted was for Rivka to be well again. But I saw that better conditions help us all."

---

* Referred to euphemistically at the Center as "birthing rooms."

Not all prospective parents had the good fortune to enter the Maternity Pavilion. In his seventh floor laboratory next door to the Center, Dr. Aby Lewin has taken on the vexatious problem of infertility in both men and women, and pre-implantation diagnosis. As a result of the lab's successes, men who had no chance of fathering children can be more hopeful.

One anxious, childless male who had been married 13 years was aided through the work in the lab and, in time, his wife gave birth to a boy through test-tube fertilization. Says Aby, "The couple could hardly believe the miracle and, to tell the truth, it was hard for me to believe it as well. Since then, we have performed the procedure many times."

"Research projects are part of the fabric of Hadassah," says Michal Roll, director of the research and development department. To get investigations moving that will hopefully turn up answers to ailments which have stumped the medical profession, Michal provides researchers with leads to funding and help in writing proposals.

A procedure is being developed at Hadassah to cure thalassemia, a crippling and ultimately fatal disease genetically transmitted. According to Avraham Israeli, Penchas's Associate Director and an internist, the procedure involves transplanting blood cells from the umbilical cord of newborn infants. Israeli says there are only six umbilical cord blood cell banks in the world, one of them being at Ein Karem.

Dermatology has one of the more active research programs at Ein Karem. The original studies of Zvi Even-Paz, who formerly headed the department, showed that extensive exposure to the sun* and bathing in the mineral rich waters in the Dead Sea region cleared skin eruptions brought on by psoriasis. The relief, brought to patients with much less risk than from the side effects of other therapies, led to the creation of a spa center that attracts thousands of sufferers to the area from abroad. The economic

---

* Long exposure to the sun at the Dead Sea is possible because Nature filters out most of the harmful rays. The mineral content of the Sea and adjacent springs are the richest in the world.

by-product has been the creation of a health industry based on the Dead Sea's unique natural resources that in 1996 earned $132,000,000 and attracted 200,000 patients. Ten percent of those were from abroad.

Dermatologist Vera Leibovici and her team corrected textbooks which have long claimed that young children are not affected by fungal infections. After examining 1,200 children aged six to 14, Vera found that fungus develops between toes and in nails, and that unless treated early, the disease can become nearly impossible to cure.

David Enk, a specialist in immunological reactions, has studied melanomas, one of the most dangerous of all cancers. With financing from an Israeli cosmetic firm, he has been looking at how a pigment produced from tomatoes may have a positive effect on the skin.

In orthopedics, Charles Howard has experimented on mending fractures, especially among the aged. In geriatric medicine, Dan Dannenberg collaborated with Arieh Ben-Yehuda to see whether a particular molecule improved the immune system in the elderly, and also explored whether it improved the effect of anti-flu vaccines.

Neurologist Oded Abramsky carried out the first trials on a drug developed in Israel that is effective against the early stages of multiple sclerosis.*

Research has benefited every branch of medicine. Noteworthy is the unremitting struggle against homo sapiens's greatest natural enemy – heart disease.

Transplanting the human heart was shown in 1967 by South African surgeon Christiaan Barnard to be one realistic solution for a diseased heart. Attempts were made, but patients did not survive long because their bodies rejected the new hearts. The transplants only became viable in 1985 with the introduction of cyclosporin, a drug that overcame the rejection

* The drug copaxone was developed by Prof. Michael Sela, Prof. Ruth Arnon and Dr. Dvora Teitelbaum, of the Weizmann Institute of Science, Rehovot. Arnon and Teitelbaum received "Women of Distinction" awards from Hadassah at its 85th anniversary celebrations in Jerusalem in January, 1997.

problem. It would be two years later when Hadassah cardiothoracic surgeon Joseph "Joe" Borman, like Barnard a South African, would perform the first successful heart transplant in Israel.*

But before Borman could proceed, Hadassah first had to obtain rabbinical permission for the procedure. Religious opposition was at times vitriolic. In ultra-Orthodox neighborhoods of Jerusalem, posters went up declaiming, "Joe Borman is a double murderer! He murders the donor and he murders the recipient!"

Discussions with individual rabbis were unsuccessful in convincing them that the donor was dead before the heart was taken and that the recipient had no chance of survival without the transplant. Finally, a day-long seminar with 30 doctors took place at the hospital with Israel's two Chief Rabbis. After the physicians presented their case with slides, statistics and explanations, the rabbis acknowledged that the overriding principle of pikuach nefesh (saving a life) applied.

Borman and his teams had the green light. But donors were scarce. Through most of 1987, the two teams were constantly on the alert. Once the heart became available they had 12 hours to begin the operation.

Borman takes up the story:

> No teams could have been better prepared than we were. While we were waiting for a donor heart, we successfully transplanted hearts in eight laboratory dogs. After eight long months, during which we grew increasingly despondent, the heart of a young donor became available.
>
> The donor died at 2.30 p.m. on August 25. We checked compatibility and at 5:00 we knew we had a match. The recipient was a grandfather, Ovadia Matzri, 51. He was given 90 minutes to turn up at the hospital. He and his family arrived at 6.30 and shortly before 10.00 p.m. the operation

---

* Two transplants in Israel were attempted in 1968 by Tel Aviv surgeons but the patients did not survive one month.

had begun. Fifteen doctors worked simultaneously in two operating rooms.

Borman continues:

> We were in a state of high tension after all the preparations but everything went like clockwork. In a long career in cardiac surgery I've had many exciting moments. But nothing before or since ever compared with that first human heart transplant when we took the clamp off the aorta and blood began flowing into the new heart.
>
> It fibrillated. We gave it an electric shock and it started to beat. I felt that heart beating through my entire body. I stood and stared down at it. In place of the huge sick heart we had cut out only a short while before, a young healthy heart was beating vigorously. I watched it and knew that the patient would be well.*

Transplants then became a common occurrence at Hadassah. A milestone was reached in 1992, when five human organs – liver, pancreas, heart and the kidneys – of a 29-year-old man were used to save the lives of four patients. The donor's two corneas were put aside for future use.

Despite all the sophisticated machines and wonder drugs available to orthodox medicine, a physician must frequently tell a patient that there is nothing more that can be done. Too often the doctor's unhappy verdict is, "You'll just have to learn to live with it."

Well, not necessarily. In the past few decades, great numbers of patients have been exploring alternative therapies. Hadassah's expert in the field is Martine Toledano, head of the unit for complementary medicine. Martine received her medical degree in Paris. At first she thought the idea of

---

* Matzri survived for three years, then died of a stroke unrelated to the transplant. The survival of transplant patients is now 80% for up to one year, 70% to five years and 50% as long as 10 years.

complementary medicine was "rubbish". But as she learned more, she says, she became enthusiastic.

"It's clear we need some additional form of medicine but in 1990 when our unit was established at Ein Karem, most doctors were unwilling to believe what they could not explain.

"Things have now changed. Most doctors recognize there are many ways to help a patient. Someone suffering backache can be treated with a course of Voltaren or with Chinese medicine or another approach. In short, complementary medicine adds therapeutic tools to the doctor's arsenal."

The Hadassah physician's armory is formidable: homeopathy, acupuncture, osteopathy, chiropractice, auricular therapy, reflexology, Feldenkreis and hypnosis. In an examination, Martine's team will look at a patient's foot or eye or test the body's energy.

"Patients used to come to us as a last resort. Now we will be the first resort. Patients who don't like taking drugs or want to avoid surgery will see first whether complementary medicine has anything to offer them. Usually we have."

Hundreds of patients go to the unit each month. "That is a sign we are succeeding," says Martine. "We treated one woman whose entire body was affected with lesions from psoriasis. Her body is now completely clean. An 80-year-old man came to us because he did not want to undergo surgery for a disc problem. After three treatments, his pain was far less and he no longer feels he needs surgery. We've had particular success in treating pain problems that Hadassah's pain clinic cannot help."

Many cancer patients apply to the unit. Says Martine, "We always encourage them to continue their chemotherapy but we help them cope with it better on an emotional level. With homeopathy and reflexology techniques we can help decrease side effects.

"We are a clinic of doctors who simply offer more treatment possibilities," says Martine.

Hadassah Ein Karem is a self-contained city devoted to healing, research and teaching. Within its precincts, a visitor can find a bank, a post office, a travel agent, a synagogue or great art. Its halls teem with men and women in white or green rushing about carrying vials, reading charts, answering emergency calls, wheeling beds – all to save life or relieve suffering.

There are those who go about their tasks but remain in the shadows. Night and day they keep the watch. These men and women work quietly and efficiently. They are directed by Hadassah's security officer who has been on guard for 14 years. He is Udi Shauloff, former captain in the Israel Defense Forces. Probably in no other city in Israel is the security of a civilian institution more vital than it is at Ein Karem or on Mt. Scopus. Says Udi:

> We have about 20,000 people on the Ein Karem campus every day in addition to as many as 50 busloads of tourists – a very mixed population. Up to 6,000 vehicles pass through our institution. We have a very large number of security personnel who are posted in the building or who walk about incognito.

Udi's most serious concern is that explosive material not be taken on to the campus. His record on that score has been good. Warnings of terror incidents or suspicious objects left lying around send his men on sweeps throughout the premises and grounds.

The constant tension between Israel and its Arab neighbors complicates the work. A well-trained reserve officer, Udi inspires confidence:

> We're ready for war. We carry out drills periodically and we are trained to handle chemical warfare. We have a sealed room in every department. We can transform this hospital to handle an emergency in hours. When the bus explosions occurred in 1996 the wounded began coming in within five

to seven minutes. We received about 30 wounded from each
bus and because of our system we saved them.

All who enter Hadassah, both great and small, are given the best that
science can offer. The two Medical Centers at either pole of Jerusalem
resonate with accomplishments that have won worldwide attention.

Says Shmuel Penchas:

> The Hadassah Medical Organization can be the envy of other
> nations. I believe in the uniqueness of what HMO must do –
> this is a brave new world where we shall not treat diseases
> after they occur, but where we will prevent their inception.
> We will be there at the cradle, preventing an early grave.
>
> What Hadassah is now enabling HMO to do is of major
> importance to humanity, to the Jewish people, to the battle
> for women's and children's health, and to the glory of the
> State of Israel.

AFTERWORD

Hadassah and I were born within months of each other on opposite sides of the globe. It, of course, was as unaware of the infant struggling into life in pre-World War I Vienna as I was of the group of determined women in New York who sent two nurses to open a health station in Jerusalem – and launched a singular medical phenomenon.

I discovered them sooner than they found out about me. By the time I reached Palestine 22 years later, Hadassah had already thrown a network of health stations across the country, one of them within reach of the swampy Kinneret shore where I went to build a new kibbutz.

It was not until the late 1940's and early 1950's, however, when I spent four years in the United States that I made contact with Hadassah on its home ground. It was then I first began to understand the single-minded vigor of these women and their involvement in the health and social services of a country 6,000 miles away.

Five years later, I was chairing the Israel Government Tourist Corporation. Around 45,000 tourists were expected that year – a small figure compared with the numbers who come today, but then as now an important injection into the country's economy.

But with the Sinai Campaign the United States placed a ban on travel to the Middle East. Tourism plummeted. Israel's hoteliers and everyone else who depended on the tourist trade faced bankruptcy. The isolation was strongly felt not only in the economic field.

Almost naturally I turned to Hadassah. I asked that they schedule a mission in Jerusalem and request State Department permission for its members to attend. Hadassah agreed and marched into action. The tourist blockade was broken and Israel, particularly Jerusalem, was turned into the international convention center it is today.

With this kind of precedent I was not at all surprised 35 years later when Hadassah moved part of its 1991 midwinter convention to Jerusalem, arriving even as Saddam Hussein's scud missiles were falling. It was a gesture of solidarity and cheer that I and other Jerusalemites appreciated – another link in the bond between Hadassah and Jerusalem.

Part of the reason this bond has endured is that Hadassah holds Jerusalem at the center of its aspirations. It is no mere chance that Hadassah opened its first health station in this most special of cities or built its hospitals and medical schools here.

One of Hadassah's hallmarks has been practical Zionism, the recognition that the road to a dream begins with the possible, building under its feet even if the ultimate goal remains over a distant horizon. For Hadassah the possible has meant providing the best and most advanced in preventive and curative health care and in medical research and education. By establishing centers of medical excellence, the organization contributes not only to the health of Jerusalem's citizens – and to the modern city's prestige – but also makes a vital and massive contribution to Jerusalem's economy, providing thousands of jobs. Indeed, Hadassah is – along with the national government, the city administration and the Hebrew University – one of Jerusalem's four largest employers.

Another vital and potentially explosive area where Hadassah has contributed so much is promoting the ideal of equality. Hadassah has, since the first day, taken in all comers, regardless of how and where they worship. That Hadassah has credibility among all sectors of the population has been borne out many times. When Jerusalem was divided, Hadassah was cut off from most of the Arab population who had come to know it before 1948, but its reputation survived. In the first days after the city's reunification, the large number of Arabs who showed up at Hadassah demonstrated that its good name was intact even beyond a hostile frontier; this is one of the greatest tributes to Hadassah.

Hadassah has done the seemingly impossible so often that it is now virtually expected of the organization. It has raised phenomenal sums of money to build and maintain high-technology hospitals that practice advanced medicine. It has solved practical and administrative, political and bureaucratic problems along the way because the objective was so clear that obstacles were seen merely as challenges to be overcome.

I'll never forget how Hadassah responded to my phone call in June 1967. Hadassah's original hospital on Mount Scopus had been behind Jordanian lines for 19 years, during which time the new medical center had risen in Ein Karem.

It was in the heady week of the Six-Day War and the battle for Jerusalem had just been won. Somewhat euphoric myself, I picked up the phone and called Kalman Mann, then director general of the Hadassah-Hebrew University Medical Center. "If you want your hospital, come and get it," I said. And come they did. First Dr. Mann and his colleagues came, renewing acquaintance with the abandoned building on Mount Scopus. Within weeks Hadassah had undertaken a massive fund-raising drive to rebuild its first hospital even though it had been replaced with the Ein Karem facility. Instead of a single hospital anchoring one end of the city, Hadassah's two hospitals would embrace Jerusalem from opposite sides.

Approaching the close of its first century, Hadassah is visibly full of vigor. Its hospitals are flourishing, its community health center is expanding, its technical college is growing, its career center is busier than ever. As always Hadassah remains flexible and responsive. Today, Soviet and Ethiopian immigrants need help and all Hadassah's multi-faceted institutions are involved. Tomorrow? I don't know as yet, nor do they, but I've no doubt that as soon as they do, they'll play their part.

I am proud to share the year of my birth with Hadassah, though I know that I will not be able to match its record for longevity. But I have no doubt that the city beloved by us all will keep pace with this extraordinary organization. And I hope that some successor of mine, some mayor of Jerusalem a hundred years hence, will be privileged to write a tribute to yet another update of *It Takes a Dream*.

— Teddy Kollek

EPILOGUE

On Sunday, March 23, 1997, Hadassah observed its 85th birthday one mile from the site* where it was born. It was the 14th day of the Hebrew month of Adar Bet, and it was Purim.

"More than any other holiday in the Jewish calendar, Purim belongs to Hadassah," former President Bernice Tannenbaum told a distinguished gathering.

The distinguished gathering in today's Temple Emanu-El included President Marlene Edith Post, New York City Mayor Rudolph W. Giuliani, the Borough presidents of Manhattan and the Bronx, Congressman Charles Schumer, Belle Simon, co-chairman of Hadassah's 85 birthday committee and five former Hadassah Presidents: Charlotte Jacobson, Deborah Kaplan, Ruth Popkin, Miriam Freund Rosenthal and Bernice Tannenbaum.

President Post spoke of the women Hadassah honored with its first "Women of Distinction" award given in Jerusalem in January 1997. By inference she referred as well to the organization's creators when she said, "The women we honored dared to dream and then did what others said

---

* A commercial establishment exists at the corner of 43rd Street and Fifth Avenue in New York City where the old Temple Emanu-El stood. No plaque distinguishes the historic site.

could not be done. Their courage, determination, discipline and vision have changed people's lives. Their example is an inspiration."

The celebration over, Hadassah's leadership prepared for the new century about to dawn and for the organization's 100th birthday. What, indeed, lay ahead for Hadassah and how would it develop by the year 2012?

"New Directions," Hadassah's third strategic planning program has set two basic goals for 2000:

To place Hadassah at the forefront in making contributions to the changing roles of family, society and spirituality and,

To form a global community for all Jewish women.

With women becoming more active in the political life of America and their greater involvement in issues of general concern, would Hadassah veer away from its Zionist moorings into a service organization? With the increase in intermarriages would Hadassah become non-sectarian? Would a man ever become President?

President Post is emphatic on at least one issue. Says she, "We will always have a Zionist mission. That is part of our strength. We have maintained an unwavering commitment to the people and land of Israel, to Judaism."

In Israel, Jewish National Fund President Moshe Rivlin describes Hadassah in terms that leave no doubt as to its meaning for the Jewish people:

"Everyone knows what Hadassah means. It is the largest Jewish women's organization and it is where the world of Israel and Judaism and Zionist heritage are being brought into hundreds of thousands of Jewish homes."

Bernice Tannenbaum, an influential thinker in Hadassah's leadership, states, "I do not see Hadassah ever becoming non-Jewish or non-Zionist. I would like to see Hadassah remain tied to the Zionist concept, maintain its programs of Jewish education, and continue being active on the American scene as an advocacy body for Israel."

She does not rule out Hadassah being a "service body to the extent that we promote medical issues of special interest to women. Philosophically, I think our basic beliefs are sound. We'll have to develop better marketing devices and find some way of adapting our structure to present and future realities. With women working, Hadassah will resort increasingly to Internet or use techniques not available in the past. We have to take advantages of new technologies," says Bernice.

To a certain extent that is already being done. Executive Committee leaders outside New York "attend" meetings via conference calls. Fax and E-mail are used to speed basic papers to leaders around the country.

Technology now being developed will make it possible to televise conference calls. National board members living outside New York will observe committee meetings in New York on large, closed circuit three-dimensional television screens in their homes. Their own images will be transmitted from their homes or offices so that it will appear that they are actually in the committee room taking part.

In medicine, Hadassah can look forward to moving from the present systematic system into cellular medicine. "We will look more and more into the sub-components of cells," says HMO Director-General Shmuel Penchas. "We will do more and more work on this cellular medicine from the point of view of molecular biology, genetics and gene therapy."

Henri Atlan, director of the Hadassah's Human Biology Research Center in Jerusalem, predicts "an unprecedented leap forward in our understanding of how the body works."

Already computer technology has sparked a revolution with the cracking of the gene code. Biochips are being developed for micro-processors that will permit researchers to look at thousands of genes simultaneously. *Fortune* (March 31, 1997) has revealed that researchers are using gene chips to determine everything from the origins of cancer to gene mutations that make the AIDS virus resistant to drugs.

By the time Hadassah is 100 years old, the chips may well be able to scan an individual's genes, determine what is wrong with any one of them and make it possible for a drug to be tailor-made to repair the gene. The result: an individual will be prevented from developing a deadly disease years before he or she falls ill.

Hadassah has already invested heavily in gene research and is orienting itself toward gene therapy.

Zvi Stern, Hadassah Hospital Director at Ein Karem, says, "Within the next ten to 20 years we will be more specialized. Diagnostic procedures, like the PET and the cyclotron, will help us to be more definite in identifying pathological processes."

The tasks for Hadassah medicine that lie ahead will be formidable. Says Stern, "We will have to give more answers to patients with more complicated sicsnesses since we will lengthen life. In microbiology, we will have to face new diseases as microbes develop resistance to drugs."

In surgery, technological innovation will make it possible, says Herbert Freund, head of surgery on Mt. Scopus, "to extend keyhole techniques to cardiac, chest, vascular, urological, plastic, ENT, pediatric and orthopedic procedures. As surgery becomes more technically complex it will be far less invasive."

Hadassah sees its relationship with Israel both as humanitarian and as a partnership.

Says President Post, "We want to create a Foundation in Hadassah for which we will raise and distribute funds for innovative and needed programs in Israel. While we are proud of our name in Jerusalem, we also want to reach out to the rest of the country as well.

In the U.S., Hadassah leaders predict that it will one day become the country's most powerful women's organization.

President Post says, "The women's movement in the U.S. is far more narrowly focused than we. We will be powerful because Hadassah will do the things women do while adding the Jewish and Zionist components."

How does one describe Hadassah? Certainly not in a word or two.

To encompass its entire history, its achievements, would require a work of encyclopedic magnitude. And how can one explain its success, its dynamism, its energy? Zionism, it has been said, is the world's only movement that began as a dream, and fulfilled that dream to become a reality in the birth of a state. Much the same can be said of Hadassah. A dream became a reality.

President Frieda Lewis wrote on leaving office in 1984: "There are three criteria by which to judge a work of art: harmony, intensity and continuity. Hadassah is indeed a masterpiece. Not only does it possess these attributes, but perhaps even more significantly, the bond that Hadassah develops with each of us is one of harmony, intensity and continuity."

Concludes President Post:

"For 85 years Hadassah has responded to the challenges of history. We have a proud history but more important, we are still on a rising curve. For every story told on these pages there are at least another one hundred to be told.

"As we enter a new century, we pray that we will be able to help build a healthier and stronger Israel unfettered by the dramatic and often violent challenges that history has presented to us. If the new age is as turbulent as the old, we will rise to the occasion."

THE END

PRESIDENTS
OF
HADASSAH

Henrietta Szold * (Founder)
1912-1921   1923-1926

Alice L. Seligsberg *
1921-1923

Irma Lindheim *
1926-1928

Zip Szold *
1928-1930

Rose Jacobs *
1930-1932   1934-1937

Rose L. Halprin *
1932-1934   1947-1952

Judith Epstein *
1937-1939   1943-1947

Tamar DeSola Pool *
1939-1943

Etta Rosensohn *
1952-1953

Rebecca Shulman *
1953-1956

Dr. Miriam Freund Rosenthal
1956-1960

Lola Kramarsky *
1960-1964

Charlotte Jacobson
1964-1968

Faye L. Schenk *
1968-1972

Rose E. Matzkin
1972-1976

Bernice S. Tannenbaum
1976-1980

Frieda S. Lewis *
1980-1984

Ruth W. Popkin
1984-1988

Carmela E. Kalmanson
1988-1991

Deborah B. Kaplan
1991-1995

Marlene Edith Post
1995-Present

INDEX